The Whole Sex Catalogue

Edited by Bernhardt J. Hurwood

D1605377

PINNACLE BOOKS • NEW YORK

This book is lovingly dedicated to my wife, Laura, who not only
contributed materially to it with a constant flow of ideas and en-
couragment, but also suffered long hours of lonely apprehension while
I streaked through the shadows of the valley of sex (in the name of
research, of course).

While acknowledgments appear throughout the book, because of space and
design limitations we herewith give grateful acknowledgment for permission
to reprint from the following:

FANNY HILL'S COOKBOOK by Lionel H. Braun and William
Adams. Copyright © 1971 by Lionel H. Braun and William Adams.
Reprinted by permission of Tuplinger Publishing Co., Inc., New
York.

THE NAKED CHEF by Billie Young. Copyright © 1971 by Billie
Young. Reprinted by permission of Ashley Books, Inc., Port
Washington, New York.

SEX IN HISTORY by G. Rattray Taylor. Copyright © 1954 by
G. Rattray Taylor. Reprinted by permission of Vanguard Press,
Inc., New York.

An original Pinnacle Books edition, published for the first time anywhere.

ISBN 0-523-00721-3

First printing, October 1975

Designed by Frank Curcio

Printed in the United States of America

PINNACLE BOOKS, INC., 275 Madison Avenue, New York, New York 10016

Contents

Introduction

Let's assume you wanted to know about massage parlors, singles clubs, gay bars, porno movies, swing clubs, sex boutiques, call girls, erotic literature, sex techniques, contraception, erotic artists, sex therapy, or where to find your friendly neighborhood sex clinic . . . you name it, *anything*, from the sublime to the ridiculous, in the wide and mysterious world of human sexuality—where would you start looking?

A trip to the public library won't do much good, right? You couldn't look it up in the Yellow Pages either. The much media-advertised *sexual revolution* of our time notwithstanding, there still are no entries under *French ticklers, dildoes*, and *vibrators* in the phone book or the classified ads. So where'd you go?

THE WHOLE SEX CATALOGUE is the answer. It fulfills a very real need for exactly the kind of practical down-to-earth sex information anyone might be desperately looking for, anywhere, anytime. We know. There were many times when we too were trying to locate such information for our research, or, to be quite frank, just for our own private fun and entertainment.

Let's say you want to inform yourself on one or another fine point of sexology. For example: transvestism, the desire or need to dress in the customary clothes of the opposite sex—men dressing up as women, women dressing like men. Not only will you find the history and psychology of transvestism in this Catalogue, but you will also find an impressive *bibliography* on this as well as on the many other sexual subjects included herein, so you can read up on it to whatever extent you may want. The Catalogue also gets down to the important *practical* points, such as where you can find fashion boutiques specializing in (often oversize!) transvestite clothes, transvestite hangouts, nightclubs featuring transvestite entertainment, etc.

Or, take a subject such as *aphrodisiacs*. Are there really some substances—pills, teas, ointments, powders, liqueurs— that enhance male potency or increase the sex drive of women?

There is no one-sentence answer to this age-old, controversial question. But there are *some* things that really seem to work, if only by *indirect* rather than direct action. Still, who cares whether it's direct or indirect—as long as you know about it and it works. Again, the Catalogue not only tells you all about it theoretically, but also in very down-to-earth, practical terms where you can buy so-called *aphrodisiacs*, which ones are more likely than others to have some kind of effect, and how much they cost. It even tells you how to mix *aphrodisiac cocktails*, some of which sound like such great-tasting concoctions that they should be fun trying, even if no more should happen with them than with gin and tonic or Scotch on the rocks.

But, to turn to more serious matters. You might have damn good reason for wanting to know something about the *sex laws* of the state you happen to be living in. Perhaps you want to know what its divorce provisions are. Or whether you've got the good fortune of living in one of the more enlightened states with a *consenting adults* law. It might mean the difference between going to jail or staying out of it for such harmless and common sex practices as oral or anal intercourse—yes, even with your own legally wedded spouse—to say nothing of homosexuality, swinging, prostitution, and the like!

Or you might want to have some erotic art pictures for your bedroom. Or you might want to wear some erotic jewelry, or you might be interested in erotic candles and candle sticks, or erotic lamps and that sort of thing. The Catalogue lists many of the most outstanding artists, shows many illustrations of their work, lists galleries and boutiques where these things are on sale and, again, puts you in immediate touch with whatever it is you might be interested in, sexually speaking.

Even with *people*, sex people, that is. For instance *swingers* and those interested in *alternate lifestyles*—alternate, that is, to the common, humdrum, monotonous, monogamous, or at least *supposedly* monogamous marriage. For those merely interested in the usual Saturday night swing, the Catalogue has some fine suggestions and daring leads to the right places on both coasts and even the midwest where, contrary to common belief, the so-called *silent majority* swings as high as anywhere else.

And for those who are seriously seeking something more— something where sexual freedom is tied in with a belief in the beauty of nudism, of emotional growth, of sharing, and of loving relationships with more than just your most important primary partner—the Catalogue can guide you to groups such as Sandstone Center in California and some other contacts where you can literally have *the best of two worlds.*

To top it all off, the Catalogue is beautifully designed, richly illustrated with over a thousand fascinating, often highly erotic, sometimes hilariously funny, and always most informative educational pictures that make the Catalogue the kind of unique publication and conversation piece that it truly is.

There is just nothing quite like it, nor, we suspect, will there be for a long time to come. We would therefore not only recommend *The Whole Sex Catalogue* unreservedly, but would urge anybody who wants to know more about sex in the most pleasant way possible, or who wants to make a good sex life even better and still more exciting, to keep the Catalogue near him/her, wherever you are.

The ancient Japanese, Chinese, and Hindus always knew that sexual knowledge ought to be presented in such a way that it would be educational as well as a turn-on. We have always tried doing so in our own work. Now *The Whole Sex Catalogue* has done likewise, and in such a superb way and with such remarkable taste that we take it as a privilege and a joy to introduce it to the discriminating, sexually alive public.

Drs. Eberhard and Phyllis Kronhausen
New York 1975

Sex Through the Ages

The Voyeur and the Couple—*15th Century Woodcut*

Have Things Really Changed?

It would be presumptuous to present, in necessarily sketchy form, a "definitive" picture of sexual attitudes since the Year One. The assorted booming utterances of historians, social scientists, churchmen, and politicians notwithstanding, sexually mature human beings—when left to their own devices—have always done whatever they chose to do, regardless of what they admitted in public. Since history has been written with one bias or another, the overall effect of accumulated writings has been confusing.

Before the introduction of Judaeo-Christian mores, sexuality was regarded in a totally different light. Primitive philosophers, recognizing the relationship between sexual intercourse and new life, looked upon sexuality with awe. Sexual union not only produced immediate sensations of ecstasy, but resulted in long-range consequences of immense importance. Obviously sex, this potent source of transcendent feelings, had to have divine or supernatural overtones.

As civilizations developed, the matter of sex became increasingly more complex. In addition to the emotional aspects of sexuality, such as love and lust, the elements of religion, politics, and law entered the picture. Although procreation was always the dominant theme, the recreational side of sex was not necessarily held in low esteem, except in certain societies where it was essential to maintain a steady birthrate for purposes of survival. For example, homosexuality

Erotic Ostrakon—New Empire

has been virtually nonexistent in cultures where the combined energies of the group were devoted to staying alive.

With the spread and growth of learning and technology, life became proportionately easier. People found themselves able to spend more time exploring new ways to express themselves sexually, without having to worry about the less enchanting aspects of existence. We must never forget, however, that humans are essentially no different now than millennia ago. The actual changes have been mainly external, evident in laws and codes of conduct. Predetermined patterns of behavior have been largely dependent upon the individual tastes of those who have had the power and authority to impose their views on everyone else.

The first sexual revolution came with the ancient Jews. Their strict adherence to monotheism and a determination not to intermarry with their polytheistic neighbors gave rise to a stringent moral code specifically designed to preclude such liaisons. Culturally they were a small group whose primary concern was survival. Propagation of the tribe was of the utmost importance to them and formed a cornerstone of their culture. The laws of Moses enjoined them to "be fruitful and multiply." On these grounds alone masturbation was forbidden; so were sodomy and bestiality—the only licit sexual activity was that which produced progeny.

Christianity appeared, with all of these concepts incorporated in a new faith, but a few new wrinkles were added. St. Paul, who was one of the most influential founding fathers of Christianity, had no use for women, and though he recognized the necessity for procreation, his personal attitude of distaste was completely embodied in the basic Christian doctrine.

Since many early Christian converts came from pagan backgrounds, a great deal of conceptual restructuring was necessary. In order to wean them away from old customs, especially those involving sexuality, every effort was made to associate pre-Christian religious practices with sin and the concept of evil. Harmless fertility gods and goddesses were redesignated as demons, devils, and evil spirits. The devil himself was physically modeled after the satyr—half-goat, half-man, and predominantly sexual in nature. Having been so cruelly persecuted by the Romans, early Christians understandably made a conscious effort to denigrate anything associated with the Romans—and Roman sexuality was an ideal target. It was only the beginning of a long crusade against sexuality. Now admittedly this is a gross oversimplification, but it provides some insight into how present-day attitudes began.

Ironically, as popes replaced caesars in the Eternal City, individual Christians did not change their sex habits appreciably; they merely began to feel guilty about them. Again, the more astute thinkers in the

Mural from the Necropolis at Tarquinia.

church hierarchy made a sensible move. They provided the masses with an infallible escape route—the confessional. They were pioneers, and like pioneers before them elsewhere, their principal concern was with survival.

The Middle Ages saw no sweeping changes in sexual behavior and attitudes. Eroticism in art was disguised by a thin veneer of religious piety. The wealthy and the powerful behaved very much as they pleased, secure in the knowledge that sexual transgressions were readily absolved by the exchange of gold. The poor and the powerless engaged in procreation to provide a labor force and cannon fodder, taking their pleasures where and when they could. During this time, holdovers from ancient phallic worship customs continued to survive. A mysterious relic alleged to be the prepuce of Christ was revered and widely sought after to ensure fertility. In areas more remote from church influence, sexual license was proportionately more open and widespread.

When Pope Innocent VIII issued his edict against witchcraft in the late fifteenth century, there was an upsurge of sexual repression and persecution. The equation of sexuality with evil was emphasized to such an extent that even some of the most influential individuals in Europe, notably Gilles de Rais, Marshal of France, fell victim to the power of Rome.

With the coming of the Renaissance and the humanist movement there was a general relaxation of sexual repression that infused art, literature, and society at large. But the advent of the Reformation brought with it a wave of puritanism that reached its peak in Cromwellian England. In that country especially, the restoration of the Stuarts to the throne gave rise to an eruption of unbridled sexuality in all strata of society, unrivaled perhaps until the 1960s.

The pendulum swung back again during the eighteenth century, although rebels like de Sade and others refused to allow themselves to be swept under the rug of history. It was during this period that modern psychiatry was born. This led eventually to the evolution of modern social scientists determined to place a proper emphasis on the study of sex, men like Krafft-Ebing, Schrenk-Notzink, Havelock Ellis, and Sigmund Freud. With the development of psychoanalysis, a major shift had been accomplished, and though it had certainly not been replaced, the confessional was now supplemented by the couch. Despite all efforts to prevent it, sex was now being regarded as far more than a necessary evil.

Now, what about America? American history texts

14th Century Erotic Quatrefoil, Musee De Cluny, Paris.

The Offering to Priapus after Hypnerotomachia Poliphil by Francesco Colonna, 15th Century.

being what they are, little has been said about sex in the new world. The early settlers were too busy worrying about survival to regard sex as anything more than a means of ensuring future generations. Nevertheless, as time passes many interesting details are coming to light about the sex lives and attitudes of earlier Americans. Certainly when a detailed and accurate sexual history of the U.S.A. is written, fascinating, little-known tidbits will come to light—not the least of which is the fact that itinerant whores were among the prime movers in the taming of the Wild West.

For those who care to examine information available in the nation's libraries, there are volumes of obscure material on sex in America during the Victorian and Edwardian eras. From that point on, thanks to better communications, it is not too diffiult to look at Western society—and sexual attitudes—as a whole.

Today, sexually speaking, the world is as topsy-turvy as it ever was. Ideas and attitudes seem to be ping-ponging about with unpredictable speed. Yesterday's puritan is today's libertine and tomorrow is up for grabs.

Despite all the advances that have been made in the direction of rational sexuality, sex is still one of society's chief scapegoats. While self-proclaimed guardians of public morality in America cry, Cassandra-like, that the Communists are corrupting us with pornography, the Communist press says the same thing about us. While border guards of Eastern bloc nations confiscate copies of *Playboy* and *Penthouse*, U.S. Customs men still seize works of art they consider pornographic.

Worse yet, in the midst of burgeoning crime and economic chaos, headline-seeking politicians and other opportunists launch periodic antismut campaigns to direct the public eye away from their own misdemeanors. Whatever the immediate future holds, the pendulum will swing as it always has, and controversies will rage. Mankind, being what it is, will continue to be the peculiar species it has been from the beginning. Until the vine eventually withers in the twilight before Armageddon, we will keep on gathering our rosebuds, continue singing praises to Eros and Venus, then be ultimately consumed by the final orgasm and returned to the swirling dust of the Cosmos.

The Congress
Anonymous Persian Miniature

Jupiter as a Dragon Approaches Olympia
Giulio Romano

Detail from a mural in the Etruscan tomb at Tarquinia

Sex As You Like It

Heterosexual - Homosexual - Bisexual

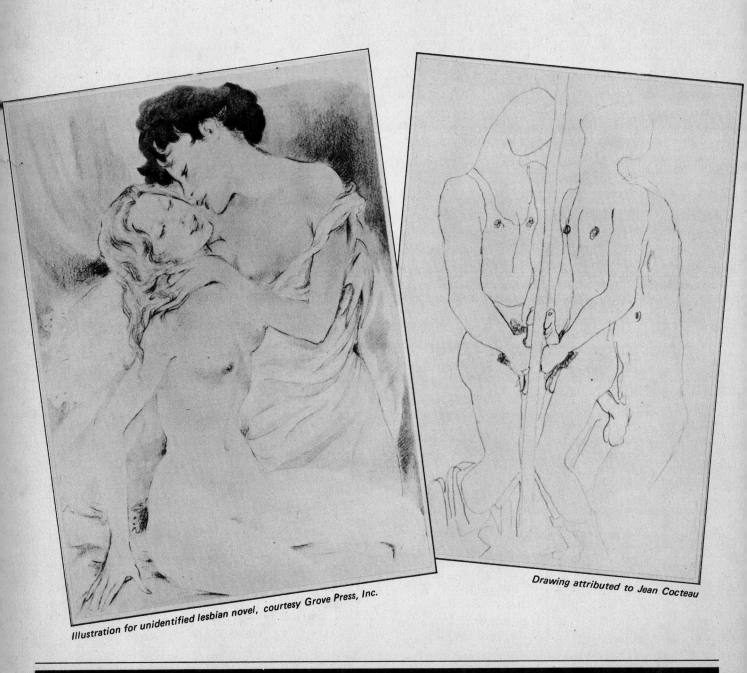

Illustration for unidentified lesbian novel, courtesy Grove Press, Inc.

Drawing attributed to Jean Cocteau

$\mathcal{E}$xcluding the more exotic methods of sexual expression, the fact remains that there are still a variety of common ways for individuals to express their sexual preferences. Although in some societies, especially ancient Greece and Rome, there was little or no stigma attached to homosexuality, the major sexual emphasis in Western culture has been strictly heterosexual. Now, if human beings were machines that could be thoroughly programmed, then it would have been a simple matter throughout time for governments to lay down rules, set whatever norms they chose, and arbitrarily impose their mores on everyone within their spheres of influence. But since this has never been so, people have always been faced with the choice of doing whatever they please or following existing rules, even if this latter course damaged them in the process. The result has been rampant hypocrisy, widespread emotional stress, bloodshed, and recurrent chaos. Establish unattainable goals, and you will inevitably produce misery, frustration, and social ills.

One of the major flaws in human nature has always been, and always will be, an irrepressible impulse to wage war against people with conflicting ideas, and this of course goes beyond sex. Certainly one of the most sensible ideas of modern times is the concept of unrestricted behavior between consenting adults, providing they do not hurt anyone. To paraphrase what George Bernard Shaw's actress friend, Mrs. Pat Campbell, said: "Let people do anything they please as long as they don't do it in the streets and frighten the horses."

Unworkable laws and benighted social customs notwithstanding, every human being has the right to decide upon his or her own sexual orientation. As long as we seek out partners whose feelings coincide with our own, what difference does it make what we or our neighbors do in the privacy of our bedrooms?

Our chief concern in this section is to provide you with information on sexual alternatives and offer you a few obscure tidbits from the past to show you how some of our predecessors expressed themselves on both male and female homosexuality.

The ancient Egyptians, for example, were even more prudish than the Victorians. Etched on the walls of many tombs was the inscription: *I may have been guilty of many things during my lifetime, but I have never been guilty of homosexuality.* A fascinating insight into the Egyptian attitude appears in a legend concerning the two gods, Seth and Horus. It was found on a papyrus dating back to the reign of Rameses V, circa 1150 B.C. Horus was the son of Osiris and Isis, and in this particular legend he is depicted as Seth's brother. After engaging in furious battles they are finally reconciled. What happens immediately afterwards is described as follows:

"Thereupon Seth spake unto Horus: Come, let us spend a happy day in my house. Thereupon Horus said unto him: I will do so, verily I will do so. And when it was eventide the bed was spread for them, and they twain lay down. And in the night Seth caused his member to become stiff, and he made it go between the loins of Horus. Thereupon Horus put his two hands between his loins, and he caught the seed of Seth. Thereupon Horus went to speak unto his mother Isis: 'Come unto me O Isis, my mother! Come and see this which Seth hath done to me!' And he opened his hand, and he caused her to see the seed of Seth. And she cried out aloud, and she seized her knife, she cut off his hand, and she cast it into the water. And she drew out for him a hand of like worth."

The ancient Greek attitude toward homosexuality was nothing like that of today. Although effeminate behavior in males was scorned, physical love between members of the same sex was condoned. With rules and taboos, it was a highly complicated matter. G.

*Engraving by Felicien Rops
Belgium, 19th century
Courtesy Drs. Phyllis and
Eberhard Kronhausen*

Rattray Taylor, in *Sex in History*, writes of one aspect, saying that the "nobler relationship was not the eccentricity of a few, but was absolutely general. It was a disgrace for a boy not to be chosen by anyone [*i.e.*, an older man]; when any boy was chosen, the arrangement was agreed to by his parents. 'I know not any greater blessing to a young man beginning life,' said Phaedrus in the *Symposium*, 'than a virtuous lover, or to the lover than a beloved youth.' Such relationships were general also in mythology, a fact which the modern editors have found difficult to disguise."

One view of the female side of the coin may be seen in this extract from Lucian's *Dialogues of the Courtesans*. The narrator is a young woman named Leaina.

Megilla and Demonassa, rich Corinthian women, smitten with the same tastes, gave themselves over to an orgy. I was taken to their house to sing and accompany myself on the lyre. The songs and the night grew longer; it was the hour for rest. They were drunk.

Then Megilla said, "Leaina, it is time to sleep. Come lie here between us."

First they gave me some male kisses, not only by joining their lips to mine, but with mouths open. I felt myself clasped in their arms. They bruised my breast. Demonassa bit me in kissing me. I knew not where all this had to end. Fianlly, Megilla, thoroughly inflamed, flung back her coiffure, pressed me, threatened me like a young, robust athlete, and . . .

"Well, Leaina," she said to me, "have you seen a handsomer boy?"

"'A boy, Megilla? I do not see any here.'"

"Cease to regard me as a woman. Today I call myself Megillus, and I have married Demonassa."

I began to laugh. "I knew not, handsome Megillus," I said to her, "that you were here like Achilles in the midst of the virgins of Scyros. Nothing is lacking in you, no doubt, of what characterizes a young hero, and Demonassa has experienced it?"

"Leaina, I am like you, but I feel in myself the wild passion and burning desires of a man."

"Desire? Is that all?"

"Deign to lend yourself to my transports, Leaina, and you shall see that my caresses are virile. Deign to lend yourself, and you shall depart. . ."

She entreated me long, made me a gift of a precious necklace and a diaphanous cloak. I offered myself, she embraced me, kissed me, writhed . . . She succumbed under the weight of voluptuousness.

The lesbian of the seventies, especially the feminist lesbian, will rightly take exception to this little scene, for though it depicts physical lovemaking between women, it emphasizes traditional role playing, and it was written by a man who imparted his own viewpoint to it.

If we may take the liberty of jumping ahead to the seventeenth century we can touch briefly on a totally different literary look at homosexuality. In one of his wittiest works, *Sodom; Or the Quintessence of Debauchery* [see Sex and the Performing Arts], the Earl of Rochester reduced a mythical society to utter absurdity. Here, the homosexual king of Sodom declares heterosexuality out and homosexuality in, by royal decree. Naturally by the time the final curtain falls, everything is going up in smoke. Any intelligent person—sexual preferences aside—can immediately grasp Rochester's point. You can't force people to follow an arbitrarily chosen mode of sexuality against their will. It is tantamount to socio-political rape. Yet

Drawing attributed to Jean Cocteau

Martin
Van Maele,
turn of
the century
Belgian master

the modern homosexual, who is forced to live under laws the reverse of those imposed by the fictional king of Sodom, is as much a victim as that monarch's hapless heterosexual subjects.

So much for ancient history.

Our primary concern here is *today*. For the first time in modern history, homosexuals—male and female—and bisexuals are asserting themselves, taking a political stand, accepting themselves, and striving to gain general acceptance by society at large. Despite the fact that they are in a better position now than they were in the 1950s, they are still very much an underdog minority group, recognizing all too well that in certain sectors they are subject to abuse, discrimination, and in many instances blatant persecution.

It is appropriate to take a brief look at what some of the more articulate members of the gay community are saying. A great deal of new awareness has sprung out of the Women's Movement, especially as a result of consciousness raising. An exceptionally revealing article by Anne Koedt, titled "Loving Another Woman,"* first appeared in *Notes from the Third Year: Women's Liberation* and was later reprinted in *Ms.* Magazine. It consisted of an interview with a woman who had been strictly heterosexual, but who eased into a love-relationship with a female friend as a result of their mutually expanded sexual awareness.

The interviewee describes her initial realization of a new feeling for her friend as it occurred one night after a meeting. She stayed overnight at her friend's and slept on the couch, recalling: "It wasn't really until I tried to fall asleep, and couldn't, that all of a sudden I became very very aware. I was flooded with a tremendous attraction for her. And I wanted to tell her, I wanted to sleep with her, I wanted to let her

*Copyright © 1971 by Anne Koedt

know what I was feeling. At the same time I was totally bewildered, because here I was—not only did I want to tell her, but I was having a hard time just facing up to what was coming out in myself. My mind was working overtime trying to deal with this new thing. . . . When I did bring it up to her in an oblique way, and told her that I was attracted to her, she replied somewhat generally that she felt the same way. You see, she was as scared as I was, but I didn't know it."

They began sleeping together after this, first non-sexually, and finally sexually. Initially the interviewee did not think that the relationship would be very physical, assuming it would be basically "warm and affectionate." She said, "I think I probably thought this because with men sex is so frequently confused with conquest. . . ." She went on to say, "Perhaps I wasn't quite sure what would happen sexually once it was removed from its conventional context. But one of the things I discovered was that when you really like somebody, there's a perfectly natural connection between love and sensuality and sexuality. That sexuality is a natural part of sensuality."

This is a point that comes up again and again in *The Bisexuals*, by Bernhardt J. Hurwood. Once she became accustomed to the new relationship, she recognized that it had "added a whole new dimension" to her own sexuality. She emphasized that, contrary to the stereotyped misconception, she was not "lost" to heterosexual relationships, and that her expanded sexual horizon did not mean she would now jump into bed with every attractive woman she met. She did not regard her involvement with another woman as a political gesture, and she emphasized that she saw no reason why she could not love a man in the future with the same intensity of feeling that she presently loved her friend. She strenuously objected to the confusing of sexual *partners* with sexual *roles*. She summed up by saying, "If you want to remove sexual roles, and if you say that men and women are equal human beings, well, the next question is: why should

you love only men? I remember asking myself that question, and I remember it being discussed in many workshops I was in—what is it that makes us assume that you can only receive and give love to a man?"

This woman's viewpoint is certainly opposed to that of the radical lesbians, but it is rational and deserving of serious attention. Yet it is still a difficult concept for those who regard homosexuality as a personal threat, and it remains a matter with which they themselves must come to terms.

Probably one of the most comprehensive handbooks for homosexuals is John Francis Hunter's *The Gay Insider/U.S.A.,* for it offers a full range of information about gay publications large and small, organizations (including religious), a state-by-state guide to gay activities, and much more. Quoting a California Gay Liberationist, Hunter writes:

"Homosexuality is *not* a lot of things. It is not a makeshift in the absence of the opposite sex; it is not genetic; it is not the result of broken homes (except inasmuch as we see the sham of American marriage). *Homosexuality is the capacity to love someone of the same sex.*"

And that, we think, synthesizes the homosexual viewpoint as concisely as it has been expressed anywhere.

Alexander the Great before the God Kim at Karnak. *Watercolor, reprinted courtesy of Drs. Phyllis and Eberhard Kronhausen*

The Two Friends. *Felicien Rops*

Oscar Wilde by Aubrey Beardsley. *From* The Collected Drawings of Aubrey Beardsley *edited by Bruce S. Harris.* © *1967 by Crescent Books, Inc. Used by permission of Crown Publishers, Inc.*

Straight Meets Gay

by Jake Millar

*W*e have all heard stories about men and women being seduced by homosexuals and being thoroughly disturbed as a result; the clichéd reaction to such an encounter is either serious trauma to the seduced or complete transformation to homosexuality. Here is another viewpoint, an actual case in which a young man had an unexpected homosexual encounter and dealt with it in objective, introspective terms. Jake Millar is the pseudonym of a young man now working in the communications field.

The Mobius Strip
Painting by Michel Desimon, 1966

Man
*Drawing by
Raphael*

*O*ne day I came face to face with a question I didn't want to face. I'd been a happily heterosexual male all my life, and suddenly I faced the prospect of finding out I was a closet fag.

I was working on an off-Broadway show with a group of people I had recently met. The leader of the group was an attractive, well-built man of open countenance and great personal magnetism. His manner was somewhat effete, but I knew this wasn't necessarily the mark of a homosexual; lots of show-business types act that way.

For three weeks we worked very closely together in his apartment, which had lots of space for rehearsal. I was working on the show only during the evenings, and I would invariably stay late, studying musical arrangements or going over script revisions. On such occasions I noticed one of the players would stay late as well, but I thought nothing of it until one particular evening.

It was to be a rehearsal for the musicians only, of whom I was one. John, the leader, was there. So was Eric, the player who spent so much time at the apartment. After the rehearsal, the three of us sat around, relaxing after a long week. Eric was sitting in an easy chair, knitting. John came from the kitchen, leaned down over Eric, and kissed him on the lips.

All the half-thoughts which had lain dormant and unformed in my brain suddenly crystallized into an obvious conclusion: these two were lovers. It fit together very neatly, and I felt rather foolish for not having figured it out sooner.

I had little time to ponder this turnabout, though. John asked me if I wanted to take a Quaalude. My experience with that drug was rather limited: I'd tried one the previous week, and it had made me feel dizzy and uncoordinated. I thought there must be some reason everyone else was taking it, so I decided to give it another try. And that was my undoing.

Detail from
The Last Judgment
by Michelangelo
The Sistine Chapel,
Rome

A very important fact to remember about soporifics is that they release inhibitions and heighten physical sensations and in this case, very pleasantly.

About ten minutes after swallowing the tablet, I felt nicely rounded about the edges. I was lying on a waterbed in the front room, and the rolling motion of the mattress made me feel languid and sensuous.

John and Eric and I had gotten to be pretty close in the several weeks we'd worked together, but I was surprised when John began to caress my chest in graceful, flowing strokes. I say surprised, but not taken aback. The drug had taken effect, and I was able to look upon myself with the peculiar detachment drugs can induce. There I was, being amorously approached by another man, and I was neither ashamed nor frightened. The part of my mind which watched me was amused and somewhat surprised by my lack of fear. After a lifetime of conditioning which had attempted to make homosexuality abhorrent to me, I was enjoying the whole scene and anticipating further developments with considerable curiosity and little anxiety.

After several minutes of gentle caresses the three of us began to shed our clothes and seek one another's mouths. I kissed both of them on their lips, and as clothing became less of a concern, in other places. By now I was aware that I was gaining an erection. The heat of their bodies, the excitement of doing something forbidden without feeling guilty or perverted, and my own waxing interest, conspired to make me grow large—a fact which didn't go unnoticed or unappreciated.

The three of us cavorted on the waterbed, three writhing bodies twisting around one another in an ever-changing erotic triangle. Mouths sought penises, and I suddenly realized that I was about to do something I'd only heard about. Eric was anointing my penis with "joy jelly." John, meanwhile, was sucking Eric's dick, and I took some of the jelly from Eric and began massaging John's organ. In the kaleidoscopic scene, I said to John, "Me and Eric?"

He only nodded his head in stuporous assent, his attention held by my active fingers. I was ready; Eric was ready. We maneuvered about so that I could enter Eric from behind. I felt strong and hard as I slowly slid my tool into the tight tube of his anus. As I did so, Eric exclaimed in joy at the pressure I put upon his central core. In and out I pumped; unlike a woman, the path was dry and hard, not wet and soft. I felt that I could do this all night without coming, but that didn't bother me because I could feel Eric shuddering with delight, moving closer and closer to release. Suddenly he came, and moments later I withdrew.

Then Eric went down on me and within minutes brought me to delightful surcease. And it was over. We all lay about, and still bathed in the warmth of sex and the mists of the drug, we fell asleep, to wake the next morning feeling refreshed and alert.

My most vivid impression of the whole thing was—okay, so this is what it's like. Well, it's just too bad that these guys don't dig women, because, while I can see the pleasure in this kind of an experience, it pales next to the mutual rewards of heterosexual love. I felt released, relieved that I wasn't drawn to homosexuality. Satisfied that I had enjoyed myself, and yet had confirmed my hopes and dispelled my fears. Pleased that I hadn't reacted with disgust, or with wild enthusiasm. It was educational, a thing to finally have known and understood as a part of the life experience.

I don't know whether it will ever happen again. Right now, I doubt it. It wasn't truly a turn-on, and after all, that's what sex is all about.

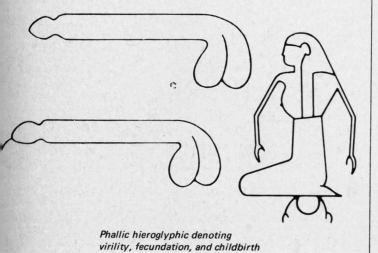

Phallic hieroglyphic denoting virility, fecundation, and childbirth

Preamble to the Constitution and Bylaws of Gay Activists Alliance / New York

"We as Liberated Homosexual activists demand the freedom for expression of our dignity and value as human beings through confrontation with and disarmament of all mechanisms which unjustly inhibit us: economic, social, and political. Before the public conscience, we demand an immediate end to all oppression of homosexuals and the immediate unconditional recognition of these basic rights:

"**The right to our own feelings.** This is the right to feel attracted to the beauty of members of our own sex and to embrace those feelings as truly our own, free from any question or challenge whatsoever by any other person, institution, or 'moral authority.'"

"**The right to love.** This is the right to express our feelings in action, the right to make love with anyone, any way, anytime, provided only that such action be freely chosen by the individuals concerned."

"**The right to our own bodies.** This is the right to treat and express our bodies as we will, to nurture, display and embellish them solely in the manner we ourselves determine, independent of any external control whatsoever."

"**The right to be persons.** This is the right freely to express our own individuality under the governance of laws justly made and executed, and to be the bearers of social and political rights which are guaranteed by the Constitution of the United States and the Bill of Rights, enjoined upon all legislative bodies and courts, and grounded in the fact of our common humanity."

"To secure these rights we hereby institute the Gay Activists Alliance, which shall be completely and solely dedicated to their implementation and maintenance, repudiating, at the same time, violence (except for the right of self-defense) as unworthy politically or socially and forbearing alliance with any group except for those whose concrete actions are likewise so specifically dedicated."

"It is finally to the imagination of oppressed homosexuals themselves that we commend the consideration of these rights, upon whose actions alone depends all hope for the prospect of their lasting procurement."

*Phallic mobile of lead and bronze
Pompeii, first century A.D.*

Gay Activists Alliance's Twenty Questions About Homosexuality

1. Who is a homosexual?

2. How is a person's sexual orientation determined?

3. Can a person change his or her sexual orientation?

4. How many homosexuals are there?

5. Are homosexuals easy to identify? By appearance? Behavior? Choice of profession?

6. Are there two types of homosexuals, active and passive?

7. Is homosexuality "against nature"?

8. Does religion tell us that it's immoral?

9. Is homosexuality socially destructive? Has it always accompanied decadent societies?

10. Is homosexuality a mental illness?

11. Are homosexuals all neurotic?

12. Are homosexuals more "promiscuous" than heterosexuals?

13. Are homosexual relationships as stable as heterosexual ones?

14. Is homosexual love different from heterosexual love?

15. Does our society discriminate against homosexuals?

16. Is there reason to bar homosexuals from certain kinds of employment? Are homosexuals security risks?

17. Should homosexuals be allowed to work with children in schools and camps? Are homosexuals child molesters?

18. Must there be any laws relating to homosexuals? What about prostitution? Public sex?

19. If there weren't any antihomosexual laws, would homosexuals be encouraged to proselytize? Would there be more homosexuals as a result?

20. Is it better, in this society, to be heterosexual?

For the pamphlet and the answers to the questions, write: Gay Activists Alliance, P.O. Box 2, Village Station, New York, N.Y. 10014. (Include 50¢ postage.)

Gay Liberation Groups around the Country

*Ancient Roman
terra cotta bas relief*

Listed below is a representative cross-country sampling of the major gay organizations. A complete state-by-state, town-by-town list is available in John Francis Hunter's *The Gay Insider/U.S.A.*, published in paperback by Stonehill for $3.95 (distributed by Dell Books and available at major bookstores across the country). For gay groups outside of the U.S. or for further information, consult the various published Gay Directories listed in this section.

CALIFORNIA

Gay Community Alliance
525 N. Laurel Ave.
Los Angeles, California 90048
c/o Jim Kepner or P.O. Box 39408

Gay Community Services Center
1614 Wilshire Blvd.
Los Angeles, California 90017

Gay Liberation Front
c/o Morris Knight
1822 W. 4th Street, or
P.O. Box 29280
Los Angeles, California 90029

Sexual Freedom League
P.O. Box 7856
Los Angeles, California 90807

Gay Liberation Front
P.O. Box 40397
San Francisco, California 94140

Mattachine Society, Inc.
348 Ellis Street
San Francisco, California

DISTRICT OF COLUMBIA

Gay Activists Alliance
P.O. Box 2554
Washington, D.C. 20013

Mattachine Society
P.O. Box 1032
Washington, D.C. 20013

FLORIDA

Gay Activists Alliance
P.O. Box 679
Miami, Florida 33133

HAWAII

Gay Community Alliance
P.O. Box R-3
Room 203
Hemenway Hall
Univ. of Hawaii, Hawaii 96822

ILLINOIS

Mattachine Midwest
P.O. Box 924
Chicago, Illinois 60690

Gay Community Center
171 W. Elm Street
Chicago, Illinois 60610

MASSACHUSETTS

Homophile Community Health Center
Boston (HUB)
P.O. Box 217
Dorchester Station
Boston, Massachusetts 02124

Boston Gay Phone: (617) 354-1555, 1556

MINNESOTA

Fight Repression of Erotic
Expression/Gay Liberation of Minnesota
Rm. B-67, Coffman Memorial Union
University of Minnesota
Minneapolis, Minnesota 55455

NEW YORK

Gay Activists Alliance
P.O. Box 2
Village Station
New York, New York 10014

Gay Switchboard
(212) 924-4036

Mattachine Society of New York
59 Christopher Street
New York, New York 10014

TEXAS

Gay Liberation Front
P.O. Box 53221
Sam Houston Station
Houston, Texas 77052

Circle of Friends
P.O. Box 35852
Dallas, Texas 75235

WASHINGTON

Counseling Service for Homosexuals
318 Malden Ave, E.
Seattle, Washington 98102

WISCONSIN

Gay Liberation Front
University of Wisconsin
10 Langdon Street
Madison, Wisconsin 53703

Gay Liberation Organization
c/o Fr. Joseph Felhausen
115 N. 21st Street
Milwaukee, Wisconsin 53211

Lesbian Organizations

ATLANTA LESBIAN FEMINIST ALLIANCE
P.O. Box 7963
Atlanta, Georgia 30309

LESBIAN FEMINIST LIBERATION
P.O. Box 243
Village Station
New York, New York 10014

GAY ADVOCATES
325 Michigan Union
Ann Arbor, Michigan 48104

GAWK/GAY AWARENESS WOMEN'S KOLLECTIVE
Feminist House
225 East Liberty
Ann Arbor, Michigan 48104

LESBIAN RESOURCE CENTER
710 West 22nd Street
Minnepolis, Minnesota 55405

LESBIAN RESOURCE CENTER
YWCA University of Washington
4224 University Way, N.E.
Seattle, Washington 98105

LESBIAN SWITCHBOARD
(212) 741-2610

For other lesbian organizations around the country, consult your favorite gay publication or your local Gay Liberation group.

Engraving by Mihaly Zichy, 19th century Hungarian artist. From The Erotic Drawing of Mihaly Zichy compiled by Drs. Phyllis and Eberhard Kronhausen. Copyright © 1969 by Grove Press, Inc. Reprinted by permission of the publisher

Bisexuality

*T*he bisexual, male or female, is faced with a dilemma. Regarded by the straight community as a homosexual who won't admit it, and by segments of the gay community as a homosexual who is copping out, bisexuals have finally come out on their own and are now insisting upon recognition as a distinct group. Many are happily married and enjoy, as they put it, a sex life encompassing the best of all possible worlds.

Bisexuals now have their own organization, National Bisexual Liberation. Founded in 1972 by Don Fass and friends, Bi-Lib now has over 1,500 members and chapters in five states.

"While being bisexual may not be for everyone," says founder Don Fass, "for those of us who have grown into it or would like to, whether coming from gay or straight, we believe bisexuality to be the fullest expression of human liberation. It is a state in which we can love and grow, reaching out with warmth, openness, and our fullest potential to any individual we care about—be they genital females or males. Our emphasis is on growth, but we're aware of our political responsibilities."

National Bisexual Liberation acts as a clearing house for bisexual information and publications. They sponsor workshops, consciousness raising groups, and social events. Membership dues are $5.00 per year, $3.00 for students. They publish a monthly newsletter, *The Bisexual Expression.*

For additional information write:

National Bisexual Liberation
345 West 85th Street
New York, N.Y. 10024

Or phone: (212) 595-5365

Bisexual Newsletters

BISEXUAL EXPRESSION, the monthly newsletter of National Bisexual Liberation. $4.00 per year. (10 issues) Suite 46, 345 West 85th Street, New York, N.Y. 10024

BISEXUALITY, Annual Magazine. Published by the National Bi-Lib. $1.50. 345 W. 85th Street, New York, N.Y. 10024

EVERYTHING YOU WANT TO KNOW ABOUT BISEXUALITY. Center for Humanistic Sexuality. 75¢ per issue. (15 or more, 40¢) Available from the National Bisexual Liberation.

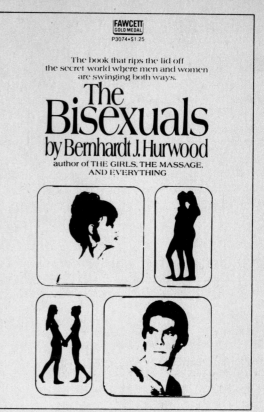

The first mass market paperback on the subject of bisexuality, and also the first original paperback ever to be excerpted in VOGUE

Homosexual Magazines and Newspapers

THE ADVOCATE
Newspaper of America's homophile community.
Box 74695
Los Angeles, California 90004
Biweekly. 13 issues/$4.00

AIN'T A WOMAN?
Gay women's radical paper.
Box 1169
Iowa City, Iowa 52240
Approx. bimonthly.

AMAZON QUARTERLY
Lesbian-feminist arts journal.
554 Valle Vista
Oakland, California 94610
Quarterly/$4.00

Lithograph attributed to Andre Dunoyer de Segonzac

BIG DAVID
A gay tabloid, published biweekly by Valerie Publications.
204 W. 20th Street
New York, N.Y. 10011
75¢ per issue

THE BODY POLITIC
Gay Liberation Journal.
139 Seaton Street
Toronto, Ontario, Canada
Bi-monthly. 6 issues/$2.00

COWRIE
Lesbian/Feminist.
359 E. 68th Street
New York, N.Y. 10021
Irregular. 10 issues /$5.00

COMING OUT
Gay women's newsletter at Oberlin College.
P.O. Box
Oberlin, College
Oberlin, Ohio
(216) 774-1221

DIGNITY
A national publication of the gay Catholic community.
755 Boylston, Room 514
Boston, Massachusetts 02116
Monthly.

FAG RAG
A gay male publication.
Box 331 Kenmore Station
Boston, Massachusetts 02215
Quarterly. 12 issues/$5.00

ECHO OF SAPPHO
A lesbian/feminist publication.
Sisters for Liberation
P.O. Box 263
Brooklyn, New York 11217
Quarterly 50¢ per issue.

FOCUS
A journal for gay women.
c/o Boston DOB
419 Boylston, Room 323
Boston, Massachusetts 02116
Monthly.

THE GAY ALTERNATIVE
Journal of gay people.
232 South Street
Philadelphia, Pennsylvania 19147
Bimonthly. 10 issues/$3.50

THE GAY CHRISTIAN
A journal of Metropolitan Community Church, MCC/New York.
Box 1757 GPO
New York, N.Y. 10001
4-6 issues a year. 12 issues/$5.00

For a complete list of major gay magazines and newspapers published around the U.S. and Canada, consult John Francis Hunter's *The Gay Insider/U.S.A.*

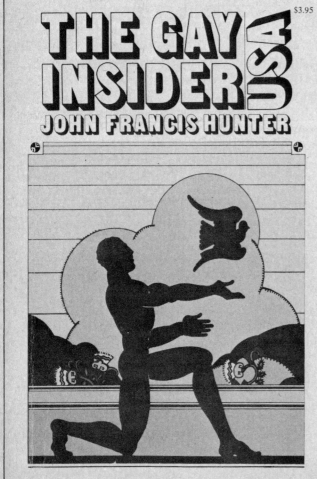

GAY LIBERATOR
A newspaper for gay activism.
Box 631-A
Detroit, Michigan 48232
Monthly.

GAY LITERATURE
A new quarterly. $2.00 per issue. A magazine devoted to literature.
Dr. Daniel Curzon
English Department
State University of California
Fresno, California 93740

GAY PEOPLE AND MENTAL HEALTH
Newsletter on events and resources.
Box 3592
Nicollet Station
Minneapolis, Minnesota 55403
Monthly.

GAY SUNSHINE
A journal of gay liberation.
P.O. Box 40397
San Francisco, California 94140
Bimonthly. 12/issues $5.00

GAY TIMES
An adult only newspaper.
17620 Sherman Way, Suite 10
Van Nuys, California 91406
$1.00 per issue

GAY WORLD SWINGER
A swinging newspaper for gay people.
$3.00 per copy or $15.00 for six issues.

HOMOSEXUAL COUNSELING JOURNAL
Quarterly.
Journal to the Helping Professions
921 Madison Avenue
New York, N.Y. 10021

INTERCHANGE
Magazine of the National Gay Student Center.
2115 S St. N.W.
Washington, D.C. 20008
Bimonthly. $3.00 per issue

IN TOUCH
A magazine celebrating gay awareness.
P.O. Box 3453
Hollywood, California 90028
1 year $15.00

IT'S TIME
Newsletter of the National Gay Task Force.
NGTF, Suite 903
80 5th Avenue
New York, N.Y. 10011
Monthly. $15.00 (including membership in NGTF).

JOURNAL OF HOMOSEXUALITY
Journal for the mental health and behavioral science professions.
Haworth Press
53 W. 72nd Street
New York, N.Y. 10023
Quarterly. $12.00

Sample table of contents IN TOUCH *popular California Gay Magazine*

THE GAY EXPERIENCE   JUNE 1975 $1.00

VECTOR

Interracial Love
Cruising
Gay Soul
The Happy Hustler

THE LESBIAN FEMINIST
A lesbian paper.
Box 243
Village Station
New York, N.Y. 10014
Monthly. $3.00

LAVENDER WOMAN
A lesbian and arts newsletter.
Box 60206
1723 W. Devon
Chicago, Illinois 60660
8-9 issues a year. $3.00

LAZETTE
The official newsletter of New Jersey Daughters of Bilitis. For price and information write:
New Jersey D.O.B.
P.O. Box 62
Fanwood, New Jersey

LONG TIME COMING
Canadian/lesbian feminist newspaper.
Box 161 Station E.
Montreal Quebec, Canada

MICHAEL'S THING
An entertainment magazine, published weekly.
37 Riverside Drive, Suite 3a
New York, N.Y. 10023
50¢ per copy. 1 year subscription, $20.00

OUT
A gay magazine.
Box E.
Old Chelsea Station
New York, N.Y. 10011
Monthly. (Cover price $1.00)

PORTCULLUS
A feminist/lesbian publication.
P.O. Box 65791
Los Angeles, California 90065
$5.00 per 12 issues.

ROOM
A quarterly publication to expand and forward the creativity of all women.
10 Laguna Street
San Francisco, California 94102.
(No fixed price, donations expected.)

SISTERS
A magazine by and for gay women.
1005 Market, Suite 402
San Francisco, California 94103
Monthly. $5.00

SO'S YOUR OLD LADY
The official magazine of the Lesbian Resource Center in Minneapolis.
LRC
710 West 22nd Street
Minneapolis, Minnesota 55405

THE TIDE
A lesbian feminist publication by and for the rising tide of women today.
The Tide Collective
373 N. Western Avenue, No. 202
Los Angeles, California 90004
Monthly. Free, but donation requested.

TRES FEMMES
Publication for women
c/o Gay Center for Social Services
2250 B. St.
San Diego, California 92102
2-4 issues a year. 4 issues/$3.50

VECTOR
A magazine celebrating the gay experience.
The Society for Individual Rights
83 Sixth Street
San Francisco, California 94103
Monthly. $1.00 per copy

Selected Homosexual Newspapers and Magazines around the World

Drawing by Pollaiolo (1430-1498)

SAPPHO
The only lesbian magazine in Europe.
BCM/Petrel
London, WCIV
England
Pay in sterling only by International money order.
Subscriptions: sealed £4.66p; wrapper £3.28p

GAY NEWS
Europe's largest circulation newspaper for homosexuals (every two weeks). 15p per issue
62a Chiswick High Road
London, W. 14
England
Subscriptions: overseas prices available on request.
England. £2.75p for 13 issues

AUSTRALIA

Sydney Gay Liberation Newsletter
P.O. Box A76
Sydney, South 2000
New South Wales

CANADA

The Gay Canadian
Canadian Gay Activists Alliance
P.O. Box 284, Station, A.
Vancouver, 1, B.C.

Gay Book News
Catalyst Press
315 Blantyre Ave.
Scarborough, Ontario

Quebecoise Deboutte!
Centre des Femmes
4319 Rue St. Denis
Montreal, 130, Quebec

DENMARK

Paedoposten
Paedofil Gruppe
BBC Box Nr. 59
Vesterbrogade 208, Denmark

DEUTSCHLAND

DON
c/o Bibipress AG
D-6000 Frankfurt 70
Postfach 700229, Germany

Him—das Magazin mit de Mann
D-2000 Hamburg 4, Postfach 102
Hein-Hoyer-Strasse 12. Hamburg
Germany

Homophiler Nachrichtendienst (Gay News)
c/o Johannes Werres
D-6242, Kronberg, Mainblick 15
Germany

ESPANA

Aghois
Movimiento Espanol de Liberacion Homosexual
c/o National Gay Task Force
80 Fifth Avenue
New York, N.Y. 10011

FRANCE

Le Fleau Social
c/o Alain Fleig,
8 Rue Linne, F-75005
Paris, France

GREAT BRITAIN

Follow-up
Don Bugsby Studios
200d Railton Road
Herne Hill
London, S.E. 24. England

Gay News
62a Chiswick High Road
London, W.4. England

Just Us
POB Ox 804
London, W.4. England

Spare Rib
9 Newburgh Street
London, W.1. England

ITALY

Homo
Via Romagna
Opera (Milano), Italy

Noi e gli altri
Via delle Fratte di Trastevere 42
Roma, Italy

NEDERLAND

Onder Anderen
Deltaboek, Postbus 92
Ridderkerk
Nederland

NEW ZEALAND

The Circle
P.O. Box 427
Wellington, New Zealand

NIPPON

Bara-zoku
5-2-11 Daizawa
Setagaya-ku
Tokyo 155, Japan

NORGE

Kontakt
Postboks 6550
Rodeløkka, Oslo 5
Oslo 5, Norway

PUERTO RICO

Pa'fuera
Comunidad de Orgullo Gay Apartado 5523
Puerta de Tierra
San Juan, Puerto Rico 00906

SWEDEN

Revolt
Revolt Press AB
Box 15, S-360 70
Aseda, Sweden

Sexualpolitik
Homosexuella Socialister
c/o RFSL Stockholm
Timmermansgatan 24, S-116 49
Stockholm, Sweden

SWITZERLAND

Hey
Schweizerische Organisation der Homophilen
Postfach 428
CH-8022,
Zurich, Switzerland

The Following Is a Recommended List of

Gay Films and Musical Recordings

HOME MOVIE by Jan Oxenberg. 16mm film, color and b/w, sound 11 mins. 1973. Multi-Media Resource Center, 540 Powell Street, San Francisco, California 94108. Est. rental $20.00. Est. purchase $100.

THE INVISIBLE MINORITY: THE HOMOSEXUALS IN OUR SOCIETY by Derych Calderwood and Wasyl Szkodzinsky. 3 color filmstrips with three records. Approx. 20 minutes each. 1972. Dept. of Education & Social Concern. Unitarian Universalist Assn. 25 Beacon, Boston, Massachusetts 02108. Purchase only $60.00.

LAVENDER by Colleen Monahan and Elaine Jacobs. 16mm film (also 8mm and video cassette), color, sound, 13 mins. 1972. Perennial Education Inc. 1825 Willow Road, Box 236, Northfield, Illinois 60093. Rental $17. Purchase $170.

ON BEING GAY. Cassette tape, 60 mins. 1973. Thesis Creative Educational Resources, Box 11724, Pittsburgh, Pennsylvania 15228. Purchase $5.98.

A POSITION OF FAITH by Michael Rhodes. 16mm film, color, sound, 18 mins. 1973. Contemporary/McGraw Hill Films. 333 W. 42nd Street, New York, N.Y. 10036. Rental $25.00. Purchase $250. Rental also at $15.00 from Office of Visual-Audios, United Church of Christ, 600 Grand Ave., Ridgefield, New Jersey 07657.

SANDY AND MADELEINE'S FAMILY by Sherrie Farrell et al. 16mm film, color, sound, 29 minutes. 1973. Multi-Media Resource Center, 540 Powell Street, San Francisco, California 94108. Est. rental $50. Est. purchase $300.

SECOND LARGEST MINORITY and **GAY AND PROUD** by Lilli Vincenz. 16mm films (one reel) b/w, sound, total 18 mins. 1968 & 1970. Lilli Vincenz, 5411 S. 8th Place, Arlington, Virginia 22204. Purchase $135, prepaid (includes sound transcript), rental by arrangement.

SOME OF YOUR BEST FRIENDS by Kenneth Robinson et al. 16mm film, color, sound, 40 mins. 1971. University of Southern California, Division of Cinema, University Park, Los Angeles, California 90007. Rental $25. Purchase $325.

Recordings

CARAVAN TONIGHT. Steven Grossman—LP record on the Mercury Label. Album of gay-lib songs. $5.98. Available from record stores and Oscar Wilde Bookstore, 15 Christopher St., New York, N.Y. 10014.

LAVENDER JANE LOVES WOMEN. Alix Dobkin and friends. A celebration of lesbian love and the Oscar Wilde Memorial Bookstore's best-selling record. $4.98 (Available from the Oscar Wilde Bookstore, 15 Christopher St., New York, N.Y. 10014.)

STONEWALL NATION sung by Madeline Davis. 45 rpm record. 50¢. Available from the Oscar Wilde Bookstore, 15 Christopher Street, New York, N.Y. 10014.

Gay Directories

THE ADDRESS BOOK. Bob Damron's 1975 edition of his guide for the United States and Canada for gay men and women. $5.00. (Available at the Oscar Wilde Bookstore, 15 Christopher Street, New York, N.Y. 10014.)

GAY ACTION IS IN FLORIDA. A handbook for homosexuals and lesbians around Florida. Published by Arthur Brickman Associates, 7228 Biscayne Boulevard, Miami, Florida 33138. $1.00 per copy.

GAYELLOW PAGES. Classified directory of gay businesses, services, organizations, publications, bars, and much more. Box 292, Village Station, New York, N.Y. 10014. Three times a year. Single issue $5.00. Four-issue subscription $10.00.

THE GAY INSIDER/U.S.A. A Stonehill book by John Francis Hunter. Lists the gay liberation groups, religious groups, gay publications, gay bars, and clubs around America. Paper edition $3.95.

THE GIRL'S GUIDE. An international guide for gay women, including Europe and the United States. $5.00. (Published in England but available at the Oscar Wilde Bookstore, 15 Christopher Street, New York, N.Y. 10014.)

INTERNATIONAL LIST OF GAY ORGANIZATIONS. (No. 4) Available from the Gay Activists Alliance, New York. Box 2, Village Station, New York, N.Y. 10014. $1.00.

SPARTACUS INTERNATIONAL. A gay guide around the world. Text in English, Deutsch, and Français. Published by Euro-Spartacus, P.O. Box 3496, Amsterdam, Holland. (Also available at major bookstores across America.) Annual

STUDENT GAY GROUPS. List of gay groups at member colleges of the National Student Association. Available from the National Gay Student Center, 2115 S Street, N.W., Washington, D.C. 20008. (25c each.)

FRANCE — NICE

Hotels
HOTEL REGENCE
21 rue Massena (87 75 08)
HOTEL DE CASTILLE
30 rue Massena (87 88 63)

Saunas
HAMMAM DU CHATEAU (M)
17 rue des Ponchette, Quai des Etats-Unis
SAUNA DES PLATANES (M)
5 rue Foncet

Outside cruising
Parc du Château (daytime)
Parc Albert I (AYOR) in front of Hotel Plaza
Parc Gustav V
Place Wilson
Promenade des Anglais (late)

Beaches
On the rocks of Cap de Nice, at far end. Illicit nude sunbathing. Very busy

Facilities
At bus station
In main railway station (quai 1 and 3 only)
In Gustav V Parc, opposite Air France (2200-?)

Gay Groups
Arcadie (c/o Arcadie Paris)
FHAR de Nice
Gedlip
B.P. 621 06 Nice

NIMES 30 (Gard)

Outside cruising
Jardin de la Fontaine
Allées Jaen Jaurès
Parking lot behind old theatre

Facilities
Behind the church, Place G. Péri
Left of, and in front of Gare SNCF

ORLEANS 45 (Loiret)
DOMAINE DE MONTAIGU (B F D P)
Tel: (38) - 80 51 68
LE REFUGE (B F P) (1700-?)
23 boulevard de Châteaudun (62 54 98)

OLIVET-ORLEANS 45 (Loiret)
LE PRADO (Hotel/Bar/Restaurant. D)
68 Ave du Loiret (66 17 51)

144

FRANCE — PARIS

To make it easier to find your way around our long lists of Paris bars and restaurants, we have listed them under Arondissments, or postal districts. This applies to men' bars, mixed bars, and restaurants. Special Lesbian bars are listed separately, as are also Baths/Saunas, Hotels, outside cruising, and facilities.

Um Ihnen die Lokalsuche ein wenig zu erleichtern, haben wir die Liste der Lokale, Clubs und Restaurants nach Arondissements (Stadt-Bezirken) aufgeteilt. Lesbische Lokale sind aber für sich aufgeführt, ebenso Bäder und Saunen, Hotels, Outside cruising und Klappen.

Pour vous permettre une recherche plus aisée parmi notre longue liste de bars et restaurants de Paris, nous l'avons établie par arrondissements. Cette liste concerne les bars homophiles, les bars mixtes, et les restaurants. Les bars lesbiens sont classés séparément, de même que bains/saunas, hôtels, promenades, et toilettes.

PARIS 1er.
AUBERGE DU PALAIS ROYAL
10 rue Jean-Jacques Rousseau (236 88 69)
★★ LE BALTHARD (B F M)
rue St Denis
NEW BOOTHS (B D P) (2000-0600)
3 rue Villedo (742 81 11)
★★ LE BRIGNOLET (B D F M YC) (1200-0600)
29 rue Montpensier (742 71 42)
★★ LE BRONX (B LJ RT) (2000-?)
11 rue St.Anne (742 60 69)
★★ LE BELVEDERE (B E F M) (1900-0200)
5 Place du Théâtre Français (260 68 06)
★★ COLONY RESTAURANT (B F M P YC) (2030-0400)
11 rue St Anne (742 60 69)
★★ CLUB 18 DU PALAIS ROYAL (B D G P YC) (2200-0600)
18 rue de Beaujolais (742 75 43)
★★ CLUB SEPT (B E F G M P R) (Expensive)
rue St Anne (742 83 99) (Ridiculously high prices)
★★ LE PETIT VENDOME (B) (2000-0200)
3 rue de la Sourdière (073 76 96)
★★ COLONY CLUB (B D M P YC) (2300-0600)
11 rue St.Anne (742 60 69)
★ SIDONI BABA (B R) (afternoon & evening)
32 rue St.Anne (742 19 98)
★★ LE VAGABOND (B F G) (1800-0200)
14 rue Thérèse (742 90 97)
I CHEZ GEORGETTE ANYS (B M RT) (1000-0900) 13 rue des Petits Champs (742 45 16)
★★ AU BEC FIN (B F M S) (dinner & théâtre)
6 bis, rue Thérèse (742 99 79)
RESTAURANT ANDRE FAURE (B F)
40 rue du Mont Thabou (073 39 15)
★★ RIVE DROIT (B D M S) (2200-0600)
33 rue des Petits Champs (742 29 53)

145

Important Pamphlet Publications

For Gay Men and Women, Covering All Subjects from Medical to Poetry Anthologies . . .

Prehistoric double dildo

American Psychiatric Association Resolutions on Homosexuality. (American Psychiatric Association.) Dec. 15, 1973. (Press release and rationale paper available free from APA, Div. of Public Affairs, 1700 18th Street, N.W., Washington, D.C. 20009.)

Amazon Expedition, a lesbian/feminist anthology, edited by Phyllis Birkby, Bertha Harris, Jill Johnston, Esther Newton, and Jane O'Wyatt. Available from Times Change Press, c/o Monthly Review Press, 116 West 14th Street, New York, N.Y. 10011. $1.75 (plus 35¢ postage).

Blair, Ralph (ed). *The Otherwise Monographs Series.* National Task Force on Student Personnel Services & Homosexuality, 1972. 15 pamphlets $20. (List of titles from Homosexual Community Counseling Center, 921 Madison Ave., New York, N.Y. 10021.)

Blamires, David. *Homosexuality from the Inside.* London Social Responsibility Council of the Religious Society of Friends, 1973. (Friends Book Store, 302 Arch Street, Philadelphia, Pennsylvania 19106. 95¢ plus p/h 30¢ single copy; 50¢ for 2 or more.)

Fluckiger, Fritz. *A Research through a Glass Darkly: An Evaluation of the Bieber Study on Homosexuality.* Privately printed, 1966. Available from Barbara Gittings, Box 2383, Philadelphia, Pennsylvania 19103. $1.00.

Homosexuality. SIECUS. Study Guide No. 2 (Revised ed). Sex Information & Education Council of the United States, 1973. Behavioral Publications, 72 5th Avenue, New York, N.Y. 10011. Single copy $1.00 prepaid.

Kameny, Franklin E. *Action on the Gay Legal Front.* Privately printed. 1974. (National Gay Task Force). 80 5th Avenue, New York, N.Y. 10011. $1.00

Lauritsen, John, and Thorstad, David. *The Homosexual Rights Movement.* Privately printed. Available from the Oscar Wilde Bookstore, 15 Christopher Street, New York, N.Y. 10014. (50¢ plus 25¢ postage.)

Lee, Ronald D. *Gay Men Speak.* Multi-Media Resource Center. *(The Yes Book of Sex Series)* 1973. Available from the Multi-Media Resource Center, 540 Powell Street, San Francisco, California 94108. $1.95

Lesbian Grapevine. 373 N. Western Avenue, No. 2024, Los Angeles, California 90004. A National Lesbian Communication incorporating the publications of magazines and pamphlets.

The Male Muse. A male gay anthology of poetry, edited by Ian Young. $3.95. Available from the Oscar Wilde Bookstore, 15 Christopher Street, New York, N.Y. 10014.

Martin, Del, and Lyon, Phyllis. *Lesbian Love and Liberation.* Multi-Media Resource Center. *(The Yes Book of Sex Series)* 1973. Available from the Multi-Media Resource Center, 540 Powell Street, San Francisco, California 94108. $1.95

Motive: Gay Men's Liberation Issue/Lesbian Feminist Issue. Two separate publications, distributed by the National Gay Student Center. 2115 S St. N.W., Washington, D.C. 20008. $1.00 per copy.

Mouth of the Dragon. A poetry anthology for gay men. Available at the Oscar Wilde Bookstore, 15 Christopher Street, New York, N.Y. 10014. $1.95

National Gay Task Force. 80 5th Avenue, New York City. Publication of resolutions and statements from various church groups. NOW, American Library Assn., Amer. Psychiatric Assn., NYC Bar Assn., etc. Complete package $2.00

National Institute of Mental Health. *Task Force on Homosexuality Final Report and Background Papers.* 1972. Superintendent of Documents, Government Printing Office, Washington, D.C. 20402. Catalogue no. HE20-2402 H75/2. $1.00

Parker, William. *Homosexuals and Employment.* San Francisco, The Corinthian Foundation et al. 1970. Council on Religion & the Homosexual, 83 McAllister, San Francisco, California 94102. $1.00

The Tenderest Lover. Erotic poetry of Walt Whitman, including "Leaves of Grass." $2.45 (Available at the Oscar Wilde Bookstore.)

Tripp, C. A. *Who Is a Homosexual?* Privately printed, 1966. (Barbara Gittings, Box 2383, Philadelphia, Pa. 19103) 50¢

Twenty Questions about Homosexuality. Gay Activists Alliance of New York, 1972. (GAA, Box 2, Village Station, New York, N.Y. 10014) $1.00 per copy.

Violet Press. A collective of women publishing literary and artwork for lesbians by lesbians. Write for listings: P.O. Box 398, New York, N.Y. 10009.

For other articles of importance on homosexuality, consult the *Readers Guide to Periodical Literature* at your local library.

Nightwood, Djuana Barnes. Harper, $6.50. New Directions, $1.50. (Lesbian fiction classic first published in 1936.)

Patience & Sarah, Isabel Miller. McGraw Hill, $5.95. (Lesbian fiction: winner of Gay Book Award of the Year, 1971.)

Satyricon of Petronius. There are numerous editions of this classic in print. Check your bookstore for a selection of different translations.

Well of Loneliness, The Radcliffe Hall Pocket Books, $1.95. (The classic story of lesbian love.)

Year in the Closet, William Carney. Warner paperback, $1.50. (A story of homosexual love; its joys and sorrow.)

The listed books are available at most major bookstores and libraries. If you have trouble locating a particular book, query Renaissance House Book Club, Box 292, Village Station, New York, N.Y. 10014. (Enclose stamped addressed envelope for reply.) For a more extensive gay fiction reading list, consult John Francis Hunter's *The Gay Insider/U.S.A.* published in paperback by Stonehill. $3.95.

Suggested Reading

The following is a suggested reading list of fiction dealing with homosexuality from classic to contemporary. It is listed alphabetically by the titles, not authors, as in a standard bibliography. We felt you might be more familiar with titles rather than the authors in this instance.

City of Night, John Rechy. Ballantine paperback, $1.95. (A novel of the seamy world of the male hustler.)

Fire From Heaven, Mary Renault, Pantheon, $7.95. Popular Library, $1.25. (The story of Alexander the Great's early childhood and his homosexuality.)

The Front Runner, Patricia Nell Warren. Morrow, $7.95. (A novel for gay men in an Olympic setting.)

Giovanni's Room, James Baldwin. Dial, $6.95. Dell, 75¢. (The controversial book about a man's love and his decision to follow his desires rather than those of society.)

The Green Carnation. First published in 1894 in London. (An underground best seller whose characters are based on Oscar Wilde and Lord Alfred Douglas.) o/p but available from libraries.

Loving Her, Ann Shockley. Bobbs-Merrill, $6.95. (The story of two women finding fulfillment.)

Maurice, E. M. Forster. W. W. Norton, $6.95. N.A.L., $1.50. (Gay male fiction written in 1914 and published after Forster's death in 1971.)

Copyright © David Paris, 1975

Extensive bibliographies on homosexual reading are available from:

A Gay Bibliography: published by the Gay Task Force of the American Library Association. 10¢.Co-ordinator, Barbara Gittings, Task Force on Gay Liberation, Box 2383, Philadelphia, Pennsylvania 19103.

Oscar Wilde Memorial Bookshop, 15 Christopher Street, New York, N.Y. 10014. (212) 255-8097.

The First Gay Catalog available from Elysian Fields, Booksellers, 81-13 Broadway, Elmhurst, New York 11373. (212) 228-0900.

Bibliography

Abbott, Sidney, and Love, Barbara. *Sappho Was a Right-On Woman*. New York: Stein & Day, 1972. $1.95

Aldrich, Ann. *Take A Lesbian To Lunch*. New York: Manor Books, 1972. $1.25

Allen, Gina, and Clement, Martin. *Intimacy*. New York: Cowles Books.

Altman, Dennis. *Homosexuality: Oppression and Liberation*. New York: Avon, 1973. $1.65

Bailey, Derrick S. *Homosexuality and the Western Christian Tradition*. London: Longmans Greene, 1955.

Barnett, Walter. *Sexual Freedom and the Constitution*. Albuquerque, New Mexico: University of New Mexico Press, 1973. $10.00

Bell, Arthur. *Dancing the Gay Lib Blues*. New York: Simon & Schuster, 1971. $5.95

Benson, R. O. *In Defense of Homosexuality*. New York: Julian Press, 1965.

Benton, Nick. *Sexism, Racism, and White Faggots in Sodomist Amerika*. n.p., n.d.

Bergler, Edmund. *Homosexuality: Disease or Way of Life?* New York: Macmillan, 1962. $1.50

Bieber, I. *Homosexuality: A Psychoanalytic Study of Male Homosexuals*. New York: Random House, 1972. $2.95

Brecher, Edward M. *The Sex Researchers*. Boston: Little, Brown, 1969.

Broderick, Carlfred, and Bernard, Jessie. *The Individual Sex & The Society: A SIECUS Handbook for Teachers & Counselors*. Baltimore: Johns Hopkins Press, 1969. $12.00 (cloth), $4.50 (paper)

Churchill, Wainwright. *Homosexual Behavior among Males*. New York: Hawthorne, 1969. $2.45

Clarke, Lige, and Nichols, Jack. *I Have More Fun with You Than Anyone*. New York: St. Martin's Press, 1972. $5.95

——. *Roommates Can't Always Be Lovers*. New York: St. Martin's Press, 1974. $6.95

Cinard, M.B. *Sociology of Deviant Behavior*. New York: Holt, Rinehart and Winston, 1968. $10.95

Cory, Donald Webster. *The Lesbian in America*. New York: Tower, 1971. 95¢

Cory, Donald Webster, and LeRoy, John P. *The Homosexual and His Society*. n.p., 1951.

Crompton, Louis. *Homosexuality and the Sickness Theory*.

De Becker, Raymond. *The Other Face of Love*. Translated by Margaret Crolland and Alan Deventy. New York: Bell, 1964.

De Martino, M. F. *The New Female Society*. New York: Julian Press, 1969.

Fisher, Peter. *The Gay Mystique: The Myth and Reality of Male Homosexuality*. New York: Stein & Day, 1972. $7.95

Ford, Celellan S. and Beach, Frank. *Patterns of Sexual Behavior*. New York: Harper & Row, 1951. $7.95; Reprint. New York: Harper & Row, 1970. $2.75

Freedman, Mark. *Homosexuality and Psychological Functioning*. Monterey, Calif.: Brooks Cole, 1971. $3.25

Gerhart, Sally, and Johnson, William R., eds. *Loving Women/Loving Men: Gay Liberation and the Church*. San Francisco: Glide Publications, 1974. $6.95

Grummon, Donald L., and Barclay, Andrew M., eds. *Sexuality: A Search for Perspective*. New York: Van Nostrand Reinhold, 1971. $6.50

Hart, George. *The Straight or Gay Book*. Los Angeles: Price/Stern/Sloan, 1974. $1.25

Hart, H. L. *Law, Liberty, & Morality*. Palo Alto, Calif.: Stanford University Press, 1963. $1.45

Hatterer, L. J. *Changing Homosexuality in The Male*. New York: Dell, 1971. $2.95

Hoffman, Martin. *The Gay World: Male Homosexuality and the Social Creation of Evil*. New York: Basic Books, 1968. $7.55

Hudson, Billy. *Christian Homosexuality: An Explosive New Side to the Gay Revolution*. New York: New Library Press.

Humphreys, Laud. *Out of the Closets: The Society of Homosexual Liberation*. Englewood Cliffs, N.J.: Prentice-Hall, 1972. $5.95 (cloth), $2.45 (paper)

——. *Tearoom Trade: Impersonal Sex in Public Places*. Chicago: Aldine, 1970. $5.95

Hunter, John Francis. *Gay Insider: A Hunter's Guide to New York and a Thesaurus of Phallic Lore*. New York: Olympic Press.

——. *Gay Insider/U.S.A.* Stonehill Publishing, 1974. $3.95

Hyde, Montgomery H. *The Love That Dared Not Speak Its Name*. Boston: Little, Brown, 1970.

Jay, Karla, and Young, Allen, eds. *Out of the Closets: Voices of Gay Liberation*. Douglas Books, 1972. $3.95

Johnston, Jill. *Lesbian Nation: The Feminist Solution*. New York: Simon & Schuster, 1973. $7.95; New York: Simon & Schuster, Touchstone. $2.95

Karlen, Arno. *Sexuality and Homosexuality*. New York: W. W. Norton, 1971. $15.00

Kirkendall, Lester A., and Whitehurt, Robert, eds. *The New Sexual Revolution*. Donald W. Brown Inc.,1971. $6.95

Klaich, Delores. *Woman Plus Woman*. New York: Simon & Schuster, 1974. $8.95

Lauristen, John, and Thorstad, David. *The Early Homosexual Rights Movement. (1864-1935)* New York: Times Change Press, 1974. $6.95 (cloth); $2.25 (paper)

Martin, Del, and Lyon, Phyllis. *Lesbian Woman*. San Francisco: Glide Publications, 1972. $7.95. New York: Bantam $1.50

McCaffrey, Joseph A. ed. *The Homosexual Dialectic*. Englewood Cliffs, N.J.: Prentice-Hall, 1972. $6.95

Miller, Merle. *On Being Different: What It Means to Be a Homosexual*. New York: Random House, 1971. $4.50; New York: Popular Library. 95¢

Mitchell, R. S. *The Homosexual and the Law*. New York: Arco, 1969.

Murphy, John. *Homosexual Liberation: A Personal View*. New York: Praeger, 1971. $5.95

Oberholzer, Dwight W. ed. *Is Gay Good? Ethics, Theology, and Homosexuality*. Philadelphia: Westminster Press, 1971. $3.50

Onge, Jack. *Gay Liberation Movement*. New York: Alliance.

Perry, Troy, and Lucas, Charles L. *The Lord Is My Shepherd and He Knows I'm Gay*. New York: Bantam, 1973. $1.50

Pittenger, Norman W. *Making Sexuality Human*. Philadelphia: Pilgrim/United Church Press, 1970. $4.33

Richmond, Len, and Noguera, Gary, eds. *The Gay Liberation Book*. New York: Ramparts Press, 1973. $7.95

Rodgers, Bruce. *The Queen's Vernacular: A Gay Lexicon*. San Francisco: Straight Arrow Books, 1972.

Romm, M. E. *Sexual Inversion: The Multiple Roots of Homosexuality*. New York: Basic Books, 1965.

Rosen, David H. *Lesbianism: A Study of Female Homosexuality*. Springfield, Ill.: Charles C. Thomas, 1974. $7.95 (cloth); $4.95 (paper)

Rosenfels, Paul. *Homosexuality: The Psychology of the Creative Process*. New York: Libra. $5.95

Roszak, Betty, and Roszak, Theodore, eds. *Masculine/Feminine*. New York: Harper & Row, 1969. $2.95

Ruitenbeek, Hendrik. *Homosexuality: A Changing Picture: Problem of Homosexuality in Modern Society*. New York: Dutton, 1974. $2.25

Saghir, Maurice, and Robins, Eli. *Male and Female Homosexuality: A Comprehensive Investigation*. Baltimore: Williams & Wilkins, 1973. $12.95

Schur, Edwin. *Crimes Without Victims*. Englewood Cliffs, N.J.: Prentice-Hall, 1965. $2.45

Schofield, Michael. *Sociological Aspects of Homosexuality*. London: Longmans Greene, 1965.

Socarides, C. W. *The Overt Homosexual*. New York: Grune & Stratton, 1968. $8.00

Szasz, Thomas S. *The Manufacture of Madness: A Comparative Study of the Inquisition and the Mental Health Movement*. New York: Harper & Row, 1970. $9.95

Teal, Don. *The Gay Militants*. New York: Stein & Day, 1971. $7.95

Tobin, Kay, and Wicker, Randy. *The Gay Crusaders*. New York: Paperback Library, 1972. $1.25

Tyler, Parker. *Screening the Sexes: Homosexuality in the Movies*. New York: Holt, Rinehart & Winston, 1972. $8.50

Valente, Michael F. *Sex: The Radical View of a Catholic Theologian*. Beverly Hills, Calif.: Bruce, 1970. $2.95

Weinberg, George. *Society and the Healthy Homosexual*. New York: St. Martin's Press, 1972. $5.95; New York: Anchor/Doubleday. $1.95

Weinberg, George, and Williams, Colin J. *Male Homosexuals*. New York: Oxford University Press, 1974. $10.95

Welge, Ralph W., ed. *The Same Sex: An Appraisal of Homosexuality*. Philadelphia: Pilgrim/United Church Press, 1969

West, D. J. *Homosexuality*. Chicago: Aldine, 1967. $9.50

Westwood, Gordon. *Society and the Homosexual in Great Britain*. Atlantic Highlands, N.J.: Fernhill, 1969. $6.50

Wolff, Charlotte. *Love Between Women*. New York: St. Martin's Press, 1971.

Wood, R. W. *Christ and the Homosexual*. New York: Vantage Press, 1960.

Wysor, Betty. *The Lesbian Myth*. New York: Random House, 1974. $8.95

Drawing by Claude Flavius Malpertuy as illustration for Baudelaire's Les Fleurs du Mal, *1876*

Love Play *by Thomas Rowlandson*

The Group Sex Scene

Swinging and Swapping

Free love, dyadic marriage with or without nonconsensual adultery, swinging, open marriage, intimate friendship, evolutionary communes, and group marriage are points on a continuum of increasing complexity in interrelationship, free love representing the least complex and group marriage the most complex relationship in which intimacy occurs.

James W. Ramey, Ed.D., Director
Center for the Study of Innovative Life Styles
Box 426, New York, New York 10956

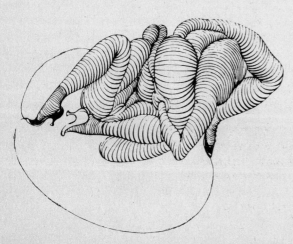

If you were to believe everything you read on the subject of swinging, you might think there was something new about group sex. In fact, if you really want to bone up on the subject, your best jumping off place would be the Old Testament. There is also a great deal of scholarly literature on the subject, dealing with fancy fuckathons which predate Christianity by many centuries.

Throughout history, and in modern times as well, there have been groups who have rationalized their proclivities toward group sex as religious and ritualistic. For centuries historians and pornographers have dwelt in lingering, luxuriant purple prose on the subject of orgies. Artists, on the other hand, have tended always to tell it as it actually is, depicting exactly what they saw. If you take the long view, you will see that essentially nothing has changed in thousands of years, except possibly the terminology and the rationale.

Burgo Partridge, in his fascinating *History of Orgies* (Bonanza Books, New York, 1960), covers the subject from ancient Greece to the twentieth century. He has defined the term somewhat clinically: "An orgy is an organized blowing off of steam; the expulsion of hysteria accumulated by abstinence and restraint, and as such tends to be of an hysterical or cathartic nature." An interesting comment, but not quite accurate today. There is certainly a *blowing off of steam*, but the contemporary swing, which is the most commonly accepted term for group sex now, is hardly hysterical. Although, to an uninvolved researcher witnessing half a dozen couples in the same room all reaching orgasm within a five- or ten-minute period, the impression of hysteria might be suggested.

Patrick M. McGrady, in his excellent book, *The Love Doctors,* summed it up much more succinctly. "The difference between swinging and the classical orgy, or *partouze,* lies precisely in the degree of organization. Swinging is heavily organized. It is terribly American, structured along lines of the sodality. It is clubby, puritanical in its exclusion of drugs (and often alcohol) and specific deviations. The few profiles of swinging groups that have been done show them as reflective of America's Silent Majority: antimale homosexual, antiblack, to right of center politically, vaguely Germanic ethnically, humorless, comfortably but not overly educated, and suburban."*

Yet despite McGrady's observation, there are exceptions.

Swingers, like any other sport enthusiasts, do not fit into a neat little slot prepared by the analytical mind of a social scientist. They come in all sizes, shapes, and colors, and from almost every walk of society. The equivalent of swinging in former times was restricted more or less to the aristocracy because the poor and the uneducated were more concerned with filling their bellies and were too fearful of Heavenly wrath to experiment.

Today, at a swing, there are no guarantees as to who you might find doing what to whom. It is not at all uncommon to find, in any given tangle of writhing bodies, such combinations as celebrity-student-police officer. There is an unspoken rule, however: if you encounter the governor of your state, in the buff, about to plunge between the waiting legs of an eminent female psychiatrist, you lose points if you talk about it afterwards. That, by the way, is one of the biggest compliments anyone can pay to swingers. Their discretion exceeds the most stringent requirements set down in the world. If the president were to

*From THE LOVE DOCTORS by Patrick M. McGrady, Jr. Copyright © 1972 by Patrick M. McGrady, Jr. Reprinted by permission of Macmillan Publishing Co., Inc.

From Aphrodisiac Cookery: Ancient and Modern by Greg and Beverly Frazier, illustrated by David and Dennis Redmond, Copyright 1970 by Greg and Beverly Frazier. Published by Troubador Press, San Francisco, Reprinted by permission.

attend a swing (provided he could give his secret-service guardians the slip) he would be safer than in a motorcade in any major city. Not only that, even if he were seen performing the most bizarre sexual act with the undergraduate wife of a theology student who was making it in the next room with the leading lady of television's top-rated children's program, no swinger would ever reveal a snippet of information of what he or she had seen, even if that person had shared a mattress with the president and his partner. It would make no difference even if the witness happened to be a reporter for The New York Times. The same rules of discretion apply no matter who you are or who you are with or what you are doing.

If you are now into swinging, heavily into swinging that is, then in all probability what you learn here will be minimal. Yet you can't afford not to include every available piece of information you find in your files. You know how things change.

If you are not yet into swinging but are contemplating it, then be sure to personally investigate everything that appeals to you. The Swingers Hotline, for example, the toll-free phone number you will see advertised, is definitely operative but usually busy. As for the ads you may find in swinging publications (see Jerry Schneiderman's piece on how to read, write, answer, and interpret a sex ad), make sure that the ones you answer are exactly what they appear to be. Sometimes you will find ringers lurking between the lines. Remember the cliché, "Look before you leap." And remember that your whole purpose is to explore new sexual horizons, not acquire new headaches.

Remember also that swinging has its rules, and the rules may vary from place to place. Find out precisely what they are in advance and abide by them. If you are a bisexual male and you get in with a group that frowns on males touching males, either find a group that digs this, or stick to women when you are in this crowd. And a word to the novice female/swinger . . . female/female contacts during group sex encounters are not frowned on. If the idea of making it with another woman is abhorrent to you, just let the others know at the outset. There is no such thing as rape in group sex. Everyone does what he or she wants to do and with whom. The expression of a preference makes things easier if you make it clear in advance. To refuse sex with someone with whom you do not feel like having contact does not constitute a psyche-damaging rejection. It is regarded in the same light in which one might refuse a drink, a cigarette, or a piece of candy. In any case, there is only one way to find out.

Okay, so you've read all the sensational magazine articles, and maybe even seen a movie or two about swinging and swapping, and you want to get in on the action yourself. You've got visions of answering a sex ad, meeting a bunch of exciting and highly sexual people, and getting in on what may be the ultimate form of liberation—the Sexual Revolution.

But wait just one moment. Most of the stuff you've read is probably sensationalism, drivel written by writers out to make a buck by exploiting what they think their readers want to hear. The potential for exciting sex play initiated through correspondence is there all right, but it's a fine art to make out well and a difficult game to play when you don't know all the rules. That's the purpose of this article: to take you slowly along the road to successful swinging, to move step by step with you, showing you all the tricks of the trade. And without much time or trouble, you'll be able to move right into the secret world of the sexual swingers, where just about anything (sexual) is possible.

But before we go any further, important questions must be answered by you. Why do you want to answer sex ads? What are you looking for? Before you glance at your first sex paper or suggestive advertisement, you've got to have a clear picture in your mind of what you hope to accomplish. You aren't about to find strawberries in a hardware store, and by the same logic, you're not about to find a conservative and faithful mate in a periodical where people advertise for playmates. There also are specialized magazines for people who are looking for different types of pleasure. There are papers for homosexuals, people looking for partners of a different race, bisexuals, and just about anything you can think of and probably much more. You have to know what you want, what you can offer, and where it can be found. We'll help you find all this out.

The first place to look for sex ads is the so-called "sex papers" like *Screw*, *Pleazure*, and the *San Francisco Ball*. They are sold mostly in adult book stores in big cities. In a few places, notably New York, they are sold openly on newsstands alongside *Reader's Digest* and *Newsweek*. All of these papers, with the exception of the half-political half-prurient *Los Angeles Free Press*, are designed totally and specifically for getting you off. The pictures are explicit, the stories to the point, and the sex ads from swingers quite blunt. All have scores of ads, mostly from men and couples with a few from women, placed by people who are looking to make new friends through the mail. The ads are all real, and not the product of a demented copywriter's imagination, as they often are in some of the lesser publications.

One way to separate the good guys from the exploiters is to check on the number of ads from single women. Gals have an easier time fulfilling their needs, no matter how far out they may be, and therefore have less reason to advertise. So if the tabloid has plenty of ads from females and charges a fee to forward communications to the person who is advertising, the chances are fairly good that the whole production is simply a scheme to separate you from your money.

In case you have any trouble finding any of the sex papers, you can get sample copies and subscription information from the following sources. (Sample copies are $1.00 each from all of the publications listed below.)

Screw: Milky Way Productions, P.O. Box 432, Old Chelsea Station, New York, New York 10011

Pleazure: TMT, P.O. Box 595, Old Chelsea Station, New York, New York 10011

San Francisco Ball: Jaundice Press, 17620 Sherman Way, Van Nuys, California 91406

The Advocate (biggest gay paper): Box 74695, Los Angeles, California 90004

How to Answer a Sex Ad

by JERRY SCHNEIDERMAN

Jerry Schneiderman, best known as *the arch smut hound of New York*, has been a columnist for *Screw* and is currently East Coast correspondent for *The National Ball*, film critic and Ralph Nader of massage parlors for *Pleazure*, as well as a regular contributor to *Naked News, Escapade, National Exposé, Dapper, National Climax,* and *The Swinger*. He has no minor vices, being a teetotaler and non-smoker; however, he can eat anyone under the table.

Photo of Jerry Schneiderman by Al Fredericks

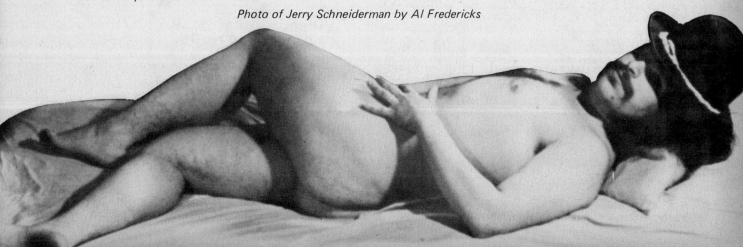

Seventeenth century engraving of an orgy in a royal household.

It's strange that while in the *newspapers* a forwarding fee for letters is an indication that something may be less than honest, every reputable and honest swingers *magazine* charges a fee, usually $1.00 per letter, to be forwarded to an advertiser. And they do it without inserting a single ringer, or phony ad.

The glossy magazines are the real heavies in mail order correspondence sex. One claims that it has forty-five hundred ads, from every state in the country and many foreign nations. Most are from couples eager to swap, and all are real. The magazines sell for about $3.50 each, and they will send you sample copies at that price.

There are many ads from single women in these publications mainly because they give them the ads for free, a practice which the tabloids don't indulge in. Many are with photos. One problem is that a sizable number of the ads from women looking for single men are for commercial rather than romantic or sensual purposes. Many of the gals are selling photos of themselves. Others want to unload their used undergarments and other intimate apparel. Some are veiled offers of prostitution, claiming to be models or escorts for out-of-town businessmen. If the ad mentions the term "generous" men, you can be sure that the only part of your anatomy that interests the advertiser is your wallet. And then only if it is chock full of money.

There are several good swingers magazines, most of which are for sale at adult bookstores all over the country. If there are any shops in your town, check them out. If not, we'll give you the addresses of several of the prominent publications. We've had good experience with several. They are *Select, The Digest, Continental Spectator* (the oldest), *Intrigue* (the only one with no censorship of the photos), and *The Rigid Bondage Roster* (for sado-masochists). Here are the addresses.

Continental Spectator: 152 West 42nd Street, Room 504, New York, New York 10011

The Digest: P.O. Box 20140, Philadelphia, Pa. 19145

In Crowd (Bondage): 210 Fifth Avenue, New York, New York 10010

Intrigue: P.O. Box 1364, Des Moines, Iowa 50305

Mature: P.O. Box 352, Freeport, New York 11520

The Players: P.O. Box 3273, Station A, Bakersfield, California 93305

The Rigid Bondage Roster: P.O. Box 411, New York, New York 10008

The Seekers: P.O. Box 781, Cherry Hill, New Jersey 08003

Select: P.O. Box 889, Camden, New Jersey 08101

One of the problems you have in answering sex ads is that you're often competing with hundreds of other interested people who all want to meet the same people you do. The advertiser probably doesn't have time to get together with or even answer all who have written. Since you want to be among the ones who are answered, there are a couple of points you should bear in mind to increase your chances.

The most important question you should ask yourself before answering an ad is "Am I what this person is looking for?" If it's a gay woman looking for another, and you're a guy, it would be a waste of everyone's time for you to answer. Likewise, if the advertiser is looking for someone shorter than 5'8", and you're over 6 feet tall. It doesn't make sense to try to succeed with someone who clearly makes his or her preferences known in advance, when you don't meet the qualifications. Stay away from these mismatches, and you'll save a lot of time that you can put to better use by answering ads that match your tastes.

When you spot an ad looking for someone like you, you still have to exercise caution in responding. Remember, the person who wrote the ad is swamped with replies. For yours to be chosen it has to stand out above the others. If the writer wants a photo, then send one. If they want it to be revealing, send them a nude if you can get one. In your response you have to sell yourself. So spend the extra couple of minutes needed to fully explain why you think you have what the other person wants, and why he or she should want to be with you. Consider before you write your letter. Any good points you think can do you good should be mentioned. If you're good looking, cheerful, sensitive, or loving, mention it. In order to get a reply to your letter, you have to make an impression.

It's easy to become confused when you go through the sex magazines if you don't understand the slang terms used. There is a special language swingers use to describe their preferences. These expressions developed in less tolerant days, when you could get in trouble for openly advertising your desires. Oral-genital relations became known as *French*. Anal-genital intercourse became *Greek*. If you enjoy being urinated on or doing it to other people, it's a *Golden Shower*. Here's a short glossary of other widely used terms.

AC/DC means bisexuality, or enjoying sex with both men and women.

B & D is bondage and dominance. Enjoyment of tying someone up before sex, or having it done to you. Dominance is the enjoyment of being ridiculed or humiliated.

S & M is sadism and masochism. The former means the enjoyment of causing pain, the latter is enjoyment of receiving it.

English Culture is the enjoyment of B & D, and S & M.

Gay means homosexual.

Roman Culture is the fun of orgies.

SASE or *SSAE* is a self-addressed stamped envelope. If you enclose one when you answer an ad, you make it easier and cheaper for the other person to write back. This increases your chances of getting an answer.

TV means transvestite, a person who enjoys cross dressing, which means wearing the clothes of the opposite sex—usually a man who enjoys wearing women's clothing. He may or may not be homosexual.

Rubber or *Leather* refer to fetishes that make it pleasurable for some people to wear clothing made out of these materials.

Foxy Lady is an old black term that has been popularized to the point that it merely signifies an attractive woman.

You may also consider writing an ad yourself rather than replying to those of other people. The same rules apply. Your ad should state what you want and what you have to offer. Your appraisal of yourself should be honest, and you should avoid any claims or exaggerations that you may not be able to live up to. You should accentuate any strong points that might make yourself more attractive to other people. But don't lie. If you're fibbing, your new friends will find out quickly enough when you meet. That can only lead to disappointment.

If you want to advertise in the sex tabloids, the rates are generally ten or fifteen cents a word. You can get the exact rates by writing to the addresses we listed earlier for sample copies. It usually takes two or three weeks from the time they get your ad until it appears in print. This is relatively quick compared to the glossy magazines.

To advertise in the glossies, you first have to become a member, which will cost approximately ten dollars a year. You than have to wait up to six months for them to print your ad. Most magazines publish four times a year, so the lag before publishing is greater than with the papers.

To test the response to unusual advertisements, we ran the following ad in *Screw, Pleasure, Continental Spectator,* and *Intrigue.* It was written as a goof, and we were curious to see what type of response an original but meaningless ad would draw.

ABSURD HETEROSEXUAL PORNOGRAPHER SEEKS UNINHIBITED WOMAN, OR NYLON FETISHIST LESBIAN DWARF TRUCKDRIVING NECROPHILIAC, PEDOPHILIAC BASKET CASE GREASER CHICK. NO SICKIES OR REPUBLICANS. (WELL MAYBE A FEW) JERRY SCHNEIDERMAN, P.O. BOX 787, OLD CHELSEA STATION, NEW YORK CITY 10011.

If you need one, the translation is as follows: "Weird guy seeks horny lady or a lezzie truckdriver into fucking children and dead people. Must be armless, legless dwarf heavily into a stocking fetish. To reply, said female must be well adjusted and not a Nixon freak. Exceptions will be made."

Quite a contradiction of terms, no? I was hoping for the best, a horny lady with a sense of humor, curious enough to reply. No such luck. I got a couple of threatening letters, one answer from a gay male truckdriver in Washington, and an appeal from the American Bible Society.

So based on that experience, you can see that although creativity is a virtuous thing, there's such a thing as going too far. Keep your ad in the realm of the believable. Spend the extra ten cents a word to state your case well. Be sincere, honest, and witty. But don't be outrageous or obviously ridiculous.

One inexpensive way of increasing your chances for meeting other like-minded folks through the mail is by enclosing a self-addressed stamped envelope with your letter every time you answer an ad. If the writer is getting a heavy response, the cost of postage alone in answering letters could be high. The easier you make it for someone to get in touch with you, the better your chances are. For that reason, you might also want to enclose a phone number where you can be reached. If it's long distance and you can afford it, tell your pen pal to call collect.

One common problem for letter writers is the fear of letting strangers know their address. One potential problem is that a strange degenerate is going to knock on their door. Or they might be "exposed" for the so-called sexual "degeneracy" of swinging. There is a simple answer to that problem. There are several mail-receiving addresses that cater to swingers. You can use their address, and even a phony name, and get your mail there. They can either hold the correspondence for you until you pick it up at their office, or they can remail it to you at home, taking your mail and placing it unopened in a larger envelope to be sent to you at your real address. The cost for this service is generally in the area of five dollars a month.

One such service is the Downstairs Mail Service in New York City. It's discreet, friendly, and even helpful in handling any problems or questions you might have. Our experience with them has been quite favorable, and they often are recommended by sex papers like *Pleazure, Naked News,* and *The National Exposé.* Even *Gallery* magazine did an article. Their address is:

Downstairs Mail Service
167 West 21st Street
New York, New York 10011

and if you write them for information, they will cheerfully send you all the details for free and with no obligation.

That's it. You should now be able to answer any sex ad that turns you on. And your letter should be guaranteed to produce a response in return. Good luck.

The Joys of Country Living. *Anonymous satirical copper engraving from the Regency period, England*

Swinging Magazines and Newspapers

Estimates as to the total number of people engaged in swinging range from five to ten million. There is no way of getting accurate statistics as yet, because the U.S. Census Bureau has not gotten around to including swinging in its questionnaires. If you want to get into the swinging scene, or merely want to find out who the swingers are and what they are doing, the following are the publications to read. Some can be found in adult bookstores, but the best way to get them is to subscribe. For those who want to plunge in, each publication gives explicit instructions as to how to contact swinging advertisers. There are forwarding fees in many cases and these vary according to the publisher and the economy.

CLUB CONTACT SWINGERS' DIRECTORY

Published by CONTINENTAL SPECTATOR in paperback book format, it contains swingers' ads with photos. 196 pages. Issued quarterly. $2.50 per issue. $10.00 for six issues.

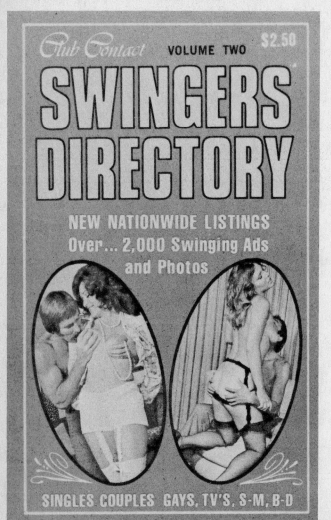

CONTINENTAL SPECTATOR

152 W. 42nd Street
New York, New York 10036
(212) 947-0949

The granddaddy of all swingers magazines, it is over eleven years old. For couples, singles, straights, bi's, and gays. Photos, personal and commercial ads, as well as feature articles. $3.50 per issue. Three-issue subscription $7.00. Twelve-issue subscription $18.00. Published quarterly.

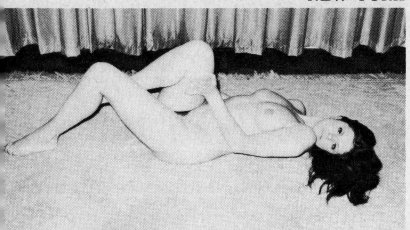

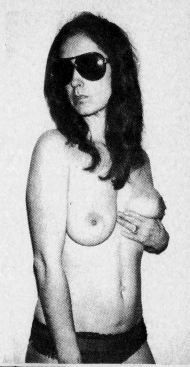

NYC-Warm and gentle but shy girl who needs to touch and be touched..but not grabbed. If that's where you could be at, it could be with me. Send stamped envelope for my picture and sensuous letter. Let's do it!

NYC-Model seeks single males for good times. I'm very cooperative. Love everything. Will answer all with SASE and photo.

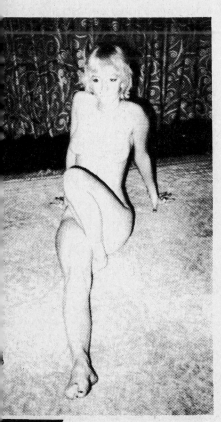

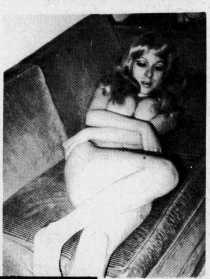

NY-Vivacious ash blonde, 30's, enjoys foreign cultures, especially French, wants to hear from secure, responsible, discreet gentleman for durable relationship. THE man who describes himself and his interests and sends envelope with stamp will be answered. No telephoning.

NYC-Nice looking married couple. She's 32, 105 lbs., and latent bi. He's 35, athletic 5'7", 140 lbs. and hetero. New to swinging and eager to learn. Desire friendship and adult pleasures. Can travel and entertain. Please send photo and phone for quick response. No singles or weirdos.

NYC-I'm not liberated yet! I love men. Am a young exhibitionist. You won't need fantasies with me because I'm for real. Enjoy most cultures. Looking for new friends. Are you one? All those that are sincere send SASE and I will send my photo.

NYC-I'm all baubles, angles and not backward. Love men and hate moderation. Love getting into all things. Let me include you. Send for my letter and picture. Will answer all who send SASE.

THE DIGEST

P.O. Box 20140
Philadelphia, Pennsylvania 19145
(215) 735-1556

"The National Swingers Magazine for Social & Sexual Encounters" is published quarterly in March, June, September, and December. All ads and photos guaranteed to be valid. Their *Club Digest* sponsors and plans parties and other group social activities. For information contact the club's social director, Heather. Single issues $3.50. Yearly subscription $10.00.

THE FLORIDA SWINGER

7228 Biscayne Blvd.
Miami, Florida 33138
(305) 757-0530

Published by Arthur Brickman Associates, this magazine covers the state of Florida only and carries personal ads, some with photos, as well as commercial ads covering subjects of interest to swingers. Published six times a year in January, March, May, July, September, and November. Single issues, $3.50. Six-issue subscription, $18.00. Available back issues, $3.00. Copy that has arrived too late to make regular issues is carried in an "Interim report" available for $1.00 per issue or $5.00 for six issues. Plans are under way for three new publications: *The California Swinger, The New York Swinger*, and *The Swingin' States.*

SELECT

Box 889
Camden, New Jersey, 08101
(609) 428-7553

Published bimonthly beginning in January, now in their ninth year of publication. This is both a magazine and a national organization. It is the biggest, best-produced, and most widely distributed swingers publication. Listings are according to state and country. International listings cover Asia, Africa, Canada, Europe, Central and South America. One year's membership/subscription is $15.00. Single issues, $3.50, and available back issues, $2.50. Women receive a free membership if they send in a photo and an ad specifying an interest in single men. *Select* also carries readers' contributions on the swinging scene, occasional fiction, letters from readers, and feature articles. *Select* also sponsors social events which are held in different cities with dates announced well in advance. Membership is approximately 95,000.

SWING

(not to be confused with any other similarly named publication)
Global Press, Inc.
926 W. North Avenue
Pittsburgh, Pennsylvania 15233

A paper claiming to offer "new horizons in sexuality." $5.00 will bring a one-year (twelve-issue) subscription. $18.50 will bring you *Swing* plus three of Global's other publications: *Truth, National Times*, and *It's Happening.*

E NATIONAL SWING
(corporating *California Ball*)
Jaundice Press, Inc.
620 Sherman Way, Suite 10
n Nuys, California 91406

very professionally put together tabloid, including feature
icles, a swingers' forum, film reviews, book reviews, humor,
d serious editorials. Swingers' personal ads come from all
er the country, and commercial ads run the entire gamut of
, films, sex products, services, massage parlors, clubs, and
u name it. There is also a directory of swing clubs, free
vironments, nude beaches, swing bars, singles pick-up spots,
ated movie motels, and adult theaters, the emphasis being
the California area. Fifty cents per single issue. Twelve-issue
scription (third class) $9.89; $12.00 (first class). First class
arantees delivery, third class can easily wind up in the hands
some horny post office employee. Foreign, $15.00. A very
tertaining paper.

THE SWINGER
Denmark Publishing Co.
P.O. Box 486, Canal Street Station
New York, New York 10013

A tabloid newspaper, fifty cents per issue. Subscriptions,
$15.00 per year in U.S.A., Possessions, and Canada; $20.00
foreign. Airmail subscriptions, $30.00 international money
order, funds payable in New York. Although the emphasis is
on swingers' ads, there are plenty of ringers—hookers, women
looking for ''generous'' men, and ads galore for films, still pix,
kinky products, and services, some even involving the occult.
There are many wild personal ads here. Although *The Swinger*
can be found at newsstands in some major urban areas, the
subscription route is your best bet.

Other Swinging Guides and Publications

Every sexpaper in print has considerable information related to swingers and swinging, but as they are not exclusively devoted to the subject they will be listed in their own section. Newcomers to swinging, however, should make it a point to scan all of them.

BLUE FLAME
Box 144
Allentown, Pennsylvania

Basically a service, for $3.00 they offer to send men a list of thirty swinging women in their vicinity.

CRITERION
P.O. Box 1345
Dallas, Texas 75221

Basically a service employing the club approach, but more of a merchandising operation. For $3.00 they offer a list of swingers including phone numbers. Women listed free.

Detail of illustration from an eighteenth century edition of Fanny Hill. *From Erotic Illustrations by Gordon Grimley. Copyright © 1974 by Gordon Grimley. Reproduced by permission of Grove Press*

INTRIGUE
P.O. Box 1364
Des Moines, Iowa 50305

The only publication with no censorship of photos.

NEW WORLD CLUB DIRECTORY
Select Products
Box 889, Camden, New Jersey 08101

Lists names, addresses, and descriptions of swinging clubs and groups in all the states and eighty foreign countries. For couples, singles, nonconformists of all races. This is marketed by *Select* magazine, so it represents money well spent for those interested. $3.00

MODERN CONTACTS
P.O. Box 544-B
Berkeley, California 94701

Claims to be the fastest growing swinging magazine, advertises "1,000 beautiful women and models waiting to do your thing." This is a thirty-six page magazine. $3.00

PERSONALITY PLUS
P.O. Box 55093
Sherman Oaks, California 91413

Another listing service. This one promises names and phone numbers of swinging women listed according to location $5.00.

THE RIGID BONDAGE ROSTER
P.O. Box 411
New York, New York 10008

Sado-masochism.

SWINGERS DIGEST
MC Distributing Co.
1133 Broadway
New York, New York 10010

$5.95 mail order item, eight by ten format. Contains photos ads; interviews with hookers and masseuses; discussing prices, what to ask for and expect; glossary of terms; names, addresses, and phone numbers of single women who are available; information on nudist camps; whorehouses (with ratings); and general related articles.

Illustration from the 1797 edition of de Sade's L'Histoire de Juliette *Reprinted in 1969 as* Sixty Erotic Drawings from Juliette. *Reproduced courtesy of Grove Press*

Organizations and Clubs

As we have pointed out, estimates on the number of Americans engaged in one form of swinging or another range from five to ten million. Many clubs are compulsively private, and they strenuously avoid publicity, relying on personal contacts and selective word of mouth. Those that advertise, however, restrict themselves to sexually oriented publications.

Many are hit-and-miss, fly-by-night operations, others are highly efficiently organized, run on a businesslike basis, and have maintained an ongoing operation over a number of years. Every attempt has been made here to offer the most comprehensive directory of existing clubs and organizations, but due to the nature of the swinging scene it is distinctly possible that some may no longer be in operation. This offers no problem, however, because you will find enough current, valid information here to find whatever you may be looking for on a nationwide basis. As you have seen so far, some of the major publications operate on a dual club/magazine basis, and certain directories maintain current information on operating clubs.

THE AMERICAN SEXUAL FREEDOM MOVEMENT
8235 Santa Monica Blvd.,
Los Angeles, California 90046,
(213) 654-4336

Founded in 1967 by John Raymond, the ASFM is one of the largest sexual freedom organizations in the country, claiming a growth of 1,500 to 2,000 members per year. California members have an advantage because personal introductions are arranged through the office nightly, and parties and frequent discussion groups are sponsored. Out of state members are listed in the organization's Master Member Library (MML). Each listing is given a code number, and updated listings are mailed out regularly to members. You check off listings that interest you, then contact ASFM headquarters, identifying yourself with your code number. You are then advised as to how you may contact the persons you have selected. This may be done by mail or by phone, depending on individual preference. No names, addresses, or phone numbers are published in the MML. Annual membership for out of California residents is $36.00. For California residents costs vary due to the frequency and variety of activities. For further information write or phone.

Here is a typical member's comment:

"I learned more about myself in the last four Wednesday night discussions than I've learned in one and a half years of analysis. I feel fantastic! I've never seen people relate to one another so openly and honestly before, especially when discussing sex.

—S.M.

From 100 Years of Eotica *by Paul Aratow*
Published by Straight Arrow Books, San Francisco
Reprinted by permission

CALIFORNIA

Although swinging is active throughout the United States, California, being the twentieth century land of the lotus eaters, has much more going on that is easily and readily located by interested parties. To list every party house would be impossible because of frequent changes. The most up-do-date and comprehensive listings can be found in Jaundice Press's *National Swing* (listed earlier), *The Berkeley Barb*, and in the other swinging and sexpapers listed elsewhere in *The Whole Sex Catalogue*.

One of the best party houses in Southern California, according to the ASFM and Drs. Phyllis and Eberhard Kronhausen, is Eden (213) 650-6212. In Northern California, specifically in the San Francisco Bay area, unquestionably the best is run by a charming couple named Shell and Barry (415) 834-5808. Their house is located in a pleasant, easy-to-find neighborhood, it is sensuously and tastefully furnished, and their parties are lavish. A writer for *The San Francisco Chronicle* recently remarked that the food is so good he suspects it to be as much of an attraction as the group scene. Shell and Barry screen everyone individually in advance to make certain that they will be compatible with their loyal regulars.

In the case of both Eden, and Shell and Barry, call for times, directions, and other pertinent information.

Sexual Freedom League list of chapters

P.O. Box 4699   (East Bay Chapter)
Hayward, California 94544

P.O. Box 0155   (San Diego Chapter)
College Grove Station
San Diego, California 92115
(714) 465-2853

P.O. Box 14034   (San Francisco Chapter)
San Francisco, California 94114
(415) 665-5260

P.O. Box 3275   (South Bay Chapter)
San Jose, California 95116
(415) 289-8524

P.O. Box 1306   (Los Angeles area chapter)
South Pasadena, California 91030
(714) 465-2852

[*Note:* although the following two chapters are not in California, they are listed here because they are under the general blanket of the Sexual Freedom League.]

(312) 258-5515   Chicago Chapter

(313) 285-4343   Detroit Chapter

OTHER CALIFORNIA GROUPS ARE:

Exchange
P.O. Box 912
Azuza, California 91702

The Players
P.O. Box 3273
Bakersfield, California 93305

A FEW MORE GROUPS AROUND THE U.S. ARE:

FLORIDA

Club Joy
Royal (SCEJ)
Box 1548
Pompano Beach, Florida 33060

ILLINOIS

DOT

c/o C&W
Box 6887-B
Chicago, Illinois 60680

Embassy
P.O. Box 166
East St. Louis, Illinois 62202

MARYLAND

Swing
P.O. Box 1934
Silver Spring, Maryland 20902

NEW JERSEY

Action Group
Box 53-J
Blawenburg, New Jersey 08504

A very active group founded in 1969. Very popular with singles as well as couples, with services for over thirty-fives as well as newcomers to swinging. Run by a very bright and lively pair of charming women, they offer a discount to *Select* members.

Our Gang
P.O. Box 803
Fair Lawn, New Jersey 07410
(201) 791-2256

In operation since 1971, this group sponsors weekend mix-and-match cocktail parties. Call or write for full details.

The Seekers
Box 781
Cherry Hill, New Jersey 08034

Another group/publication that has been in business for several years. They concentrate on weekend action primarily and advertise nationally.

NEW YORK

J.S. Exchange
P.O. Box 527
New York, New York 10010
(212) 761-6641

One of the oldest, most active swinging clubs in New York, the J.S. Exchange sponsors get-togethers Wednesdays through Sundays at 8:30 p.m. at selected locations in Manhattan. Members are notified as to time and place in the event of changes. They also sponsor periodic weekend swings at which time they take over entire hotels. All queries are cheerfully and promptly answered.

The Underground
P.O. Box 197
Village Station
New York, New York 10014
(212) 223-7448

A relatively new club that meets at selected Manhattan spots. They have ambitious plans that include travel and exchange of information with other clubs around the country. For further details write or call Don or Jo Jo.

OHIO

Club Modern
P.O. Box 6267
Cincinnati, Ohio 45206

The Mixers Club
P.O. Box 19057
Cincinnati, Ohio 45219

PENNSYLVANIA

Exchange Scene Club
P.O. Box 14756
Philadelphia, Pennsylvania 19134

INTERNATIONAL

World League of Swingers and Swingers' clubs (W.L.S.)
P.O. Box 11
Camden, New Jersey 08101

A new international organization set up to provide service and information to swingers all over the world. At present there are approximately a hundred clubs around the United States participating, all of whom honor W.L.S. membership cards. For full details write at the above address.

Photo by Bernhardt J. Hurwood

Swingers' Hangouts

From The International Sex Maniacs Desk Diary 1975.

The following list of groups and/or listing services is offered here without comment. At the time the Whole Sex Catalogue went to press all were in operation. It is possible, however, that between then and the on-sale date changes may have taken place.

It would be counterproductive to attempt a comprehensive listing of every swinging hangout in the country, chiefly because there is a tendency on the part of swingers to switch locations from time to time. Here, however, is a representative sampling. Since swingers tend to maintain a very active grapevine, all one has to do to find out where the current action can be found is to get acquainted with other swingers. Use the various channels presented here, and there will be no problems involving the acquisition of further current information.

CALIFORNIA

Brass Rail
160 Mt. View-Alviso Road
Sunnyvale, California
(408) 734-1454

(On the Peninsula, about thirty miles south of San Francisco)

The Swing
Ventura Blvd at Coldwater Canyon
Studio City, California
(213) 783-7171

FLORIDA

Ivy Inn
1224 South Dixie Highway
Hollywood, Florida
(305) 925-9897

ILLINOIS

Executive North Lounge
Chicago, Illinois
(312) 777-2225

This is both a meeting place and the only permanent swingers club in Illinois. Their mailing list includes approximately 2,000 couples and their regular membership roster is over four hundred. Dues are $40.00 per year. Singles are welcome on Mondays through Thursdays, but on weekends entrance is restricted to couples who pay a $5.00 cover charge. The atmosphere is relaxed, and the back room has a pool table and assorted electronic games—hockey, ping pong, bowling. Interested parties should contact the club's president, La Croix, or his wife, Pat, who will cheerfully answer all questions. "Our main key to success," says Mr. La Croix, "is that we provide a neutral meeting place where couples can go to meet other couples without obligations."

NEW YORK

The Botany Talk House
803 Avenue of the Americas (6th Ave to natives)
New York, New York
(212) 255-9848

WASHINGTON, D.C.

The Class Reunion
1726 H Street N.W.
Washington, D.C.
(202) 298-8477

To Swing or Not to Swing

From *The Love Test*
by Lawrence Schwab,
© 1974 by Lawrence Schwab

Zebra Books,
New York 1974 ($1.25)

Reprinted by permission

Illustration from the 1797 edition of de Sade's L'Histoire de Juliette. *Reprinted in 1969 as* Sixty Erotic Drawings from Juliette. *Reproduced courtesy of Grove Press, Inc.*

*T*he Swinger's pendulum performs a wide arc. At one apex are those who proselytize swinging as the most advanced sign of maturity. At the other pole, in opposition, are sexual conservatives who abhor swinging and label it bad, immoral, degrading, denigrating, animalistic . . .

In the middle, humanistic psychologists and psychiatrists picture swinging as the fulfillment of our unlived exploratory sex life. They say you "should" be able to engage in it comfortably, then take it or leave it.

Reality notes: swinging is a social phenomenon that is growing rapidly, especially among middle-class couples in their thirties; but it is by no means limited to this slice of our population.

Couples who have successfully made the swinging scene tend to have a firm primary bond relationship. The main hindrance to swinging stems from feelings of inferiority, possessiveness and sexual exclusivity. If a relationship is grooving outside of sex, it stays that way with the addition of swinging. Shaky sexual or nonsexual problems are magnified when swinging.

Body acceptance becomes an integrated part of the swinger's life. Many swingers have found that swinging enhances their sex life. It certainly gives them something to talk about on the way home.

Whatever your views, there is an introductory quiz that'll compare your attitudes with those who have successfully embraced swinging. And, for those who need a definition of swinging, it is the exchanging of sexual partners within the confines of an organized sexual plan.

Choose a response to each question that *most closely represents* your feelings and probable reaction:

1. Your partner suggests that the two of you join a swing club. You:
   a. Are horrified!
   b. Are excited with the proposal.
   c. Wonder why you aren't "enough" for your partner.
   d. Are willing to talk about it.

2. Looking across the room at a swing party you see your partner in an intimate embrace. You probably would:
   a. Feel a little left out and uncomfortable.
   b. Be unconcerned, because that is why you are here.
   c. Find someone to become involved with yourself.
   d. Be furious and leave.

3. You watch as your partner goes into a bedroom to swing. You probably would:
   a. Be unconcerned and continue with what you are doing.
   b. Take it for a while, then go to the bedroom to get your partner.
   c. Find someone to swing and/or talk with.
   d. Become furious and distressed, and take the car.

4. You are swinging and your partner enters the bedroom to swing. You probably would:
   a. Go on with your swinging, unconcerned.
   b. "Freeze up" and suffer until they finish and leave.
   c. Continue to swing, enjoying the sights and sounds of your mate's swinging.
   d. Leave the room.

5. Another couple invites the two of you to swing with them in a foursome. You:
a. Are delighted!
b. Would like to, if your partner agrees.
c. Wouldn't have anything to do with such a thing!
d. Would decline because of uneasiness about swinging in the same room with your partner.

6. You are in a bedroom swinging but don't enjoy your swinging partner's technique. You would:
a. Get up and leave the room.
b. Talk it over with your partner to improve mutual pleasure.
c. Endure the situation unhappily.
d. Try to shorten the experience as much as possible.

7. You are in a group scene and one of the participants of your own sex comes on to you sexually.
a. You are surprised, but decide to see what happens.
b. You "turn off" and leave the scene.
c. You are horrified and disgusted, and say so.
d. It's not your thing, and you discreetly stop it.

8. You have often thought you would like to swing. You are:
a. Afraid of venereal disease.

b. Afraid you'll find swinging so stimulating you'll be dissatisfied with your partner and split.
c. Afraid that your partner will enjoy it more than you will.
d. Afraid of what your partner will think of you if you bring it up.

9. There's a wide range of age and ethnic groups among members of the swing club you are considering. You find this:
a. Stimulating
b. Of some concern and discomforting.
c. Doesn't matter.
d. A "turn off" and unacceptable.

10. The swing club you are considering also offers social nonsexual activities. This:
a. Increases your interest.
b. Is of some slight interest.
c. Bothers you, as you don't want to mix "fucking" with social activities.
d. Might lead to the so-called "straights" finding out about you and your swinging.

Here's your swinging potential: circle the number that applies to each question.

SCORE POINTS

Question	1	2	3	4
1	b	d	c	a
2	b	d	a	c
3	a	c	b	d
4	c	a	d	b
5	a	b	d	c
6	b	a	d	c
7	a	d	b	c
8	a	b	c	d
9	a	c	b	d
10	a	b	d	c

Total Points

10-15 points: You have no hangups to hamper swinging. You will be an exciting addition to any swing group. Openness and adventure are two words underlined in your dictionary.

16-21: You are pretty healthy emotionally. You will enjoy swinging. You are open to new things, which is the sign of the person who is on the way to "peak" experiences.

22-25: Swinging is a pretty threatening jump for you to take. You waver between wanting to and being afraid.

26-31: You are likely to encounter some difficulty if you try swinging. However, swinging presents an excellent way to grow, so if you are open to a horizon-expanding trip, swinging could be beneficial to you.

32-35: Swinging would offer too many contradictions to your restricted moralistic behavior. You have often given it thought, but quickly pushed it to the back of the bus.

36-40: Swinging is not for you. Forget it! Fantasies and clandestine affairs are more your thing.

Anonymous illustration for a nineteenth century edition of Restif de la Bretonne's L'Anti Justine. From Erotic Illustrations by Gordon Grimley. Copyright © 1974 by Gordon Grimley. Reproduced by permission of Grove Press, Inc.

Bibliography

Athenaeus of Nanclia, The Deipnosophists or: The Banquet of the Learned. Translated by G. B. Gulick. New York: Heinemann, 1927.

Bartell, G.D. *Group Sex: A Scientist's Eyewitness Report on the American Way of Swinging.* New York: Peter H. Wyden, 1971.$6.95.

Becker, H. S. *Outsiders.* New York: The Free Press, 1963. $7.95

Beltz, S. E. "Five Year Effects of Altered Marital Contracts." In *Extramarital Relations.* Englewood-Cliffs, N.J.: Prentice-Hall.

Bernard J. *The Sex Game.* Englewood Cliffs, N.J.: Prentice-Hall, 1968. $3.95

Boyland, B. R. *The New Marriage.* New York: Pinnacle, Zebra, 1974. $1.50

Brandston, Garth. *The Crowd in the Bedroom.* Chatsworth, Calif.: Brandon Books, 1974. $1.95

———. *Mate Swapping: The Search for Sexual Ecstasy.* Chatsworth, Calif.: Brandon Books, 1972. $1.95

Breedlove, W., and Breedlove, J. *Swap Club.* Los Angeles: Sherbourne Press, 1964.

[Carol and Tim.] *The Swinger's Handbook.* New York: Pocket Books, 1974. $1.50

Constantine, Larry L., and Constantine, Joan M. *Group Marriage.* New York: Collier Books, 1974. $2.95

Ellis, Albert. *The Search for Sexual Enjoyment.* New York: MacFadden-Bartell, 1966. o/p

Foote, N. N. "Sex as Play" In *Mass Leisure.* ed. E. Larabee and R. Nyersohn. New York: The Free Press, 1958.

Fuller, R. *Hell Fire Francis.* London: Chatto & Windus, 1939.

Gagnon, J. H., and Simon, W., eds. *The Sexual Scene.* Chicago: Aldine, 1970.

Galant, M., and Galant K. *The Lesbian in Group Love.* Cleveland: Century Books, 1967.

———. *Wife Swapping in Business.* Cleveland: Century Books, 1967.

———. *Wife Swapping, The People.* San Diego, Calif.: Publishers Export Company, 1967.

Hamilton, G. V. *A Research in Marriage.* New York: Albert and Charles Boni, 1929.

Hartman, William E., Fithian, Marilyn, and Johnson, D. *Nudist Society.* New York: Avon, 1971. $1.50

Hudston, Ted, and Saddens, Anne. *Sex Initiations for Cliques and Clubs.* Chatsworth, Calif.: Brandon Books, 1973. $1.95

Jones, Louis C. *The Clubs of the Georgian Rakes.* New York: Columbia University Press, 1942. $25.00

Lindsey, B. B., and Evans, W. *The Companionate Marriage.* New York: Garden City, 1929.

Lobel, John, and Lobel, Mimi. *The Complete Handbook for A Sexually Free Marriage.* New York: Pinnacle Books, 1975. $1.95

———. *A Free Marriage.* New York: Bantam Books, 1974. $1.50

Margolis, Jack. *The Ins and Outs of Orgies.* Los Angeles: Price/Stern/Sloan, 1974. $2.95

Marks, P. J. *A New Community.* San Diego: Youth Resources, 1969.

Moran, Jim. *How I Became An Authority on Sex.* New York: Bantam Books, 1974. $1.50

O'Neill, Nena, and O'Neill, George C. *Open Marriage.* New York: M. Evans & Co. Inc. 1972, $6.95.; New York, Avon: 1973. $1.95

Otto, H. A., ed. *The Family in Search of a Future.* New York: Appleton, Century, Crofts, 1970. $3.95

Parker, Morton. *Five Steps to an Orgy.* New York: Brandon Books, 1973. $1.95

Partridge, Burgo. *A History of Orgies.* New York: Bonanza Books, 1974.

Richards, Eugene, and Saddens, Anne. *Group Sex, The Sensuous Five.* Chatsworth, Calif.: Brandon Books, 1973. $1.75

Rimmer, Robert H. *Adventures in Loving.* New York: Signet, 1973. $1.50

———. *The Harrad Experiment.* New York: Bantam Books, 1967. $1.50

———. *Proposition 31.* New York: Signet, 1971. $1.25

Robinson, Frank, and Lehrman, Nat., eds. *Sex American Style.* Chicago: Playboy Press, 1971. $7.50

Rubenstein, P., and Margolies, H. *Group Sex Tapes.* New York: David McKay, 1971. $6.95

Smith, J. R., and Smith, L. G. *Beyond Monogramy.* Baltimore: The Johns Hopkins University Press, 1974. $3.95

———. *Consenting Adults: An Exploratory Study of the Sexual Freedom Movement,* forthcoming.

Trimble, John F. *The Group Sex Scene.* New York: Pinnacle Books, 1971. $1.25

Whitefield, Ann. *The Joy of Swinging.* * New York: Pinnacle Books, 1975. $1.75

Wilson, T. J. B. and Meyers, E. *Wife Swapping: A Complete Eight Year Survey of Morals in North America.* New York: Volitant Press.

[X, Mrs.] *Adultery Game.* New York: Pyramid Books. $1.50

This new book contains the most comprehensive listing of swinging clubs in the United States broken down geographically.

Illustration for Le Diable du Corps by Andrea de Nerciat, 1865. From Erotic Illustrations by Gordon Grimley. Copyright © 1974 by Gordon Grimley. Reproduced by permission of Grove Press.

Rare Books

The Hellfire Club, kept by a Society of Blasphemers, n.p., 1721.

The Irish Blasters, or the Votaries of Bacchus, Dublin, 1738.

Records of the Most Ancient and Puissant Order of the Beggar's Benison and Merry and Anstruther, Privately Printed, 1892.

Illustration from an eighteenth century edition of Fanny Hill *From* Erotic Illustrations *by Gordon Grimley. Copyright © 1974 by Gordon Grimley Reproduced by permission of Grove Press.*

Periodicals

Babchuck, N., and Bates A.P. "The Primary Relations of Middle Class Couples: A Study in Male Dominance." *American Sociology Review* 28: 377-84.

Bartell, G. "Group Sex Among the Mid Americans" *Sex Research* 6, no. 2, pp. 113-30.

Beigel, H. "In Defense of Mate Swapping." *Rational Living* 4, no. 2, pp. 15-16.

Collier, James L. "Communes, Togetherness Sixties Style," *True*, February, 1969.

Constantine, Larry L., and Constantine, Joan M. "How to Make a Group Marriage," *Modern Utopian*, 4 (Summer).

——. "Personal Growth in Multiperson Marriages." *Radical Therapy* 2, no. 1, pp. 18-20.

——. "Where is Marriage Going." *Futurist,* Spring, 44-46.

Denfield D., and Denfield, Gordon M. "The Sociology of Mate Swapping: or The Family That Swings Together Clings Together." *Journal of Sex Research* 6, no. 2, 85-100.

Eysenck, H. J. "Introverts, Extroverts, & Sex." *Psychology Today,* January 1970, pp. 14-19.

Fonzi, G., and Riggio J. "Modern Couple Seeks Like-Minded Couples, Utmost Discretion." *Philadelphia* (1969) no. 9, pp. 76-89.

Gourley, H. W. "A Utopian Answer: Walden House Plus Group Marriage." *Modern Utopian* 1 (1967), no. 1.

Griebe, K. "Walden House Talks Back." *Modern Utopian* 1, 1967, No. 2.

Henshel, A. M. "Swinging: A Study of Decision Making in Marriage." *American Journal of Sociology* 78 (1973): 885-91.

Kanter, R. M. "Commitment and Social Organization. A Study of Commitment Mechanisms in Utopian Communities." *American Sociology Review* 33: 499-517.

Kanter, R. M. "Communes." *Psychology Today* 4, (1970): 53-78.

Kirkendall, L. A., and Libby, R. W. "Interpersonal Relationships/Crux of the Sexual Renaissance." *Sociological Issues* 22 (1962): 45-59.

Krippner, S., and Fersch, D. "Mystic Communes." *Modern Utopian* 4 (Spring 1970), pp. 433-48.

Levinger, G. "Task and Social Behavior in Marriage," *Sociometry* 27 (December 1964), pp. 433-48.

Lewis, R. W. "The Swingers." *Playboy* 16 (1969), pp. 149-228.

Neubeck, G., and Schletzer, V. M. "A Study of Extramarital Relationships." *Marriage and Family Living* 24 (1962): 279-81.

O'Neill, Nena, and O'Neill, George C. "Patterns in Group Sexual Activity." *Journal of Sex Research* 6 (1970), no. 2, pp. 101-12.

Ramey, J. W. "Communes, Group Marriages and the Upper Middle Class." *Journal of Marriage and the Family* 34 (1972): 647-55.

——. "The Relationship of Peer Group Rating to Certain Individual Perceptions of Personality." *Journal of Experimental Education* 27 (1958): 143-49.

Renne, K. "Correlates of Dissatisfaction in Marriage." *Journal of Marriage and the Family* 32 (1970): 54-67.

Roy, R., and Roy, D. "Monogamy, Where We Stand Today." *Humanist,* March/April, 1970;

Smith, J. R., and Smith, L. G. "Co-marital Sex and The Sexual Freedom Movement." *Journal of Sex Research* 6 (1970), no. 2, pp. 131-142.

Stein, R. "Not Just An Ordinary Family," *San Francisco Chronicle,* August 28, 1970.

Symonds, Carolyn. "Sexual Mate Swapping and the Swingers." *Marriage Counseling Quarterly,* Spring 1971, pp. 1-12.

Willie, Lois. "The Spouse Swappers," *Chicago Daily News,* June 27, 28, 29, 30, 1967.

Wollach, L. "Change Partners", *Penthouse,* January 1973, p. 111.

Zetterberg, H. L. "On Sexual Life in Sweden as Cited in the New Contraceptive Society," *Look,* February 4, 1969.

Detail from illustration by Wallace Smith to Ben Hecht's Fantazius Mallare.

Unpublished Papers

Bell, R.R., and Bell, Silvan L. "Swinging, The Sexual Exchange of Marriage Partners." Paper read at the meeting of the Society for the Study of Social Problems, August 1970, Washington, D.C.

Constantine, Larry L., and Constantine, Joan M. "Report on Ongoing Research in Group Marriage." Paper read at the meeting of Society for the Scientific Study of Sex, January 1971, New York.

Palson, C., and Palson, R. M. "Swinging: the Minimizing of Jealousy." Mimeographed. Philadelphia: University of Philadelphia, 1970.

Schuff, C. "An Analysis of some sociopsychological factors which operate in the functioning of relationship of married couples who exchange mates for the purpose of sexual experience." Ph.D. dissertation, United States International University, 1970.

Spanier, G. B., and Cole, D. L. "Mate Swapping. Participation knowledge and values in a midwestern community." Paper read at the annual meeting of the Midwest Sociological Society, 1972, Kansas City, Mo.

Symonds, Carolyn. "Pilot study of the peripheral behavior of sexual mate swappers." Master's thesis, University of California, Riverside, 1968.

"The utopian aspects of sexual mate swapping." Paper read at the annual meeting of the Society for the Study of Social Problems, September 1970, Washington, D.C. Mimeographed.

Twitchell, Jon. "Co-marital Sex. The incorporation of extramarital sex into the marriage relationship." Paper read at 61st annual meeting of the American Psychopathological Association, February 1971, New York.

Varni, C. "An Exploratory Study of Spouse Swapping." Master's thesis, San Diego State College, 1970.

——. "A Participant Observer Study of Sexual Mate Exchange among Married Couples." Paper read at the meeting of the Pacific Sociological Association, April 1971, Honolulu.

From Aphrodisiacs to Contraception

Recreational Sex and How to Avoid Procreation

On the surface it might seem a bit obscure to combine these two categories in a single section, but when you think about it there is a logical connection and a practical reason. If you and your partner get turned on by the aphrodisiacs, then assuming you are heterosexual, there is always the possibility of long-range complications—especially ones that take nine months to gestate. Here are a great many of the elements essential to making sexual activity appetizing, satisfying . . . and secure.

Aphrodisiacs

Aphrodisiacs, named after Aphrodite, the Greek Goddess of Love, are substances capable of stimulating sexual desire. They include—in addition to those substances taken internally—visual, aural, tactile, and olfactory stimulants, in short, anything that excites sexuality. Aphrodisiacs have occupied the searches and researches of man from ancient to modern times, and almost no culture, primitive or civilized, is without its pharmacopoeia of love foods and potions.

Probably the earliest recorded mention of aphrodisiacs comes from undated Egyptian medical papyri believed to be from the Middle Kingdom which flourished between 2200-1700 B.C. Aphrodisiacs are mentioned in the Bible and many of the world's sacred

LE GOURMAND

From *1001 Ways to Make Love* by Tuli Kupferberg Copyright © 1969 by Tuli Kupferberg. Reprinted by permission of Grove Press, Inc.

books, so that those who make a moral issue out of their use do not base their objections on literary reality. Ancient literature is filled with glowing accounts of aphrodisiac foods, and by the time of the Golden Age of Greece, their use was fairly commonplace. The Romans, who inherited their culture from the Greeks, were also intimately familiar with the art of culinary seduction. Aphrodisiac lore passed from the Romans to the early Christian era, the Middle Ages, the Renaissance, and into modern times. This is not to say that aphrodisiacs are strictly a Western phenomenon. Simultaneous with the proliferation of love foods in the Western world was a corresponding awareness of their powers in the mystic East; in fact, some connoisseurs insist that Oriental aphrodisiacs are among the most potent. Today we are bombarded by advertisements alleging that certain products enhance sexuality, advertisements that echo in contemporary terms the claims of the most ancient of aphrodisiacs.

Modern science lends little credibility to the belief in the sexually stimulating properties of certain foods, recognizing only two "true" aphrodisiacs: *cantharides* (Spanish fly), and *yohimbine*, a yellowish powder derived from the bark of the yohimbe tree. Science does, however, recognize the psychological lure of aphrodisiacs. Many psychologists maintain that aphrodisiacs work if one *believes* they will work.

When one speaks of the "hunger" for food and the

Anonymous
sixteenth century
woodblock

"hunger" for sex, he is hinting profoundly at the inseparable physical and psychological relationship between these two of man's most basic needs. Somewhere, over the long evolutionary process, the need to find food and the need for sexual expression have merged and become confused in man's psyche. This psychological short-circuiting has resulted in the concept of the "Doctrine of Signatures" (the ancient belief in the therapeutic efficacy of resemblances), and sympathetic magic—today described as the "you-are-what-you-eat" syndrome. Primitive man copulated in the fields in the belief that the crops would share his fertility. He observed the sexual behavior of animals and deduced that if he ate of the flesh of the more virile species that virility would be passed on to him. It didn't take much imagination to conclude that eating the sexual parts of the animal would be even more effective. Foods that resembled, tasted, or smelled like male and female genitalia were also used as aphrodisiacs. One person may include the carrot among the most erotic of foods; another is stimulated by the appearance and texture of raw oysters; and a third is sent into ecstasy by a cream puff.

Set (attitude), setting (atmosphere), and the power of suggestion are primary considerations when plying a loved one with aphrodisiacs. When Madame Du Barry fed her spiked bon-bons to the aging Louis XV, she was sure to casually mention that the recipe for those delicious titbits had been handed down by an Arabian sheikh who not only satisfied a harem of one hundred and fifty concubines, but also managed to deflower one hundred sixty virgins in a fortnight. Her elegant table was most likely laden with rich and succulent foods, served by candlelight to the romantic strains of the court fiddlers. And as the voluptuous Madame purred her deceit into the old king's ear, his "spirits" were certain to rise.

Surely eating, like sex, is most enjoyable when all the senses are called into play, making a feast for the total organism. The combination of various sensuous reactions—the visual satisfaction of the sight of appetizing foods, their pleasing aroma and varying consistencies—tends to create a state of pleasurable relaxation conducive to sexual expression. Even the most naive schoolboy out on his first date is well aware of the seductive atmosphere of candlelight and wine.

The French, gourmets and lovers all, have made a veritable art of culinary seduction. In the nineteenth century many Parisian restaurants featured private dining rooms, called *cabinets particuliers*, which catered to more amorously inclined customers. These dining-cum-boudoir suites were luxuriously furnished and specialized in creating an atmosphere rich in sensual delights. The bed was a mere few feet from the table, making the transition from sitting to lying an easy one.

These sumptuous establishments may have been unique to the French, but they were not unique to France. In the Gay Nineties, during the Champagne days of San Francisco, many similar French restaurants with "upstairs suites" were the pride and scandal of the city. The bill of fare included oysters Kirkpatrick, broiled terrapin, and fourteen-course dinners served with seven varieties of wine. The customer could choose from the live frogs displayed in the windows for his dish of frogs' legs *a la poulette*. After seducing their palates with fine foods, a gentleman and his lady would climax the evening in one of the canopied beds discreetly supplied by the management. The proprietors of these love nests were well

For those whose desire responds to a more diabolically planned diet!
From THE NAKED CHEF, *An Aphrodisiac Cookbook by Billie Young*
Copyright © 1971 by Billie Young.
Reprinted by permission of Ashley Books, Inc., *Port Washington, New York*

Detail from Botticelli's Primavera

instructed on the erotic results of a satisfying meal by the Marquis de Sade: "A plenteous meal may produce voluptuous sensations."

Nowhere is the psychological relationship between food and sex more evident than in language. Many terms for food have sexual connotations. These terms, called *erotolabia*, appear in English and other foreign languages, and their existence is no mere accident, but proof of man's universal preoccupation with the erotic character of foods. Words like "cherry," "nuts," "wiener," "dish," "tart," to name but a few, refer to some aspects of human sexuality. Others, like "sweetheart" and "dumpling," are used as terms of affection. Food, sex, and language are all intricately entwined in a psychological maze providing literal food for thought.

The marriage of food and sex is not only psychological, but physical as well. Before eating, animals salivate to prepare the mouth and esophagus to receive food. In much the same way, the sexual organs secrete mucous before coitus. The German nutritionist, Balzli, points out that "the sensual internal surface areas of the sex organs correspond to the taste-buds of the mouth." Certain nerve structures which are extremely sensitive to stimulation, called "Krause's end-bulbs," are found principally in the penis, clitoris—and lips. Man's urge to engage in oral-genital contact is as natural and healthy as his desire to partake of tasty and satisfying foods. As the Song of Solomon so poetically puts it: "I sat down under

his shadow, whom I desired; and his fruit was sweet to my palate."

The list of aphrodisiac foods ranges from the exotic to the commonplace. Even such unromantic items as the potato and the bean were once considered powerful love stimulants. The idea that a potato in the dining room can lead to a frolic in the bedroom is not as ridiculous as it sounds. Take the strange case of the barbasco.

The barbasco is a wild yam native to Mexico, Central and South America, Africa, and India. From the roots of the barbasco is extracted the basis for many modern drugs, including diosgenin, a steroid chemical used in the manufacture of birth control pills. In the laboratory, diosgenin is transformed into a *synthetic sex hormone*. Prior to the discovery of this amazing chemical, one European firm had to process a ton of bulls' testicles to produce one one-hundredth of an ounce of a certain type of sex hormone. Sex hormones *do* have an aphrodisiac effect, and they are used to treat frigidity and impotence in humans. Is it inconceivable, in this cybernetic era of space flight and miracle drugs, that some brilliant scientist will extract a true aphrodisiac from a common food like the bean or potato?

All sensation is ultimately located in the brain. We already have drugs that can stimulate, tranquilize, and depress. If there is a button in the brain's control panel marked *sex*, then there is a substance to push it, even if it is as yet undiscovered. Time, which brings knowledge, is all that separates the modern chemist from the ancient alchemist.

Reprinted from Aphrodisiac Cookery: Ancient & Modern *by Greg and Beverly Frazier. Copyright © 1970 by Greg and Beverly Frazier. With permission of Troubador Press, San Francisco*

Reproduced by courtesy of Troubador Press, San Francisco. Copyright © 1970 by Greg and Beverly Frazier

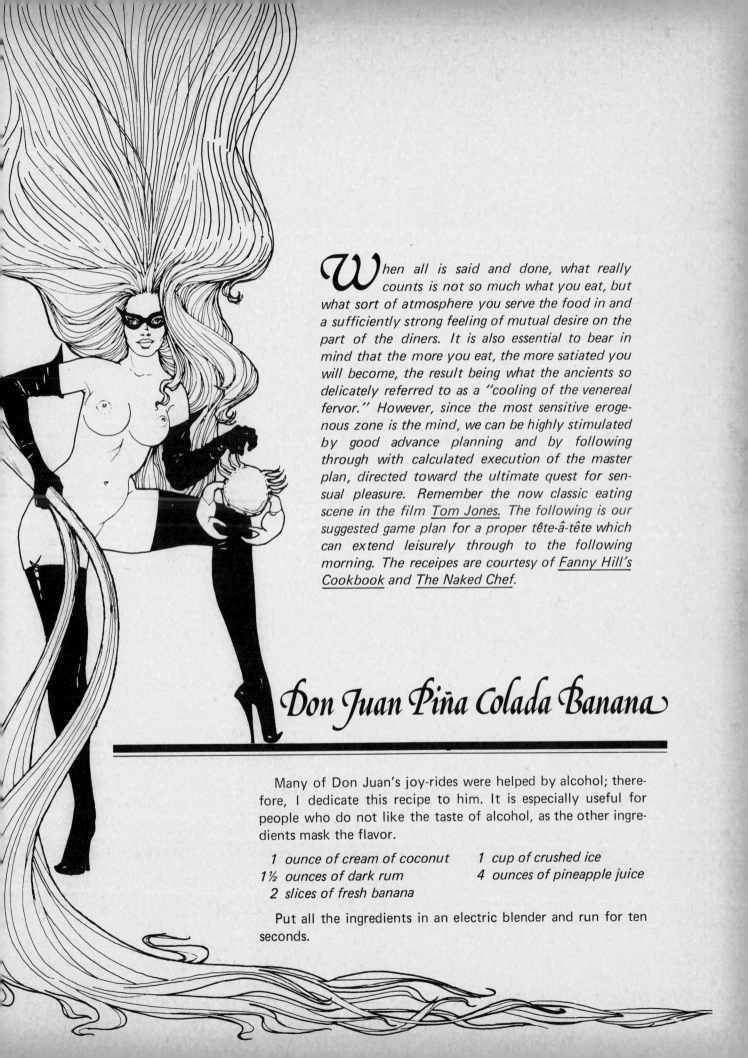

When all is said and done, what really counts is not so much what you eat, but what sort of atmosphere you serve the food in and a sufficiently strong feeling of mutual desire on the part of the diners. It is also essential to bear in mind that the more you eat, the more satiated you will become, the result being what the ancients so delicately referred to as a "cooling of the venereal fervor." However, since the most sensitive erogenous zone is the mind, we can be highly stimulated by good advance planning and by following through with calculated execution of the master plan, directed toward the ultimate quest for sensual pleasure. Remember the now classic eating scene in the film Tom Jones. The following is our suggested game plan for a proper tête-à-tête which can extend leisurely through to the following morning. The receipes are courtesy of Fanny Hill's Cookbook and The Naked Chef.

Don Juan Piña Colada Banana

Many of Don Juan's joy-rides were helped by alcohol; therefore, I dedicate this recipe to him. It is especially useful for people who do not like the taste of alcohol, as the other ingredients mask the flavor.

1 ounce of cream of coconut   1 cup of crushed ice
1½ ounces of dark rum   4 ounces of pineapple juice
2 slices of fresh banana

Put all the ingredients in an electric blender and run for ten seconds.

Marquise d' Salade

With Crafty Ebbing Undressing

Here's how to toss a green goddess until she comes across with delight. Dig your whisk into her bowl! Toss her around until she's creamy! Now draw and quarter your tomato, and give her the meat with a vengeance!

1 lb. back-fin lump crab meat, seasoned in bowl with ½ cup sherry
1 bunch fresh romaine, cut into strips, then quartered
3 large stalks Pascal celery, chopped
½ cup watercress
2 medium tomatoes, quartered

Toss salad thoroughly with crab meat mixed in.
Serve with the following dressing:

1 cup mayonnaise	*¼ tsp. dry mustard*
¼ cup minced parsley	*½ tsp. garlic powder*
¼ cup chopped chives	*2 tsps. anchovy paste*
½ tsp. tarragon	*¼ tsp. pepper*
½ cup sour cream	

Passion Fruits with Cointreau

Aphrodite, the Greek Goddess from whose name aphrodisiac stems, was called by the Roman poet, Lucretius, "the delight of men and gods." Sometimes, as the finis to an extraordinary meal where the mind is scorched with lust, both men and gods will hasten to quench love's thirst after a fast skirmish with passion fruit.

Cantaloupe, very sweet, cut into bite size pieces	*Wild raspberries Cointreau*

The Morning After
Lazy Lovers Nova Scotia

Thin sliced tomatoes
Drained capers
Thin sliced black pumpernickel bread
Sweet butter
Lemon wedges
Freshly ground black pepper
Nova Scotia salmon (smoked)

I know, you're lazy and impatient to resume the love match. You want just enough food to water your libido. Pile everything on pretty plates on a big tray, add a pot of coffee and real sweet cream. By the time you've finished eating, your erotogenic zones will be so stimulated, you'll barely have enough time to kick the tray out of reach. My sex symbol and I particularly enjoy this in our electric bed where a flick of the finger regulates the mattress as we rocket up, up, and away!

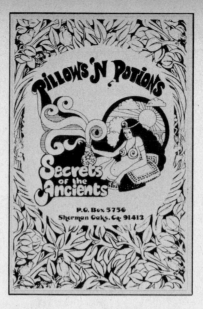

Erotic Cookbooks

Some suggested erotic cookbooks to delight both your palate and appetite . . .

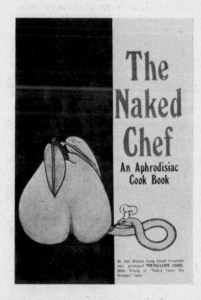

Lot and His Daughters
Painting by Lucan van Leyden, 1530.

THE NAKED CHEF prepared by Billie Young (Penelope Ashe), published by Ashley Books, $8.95. This book offers you menus for "before seduction" and "for after the seduction." There is a variety of recipes, ranging from "Instant Rejuvenation" seafood, "Salads for Sensualists," and the "Forbidden Fruits," to cures for the morning after's hangover.

There are chapters dealing with food for "Risqué Lovers with Lecherous Palates," with suggested dishes such as "Roast Ass," "Marinated Vulvas," or her "Meat & Poultry Stimulants" with such appetizing meals to begin the evening as:

Sinful Beef in Wine with Olives
2 lbs. stewing beef (chuck is very good for this) chunked, boneless
4 tablespoons heated brandy
1 crumbled bay leaf
1 small piece fresh orange peel
2 cloves garlic, minced
1 big glass dry red wine
Salt and pepper to taste
4 pieces parsley, cut small
1/8 teaspoon thyme
1/8 teaspoon chervil
¾ cup pitted black olives
Olive oil
1/8 teaspoon marjoram

Sauté the meat in a small amount of pure virgin olive oil; sear on all sides until it is brown. Pour the brandy over it and ignite, shaking the pan so that all the meat is touched by the flaming brandy. Relight the brandy if the flame dies, because it is the brandy in this recipe that will help light your fire later. Then, when the flame is finished, add everything except the olives. Simmer for three hours on a very low flame, tasting for seasoning. Then add the olives, simmer for fifteen minutes more, and serve, eating until . . . until . . .

All the menus in *The Naked Chef* have been tried and tasted before inclusion in the book by the author.

APHRODISIAC COOKERY by Greg and Beverly Frazier, illustrated by David and Dennis Redmond, published by Troubador Press, San Francisco, $4.95. This book contains a combination of "ancient and modern" recipes. The ancient recipes are compiled from folklore and literature, and the modern were invented with the authors' philosophy in mind: "It is not what the food brings to you, it is what you bring to the food." Bearing that in mind, it would be almost impossible not to find this collection of cooking delights capable of stimulating even waning sexual desire.

The book is broken down into chapters encompassing the many different varieties of food: fruits and nuts, wines and spirits, soups and potions, vegetables and exotic plants, fish and fowl, and the vitamins and minerals that make you virile. And—as the book quotes from nutritionist Dr. Hans Balzli, "After a perfect meal we are more susceptible to the ecstasy of love than at any other time . . ."—surely no more needs to be said.

LEWD FOOD, the complete guide to aphrodisiac edibles or how to sate *all* the hungers of the bawdy, written by Robert Hendrickson, published by Chilton Book Company, $10.95.

The opening words of Hendrickson's book are a quote from Lucretia, sixth century B.C. "The sole love potion I ever used was kissing and embracing, by which alone I made men rave like beasts and compelled them to worship me like an idol." Few people will dispute that, but as Hendrickson points out "food and wine are highly amatory aids to make the quest for sex more pleasurable and heighten the sexual act itself." In his book he offers any daring person an exotic bill of fare, divided into twenty-three courses from "Course One: Shall We Eat in the Nude, the Twin Breasts of Love"; "Course 17: Herculean Herbs and Spices for Various Vices"; "Course 20: Sweets between the Sheets and Desserts before the Piece de Resistance"; to "Course 21: The Sex Maniac's Quick Weight Loss Lust Diet—a Low-Calorie, Low-Cost Love Feast" to delight his or her lover with.

Detail from anonymous Dutch painting, circa 1600

FANNY HILL'S COOKBOOK by Lionel H. Braun & William Adams, illustrations by Brian Forbes, published by Taplinger, $4.95. Dedicated to "all the sons of Adam who've gone astray, and all daughters of Eve who would like to. To all who've reached the age of reason and reasoned, 'Why not!' And all who've reached the age of consent and just loved to," this cookbook bearing the name of one of fiction's bawdiest characters contains recipes and illustrations designed to whet anybody's palate. Offering a variety of dishes, from "Cheesed Balls," "Pickled Peckers," "Venusburgers," "Fellatio Mignon" to "Climax Pudding," the book guarantees "the carefully tested selections will answer any mood and make it more so (with enlightenment) like a candle in an old maid's hand. A touch of Venus, a little glass of wine, and a meal to commemorate the lasting moment's fancy, and a long goodnight with Fanny Hill."

COOKING FOR ORGIES AND OTHER LARGE PARTIES by Jack S Margolis and Daud Alani. Cliff House Books, $3.95. This book deals mainly with cooking fabulous six-course gourmet-style meals for large numbers of people in the shortest time possible at an average cost of only $1.00 per person.

The book is divided into menus giving you a step-by-step guide to the use of the cooking equipment and utensils you will need; a shopping list with estimated prices; and instructions on how *not* to spend the entire day sweating over a hot stove preparing the food for your orgy, so that when the meal is eaten you will have some energy left!

A sample menu is: Lamb Bathanjan; baked potatoes with elixir of crab; almond *cous cous*; crab ecstasy; vegetables in peanut butter sauce; and halcyon salad. The approximate cost is $29.26 (not estimating inflation); preparation time is one hour; and the result is enough food to feed from ten to thirty people.

Bon Apetit!

Aphrodisiac Bibliography

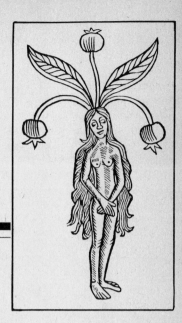

Mandrakes depicted in male and female form from the book
Hortus Sanitatis *by Johannes de Cuba, 15th Century*

Adams, Leon D. *Commonsense Book of Wine.* New York: David McKay, 1958. $3.95

Anand, Mulk Raj. *Kama Kala.* Secaucus, New Jersey: Lyle Stuart, 1959. $28.00

Apicius. *The Roman Cookery Book.* Translated by B. Flower and E. Rosenbaum, London: George G. Harrap & Co, 1958.

Bauer, W. W. *Potions, Remedies, and Old Wives Tales.* Garden City, New York: Doubleday, 1969

Bey, Pilaff. *Venus in the Kitchen.* Edited by Norman Douglas. London: William Heinemann, 1952.

Bishop, George. *The Booze Reader.* Los Angeles: Sherbourne Press, 1965. $4.50

Bloch, Iwan. *Odoratus Sexualis.* New York: American Anthropoligical Society, 1933. Reprint. New York: AMS, 1975.

Connell, Charles. *Aphrodisiacs in Your Garden.* New York: Taplinger, 1966. $3.50

Culpeper, Nicholas. *Culpeper's Complete Herbal.* New York: Sterling Publishers, 1959. $6.95

Davenport, John. *Aphrodisiacs and Anti-Aphrodisiacs.* New York: Award Books, 1970. 95¢

Davenport, John. *Aphrodisiacs & Love Stimulants.* Secaucus, New Jersey: Lyle Stuart, 1966. $6.00

Ellis, Albert. *The Art and Science of Love.* Secaucus, New Jersey: Lyle Stuart, 1969. $7.95

Ellis, Albert. *The Folklore of Sex.* New York: Charles Boni, 1951.

Gifford, Edward S. Jr. *The Charms of Love.* Garden City: New York: Doubleday, 1962.

Heartman, Charles F. *Cuisine de l'amour.* New Orleans: Gourmet's Company, 1942.

Henriques, Fernando. *Love In Action.* New York: Dell Books, 1962. 75¢

Legman, Gershon. *The Horn Book — Studies in Erotic Folklore.* New York: New York University Books, 1963. $6.95

Licht, Hans. *Sexual Life in Ancient Greece.* Reprint. New York: AMS, 1972. $32.50

Mathison, Richard. *The Shocking History of Drugs.* New York: Ballantine Books, 1958.

Nefzawi, Shaykh. *The Perfumed Garden of the Shaykh Nefzawi.* Translated by Sir Richard Burton. New York: G. P. Putnam's Sons, 1964.

Rocco, Sha. *Ancient Sex Worship.* New York: Commonwealth Company, 1904.

Tabori, Paul. *A Pictorial History of Love.* London: Drury House, 1966.

Van Gulik, Robert H. *Sexual Life in Ancient China.* New York: Humanities Press, 1961. $21.50

Vatsayana. *Kama Sutra.* Translated by Sir Richard Burton. (Many editions available.)

Wallnofer, Heinrich, and Von Rottauscher, Anna. *Chinese Folk Medicine.* New York: New American Library, 1974. $1.25

Walton, Alan Hull. *Aphrodisiacs: From Legend to Prescription.* New York: Associated Books, 1958. $7.95

——. *Stimulation for Love.* London: Tandem Books, 1966.

Wedeck, Harry E. *Dictionary of Aphrodisiacs.* New York: Citadel Press, 1960.

——. *Love Potions through the Ages.* New York: Citadel Press, 1963.

Contraception

Drawing by G. Mouton satirizing the chastity belt, 1910

*T*hroughout recorded history, man has always been faced with certain problems arising from the process of consequences of gathering rosebuds. Although the problems have varied from age to age, depending on tradition, custom, and geography, there are basic ones that are no different today from at the dawn of time.

Ever since boys and girls learned that pregnancies were not prevented by running around certain trees a prescribed number of times the morning after a healthy frolic in the hay, they have sought more practical means of prevention. This has been especially true with couples who were unmarried, or married to persons not present.

Often the problem was taken out of their hands by unbending, unsympathetic elders who believed in prevention before the fact, as it were. Thus, we find the pages of history littered with harrowing descriptions of chastity belts, nonremovable chain-mail drawers, genital padlocks (male and female!), and fibulae. Fibulae (so-called because the word derived from the Latin expression for buckle) were metal rings, loops, or locks that effectively prevented sexual intercourse. Some were made of leather thongs or threads, but wearers were so thoroughly intimidated by the dire consequences of removal that they usually remained securely in place.

Other antisex authoritarians of antiquity tried to frustrate the efforts of youthful swingers by chemical means, concocting antiaphrodisiac potions. Most of these were noxious brews so offensive to the senses that they would render the users incapable of anything more erotic than retching. Typical preventions were mouse dung, snail excrement, pigeon dung with oil and wine, lizard-drowned-in-urine, and eunuch's urine. Some antiaphrodisiacs were so far out that one can only wonder today at their originators.

The ancient Egyptians recommended hemlock, among other things, the implication being that whosoever got laid in a tomb became a mummy. But the *ne plus ultra* of aphrodisia was described by a medieval pundit named Alexander Benedictus, who recommended, "Take a Topaz, which has been previously rubbed against the right testical of a wolf, then steeped in oil of rose water, and wear as a ring. It will induce a disgust for venereal pleasure." Chances were, though, that anyone who succeeded in holding the wolf down long enough to rub the topaz properly was unlikely to feel very horny . . . never mind the oil and rose water.

Anonymous eighteenth century French engraving

Of course, for every sour-faced killjoy who tried to squelch sexual desire, there were two or three positivists sitting up nights cudgeling their brains, devising ways to kindle it. Consequently, over the centuries they positively guaranteed that aphrodisia would spring from a startling catalogue of substances. These ranged from phallic-shaped mandrake root to urine voided by a bull immediately following his copulation. Other hair-raising substances included powdered partridge brains with red wine, and contained such ingredients as ants, wood lice, bees, semen, blood, and specially prepared genitals of every creature, from rooster to stag. An old French account tells of an apothecary once prescribing fifty francs worth of pure gold per day in powdered form. And Saladin, the celebrated Saracen, was said to recommend a strict diet of fish.

Fish, of course, has always been associated with sexuality, having been sacred to the goddess of love. This probably explains a unique fishy aphrodisiac which is mentioned in an Old English verse that goes like this:

When I was a young girl, and wash't my mother's dishes, I stuck my finger in my cunt and pull'd out little fishes.

The lines actually refer to a method of preparing fish by young girls who wanted to arouse the amorous ardor of their swains. Such fish, after being properly cooked, and fed to the young men in question were supposed to be a surefire means of turning them on beneath the sheets.

Actually, all this business about aphrodisiacs and antiaphrodisiacs was never taken too seriously by younger generations of any age. They were always capable of functioning without chemical assistance, and their attitude was quite clearly expressed by a fictional sixteenth century courtesan appearing in a play by Pietro Aretino, who made a reflective declaration identical to the quote from Lucretia cited by Hendrickson in his introduction to *Lewd Food,* to the effect that the only aphrodisiac she ever needed to arouse men was that produced by her embraces and kisses.

This quite naturally brings us right back to where we started. The chief problem plaguing the sexes at play was always the mathematical one: namely, how to avoid multiplying. Sir Isaac Newton, the celebrated mathematician, effectively solved the problem for himself by keeping his multiplication tables on paper and avoiding the opposite sex altogether. Such drastic measures may have resulted in his discovering the law of gravity, but hardly recommended themselves to those who were desirous of discovering more intimate natural laws.

Barring exotic sex acts which precluded conception, or painful surgical procedures that proved more fatal than contraceptive, our ancestors sought more practical methods. For centuries this boiled down to *coitus interruptus.* Although condemned by the church and less than one hundred percent reliable, it was better than nothing at all and certainly worth the gamble for those lovers who couldn't bear the thought of tiny feet pattering into their future.

As for libertines, as swingers called themselves in times of old, there were few problems. Wives were supposed to bear children, and when occasional lovers crept into their knickers, accidental offspring automatically became property of the house. If one of the lovers happened to be a king, it was another story, of

The Intimate Wash. Oil painting by Francois Boucher (1703-1770)

course, because the little nipper was almost guaranteed a dukedom and a lifetime income. Royal bastards rarely fared badly.

Wenches of the lower classes were also supposed to bear children, and if they found themselves pregnant from time to time, there were few problems. The infant mortality rate was high, and perfectly formed girl babies could always be sold to enterprising madams who were constantly on the lookout for fresh talent.

According to most authorities, it was the discovery of America that indirectly changed everything. While the intrepid Columbus concentrated on business, his crew went ashore with more frivolous intentions, and in the process, made their own discoveries. Historians generally acknowledge that the most devastating of these was *Treponema Pallidum*, the sneaky spirochete who returned with them on their homeward voyage to make his European debut under the less formal *nom de guerre* of pox.

But until receiving a more permanent name, the pox was called by the English the French disease, by the French the Italian disease, by the Russians the Polish disease, by the Japanese the Portuguese disease, and so on. In 1530 the Italian physician, scientist, and poet Girolamo Fracastoro wrote his now-famous opus, *Syphilis sive Morbus Gallicus*, in which the hapless hero, a swineherd named Syphilos, is depicted as the first man to have the disease.

So sweeping was the spread of syphilis, that it has been said that civilization and syphilization advanced side by side. There was no prevention and no cure until around the middle of the sixteenth century, when another Italian physician, the peripatetic anatomist, Gabriel Fallopius, invented the first condom. Consisting of a linen sheath worn beneath the prepuce, it was less than comfortable and it did not prevent conception. But it apparently provided some protection against disease. The most apt comment on these primitive condoms was made by the witty seventeenth century lady of fashion, Madame Marie de Sévigné, who said that they were gossamer against infection, and steel against love.

By the eighteenth century they had been improved sufficiently to achieve a more solid reputation as the first line of defense against disease. It was said, however, that they blunted sensation to such a degree that many a rake preferred to risk the pox for the sake of his pleasure. Nevertheless, condoms gained in popularity, not only for their prophylactic virtues,

but as contraceptives, because by now they were being fabricated out of sheep gut.

For many years, a London *entrepreneuse* named Mrs. Philips cornered the market on these "machines" as they were quaintly called, dispensing them cheerfully to all comers from her establishment, the Green Canister in Half-Moon Street in the Strand. After making a fortune, she finally retired, to the consternation of her customers, until—according to a contemporary account—"learning that the town was not well served by her successors, she, out of patriotic zeal for the public welfare, returned to her occupation; of which she gave notice by diverse handbills in circulation in the year 1776."

Naturally, along with progress in general, there were undeniable advances in contraception, aphrodisia, and so on. Certainly, as we have clearly seen in recent years, the Victorians, with all their outward manifestations of an armor-plated, antisexual morality, reached fantastic heights of covert eroticism, not only in literature, but in actual practice.

The true turning point, however, did not actually come until relatively recent years. As G. Rattray Taylor pointed out in his admirable *Sex in History*, "The invention, in the early thirties, of the latex process for the manufacture of condoms is undoubtedly a landmark in social history, and has drastically altered the circumstances attending sexual activity." Next, with science advancing rapidly as old sexual taboos crumbled, revolutionary technology became the nucleus of a dynamic sexual revolution in the sixties and seventies.

In days of old when knights were bold

And rubbers weren't invented

They wrapped their socks

Around their cocks,

And babies were prevented.

The following provides information on the most commonly accepted methods of contraception in use today.

The Rhythm Method

The rhythm method appears to be the simplest of all contraceptive procedures. It is also one of the most ineffective because of the complexities involved in determining the "safe" days.

Three well-known biological facts provide the scientific basis for the rhythm method.

1. A woman usually produces only one egg during each menstrual cycle.

2. The egg has an active life of approximately twenty-four hours, and it is only during this length of time that it can be fertilized by the sperm.

3. The sperm is capable of living for approximately forty-eight hours after being released into the vagina. It is only during this span of time that it can fertilize the egg.

The obvious conclusion is that there are only approximately seventy-two hours each month when intercourse can lead to pregnancy: the forty-eight hours before the egg is released—and the twenty-four hours thereafter.

If a woman avoids having intercourse during this time, then, theoretically, she should not be in danger of becoming pregnant.

A woman using the rhythm method must refrain from having intercourse on the days when she can become pregnant, limiting her sexual activities to those days during each menstrual cycle which are supposed to be "safe."

What makes this simple concept difficult to put into practice, however, and what limits its effectiveness, is that no definite system has yet been found to determine precisely which days are safe and which are not.

THE ADVANTAGES:

1. No special equipment or contraceptive materials (prescription or otherwise) are required. (It is necessary, however, to have a calendar and a thermometer and to seek guidance from a physician. Without this the chances of success with this method will be slim.)

2. There is no need to interrupt relations with your partner in order to arrange for adequate protection. (It is, however, absolutely necessary to avoid intercourse completely on those days which are suspected of being unsafe.)

3. There is no possibility of side effects or allergic reactions from contraceptive materials.

THE DISADVANTAGES:

1. Its success depends on accurate prediction of the time when a woman is ovulating. No totally reliable system for doing this has yet been devised. Ovulation usually takes place between twelve and sixteen days before the beginning of the next menstrual flow, but both ovulation and menstruation are apt to occur irregularly. The number of days between periods varies from one woman to another. It also varies with the same woman at different times of her life, such irregularity being common in the years just prior to menopause and among very young women. And irregularity may also occur at any time when a woman experiences physical or emotional stress.

JUNE						
S	M	T	W	T	F	S
					?	?
?	?	?	?	?	?	?
?	?	?	?	?	?	?
?	?	?	?	?	?	?
?	?	?	?	?	?	

2. To use this method successfully, a woman must calculate just how much variation there is in the length of her menstrual cycles. This requires keeping a written record of menstrual periods for at least one year before attempting to use the rhythm system. (Once she has such a record, her physician can show her how to calculate the number of days each month during which intercourse must be avoided.) However, a formula for making this calculation exists when no record has been kept. This is done on the basis of "imaginary" cycles of varying length. Women who are certain that the variation in the length of their periods is never more than ten days may be able to use this formula under careful supervision of a physician.

3. This method restricts the total number of days in which a woman can safely have intercourse. (The average woman should avoid intercourse for two or three weeks out of every month for maximum protection.)

4. Not every woman can use this method. Approximately fifteen percent of all women menstruate with too much irregularity to use it at all.

5. This method is not recommended for any women during

the first few months after childbirth—usually being considered ineffective until after the third menstrual period following completion of a pregnancy.

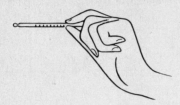

6. It is advisable to keep a daily record of body temperature in addition to the calendar record. This is done with a special thermometer known as a basal body temperature thermometer. It is marked off in tenth-of-a-degree indications and measures slight variations in temperature between 96°F and 100°F. The temperature must be taken on awakening every morning—before getting out of bed, drinking water or coffee, or smoking. Generally, a slight dip in temperature below a level that has been constant for a week or ten days provides a signal that ovulation has begun. This dip in temperature is usually followed by a rise of 1/2 to 3/4° over a period of twenty-four to seventy-two hours. After two days of elevated temperature—above the basal level—it may be assumed that a safe period has begun. This record provides a check on the accuracy of the calendar record. It should not be used alone, however, because illness or activity may cause fluctuations in daily body temperature which have nothing to do with the time of ovulation. It is essential that daily temperature readings be made under the same conditions and at the same time every day.

THE ADVANTAGES:

1. Condoms are readily available in any drugstore without prescription.

2. The main responsibility is on the male partner. Some women consider this a distinct advantage.

3. The cost is relatively low (as little as 20¢ each).

4. It can be useful as a "back-up" method to provide extra protection (when a woman forgets to take her pills, for example).

5. There is no applicator and the condom is discarded after a single use.

THE DISADVANTAGES:

1. The condom must be put on before intercourse and for that matter before any contact is made between the penis and the vagina.

2. It must be withdrawn from the vagina very cautiously, being careful that it does not break and that no sperm are allowed to escape.

3. If it is not removed immediately after intercourse, the condom could slip off as the erection subsides.

4. Vigorous or prolonged intercourse may cause it to slip off.

5. It is easily punctured.

6. Some men find it unpleasant to use, since it interferes with sensation.

7. If intercourse is repeated, a new condom must be used each time.

8. When the vaginal tissues are not very moist the condom may be irritating, unless it is lubricated.

The Condom Method

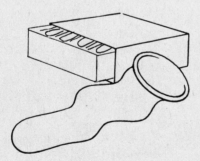

*T*he condom method depends primarily upon the man.

The condom is a thin, skin-tight sheath which is pulled on over the erect penis prior to intercourse. The tip of the condom catches the seminal fluid and prevents the sperm from being released into the vagina.

The condom may prove more effective if it is used in combination with a vaginal spermicide, any number of which are available at a drugstore without prescription.

The Diaphragm Method

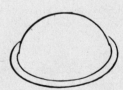

*T*he diaphragm method is an approach to contraception which has been used successfully by many women for nearly a century. It involves the use of a contraceptive cream or jelly in combination with a vaginal diaphragm—made of soft rubber, shaped like a bowl, with a flexible spring at the outer edge.

First you place a small amount of contraceptive cream or jelly in the bowl of the diaphragm, then spread a little around the edge of the rim with the fingertip.

Then the opposite sides of the rim are compressed together so that the diaphragm folds in the middle. The now flattened shape is ready for insertion into the vagina. The flexible rim enables it to resume its original shape once it is inserted and in place.

Insertion can be accomplished quite simply with the fingers, or if a woman prefers, she can use a special plastic inserter specifically designed for the purpose.

When properly placed, the diaphragm fits securely and comfortably between the rear wall of the vagina and the upper edge of the pubic bone. In that position, it completely covers the cervix and holds the contraceptive cream or jelly tightly cupped over the entrance to the womb. This provides a chemical barrier that kills the sperm.

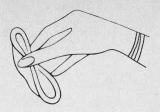

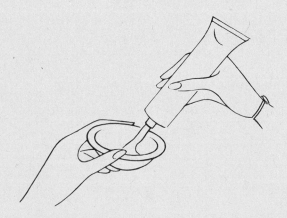

THE ADVANTAGES:

1. Women who use the diaphragm method need only concern themselves with being protected at those times when they expect to have intercourse.

2. The diaphragm and jelly need not be inserted just before intercourse. They may be inserted as much as six hours before and still be effective.

3. When the diaphragm is properly positioned in the vagina, the woman should not feel it, no matter how active she may be. (If it can be felt either it has been inserted incorrectly or it is not the correct size.)

4. You do not have to get up after intercourse to douche or to remove the diaphragm. In fact, to be most effective, the diaphragm must be left in place for at least six hours after intercourse. Douching is not necessary at all, but if a women does desire to douche, she should wait until the diaphragm is removed.

5. Whether or not intercourse actually takes place, the diaphragm may be left in place for as long as twenty-four hours. However, if intercourse takes place more than six hours after the diaphragm is inserted, an additional amount of contraceptive jelly or cream should be used. This may be inserted into the vagina with an applicator made for the purpose. It is not necessary to remove the diaphragm.

6. If properly cared for, the same diaphragm may be safely used for a year or longer.

THE DISADVANTAGES:

1. It is essential for a doctor to determine the proper size diaphragm for each woman if this method is to be at all effective. The diaphragm is obtainable only by prescription.

2. At the time of the fitting, if the woman has not used a diaphragm before, the doctor will instruct her in how to insert it properly; how to determine it is correctly placed; and how to remove it. Some women find both the prospect and the actual rehearsal of this method embarrassing.

3. The diaphragm must always be used whenever intercourse takes place. In fact it is recommended that the diaphragm be inserted at bedtime as a matter of routine so the woman will always be prepared.

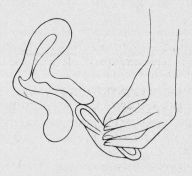

The Vaginal Spermicide Method

The vaginal spermicide method employs a very simple technique. Statistics evaluating clinical studies of modern spermicides indicate few women become pregnant, suggesting that vaginal spermicides are significantly more effective as contraceptives than rhythm, withdrawal, condoms, suppositories, or douching.

Vaginal spermicides are available in different forms: cream, gel, foaming tablets, suppositories, or aerosol foam. Each is designed to be used without a diaphragm or other contraceptive device. The woman merely inserts a measured dosage of the spermicide into the vagina (just prior to each intercourse) with a special plastic applicator designed for that purpose.

The contraceptive action of these preparations is two-fold. The spermicidal ingredients work to kill the sperm while the foam, cream, or gel base provides a "barrier" over the cervix that helps prevent sperm from migrating into and impregnating the womb.

These vaginal spermicidal products are *not* the same as the creams and jellies intended for use with a diaphragm. Each product is designed specifically for its intended use only. It is not advisable to use a preparation designed for use with a diaphragm in any other fashion.

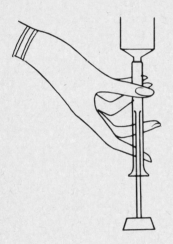

THE ADVANTAGES:

1. Vaginal spermicides can be bought without a prescription. (Not all of these products are equally effective, however, so your doctor is still the best guide to which one is best.)

2. No fitting is necessary (such as that done before obtaining a diaphragm).

3. There is no special training or technique to be learned. The instructions that come with each product provide complete directions for use.

4. There is nothing to remove after intercourse.

5. Douching is entirely unnecessary. If a woman does desire a douche, she should wait six hours after intercourse.

6. Women who use this method need concern themselves with it only at those times when intercourse takes place.

7. Some of these preparations are mildly lubricating. To women whose vaginal tissues may not be sufficiently moist to permit intercourse without difficulty, this can be a distinct advantage.

THE DISADVANTAGES:

1. Vaginal spermicides *must be applied just before intercourse.*

2. If intercourse is repeated, another full applicator of spermicide must be inserted into the vagina beforehand since each application of spermicide provides protection for only one intercourse.

3. The applicator must be washed with soap and water after each use.

4. Occasionally, an allergic reaction may result in either the male or female.

Oral Method

The oral method requires that a woman take a contraceptive pill or tablet every day for approximately three weeks. The first pill is taken on the fifth day of her menstrual period. (The day her period begins is counted as Day 1.) She takes one pill every day until she has taken twenty or twenty-one pills (the quantity depends on the pill which is specifically prescribed.) Within two or three days after taking the last pill her next period should begin.

Five days from the first day of the period, generally one week after taking the last tablet, she begins taking the pill again—one each day for the next twenty or twenty-one days.

Should she fail to have a period (this can sometimes happen), she should start taking the pills again seven days after finishing the last pill in her previous month's supply.

If two consecutive periods are missed (this occurs very infrequently), a physician should be contacted and a test for pregnancy should be done. In the event she is pregnant, she should immediately stop taking the pills.

The pills, essentially, imitate some of the normal body reactions that take place during pregnancy. Such as, during pregnancy a woman stops producing eggs until after the baby is born. When a woman takes the pills, many of the same things happen even though she isn't really pregnant.

Should you decide to use oral contraceptives, we recommend you ask your doctor for a copy of the booklet that the Food and Drug Administration has required the manufacturers of oral contraceptives to prepare providing potential users with necessary information. Briefly, this booklet says:

a) Oral contraceptives, when taken as directed, are extraordinarily effective.

b) As with any medicine, side effects are possible, the most serious being abnormal blood clotting.

c) Serious problems are rather infrequent and the majority of women who would like to use the pill can do so safely and effectively.

d) See your physician regularly, ask him any questions you may have about the use of the pill, and report to him any special problems that may arise.

THE ADVANTAGES:

1. When used properly, this is considered the most effective method.

2. The pill begins working as soon as you take your first one as directed and continues to work for as long as you take them according to instructions.

3. No special preparations are necessary before intercourse.

4. No special equipment or technique has to be learned. Oral contraceptives are taken just like any other pills. They are easy to swallow since most are considerably smaller than aspirin and practically tasteless.

5. Since the pills are taken daily whether intercourse takes place or not, there is less temptation to take a chance on going without protection.

6. Since it is not necessary to insert anything into the vagina before or after intercourse, women who find such procedures objectionable often find the oral method more satisfactory.

7. No measuring or fitting must be done by a physician as with some other methods, such as the diaphragm.

THE DISADVANTAGES:

1. To be effective, the pills must be taken as directed whether intercourse takes place or not. Women who have intercourse very infrequently may find the pills are an unnecessary precaution or that the expense is not worth it.

2. Some women, when they first begin taking oral contraceptives, experience one or more minor discomforts similar to complaints women have in the early stages of pregnancy (nausea or morning sickness, spotting or bleeding between periods, some gain or loss in weight, slight enlargement or tenderness of the breasts, darken-

ing of patches of skin on the face or elsewhere). Most women don't have these complaints and among those who do, they generally last only a few days, rarely more than a few months. There have been a few instances, however, where the discomforts were persistent enough that women chose to stop taking the pills.

3. Some women have trouble remembering to take a pill every day and sometimes forget whether they have taken a pill or not. Since the pills are supposed to be taken once every twenty-four hours, doctors advise women to connect taking their pill with some other part of their daily routine (such as brushing their teeth at night before retiring).

4. Although protection begins on the day the first pill is taken as directed, a woman who forgets one or more pills risks losing that month's protection. She should use another method of contraception (while continuing to take the pills for the remainder of the month) as an extra safeguard until her next period.

5. Some women, after they stop taking the pills, may take several months before they return to their pre-pill menstrual pattern—some may take longer.

6. The pill can only be obtained by prescription.

The IUD Method (Intrauterine Device)

The IUD method differs considerably from any other method discussed here, because the woman using it bears almost no responsibility for its effectiveness. In fact, apart from self-examination, she need hardly be concerned with it at all, after it is inserted.

The IUD, or Intrauterine Device, is inserted into the uterus, through the cervix, by a physician and left in place for as long as he feels it is appropriate to do so. No other contraceptive protection is necessary once the IUD is in position, and the woman wearing it should be totally unaware of its presence.

The intrauterine devices are slightly less effective than the oral contraceptive tablets. Occasionally a woman may become pregnant even though the IUD is still in place. If pregnancy occurs, the device is left in the uterus and should be expelled at delivery. When pregnancy is desired, the device is removed by the physician.

THE ADVANTAGES:

1. Once the IUD has been inserted, little or no thought need be given to the subject of contraception by either the woman or her partner.

2. The IUD may be left in place for a year or more.

3. After the initial cost of the IUD itself and the medical fee for insertion, there are no additional expenses. (A gynecological check-up is advisable periodically; however, this should be standard procedure regardless.)

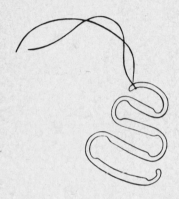

THE DISADVANTAGES:

1. A woman using an IUD should examine herself once every week to make certain it is still in place. This is done by inserting the index finger well into the vagina to feel for a short thread protruding from the opening of the cervix.

2. Some women are unable to retain the IUD and it is expelled by the uterus. This is more apt to happen to women who have had no children than to those who have had one or more babies. Of course, if the IUD is expelled there is no longer any contraceptive protection. It is important to understand that this expulsion can go unnoticed, which further emphasizes the need to regularly check for placement.

3. Women using this method usually have a considerably heavier flow during the first and often the second period after insertion of the IUD.

4. Some women, particularly those who have not had children, may complain of cramps and backache during the first few days after insertion. Usually these discomforts disappear. Occasionally, however, they persist long enough for the woman to ask that the IUD be removed.

5. A small number of women may have some spotting or bleeding between periods during the first several months. This bleeding is something of an inconvenience. If the bleeding persists, you should contact your physician.

6. The IUD can *only* be inserted by a physician.

Contraceptive products (excluding birth control pills, diaphragms, and I.U.D.s, which require doctor's examination and prescription), are available over the counter at most pharmacies throughout the nation.

The largest mail-order retailer of contraceptive products is:

ADAM & EVE
P.O. Box 2556
105 N. Columbia Street
Chapel Hill
North Carolina, 27514

For free catalogue contact them direct.

For sterilization (both male and female)
and the menstrual extraction form of
an abortion used as alternative contraception
methods see SEX AND MEDICINE.

International Planned Parenthood Federation

There are International Planned Parenthood Member Organizations all across the world.

Countries that are affiliated and involved in family planning are: Australia, Barbados, Belgium, Bermuda, Burma, Canada, Ceylon, Denmark, Egypt, Fiji, Finland, France, West Germany, Honduras, Hong Kong, India, Jamaica, Japan, Jordan, Kenya, Korea, Malaya, Mauritius, Nepal, Netherlands, New Zealand, Okinawa, Pakistan, Phillippines, Poland, Puerto Rico, Singapore, South Africa, Sweden, Thailand, Trinidad & Tobago, Uganda, United Kingdom, United States.

For further information contact: Planned Parenthood, World Population Inc., 515 Madison Avenue, New York, New York 10022.

Planned Parenthood Affiliates in the United States Regional Offices.

WESTERN, (Alaska, Arizona, California, Hawaii, Idaho, Nevada, Oregon, Utah, and Washington), 655 Sutter Street Room 500, San Francisco, California 94102.

SOUTHWEST, (Arkansas, Louisiana, New Mexico, Oklahoma, and Texas), 2928 Burnet Road, Room 204, Austin, Texas 78756

MIDWEST, (Colorado, Iowa, Kansas, Minnesota, Missouri, Montana, Nebraska, North Dakota, South Dakota, and Wyoming). 406 West 34th Street, Room 725, Kansas City, Missouri 64111

MIDEAST, (Illinois, Indiana, Kentucky, Michigan, Ohio, and Wisconsin), 111 East 54th Street, Room 207, Indianapolis, Indiana 46220

SOUTHEAST, (Alabama, Florida, Georgia, Mississippi, North Carolina, South Carolina, Tennessee, Virginia, and West Virginia), 303 Peachtree Road, N.W. Rooms 301-303, Atlanta, Georgia, 30305.

MID-ATLANTIC, (Delaware, District of Columbia, Maryland, New Jersey, and Pennsylvania), 1605 Race Street, Suite 5, Philadelphia, Pennsylvania 19103.

NORTHEAST, (Connecticut, Maine, Massachusetts, New Hampshire, New York, Rhode Island, and Vermont), 515 Madison Avenue, Room 914, New York, New York 10022.

For local offices in your town contact your regional offices or telephone directory.

Left: Published by Planned Parenthood Federation of America, Inc. 810 Seventh Avenue, New York, New York 10019   25¢
50 copies $2.50   100 copies $4.50   1000 copies $30.00

Right: Published by Planned Parenthood Federation of America, Inc. 810 Seventh Avenue, New York, New York 10019   25¢
Quantity rates: 50 copies $3.50   100 copies $6.00
(postage extra)

Pamphlets

The Planned Parenthood Federation of America publishes many pamphlets on sex education and the alternative methods of contraception and birth control. Listed below are some of their more important publications. For complete catalogues, orders, or more information write directly to:

Publications Department
Planned Parenthood Federation of America, Inc.
810 Seventh Avenue
New York, New York 10019
Or your local Planned Parenthood Office.

ABC's of Birth Control. Methods, simplified and illustrated cartoon-style. (Single copy 25¢.)

Basics of Birth Control. All the methods in chart form. (Single copy 25¢.)

Contraceptive Technology by Emory University. For medical students and physicians. (Single copy $1.00.)

Modern Methods of Birth Control. 1973 revision includes latest information. (Single copy 25¢—also available in Spanish.)

Questions and Answers About the Pill. (Single copy 25¢—also available in Spanish.)

Questions and Answers about Intrauterine Devices. (Single copy 25¢—also available in Spanish.)

To a Special Couple. Family planning reminder for newlyweds. (Single copy 25¢.)

Voluntary Sterilization for Men and Women. Explains both operations. (Single copy 25¢—also available in Spanish.)

We Are Planned Parenthood. Description of program and services. (Single copy 25¢.)

Information on bulk sale prices are available from the Planned Parenthood Federation of America.

Contraception Bibliography

Arms, Suzanne. *Immaculate Deception: A New Look At Childbirth in America.* San Francisco: San Francisco Book Co, 1975. $10.00

Arms, Suzanne, and Arms, John. *A Season To Be Born.* New York: Harper & Row, 1973. $2.95

Bailey, E. H. *Astrology & Birth Control.* London: W. Foulsham & Co.,1929.

Barrett, Florence Elizabeth. *Contraception Control and the Effects on the Individual and the Nation.* London: J. Murray, 1923.

Bates, Marston. *The Prevalence of People.* New York: Charles Scribner's Sons, 1955.

Berelson, Bernard. *Family Planning and Population Programs: A Review of World Developments.* Chicago: University of Chicago Press, 1966. $15.00

———. *Family Planning Programs: An International Survey.* New York: Basic Books, 1969. $7.95

Biezanck, Anne. *All Things New: A Declaration of Faith.* New York: Harper & Row, 1965.

Billings, John. *The Ovulation Method.* Los Angeles: Borromeo Guild, 1972. $2.65

The Boston Women's Health Collective. *Our Bodies, Ourselves: A Book by and for Women.* New York: Simon & Schuster, 1973.

Cavanagh, John R. *The Popes, The Pill, The People: A Documentary Study.* Milwaukee: Bruce Publication, 1965.

Draper, Elizabeth. *Birth Control in the Modern World.* Gloucester, Mass.: Peter Smith, 1965. $3.25

Finch, Bernard E., and Green, Hugh. *Contraception Through The Ages.* Springfield, Ill.: C.C. Thomas, 1963.

Fryer, Peter. *The Birth Controllers.* London: Seeker & Warburg, 1965.

Gordon, Sol. *Protect Yourself from Becoming an Unwanted Parent.* Syracuse, N.Y.: Education University Press, 1973.

Groden, Harold M. *Secure Rhythm.* Walpole, Mass.: Michael Press, 1967.

Guttmacher, Alan Frank. *Birth Control & Love, The Complete Guide to Contraception and Fertility.* New York: Macmillan, 1969. $6.95

———. *Population, Birth & Family Planning.* New York: New American Library, 1973. $1.75

Haire, Norman. *Birth Control Methods: Contraception, Abortion, Sterilization.* London: G. Allen & Unwin, 1936.

Hardin, Garrett James. *Birth Control.* Indianapolis: Pegasus, 1970. $2.15

———. *Population, Evolution and Birth Control.* San Francisco: W. H. Freeman, 1969. $3.50

Henshaw, Paul S. *Adaptive Human Fertility.* New York: McGraw Hill, Blakison, 1955.

Hinman, Helen R. *Population Pressure, War and Poverty.* Newark, N.J.: A. W. Cross Inc., 1945.

Lacey, Louise. *Lunaception; A Feminine Odyssey into Fertility and Contraception.* 1975. $7.95

Lader, Lawrence. *The Margaret Sanger Story, and the Fight for Birth Control.* 1955. Reprint. Westport, Conn.: Greenwood. $13.75

Lader, Lawrence, and Meltzer, Milton. *Margaret Sanger: Pioneer of Birth Control.* New York: Dell, 1974. 95¢

Loebl, Suzanne. *Conception, Contraception: A New Look.* New York: McGraw Hill, 1975. $6.95

Neubardt, Selig. *Concept of Contraception.* New York: Trident, 1967. $3.95

Ostrander, Sheila, and Schroeder, Lynn. *Astrological Birth Control.* New York: Bantam Books, 1973. $1.25

Pincus, Gregory. *The Control of Fertility.* New York: Academic Press, 1965. $14.50

Quinn, Francis X. *Population Ethics.* Washington: Corpus Books, 1968.

Rock, John Charles. *Voluntary Parenthood.* New York: Random House, 1949.

Rosenblum, Art. *Natural Birth Control.* Boston, Maine: Tao Books, 1973. $2.00

Sanger, Margaret. *Appeals from American Mothers.* New York: Women's Publishing Company, 1921. o/p

———. *Margaret Sanger: An Autobiography.* New York: Dover, 1938. $4.00

———. *My Fight for Birth Control.* Elmsford, N.Y.: Pergamon, 1972. $17.50

———. *The New Motherhood.* Reprint. Elmsford, N.Y.: Maxwell, 1970

———. *Works of Margaret Higgens Sanger.* Elmsford, N.Y.: Pergamon, 1972. $25.00

Seaman, Barbara. *The Doctors' Case Against the Pill.* New York: Peter H. Wyden, 1969. $5.95; New York: Avon, 1970. 95¢

Trussell, James, and Chandler, Steve. *The Loving Book: Toward An Understanding of Birth Control and Human Sexuality.* New York: New American Library, 1972. $5.95

Vaughan, Paul. *The Pill on Trial.* New York: Tower Books, 1971. 95¢

Wood, Clive. *Human Fertility; Threat and Promise.* New York: Funk & Wagnalls, 1974. $6.95

Wood, Haratio Curtis. *Sex Without Babies.* Philadelphia: Whitmore Publishing, 1967. $5.00; New York: Lancer, 1972. $1.25

The Five Senses *by Thomas Rowlandson*

Sensual Awareness and the New Sexuality

There is but one temple in the Universe, says the devout Novalis, and that is the human body. Nothing is holier than that high form. We touch heaven when we lay our hand on the human body.
—Thomas Carlyle, *The Hero As Divinity*

The definitive book on sensual awareness and the new sexuality has yet to be written. There is such a wide range of dynamic, ongoing activity that it is difficult to tie it up in a neat little package. So much is happening that such a book is definitely needed. However, to capsulize the whole idea, the most accurate statement would be that it is an expanding movement to make people aware that sensuality need not be restricted to the genitals, and that the concept of guilt must be expunged from sexual pleasure: that recreational sex is an essential ingredient in the totality of healthy mind and body.

One of the prime movers in pioneer efforts to bring about sexual awareness was Havelock Ellis back in the 1890s. Following in his wake were others such as Marie Stopes, whose *Married Love*, published in the 1920s, was revolutionary. Other writers and researchers—W. F. Robie, Theodore H. Van de Velde,

Eustace Chesser, and Kinsey—kindled more torches and began spreading light. The real father of the movement, however, was Albert Ellis, who began beating the drum for rational thinking about sex in the 1950s. He stated the case without pulling any punches in 1972 observing that the general public's attitude toward what constituted a sensuous person was for the most part confused. He hypothesized that few people had the slightest awareness of sensuality, sensuousness, or, for that matter sexuality itself until the year 1969. Could it be, he asked hypothetically, that suddenly writings on the subject of sexual problems and overcoming them had finally come into their own? Ellis's reply to his own question was a coarse expletive.

He went on to point out that books in the sexual how-to-do-it genre had enjoyed immense success here and abroad for over a century. By the mid-1800's he said, "how many zillions of pamphlets and books on the 'sensuous' technique alone were distributed in the United States?" The technique he referred to specifically was coitus reservatus, popularly known as *karezza,* which was first advocated here widely by John Humphrey Noyes, founder and head of the then infamous Oneida community in New York State, where open sexuality was an accepted practice.

Perhaps one of the best summations on what "the new sexuality" is appears in Dr. Herbert A. Otto and Roberta Otto's book, *Total Sex*, published by Peter H. Wyden, Inc. in 1972 and now generally available in a Signet edition ($1.50). "A movement called the New Sexuality has provided the base for the development of holistic sex. The New Sexuality has its roots in the 1950s in the work of A. Kinsey, W. Pomeroy, and associates; in the writings of Albert Ellis and R. L. Dickenson; in Van de Velde's *Ideal Marriage* and the work of Havelock Ellis. By no means restricted to the United States, the New Sexuality has made itself felt in the Scandinavian countries, Great Britain, West Germany, Australia, and a host of other nations. One hallmark of the New Sexuality is greater openness about man's sexuality—in the media as well as in verbal communication—and a clearer awareness of the impact of the Puritan/Victorian heritage on sexual functioning. Another major characteristic is a renewed emphasis on sex research and sex education."

Now, what we can provide you with here is a cross section, giving you a perspective from which you can embark on your own expedition into whatever area of human potential you may care to explore.

*Copyright © 1972 by Herbert Otto

$\mathcal{M}$any people have difficulty coming to terms with their own sexuality insofar as being able to discuss it with anyone, even those closest to them, let alone strangers (*i.e.*, friends, therapists, their doctors). Despite this, most are anxious to learn about themselves specifically. They wish to go beyond finding answers published in books. For these individuals an ideal vehicle is the Feminist Sexuality Project being conducted by Shere Hite, N.O.W., New York. For the past two years Ms. Hite has been sending detailed questionnaires on sexuality to men and women throughout the country, dealing with such subjects as orgasm, masturbation, intercourse, oral and anal stimulation, as well as love, marriage, passion, and romance. In short the entire range of physical and emotional sexuality. Anyone who honestly answers one of these questionnaires is bound to learn a great deal about himself or herself. All questionnaires are anonymous. The project is ongoing and further results will be published.* For further information, and to receive a questionnaire, write:

Shere Hite
Feminist Sexuality Project
N.O.W., New York
47 East 19th Street
New York, New York 10001

*A synthesis of the first questionnaire on female sexuality appeared as *Sexual Honesty* by Shere Hite. Warner Paperback Library, 1974, $1.50.

In the continuously expanding movement of sexual self-help and awareness almost every major university in the country now has some programs and courses in Human Sexuality, as well as many of the organizations. Here are examples of some of the workshops and centers across the country:

CALIFORNIA

Cromey's House
716 Arguello Blvd.
San Francisco, California 94118

Cromey's House holds one-day sexuality workshops for adults. The focus of these encounters is on each participant's sexuality. Identifying sexual feelings in one's self, allowing them to exist, and communicating them to others.

They also hold sexuality workshops for children and parents, dealing with sex education for preteens and teenagers and an intensive exploration into the various forms of sexual activity, i.e., heterosexuality, homosexuality, masturbation, etc.

EST
1111 Kearney Street
San Francisco, California 94133
(415) 441-0100

Erhard Seminars Training transforms one's ability to experience living on all levels so that what you have been trying to change, or have been putting up with, clears up in the process of life itself. Available nationwide in many cities.

Resource Center for Human Relations
6201 Harwood Ave.
Oakland, California 94618
(415) 653-8901

The Resource Center is currently conducting a series of intensive live-in weekends aimed at enriching human intimacy, using honest communication, self- and sensory awareness, ways to give and receive pleasure. The course is for both couples and individuals and is only part of the Center's sexual enrichment services.

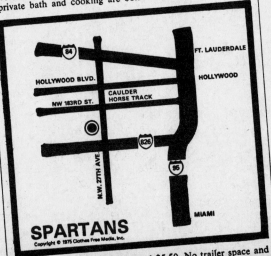

Wilbur Hot Springs
3119 Clement Street
San Francisco, California

The Hot Springs offers massage workshops the second weekend of each month in an atmosphere of these historic curing springs.

MASSACHUSETTS

New England Center
Box 575
Amherst, Massachusetts 01002
(413) 549-0886

The New England Center holds workshops exploring areas in which conflicts between cultural conformity and individual inclination distort sexual feelings, attitudes, and behavior at the cost of emotional integrity.

Stepping Stone
Four Potter Park
Cambridge, Massachusetts 02138

Stepping Stone is a small New England growth center concentrating on body awareness and massage. The center uses the Esalen form of massage as not only a way of receiving deep muscular relaxation but also as a form of communication and understanding of your total body.

NEW JERSEY

CUSP *Donald J. Maroun, Director*
Center for Understanding Sexual Preferences
304 Morris Avenue, Elizabeth, New Jersey
(201) 353-2460

This educational center exists for the purpose of creating a format for exploration whereby individuals can become aware of the ways in which their sexuality is a part of their total being. No room for labels: straight, gay, or bi. They are taking a step toward reeducating people to understand and trust their sexuality as a natural function of the body. In programs in New York and New Jersey, men and women can chart their own growth development in seminars congruent with their sexual needs and their sexual preferences.

NEW YORK

Anthos Growth Center
24 E. 22nd Street
New York, New York 10010
(212) 673-9067

Anthos is a nonprofit educational institute registered with the state of New York . . . a place where you can be yourself, and where you can continue to develop that self.

Anthos activities include ongoing encounter groups, sexual creativity workshops; do-it-youself psychotherapy program; gay is good; developing self-esteem; integrating the mind and body through the Eastern philosophies of exercise and meditation. The Growth Center offers more than forty different kinds of experiences, such as Pauline Abrams' Sex and the Joys of Loving. "Everyone has the potential for deep sexual satisfaction. This workshop will make available techniques to heighten sexual awareness and will focus on: 1) intimacy, 2) sensuality, 3) inhibitions, 4) sexuality, 5) personal identity, and 6) body image. It is designed to help you get more deeply in touch with your own sensuality. A holistic approach, utilizing techniques employed by Masters & Johnson, Marriage Encounter, and other contributors to the field of human sexuality will be used." The fee for such a program is $75.00 per person for a two-day weekend workshop. For a complete brochure on all of Anthos's awareness programs, write them directly.

The Center for Humanistic Sexuality
Director: Don Fass
345 West 85th Street (Suite 46), New York, New York
(212) 595-5365

The Center for Humanistic Sexuality is a nonprofit educational, social, and research organization in which the importance of growth is seen as a vital prerequisite to sexual politics and awareness, and as a path to a more fulfilling life for us and all our sisters and brothers. Sexuality is not viewed as some separate portion of the human experience, but as an extension and expression of our total and most actualized being. Fusing humanistic, nonsexist values from the feminist, gay, men's and bisexual movement as well as the human potential movement, the center will offer specialized programs, but primarily seeks to bring about a communion of loving, sexually free and open people.

The center also sponsors an annual weekend conference of workshops, films, and speakers on "Intimacy and Human Sexuality."

The center publishes a monthly newsletter called *Sexual Sources*, and sponsors workshops in sensory awareness, massage, etc.

Horizons
The Riverside Church
490 Riverside Drive
New York, New York 10027
(212) 749-7000 ext. 238

Horizons' *Sexual Being* is a series of eight seminars based on S.A.R. (sexual attitude restructuring). The lectures include the showing of sexually explicit films and slides, and they cover such topics as: sexual attitude reassessment, body image and awareness, the sexual life cycle, sexual orientation, human sexual responses. For information on dates and costs, contact Horizons directly.

OHIO

The Akron Forum, Inc.
Cascade Plaza
Akron, Ohio 44308
(216) 253-4684

Akron Forum offers programs to professionals and graduate students who are seeking a better understanding of sexuality. The goals of the Forum programs are to expose participants to an emotionally supportive atmosphere, to reassess their feelings about their own sexuality and the sexuality of others. The workshops involve the screening of sexually explicit films, tapes, and intensive study lectures.

Esalen

Esalen Institute
1793 Union Street
San Francisco, California 94123
(408) 667-2335

Esalen Institute is a center to explore those trends in education, religion, philosophy, and the physical and behavioral sciences which emphasize the potentialities and values of human existence. Its activities consist of seminars and workshops, residential programs, consulting, and research. They exist to sponsor, encourage, synthesize, and attempt evaluation of work in these areas, both inside and outside their own organizational framework.

Esalen/Big Sur lies 300 miles north of Los Angeles and 175 miles south of San Francisco. It is directly over the shoreline of the Pacific, with the Santa Lucia Range rising sharply behind. The property, which has natural hot baths, was once the home of a North American Indian tribe known as Esalen.

Programs at Esalen are usually conducted over a weekend, five-day group, two-week, or monthly period. Some of the methods and therapies they use as approaches to human growth are: bioenergetic analysis, encounter, gestalt, massage, psychosynthesis, structural integration (rolfing), and t'ai chi chuan.

Esalen publishes a catalogue quarterly. Subscription cost is $2.00, although those attending Esalen workshops and conferences receive them free. The pamphlet lists all their programs both at Big Sur San Francisco and in the Bay Area. Information on fees is available in the catalogue. And a single inspection copy is available free upon writing to their San Francisco office.

The National Sex Forum

THE NATIONAL SEX FORUM is a community service developed by the Glide Urban Center in affiliation with San Francisco's Glide Memorial Methodist Church, under the direction of Rev. Red McIlvenna, cofounder of the National Sex Forum, and Laird Sutton, Media Director of the Multi-Media Resource Center.

The headquarters for the National Sex Forum and the Multi-Media Resource Center are at 540 Powell Street, San Francisco, California 94108 (415) 421-5035.

The National Sex Forum offers extensive sexual self-help and awareness programs for professionals and individuals. They hold regular S.A.R. seminars and weekends. The techniques of S.A.R. were first developed at the University of Minnesota Medical Center and they were designed to assist professionals and counselors to evaluate their own sexual attitudes enabling them to pass these attitudes on to their patients and clients. S.A.R. is a very comprehensive and intensive study of human sexuality (for more detail see Sex Therapy: Better Techniques for Better Loving), encompassing a multitude of sexual attitudes such as: sexual mythology, the heightening of sexual sensitivity, sexual identification, sexual attitude reassessment, human sexual responses, sexual life styles, body image, and awareness.

S.A.R. is one of many programs and activities that the National Sex Forum is involved in. It conducts periodic courses in human sexuality, demonstrating effective methods of using the explicit material that the National Sex Forum together with the Multi-Media Resource Center has available. The center's films, video tapes, and educational literature depicting a wide variety of authentic sexual activity, from heterosexual, homosexual, lesbian, to sexual activities for the elderly and the handicapped, are slowly pushing ahead in another of the Forum's pioneer attitudes towards sexuality.

For catalogue and more information on either the National Sex Forum or the Multi-Media Resource Center please write directly to 540 Powell Street, San Francisco, California 94108.

The Multi-Media Resource Center publishes the *Yes* adult sex education booklets to help both men and women discover and learn more about their own sexuality. The books are part of the Forum's Yes Program of Sex, the use of the word "Yes" emphasizing the Forum's positive attitude towards human sexuality.

Getting in Touch. Self Sexuality for Women: a comprehensive booklet on how to masturbate; accepting masturbation as a totally normal and healthy way of expressing sexual desire and release, in order to develop your own sexual understanding of your mind and body. ($1.95 available from the Multi-Media Resource Center, 540 Powell Street, San Francisco, California.)

When You Don't Make It: a sexual self-help book for a man who may be dissatisfied with his sexual functioning. The book is written simply in a very understanding manner to help men get in touch with their bodies both sexually and mentally. ($1.95 available from the Multi-Media Resource Center, 540 Powell Street, San Francisco, California.)

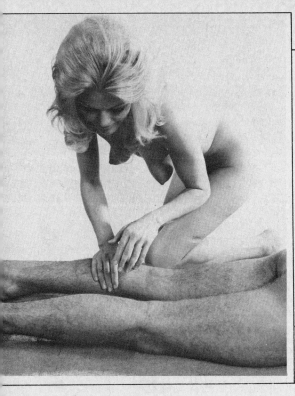

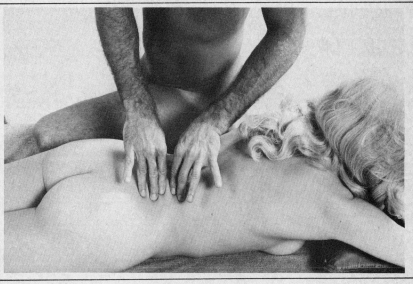

Photos by Charles Stewart

From: *Massage: The Loving Touch* by Stephen Lewis.
Copyright © 1973 by Stephen Lewis.
Reprinted by permission of Pinnacle Books, Inc.

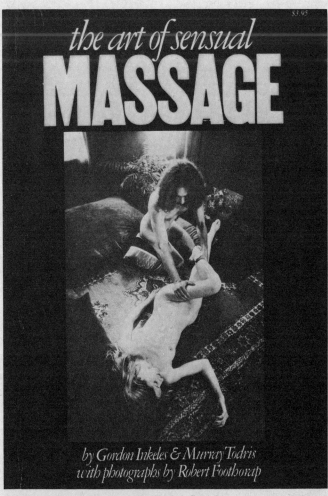

Published by Straight Arrow Books, San Francisco.
Reproduced by permission

Sandstone

Sandstone

Topanga, California 90290 (213) 455-2530

Sandstone is nestled near the top of a secluded coastal canyon in the Santa Monica Mountains. The elegance of Sandstone is enhanced by a spectacular view of Malibu, the Pacific Ocean, and the distant Catalina Island.

The setting offers a welcome relief from city tensions to the relaxing serenity of natural privacy, fresh air, and a variety of activities.

At Sandstone you may float in a skin-temperature swimming pool, play volley ball, take a hike, or unwind in the hot Jacuzzi. Lounge and dine in the luxurious lodge or on the terraced lawn. Bask in the high-altitude sun with or without clothing and feel free to express your enjoyment of sensual pleasure. While neither nudity nor sexual sharing is required, Sandstone does offer a serene setting where the real worth and dignity of human sexuality may be experienced.

The Sandstone philosophy: sexuality represents to us a door through which we must pass to reach another level of relating, where intimacy and response are not clouded by restrictive possessiveness and denial of the feelings and needs of the body, prohibitions, human nature. It is an experiment in social and recreational alternatives and a center to explore those trends in education, religion, philosophy, and the physical and behavioral sciences which emphasize the potentialities and values of human existence. Its activities consist of seminars and workshops, residential programs, consulting, and research.

The membership consists of adults from many social, economic, educational, racial, occupational, and religious backgrounds. Their reasons for coming to Sandstone are many and varied. Their unity lies in a common need for sharing, personal freedom, and growth.

Some of the seminars and programs offered are: The Sandstone Experience Seminar, Massage and Body Awareness, Freeing the Body and Feelings, Sexual Energy-Life Excitement, Bioenergetics, Gestalt and Massage, and Exploring Pleasure and Human Potential.

SANDSTONE—MEMBERSHIP DETAILS

Annual participation fee for singles or couples	**$500.00**
Quarterly maintenance fee in addition	**$ 60.00**
Guests, per person per day	**$ 10.00**

Hours: *couples,* 11:00 A.M. through midnight, Wednesday through Thursday
11:00 A.M. through midnight, Friday through Sunday

singles, * 11:00 A.M. to 5:00 P.M., Wednesday and Thursday
11:00 A.M. Friday through 5:00 P.M. Saturday

If you drink wine or beer, bring your own. No hard liquor.
Minimum age, eighteen.
Advance reservations required for guests.
Membership interviews by appointment only.
For further details call during business hours
(213) 455-2530.

*unaccompanied member

Photos by Charles Stewart

From: *Massage: The Loving Touch* by Stephen Lewis.
Copyright © 1973 by Stephen Lewis.
Reprinted by permission of Pinnacle Books, Inc.

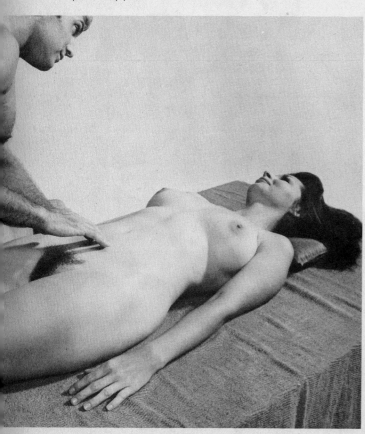

Pencil drawing by Budd Hopkins
Reproduced courtesy of Drs. Phyllis and
Eberhard Kronhausen

Liberating Masturbation

In the new era of a growing sexual awareness and self-help more and more women are discovering better techniques of sexual intercourse by developing and putting to use their vaginal and pelvic muscles. Several books and magazine articles have been written suggesting various exercises that will strengthen these muscles. Here are three basic exercises:

1. Sit on the edge of a comfortable chair, put your index finger and middle finger of one hand into your vagina, as far as your uterus. Then contract the muscles of your rectum. Release. Contract. Release. Contract. You will feel the wall of the vagina just above the rectum rise against the back of your fingers. The harder you contract the sphincter muscle, the higher the vaginal wall rises.

2. Stand up, insert the same two fingers again into your vagina, and again contract your sphincter muscle. Release. Contract. Release. Contract. You will feel the lower end of your vagina (approximately by your second knuckle) being squeezed too.

3. Sit on the toilet and once again insert two fingers into the vagina and push down, hard from inside, as if you were trying to push something out of your vagina. You'll be pushing out with the sphincter muscle. Relax. Again push down hard. What you are feeling is your uterus pushing down against your fingers. If you push down hard, the uterus will meet the fingers (or later the penis) with greater force than if you push down gently. Practice pushing down hard, then gently, then hard, then gently. But don't overdo it; always give yourself time to rest in between exercises. When you contract your muscles, try to count slowly to eight before relaxing the muscles.

Photographer: Grant Taylor

A good way to discover which muscles are which is suggested in Betty Dodson's book, *Liberating Masturbation*: "Very often women are confused about which muscles do what and how to use them. A good way to experiment is to stop the flow of urine by tightening and pulling up." That will allow you to feel yourself moving and working your own vaginal muscles. A suggested article to read that gives more comprehensive exercises and information is "*Vaginal Exercises*," by Anne R. Schneider, in the October '74 edition of *VIVA*; pages 130-131 in Jodi Lawrence's book, *The Search for Perfect Orgasm* (published in paperback, Signet $1.50; or The Multi-Media Resource Center's *Yes Book—Getting In Touch: Self Sexuality for Women*. $1.95 available from the MMR, 540 Powell Street, San Francisco, California 94108.

Under the subheading "Self Examination" Ms. Dodson says: "Reclaiming our genitals from the gynecologists starts with a plastic speculum, a good light, and a standing mirror," and many women today are insisting on examining their own genitals, and participating in the gynecological internal exam. Clinics using these sexual self-help and awareness approaches to the otherwise standard and often uninformed methods of gynecological examination have been spreading rapidly across the United States.

For information on these clinics contact your local chapter of N.O.W. (National Organization of Women), regular clinic, or doctor.

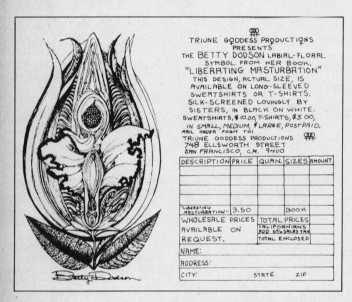

from FREE BEACHES,
by Leon Elder,
Copyright © 1975,
Capra Press.
Tim Crawford photo.

COSMIC JOY FELLOWSHIP

P.O. Box 792/Sausalito, California 94965/(415) 332-2149

Since its founding in 1967, hundreds of people have opened their own doorway to awareness by participating in workshops conducted by Cosmic Joy Fellowship. The fellowship provides the means for those living in Western society to become acquainted with ancient and modern practices from other cultures that alter awareness and release a sense of aliveness.

The fellowship conducts lecture-demonstrations, workshops, and training sessions in the San Francisco Bay area. Examples of their programs are:

The Tantra Experience: Self realization through sexual union. Two-day workshops in the philosophy and practices of tantra with games and processes to free the mind/body of imprinted habits that constrict aliveness:

Pleasuring: An all-day workshop in techniques for inducing and sharing well-being. Participants practice techniques for imparting pleasure to themselves and others based on the research of Masters and Johnson, as well as special sensuality exercises, breathing methods derived from ancient sources, and the authentic Von Newman Method ritual.

Sex Karma Workshop: An all-day workshop to understand that which stands between us and the realization of our potential as sexual beings.

All programs are limited to thirty participants. It is not necessary to bring a partner to attend. For additional information and exact costs (past program prices have ranged from $25 per person/$45 couple for the Sex Karma Workshop, $50 per person/$90 couple for the Tantra Experience) please contact the address listed above.

THE ELYSIUM INSTITUTE 5436 Fernwood Avenue /Los Angeles, California 90027/ (213) 465-1721

*T*he **Elysium Institute** is a nonprofit organization whose purpose is the support of research in the behavioral sciences and the dissemination of practical and experiential information relating to the development of human potential. It promotes self-acceptance and acceptance of others through a wholesome attitude toward the human body and its functions, both physical and emotional and including human sexuality. The Elysium Institute does not offer psychotherapy, medical therapy, sex therapy, or other such remedial services. It does, however, cooperate with experienced professionals in a wide variety of disciplines to offer seminars, workshops, discussion groups, and demonstrations.

It is the Elysium Credo that there is an essential wholesomeness in the human body and all its functions. Exposure to nature and all the elements is a basic factor in building and maintaining positive attitudes of mind in the development of a healthy body. Human sexuality is part and parcel of our living and no separation or division is possible without a denial of our essential human qualities.

Institute Facilities

Elysium Field, a country estate in Topanga Canyon, fifteen miles from Los Angeles, offers the experience of activities in which nudity is enjoyed on a clothing-optional basis. This environment is especially valuable for children, who are naturally free spirits until the body taboo is imposed. Experiential workshops and seminars sponsored by the institute are offered on an individual registration basis and it is not necessary to be an ongoing member of Elysium Institute in order to participate.

Elysium In-Town Center, on Western Avenue near Sunset Boulevard, in Los Angeles, offers illustrated lectures, discussion groups, demonstrations, workshops, get-acquainted social events, and other guided group activities appropriate to a metropolitan setting where clothing is required.

The *Elysium Journal of the Senses* is a quarterly publication of the Elysium Institute for the advancement of human sensual and sexual rights and delights, reporting on significant developments in the human-potential field.

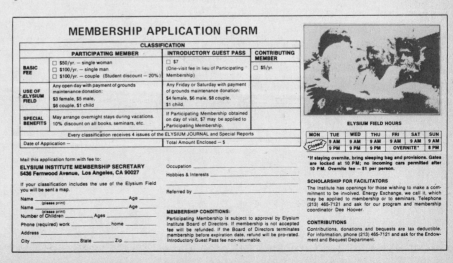

-81-

Mens' Center of New York

Men's Center of New York (Telephone: (212) 989-1313)

The first center for men in New York opens up a communications network, springing from various consciousness-raising groups around the State. The men's center is a new venture run by Warren Farrell and Andrew Rock and is designed to help men rethink their approaches to their own sexuality, their bodies, and their relationships. Andrew runs a Body Awareness Workshop—one night a week for a month, three hours a night, $45.00 for the four evenings. He calls it his "love your body workshop." It is a structured experience, beginning with Yoga and exercises to improve the body's flexibility and help break down the the accepted "hard rigid condition" of the male body; the second evening is set aside for massage, both group and individual, a learning of a new awareness of the body's sensuality; the third session follows up with talks and discussions on male masturbation; and the final evening concentrates on body maintenance and self-care.

Andrew Rock is a disciple of Betty Dodson, and much of the format for his Body Awareness Workshop is taken from her Bodysex Workshops held for women.

SIECUS

(The Sex Information and Educational Council of the U.S.)

You're born with it.
It's yours till you die.
Most people enjoy it.
Some people are afraid of it.
Some are embarrassed by it.
Some would like to change theirs.
Without it, the world would end.
What is it?

It's sex. And that's what SIECUS is all about.

SIECUS is a nonprofit voluntary health organization, dependent on individual contributions for income.

SIECUS acts as a resource center for unbiased, extensive information about sexuality. It provides consultation services to educators and counselors and other organizations and groups.

SIECUS publishes a bimonthly report called the *Siecus Report*.

Many established organizations support SIECUS and its work. Here are a few of them: American Academy of Pediatrics; American College of Obstetricians and Gynecologists; American Medical Association; National Association for Mental Health; National Council of Churches; United States H.E.W.; and the White House Conference on Children and Youth.

For further information please contact:
SIECUS 1855 Broadway
New York, New York 10023

Sounds for Sex

Syntonic Research introduces the Environment Recording Series in psychoacoustics relating to sexual and meditational experiences. The eight records in the series include:

Disc One: *The Psychologically Ultimate Seashore*—the sounds of the ocean. *Optimum Aviary*—no less than thirty-two types of birds.

Disc Two: *Tintinnabulation*—bells so dulcet and beautiful that they affect the subconscious. *Dawn at New Hope, Pa.*—the aural environment of a beautiful morning in late spring.

Disc Three: *Be-In*—recorded in Central Park, New York, April 1969. *Dusk at New Hope, Pa.*—sounds of night in the country.

Disc Four: *The Ultimate Thunderstorm*—a true colossus of a thunderstorm. *Gentle Rain in a Pine Forest*—summer rain gently dripping upon pine needles.

Disc Five: *The Ultimate Heartbeat*—this recording of a real human heart is specifically designed as an aid to lovemaking. *Wind in the Trees*—a soft breeze rustling the leaves of a grove of trees on a golden autumn day.

Disc Six: *Dawn in the Okefenokee Swamp*—the full range of myriad sounds only to be found deep in the very heart of this vast, largely undisturbed wilderness.

Disc Eight: *Sailboat*—whether your mind's ear demands a sunny afternoon off Sandy Hook or yachting on the Riviera, simply close your eyes and you're there. *Country Stream*—the rippling of the stream, the hum of insects, the song of an occasional bird, and the serene peace of the scene have been faithfully captured in this recording.

Syntonic Research has received many letters from satisfied listeners. Here are some comments:

"The ocean sounds are especially successful when listened to on a water bed!"—Paula T., Illinois

"This record makes sex sexier."—Michael D., Utah

"These records are the unique sensory experience."—Michael R., Oregon

"Believe it or not, my girl friend had her first multiple orgasm while this record was playing. Hmmm."—Sheldon R., Connecticut.

"Fantastic to make love to—wow!"—Jennifer W., Texas

"Love tripping to this record is unbelievable—outasite!"—Michael G., Ohio

These environment recordings are available from record stores and departments, or directly from the mail order department of Syntonic Research Inc., 175 Fifth Ave., New York, New York 10010. Send $6.98 for each record (plus 8% sales tax for New York State residents) or write for order forms.

First Sex Communication Teaching Album:

The Pleasures of Love, a new sex teaching record album—first of its kind, unveiled for public purchase—offers techniques tested in therapy practice designed to increase communication and understanding between lovers.

"This two-record stereo album is a breakthrough in sex teaching technique," says Dr. Don M. Sloan, president of the Eastern Academy of Sex Therapy and editor of the album. "It distills basic therapeutic theory into nearly ninety minutes of simple but effective demonstrations in sex communciation. It will aid many couples who have found it hard to verbalize their likes and dislikes in sexual activities."

The album contains music created to enhance the narrative. Included with the album is a booklet which contains low-key photos of a couple in various sexual communication situations. Booklet sections correspond to the recording.

The two-record 33-1/3 stereo album, *The Pleasures of Love,* is available for $9.95 from The Life Workshop, 211 East 49th Street, New York, New York 10017.

V.J.B.

V.I.B.—Great News for the Nudist Travelers!

(VACATIONS IN THE BUFF) a division of Lotus International has winter and summer tours available to such places as the Caribbean island of Guadeloupe. Complete cost of the tour including round-trip jet via Air France from New York, accommodations for eight nights, daily breakfast, transfer to/from the airport, and tips and taxes is $254.00, plus $20.00 tax and services per person, double occupancy; single supplement is $60.00. An informative brochure on all other tours is available for this year and next. Please write: VIB Tours, (Div. Lotus International), 244 East 46th Street, New York, New York 10017. (212) 661-5040.

Reading

There are three recent books which most accurately synthesize the present state of nudism as we know it today. Rod Swenson, Jr.'s *Nude Resorts and Beaches* (Popular Library $1.50) is a detailed guide with maps and evaluations of specific locations in the United States, Canada, and nearby islands where nudism is accepted. *Free Beaches*, by Leon Elder, is an oversized book with lavish black and white photographs by Tim Crawford and an introduction by Alex Comfort. Published by Capra Press, Santa Barbara, California ($4.95), it deals with the phenomenon of nude beaches on the California coast. The third book, also by Leon Elder, again in the oversized format, is *Hot Tubs* (Vintage Press, $3.85), and treats another California phenomenon, the activity of naked people sloshing about together in oversized tubs, wine vats, and/or any other receptacle large enough to accommodate a frolicsome group.

Liberating Masturbation *by Betty Dodson.*
Published and distributed by Bodysex Designs
121 Madison Ave., New York, New York 10016

Betty Dodson's book is "a meditation on self love" and is dedicated to all women. It attempts to raise women's consciousness to understanding that masturbation is a totally healthy and normal sexual activity. Illustrated with Betty's own drawings, it explores the *Romanticized Image of Sex*, how to *Share Masturbation* and *Become Cunt Positive*, talks about Ms. Dodson's *Bodysex Workshops*, and explains how to turn *Masturbation into Meditation*.

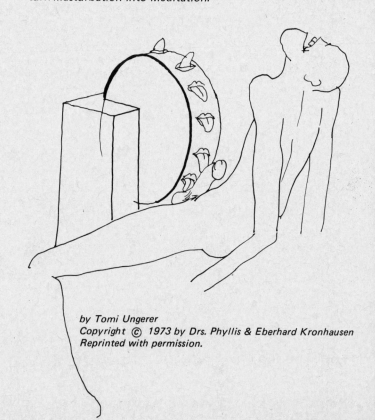

by Tomi Ungerer
Copyright © 1973 by Drs. Phyllis & Eberhard Kronhausen
Reprinted with permission.

Bibliography

Allen, Gina Martin, and Clement, G. *Intimacy, Sensitivity, Sex and the Art of Love.* New York: Cowles Book Co., 1971. $1.50

Beigel, Hugo G. *Sex from A to Z.* New York; Frederick Ungar Publishing Co. 1961 o/p

Belliveau, Fred Richter, and Belliveau, Lin. *Understanding Human Sexual Inadequacy.* New York: Bantam Books, 1970. $1.25

Bergler, Edmund and Kroger, William. *Kinsey's Myth of Female Sexuality.* New York: Grune & Stratton, 1954

Berne, Eric. *Games People Play.* New York: Ballantine, 1974. $1.50

——. *Sex in Human Loving.* New York: Simon & Schuster, 1970. $6.96

Bonaparte, Marie. *Female Sexuality.* New York: International Universities Press, 1956. $10.00

Brecher, Edward, and Brecher Ruth. *Analysis of Human Sexual Response.* New York: New American Library, 1966. $1.25

Brenton, Myron. *The American Male.* New York: Fawcett, 1970. 95¢

Broderick, C. B., and Bernard, J. *The Individual Sex and Society, A SIECUS Handbook for Teachers and Counselors.* Baltimore: Johns Hopkins Press, 1969. $4.50

Calderone, Mary. *Release from Sexual Tensions.* New York: Random House, 1960.

——. *Sexuality and Human Values.* New York: Associated Press, 1974. $7.95

Caprio, Frank S. *Variations in Lovemaking.* New York: Citadel Press, 1967. $2.25

Chartham, Robert. *Mainly for Wives.* New York: Tower, 1970. $1.25

——. *The Sensuous Couple.* New York: Ballantine, 1971. $1.25

Clark, L. *Sex and You.* Indianapolis: Bobbs-Merrill, 1950.

Comfort, Alex. *Come Out to Play.* London: Eyre & Spottiswoode, 1967.

——. *The Joy of Sex: A Gourmet Guide to Lovemaking.* New York: Crown, 1972. $12.95; New York: Simon & Schuster, 1974. $4.95

——. *More Joy: A Lovemaking Companion to the Joy of Sex.* New York: Crown, 1974. $12.95

——. *Sex in Society.* New York: Citadel Press, 1966. $1.75

——. *Sexual Behavior in Society.* New York: Viking, 1950.

Copelan, Rachel. *The Sexually Fulfilled Man.* New York: New American Library, 1972. $1.50

——. *The Sexually Fulfilled Woman.* New York: New American Library, 1971. $1.50

Davis, Katharine B. *Factors in the Sex Life of Twenty-two Hundred Women.* Reprint. New York: Arno, 1974. $20.00

Davis, Maxine. *The Sexual Responsiblity of Women.* 2 vols. New York: Dial Press, 1956.

De Beauvoir, Simone. *The Second Sex.* Reprint. New York: Random House, 1974. $2.95

DeRopp, Robert S. *Sex Energy.* New York: Delacorte Press, 1969. $6.95

Deutsch, Helen. *The Psychology of Women.* 2 vols. New York: Grune & Stratton, 1945. Vol I. $9.00/Vol. II. $10.00

Deutsch, Roland M. *The Key to Feminine Response in Marriage.* New York: Random House, 1968. $6.95

Ditzion, Sidney. *Encyclopedia of Sexual Behavior,* 2nd ed. New York: Hawthorn Books, 1969.

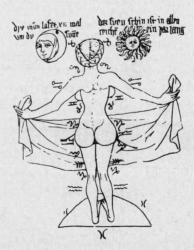

From 1001 Ways to Make Love *by Tuli Kupferberg. Copyright © 1969 by Grove Press, Inc. Reprinted by permission of Grove Press, Inc.*

——. *Marriage, Morals & Sex in America*. New York: Octagon, 1970. $15.00

Dodson, Betty. *Liberating Masturbation*. New York: Bodysex Design, 1974. $3.95

Eichenlaub, John. *The Marriage Art*. New York: Dell, 1969. $1.25

Eisner, Betty Grover. *The Unused Potential of Marriage and Sex*. Boston: Little, Brown.

Ellis, Albert. *The American Sexual Tragedy*. Rev. ed. Secaucus, N.J.: Lyle Stuart; New York: Grove Press, 1962.

——. *The Art and Science of Love*. New York: Bantam, 1960. $1.50

——. *The Civilized Couple's Guide to Extramarital Adventure*. New York: Peter Wyden, 1972. $4.95

——. *If This Be Sexual Heresy*. Secaucus, N.J.: Lyle Stuart, 1964. $4.95

——. *The Intelligent Woman's Guide to Manhunting*. Secaucus, N.J.: Lyle Stuart, 1963; New York: Dell Books, 1965 95¢.

——. *Sensuous Person: Critique & Corrections*. Secaucus, N.J.: Lyle Stuart, 1974. $6.00

——. *Sex without Guilt*. Secaucus, N.J.: Lyle Stuart, 1966. $4.95

——. *Sex and the Single Man*. New York: Dell Books, 1966. 75¢.

Ellis, Albert, and Abarbanel, Albert, eds. *The Encyclopedia of Sexual Behavior*. New York: J. Aronson, 1973. $25.00

Ellis, Albert, and Conway, R. O. *The Art of Erotic Seduction*. Secaucus, N.J.: Lyle Stuart, 1968. $4.95

Ellis, Albert, and Harper, R. A. *Creative Marriage*. Secaucus, N.J.: Lyle Stuart, 1961. $4.95

Ellis, Albert, and Sagarin, E. *Nymphomania: A Study of the Oversexed Woman*. New York: Manor Books, 1965. 75¢

Ellis, Havelock. *On Life and Sex*. New York: New American Library, 1922.

Encyclopedia of Love and Sex. Stamford, Connecticut: Crown-Castle, Ltd.,1974. $10.95

Farrell, Warren. *The Liberated Man*. New York: Random House, 1974. $8.95

Fast, Julian. *Body Language*. New York: M. Evans & Co., 1970. $4.95

Firestone, Shulamith. *The Dialectic of Sex: The Case for Feminist Revolution*. New York: Morrow, 1970. $2.95; New York: Bantam Books, 1971. $1.25

Fisher, Seymour. *The Female Orgasm*. New York: Basic Books, 1973. $15.00

Ford, Clellan S., and Beach, Frank A. *Patterns of Sexual Behavior*. New York: Harper & Row, 1951. $7.95

Frankfort; Ellen. *Vaginal Politics*. New York: Quadrangle, 1972. $6.95, New York: Bantam Books, 1973. $1.95

Franzblau, Abraham. *The Road to Sexual Maturity*. New York: Simon & Schuster, 1954.

Freud, Sigmund. *Collected Papers*. Reprint. New York: Collier Books, 1963. $2.95

——. *Sexuality and the Psychology of Love*. Reprint. New York: Macmillan, 1963. $1.50

———. *Three Essays on the Theory of Sexuality.* Reprint. New York: Basic Books, 1963. $6.45

Friedan, Betty. *The Feminine Mystique.* New York: Norton, 1964. $7.95; New York: Dell Books, 1965. $1.25

Fromm, Erich. *The Art of Loving.* New York: Harper & Row, 1956. 95¢

Gagnon, John H. and Simon, William, eds. *The Sexual Scene.* New Brunswick, N.J.: Transaction Books, 1973. $3.95

Garrison, Omar. *Tantra, the Yoga of Sex.* New York: Avon, 1964. $1.65

Garrity, Joan Terry ["J"]. *The Sensuous Woman.* Secaucus, N.J.: Lyle Stuart, 1969; New York: Dell Books, 1970.

Garrity, Joan Terry, and Garrity, John ["M"]. *The Sensuous Man.* Secaucus, N.J.: Lyle Stuart, 1971; New York: Dell Books, 1972.

Gillette, Paul J., ed. *The Layman's Explanation of Human Sexual Inadequacy.* New York: Award Books, 1970. 95¢.

Gillette Paul J. *Yes You May.* New York: Award Books, 1972. $1.25

Goldstein, Martin, and Haeberle, Erwin. *The Sex Book: A Modern Pictorial Encyclopedia.* New York: Bantam Books, 1973. $1.95

Gordon, David. *Self-Love.* Baltimore: Penguin, 1972. $1.00

Greer, Germaine. *The Female Eunuch.* Reprint. New York: Bantam, 1970. $1.95

Grummon, Donald L., and Barcley, Andrew W., eds. *Sexuality: A Search for Perspective.* New York: Van Nostrand Reinhold, 1971. $6.50

Gunther, Bernard. *Sense Relaxation, Below Your Mind: A Book of Experiments in Being Alive.* New York: Pocket Books, 1973. $1.50

Harding, M. Ester. *Women's Mysteries.* New York: Bantam Books, 1973. $1.95

Harper, R. A., and Stokes, W. *Forty-Five Levels to Sexual Understanding and Enjoyment.* Englewood Cliffs, N.J.: Prentice-Hall, 1972. $6.95

Hegeler, Inge, and Hegeler, Sten. *An XYZ Of Love.* New York: New American Library, 1974. $1.50

———. *Living Is Loving.* New York: Stein & Day, 1973.

Henry, George. *Masculinity and Femininity.* New York: Macmillan, 1973. $1.95

Hirsch, E. W. *Modern Sex Life.* New York: New American Library, 1957.

———. *The Power to Love.* New York: Knopf, 1934.

Hunt, Morton M. *The Natural History of Love.* New York: Funk & Wagnalls, 1967. $3.50

Inkeles, Gordon, and Todris, Murray. *The Art of Sensual Massage.* San Francisco: Straight Arrow, 1972. $3.95

Johnson, W. R. *Human Sexual Behavior and Sex Education.* Philadelphia: Lea & Febiger, 1968.

Katchadourian, Herant, and Lunde, Donald. *Fundamentals of Human Sexuality.* New York: Holt, Rinehart & Winston, 1972. $10.25

Kirkendall, Lester A., and Whitehurst, Robert, eds. *The New Sexual Revolution.* New York: Prometheus Books, 1974. $6.95

Koedt, Anne. *The Myth of the Female Orgasm.* New York: Free Press, 1970.

Kronhausen, Phyllis, and Kronhausen, Eberhard. *The Sexually Responsive Woman.* New York: Ballantine, 1965. $1.25

Legman, G. *The Intimate Kiss.* New York: Paperback Library, 1969. $1.95

Leigh, Malcolm. *Naked Yoga.* New York: New American Library, 1972.

Lewis, Harold, and Streitfeld, Harold. *Growth Games.* New York: Bantam, 1970. $1.25

Llewellyn-Jones, Derek. *Everywoman and Her Body.* New York: Lancer, 1971. $1.50

Lowen, Alexander. *Language of the Body.* New York: Macmillan, 1971. $2.45

——. *Love and Orgasm.* New York: New American Library, 1965. $1.25

——. *Pleasure.* New York: Lancer, 1972. $1.50

McCary, James J. *Human Sexuality.* Princeton: D. Van Nostrand, 1967. $3.50

——. *Sexual Myths and Fallacies.* New York: Schocken, 1971. $1.95

Maslow, Abraham H. *Toward a Psychology of Being.* Princeton: D. Van Nostrand, 1962, $5.95

Masters, William H., and Johnson, Virginia E. *Human Sexual Inadequacy.* Boston: Little, Brown, 1970. $13.50

——. *Human Sexual Response.* Boston: Little, Brown, 1966. $13.50

Masters, William H; Johnson, Virginia E.; Levin, Robert J. *The Pleasure Bond.* Boston: Little, Brown, 1975. $8.95

Mayeroff, Milton. *On Caring.* New York: Harper & Row, 1971. $5.95

Mead, Margaret. *Male & Female.* New York: Dell, 1972. $1.25

Mill, John Stuart, and Mill, Harriet Taylor. *Essays on Sex Equality.* Reprint. Chicago: University of Chicago Press, 1970.

Miller, Sigmund Stephen. *The Good Life, Sexually Speaking: The Antimanual Sex Book.* Englewood Cliffs, N.J.: Prentice-Hall, 1974. $6.95

Keleman, Stanley. *Sexuality, Self and Survival.* New York: Random House, 1972. $5.95

Kennedy, Eugene C. *The New Sexuality.* Garden City, N.Y.: Doubleday, 1972. $5.95

Kinsey, Alfred C.; Pomeroy, Wardell; Martin, Clyde; Gebhard, Paul. *Sexual Behavior in the Human Female.* Philadelphia: Saunders, 1953. $10.25; New York: Pocket Books, 1965. $2.50

Kinsey, Alfred C.; Pomeroy, Wardell, Martin, Clyde. *Sexual Behavior in the Human Male.* Philadelphia: Saunders, 1948. $10.25

Kirkendall, Lester A. *Premarital Intercourse and Interpersonal Relationships.* New York: Julian Press, 1961.

Millet, Kate. *Sexual Politics.* New York: Avon, 1971. $1.95

Newhorn, Paula. *Primal Sensuality.* New York: Fawcett Books, 1975. $1.75

Noyes, J. H. *Male Continence.* Oneida, N.Y.: Gordon Press, 1948. $25.00

O'Connor, L. R. *The Photographic Manual of Sexual Intercourse.* New York: Pent-r-Books, 1974. $12.98

O'Relly, Edward. *Sexercises.* New York: Crown, 1974. $4.95

Otto, Herbert A., ed. *Love Today: A New Exploration.* New York: Association Press, 1972. $9.95

——. *The New Sexuality.* Cupertina, Calif.: Science & Behavior Books, 1971. $8.95

Otto, Herbert A., and Otto, Rachel. *Total Sex.* New York: Wyden, 1972. $7.95; New York: New American Library, 1973. $1.50

Packard, Vance. *The Sexual Wilderness.* New York: Pocket Books, 1972. $1.25

Padget, Desmond. *Transcendental Sensuality.* New York: Lancer, 1973.

Perls, Frederick. *Gestalt Therapy Verbatim.* Lafayette, Calif.: Real People Press, 1969. $3.50

Phelan, Nancy, and Volin, Michael. *Sex and Yoga.* New York: Harper & Row, 1968. $4.95

Poland, Jefferson F., and Allison, Valerie. *Records of the San Francisco Freedom League.* New York: Olympia Press, 1971.

Pomeroy, Wardell. *Dr. Kinsey and the Institute for Sex Research.* New York: New American Library, 1973. $1.95

Reich, Wilhelm. *Function of the Orgasm.* Translated by Theodore Wolfe. New York: Simon & Schuster, 1970. $3.95

Reich, Wilhelm. *The Sexual Revolution.* Translated by Therese Reich. New York: Simon & Schuster, 1974. $2.95

Reik, Theodor. *Of Love and Lust.* Reprint. New York: Aronson, 1973. $12.50

Reuben, David. *Any Woman Can!* Reprint. New York: Bantam, 1972. $1.95

——. *Everything You Always Wanted to Know About Sex, But Were Afraid To Ask.* New York: David McKay, 1969, New York, Bantam, 1971. $1.95

Robbins, Jhan, and Robbins, June *An Analysis of Human Sexual Inadequacy.* New York: New American Library, 1970. 95¢

Robie, W. F. *The Art of Love.* Ithaca: Rational Life Press, 1925.

Robinson, Marie. *The Power of Sexual Surrender.* New York: New American Library, 1962. $1.25

Roen, Philip R. *Male Sexual Health.* Freeport, N.Y.: Jay Norris Corp., 1974. $6.95

Rosenberg, Jack Lee. *Total Orgasm.* New York: Random House, 1973. $3.95

Roszak, Betty, and Roszak, Theodore, eds. *Masculine/Feminine.* New York: Harper & Row, 1969. $2.95

Rush, Anne Kent. *Getting Clear: Body Work for Women.* New York: Random House, 1973. $4.95

Sagarin, Edward, and MacNamara, Donald E. J. *Problems of Sex Behavior.* New York: Thomas Y. Crowell Co., 1968. $3.50

Scheinfeld, Amram. *Women and Men.* London: Chatto & Windus, 1947.

Scott, Byron. *How the Body Feels.* New York: Ballantine, 1973. $2.95

Sherfey, Mary Jane. *The Nature & Evolution of Female Sexuality.* New York: J. Aronson, 1974. $10.00

Simons, Joseph, and Reidy, Jeanne. *The Risk of Loving.* New York: Seabury, 1971. $2.95

Stekel, Wilhelm. *Frigidity in Women.* (Vols. I and II.) New York: Boni and Liveright, 1926. $14.95

Stiller, R., ed. *Illustrated Sex Dictionary.* New York: Association Press, 1968. $2.00

Swenson, Rod, Jr., ed. *Nude Resorts & Beaches.* New York: Popular Library, 1975. $1.50

Tuffill, S. F. *Sexual Stimulation. Games Lovers Play.* New York: Grove Press, 1973.

Van Deusen, Edmund L. *Contract Co-habitation.* New York: Grove Press, 1974. $6.95

Vatsayana. *Kama Sutra.* Translated by Sir Richard Burton. (Many editions available.)

Von Krafft-Ebing, Richard. *Psychopathia Sexualis: A Medico-Forensic Study.* Translated by F. J. Rebman. Reprint. New York: Putnam, 1969. 95¢.

Winick, Charles. *The New People: Desexualization in American Life.* Indianapolis: Bobbs-Merrill, 1968. $2.25

Young, Constance. *Self Massage.* New York: Bantam, 1973. 60¢

Sex Therapy:

Better Techniques for Better Loving

$\mathcal{S}$ex therapy *per se* is very new. Technically it is an outgrowth of traditional psychotherapy, but increased awareness has dictated that the body and the mind must not be separated; they must be dealt with as a totality in order to achieve a successful resolution. This concept was first put into practice by Masters and Johnson, who insisted that patients with sexual dysfunctions had to bring their bodies as well as their minds to the therapist. During the course of their clinical investigations they totally broke down many old Freudian concepts, such as penis envy, the basic passivity of women, the idea that "real" women only experience vaginal orgasm, and general attitudes of guilt about enjoying sexual pleasure for its own sake.

One of the most startling facts to emerge from their research and practice was that over half of the married couples in the United States were plagued by sexual problems. Serious problems that had previously been ignored or swept under the rug are now being realistically confronted and dealt with like any other physical and emotional dysfunctions.

The first step anyone must take before seeking sex therapy is admitting that a problem exists, then bringing it into the open. Once this barrier has been crossed, solutions may be found. There is one basic problem: an inability to communicate with one's sexual partner verbally and physically. The most common symptoms stemming from this are inability to reach orgasm, impotence, premature ejaculation, inability to ejaculate, vaginismus (involuntary constriction of the vaginal muscles), and pain during sexual intercourse.

Treatment varies, but essentially involves an educational process. Patients are taught to break down their inhibitions, to verbalize their sexual feelings, and are given exercises designed to help them function sexually. Most therapists treat couples only. Those who treat single individuals sometimes employ sexual surrogates, trained persons who serve as therapeutic sex partners. The use of surrogates is the most controversial aspect within the sex therapy profession, and consequently surrogates require specialized training.

The most widely recognized training program for surrogates is conducted by the Sensory Awareness Center, 3939 Newmark Avenue, San Bernardino, California 92405. The program consists of a forty-four-hour intensive workshop that prepares persons of either sex to work as professional surrogate sex partners in therapeutic modalities which are designed for couples. The training is done by a dual sex team, one member of which has had surrogate experience. Candidates must be referred in writing, either by a sex therapist who wishes to employ their services or by the membership committee of IPSA (International Professional Surrogate Association), whose headquarters are maintained at the Sensory Awareness Center. The cost of the surrogate training course is $200.00. The principal purpose of IPSA is to give surrogates a professional standing and to protect them from dubious labels. Membership automatically assures therapists who employ surrogates that they are properly qualified to function in the therapeutic situation. Clinics tend to avoid the use of surrogates, however. Single patients seeking therapy should obtain specific information from the clinic or therapist from whom they are receiving treatment. Any further details can be obtained directly from the Sensory Awareness Center.

Many people ask how one determines whether a therapist or a clinic can be rated as to good, bad, better, or so-so. The quality of therapy is a highly subjective matter and depends largely on how well individual patients relate to their therapists.

One aspect of sex therapy that is rarely discussed in print is the cost. It is expensive. The price may range from several hundred dollars for three or four sessions to three thousand dollars for a full course lasting as long as a year, but as a prominent New York sex therapist pointed out, most legitimate clinics will not turn away anyone who can prove need and inability to pay. Another point to bear in mind is that most sex therapy clinics accept patients on a referral basis only, *i.e.*, from a physician, psychiatrist, psychologist, or recognized social agency.

Many sex therapists have made statements on the subject that tend to be difficult for the layman to

understand. One, however, has clearly explained his philosophy in terms that leave no questions in the reader's mind. He is Don Sloan, M.D., codirector of the Sex Therapy Unit at New York Medical College and president of the Eastern Academy of Sex Therapy. His statement is included in a booklet accompanying his innovative sex teaching record album, *The Pleasures of Love* (see Sensual Awareness and the New Sexuality). Dr. Sloan says:

I imagine there is no one who would disagree that our understanding of ourselves as sexual human beings has increased dramatically in the last ten to fifteen years. From the first big disclosures of Freud earlier in this century up to our present-day researchers like Masters and Johnson, our daily acceptance of our sexual function as a natural function has started to take hold. Yet it has only been in the last decade that we have found some general acceptance of sex education in our schools and only in the last few years (coincidental with the rise in female sexual awareness through Women's Liberation and the youth movement) that we find sex to be a pre-

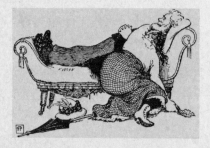

sentable subject in our mass communication media.

Yet, as a doctor and therapist, I have continuously faced problems produced primarily by unnecessary sexual ignorance and inhibition. I have found that despite the dozens of sex manuals . . . the authority and intimacy of the spoken word is far more effective in achieving rapport and understanding between and with couples. I have found too, that a simple conversation describing each other's sexual feelings is worth a thousand-word treatise on the subject. I therefore impress upon you: "Talk to each other . . . communicate."

Learning of love's pleasures can be simple, fun, and very rewarding. However, simple doesn't always mean easy. Most of life's rewards correlate with the amount of effort we put into achieving them. The great riches of a full, naturally satisfying love relationship can be gained by finding all the pleasures of love. Finding these pleasures takes commitment to the goal and to each other.

Caring for the other's feelings—wanting to give the person you love all the pleasure you can create—means knowing and understanding all about his or her total physical makeup. Giving yourselves, one at a time, to learning what pleasures the other most. Your feelings are your responsibility, just as your partner's feelings are his or her responsibility, and you are able to create pleasure only if each partner lives up to his or her responsibility to communicate those feelings.

No one can teach you how to love or make love to another. What you can be shown is how to express to your partner what pleases and displeases you, so that your partner, through his or her desire to give pleasure, will act in a way that is rewarding. The skills and art of lovemaking come later, just as the practice of any natural function, such as talking or singing, leads to an improved performance. Remember that your response to sexual pleasure is your own and cannot be compared to any other's. Its amount and quality are directly proportional to how well you have conveyed your knowledge of it to your lover.

Don Sloan, M.D.
Codirector of Sexual Therapy
New York Medical College

We can now best sum up by quoting an article, "All About the New Sex Therapy," which appeared in *Newsweek*, November 27, 1972.

Sex Therapy is new, and only time will tell how effective it is as a long-term cure. Up to now, there have been no controlled studies comparing the results of the sex therapists with those of their colleagues using conventional psychotherapy. Masters and Johnson have treated nearly 2,000 patients, most of whom had failed at psychotherapy and other forms of counseling. About 80 percent were cured of their problem and continue to have satisfactory sex lives five years after treatment. Most of Masters and Johnson's disciples haven't been in practice long enough to provide such a long-range picture. But their initial results are about the same as the pioneers, and few patients regress once they've overcome their sexual inadequacy. "It's like learning to ride a bicycle," says Dr. Alexander Levay of Columbia. "Once you get the hang of it, you never forget."

The Lacedemonian Ambassadors
From *The Collected Drawings of Aubrey Beardsley* edited by Bruce S. Harris © 1967 by Crescent Books, Inc. Reprinted by permission of Crown Publishers, Inc.

Who Makes Up the Sex Establishment?

Anonymous 19th century French illustration

"Membership in the Sex Establishment is determined by a tacit consensus of the members. Although it is basically anti-Freudian, it includes psychoanalysts like Judd Marmor and Harold Lief. Although Albert Ellis is *a*, if not *the*, founding father, his independence and earthiness have disqualified him from today's inner circle. Other "in" officers of the Sex Establishment include William Masters, Virginia Johnson, John Money, Wardell Pomeroy, Paul Gebhard, John Gagnon, Mary Jane Sherfey, Hugh Hefner (by virtue of his tie to Masters and Johnson—not the Playboy philosophy), Mary Calderone, William Simon, Edward S. Weinberg, David Mace, and Robert Stoller.

Those who are too candid about their own sexual behavior, or show the slightest hint of bon vivantism, haven't a prayer of joining. Thus the exclusion of Harry Benjamin, Tom Palmer, Martin Shephard, and William Bryan. Ideological deviation keeps out Rollo May, Natalie Shainess, and David Reuben. Eugene Schoenfeld is certainly candidate material. Bill Hartman and Marilyn Fithian would be in the inner circle, were it not for the seniority of Masters and Johnson. Alex Comfort would be welcome, but is too catholic an intellectual to join.

Very few writers have made the Sex Establishment. Morton Hunt, Ed Brecher, and Nat Lehrman have. Barbara Seaman came very close, but, again, is a victim of the Masters and Johnson veto. Most foreign sex specialists are merely names to the inner circle and are automatically excluded. . . ."

From *The Love Doctors* by Patrick M. McGrady, Jr. The Macmillan Company $7.95
© 1972 by Patrick M. McGrady, Jr. Reprinted by permission of the author.

Patrick M. McGrady, Jr., was born in Shelton, Washington, in 1932. He majored in International Relations at Yale, and is fluent in French, Russian, and Yiddish. He has been a newsman for the United Press, the Associated Press, the *Chicago Sun-Times* and NBC. He was also Moscow correspondent for *Newsweek*. A member of the Society of Magazine Writers, he is an active crusader for First Amendment rights. He currently lives and works in New York.

S.A.R. (SEXUAL ATTITUDE RESTRUCTURING)

S.A.R. (Sexual Attitude Restructuring) is an educational program which was first developed during the early 1960s at the University of Minnesota Medical Center for the training of counselors, semiprofessionals, and educators in the field of sex therapy and sex education, to help *restructure* and evaluate their own attitudes towards all forms of human sexuality, thus improving their own sexual counseling with patients, clients, and students.

Since then, other universities and institutions have adopted the S.A.R. method. However, the major educational facility offering the program on a regular schedule is the National Sex Forum (540 Powell Street, San Francisco, California, 94108). It is an intensive educational and experiential event with full-time participation, over a period of eight days, in seminars, lectures, encounter groups, films, and slide shows.

The eleven units of the S.A.R. restructuring method are:

1. Endorsement
2. Information giving, general
3. Information giving, reproductive biology
4. Masturbation
5. Lesbianism and homosexuality
6. Sexual desensitization and resensitization
7. Female and male sexuality
8. Sexual enrichment
9. Sexual inhibitions stemming from special problems: medical, physical dysfunction, or religious
10. Therapy: the elements of what sex therapy is, the main dysfunctions, and the methods used to help patients
11. Cultural expression (through art, film, dance, and music)

The eight-day working sessions also include counseling on bisexuality, open marriage, "bizarre" sex practices, and how to give a sexological examination (a method of teaching women how to self-examine their internal and external genitalia).

However, since S.A.R.'s inception at the National Sex Forum they have now established it as an eight-day educational course on Human Sexuality which is available to any individual or couple who wishes to participate. The cost is approximately $250.00 per person or $450.00 per couple. This fee does not include housing (for residents outside of San Francisco) or meals (with the exception of breakfast each day).

For more information, application forms, and schedules, please write:
The National Sex Forum
540 Powell Street
San Francisco, California 94108

Anonymous illustration of illicit love, approximately sixteenth century

Therapists and Treatment Centers

A Bagnio, Hot House, or Stew (England). This reproduction of a woodcut is a rare broadside issued in the reign of James I; it shows the ladies of the bagnio bathing, partaking of refreshments, and gossiping.

*I*t is difficult to say, with any degree of certainty, how many self-appointed sex therapists exist around the country. All too many have credentials ranging from the dubious to the fictitious. Sex therapy, like any other form of treatment, should be supervised only by qualified professionals. The following list, broken down according to state, is limited strictly to recognized therapists and treatment centers. As we stated earlier, most of them take patients only on a basis of professional referrals. For further information it is suggested that you contact the therapist or center nearest you.

(Note: In view of the fact that there are more listings in California than in any other geographical area they are broken down alphabetically according to locality within the state).

California (North & Central)

Nathan E. Liskey, H.S.D. & Jean Lisky, M.S.
6061 N. Winchester
Fresno, California 93704

Dr. Jerry Nims & Martha Nims
The Tahoe Institute
P.O. Box 796
South Lake Tahoe, California 96705

Kenneth W. Fors, M.S.W. & Mrs. Beverlee H. Filloy, M.S.W.
3333 Watt Avenue, Suite 209
Sacramento, California 95825

Greek Courtesans—from a design by Garnery, gravure by R. De Launay

California (Bay Area and the Peninsula)

Gerald Smith, Ed.D
1080 Alameda de Los Pulgas
Belmont, California 94402

Dr. Bernard Apfelbaum
The Berkeley Group for Sexual Development
2614 Telegraph Avenue
Berkeley, California 94704

Dr. Tom Durkin
North Berkeley Community Counseling Center
919 The Alameda
Berkeley, California 94707

Lonnie Garfield, M.A.
925 The Alameda
Berkeley, California 94707
(Associate, Sex Advisory & Counseling Unit, University of California Medical School. Groups for nonorgasmic women.)

Dr. Daniel Goldstine & Shirley Zuckerman, M.S.W.
Berkeley Therapy Institute
1749 Grove Street
Berkeley, California 94720
(Directors, Sex Therapy Program, Cowell Hospital, University of California at Berkeley.)

Paul Schaeffer, M.D.
919 The Alameda
Berkeley, California 94707

Lynn G. Smith, Ph.D. & James R. Smith, M.A.
1185 Sterling Avenue
Berkeley, California 94708

North County Mental Health Center
45 South Gate Avenue
Daly City, California 94015

Bernard Zilbergeld, Ph.D.
139 Behrens
El Cerrtop, California 94530

Dr. Frank E. Humburger
Interpersonal Relations, Lafayette Center for Counseling & Education
Brook Dewing Medical Building
914 Dewing Avenue
Lafayette, California 94549

Santa Clara Valley Sexual Behavior Clinic
248 Blossom Hill Road
Los Gatos, California 95030

Shirley Lewis
Center for Intimacy & Sexuality
6169 Harwood Avenue
Oakland, California 94618

Dr. Arnold Kresch
Department of Psychiatry
School of Medicine, Stanford University
Palo Alto, California 94305

California (San Francisco)

Dr. Ben Ard
Department of Psychology, San Francisco State University
1600 Holloway Avenue
San Francisco, California 94132

Dr. Joel Fort
Fort Help
199 10th Street
San Francisco, California 94103

Ben Handelman, M.S.W.
3838 California Street
San Francisco, California 94118
(Associate, Sex Advisory Counseling Unit, University of California Medical School.)

Dr. Len Laskow
3838 California Street
San Francisco, California 94118
(Associate, Sex Advisory Counseling Unit, University of California Medical School.)

Dr. Herbert Vendervoort & Dr. Jay Mann
Sex Advisory & Counseling Unit
University of California Medical School
San Francisco, California 94122

California (Southern)

Ernest Bruni, Ph.D. & Judi Gibbs, Ph.D.
11565 Paramount Boulevard
Downey, California 90241 (or)
1888 Century Park East, Suite 1022
Los Angeles, California 90067

The Center for Behavior Therapy
211 South Beverly Drive
Suites 207 & 208
Beverly Hills, California 90212

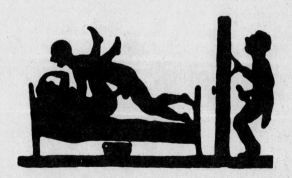

Dr. William Hartman & Marilyn Fithian
Center for Marital & Sexual Studies
5199 East Pacific Coast Highway
Long Beach, California 90804

Thomas R. Krause, M.A.
Beach Cities Counseling Center
112 18th Street, Suite A
Huntington Beach, California 92646

Jeremy More, Ph.D. & Virginia More, M.B.A.
Glenmore Institute for Sexual Therapy
10745 Riverside Drive
North Hollywood, California 91602

Robert Reitman, Ph.D.
19100 Nashville Street
Northride, California 91324

Dr. Alexander Runciman
4911 Van Nuys Boulevard
Sherman Oaks, California 91403

Carolyn Symonds, M.A.
Sensory Awareness Center
5098 Wilder
Soquel, California 95073

Emerson Symonds
Sensory Awareness Center
3939 Newmark Avenue
San Bernardino, California 92405

Connecticut

Dr. Eleanore Luckey
Department of Child Development
University of Connecticut
Storrs, Connecticut 06268

Dr. Philip M. Sarrel
School of Medicine
Yale University
333 Cedar Street
New Haven, Connecticut 06510

Hawaii

Dr. Jack Annon
1481 South King Street
Honolulu, Hawaii 96814

Dr. Vincent De Feo
School of Medicine
University of Hawaii
1960 East-West Road
Honolulu, Hawaii 96822

Illinois

Dr. Daniel Offer
Associate Director, Psychosomatic Institute
Michael Reese Hospital
2929 South State Street
Chicago, Illinois 60616

Indiana

Dr. Alan Bell
Institute for Sex Research
Indiana University
Bloomington, Indiana

Dr. Edward T. Tyler
School of Medicine
Indiana University
1100 W. Michigan
Indianapolis, Indiana 46202

Kentucky

Ernest E. Jordon, Ed.D.
1499 Forbes Road
Lexington, Kentucky, 40505

Maryland

Dr. Armando Demoya
11125 Rockville Pike
Rockville, Maryland 20852

Dr. John Money
Office of Psychohormonal Research, Department of Psychiatry & Pediatrics
School of Medicine
Johns Hopkins University Hospital
Baltimore, Maryland 21205

Dr. Harvey Resnik
4740 Chevy Chase Drive
Chevy Chase, Maryland 20015

Richard F. Tyson, M.D. & Joanne H. Tyson, R.N.B.S.N.
Institute for Marriage Enrichment and Social Studies
Century Plaza
10632 Little Patuxent Parkway, Suite 224
Columbia, Maryland 21044

Minnesota

Titus P. Belleville
Department of Psychiatry
University of Minnesota
Minneapolis, Minnesota 55455

Rick Chilgren
School of Medicine
University of Minnesota
Minneapolis, Minnesota 55455

Missouri

Larry N. Edson, D.O. & Marilyn Edson
Department of Psychology
Kirksville College of Osteopathy & Surgery
Kirksville, Missouri 63501

Dr. William Masters & Virginia Johnson
Reproductive Biology Research Foundation
4910 Forest Park Boulevard
St. Louis, Missouri, 63108

New York

Hugo C. Beigel, Ph.D.
138 E. 94th Street
New York, New York 10028

Dr. Albert Ellis
Institute for Advance Study in Rational Psychotherapy
45 East 65th Street
New York, New York 10021

Dr. Helen Kaplan, Director
Payne-Whitney Psychiatric Clinic
525 East 68th Street
New York, New York 10021

Dr. Harold Lear
Human Sexuality Program
Department of Community Medicine
Mount Sinai School of Medicine
Fifth Avenue at 100th Street
New York, New York 10029

Dr. Wardell Pomeroy
215 East 68th Street
New York, New York 10021
(Consultant, Payne-Whitney Psychiatric Clinic.)

Dr. Donald Sloan
New York Medical College
Fifth Avenue at 106th Street
New York, New York 10029
(Sex Therapist, Fertility Research Foundation.)

Dr. Joseph Lo Piccolo
Department of Psychology
State University at Stony Brook
Stony Brook, New York 11794

Lynn G. Smith, Ph.D. & James R. Smith, M.A.
Self Actuation Laboratory
Lake Titus
Malone, New York 12953

Dr. Leon Zussman, Acting Director, &
Dr. Shirley Zussman, Acting Assistant Director
The Human Sexuality Center
Long Island Jewish Hospital
270-05 76th Avenue
New Hyde Park, New York 11040

North Carolina

Dr. Takey Crist
Department of Obstetrics & Gynecology
University of North Carolina
Chapel Hill, North Carolina 27514

Dr. Clark Vincent
Bowman Gray School of Medicine
300 S. Hawthorne Road
Winston-Salem, North Carolina 27103

Ohio

Elmer D. Fenner, Ph.D. & Carol Ann Fenner
1009 Beachside Lane
Huron, Ohio 44839

Oregon

Dr. Selby Clark
Director Counseling Center
Portland State University
P.O. Box 751
Portland, Oregon 97207

Dr. Daniel Labby
School of Medicine
University of Oregon
3181 Sam Jackson Park Road
Portland, Oregon 97201

Dr. Ira Pauley
School of Medicine
University of Oregon
3181 Sam Jackson Park Road
Portland, Oregon 97201

Dr. Arnold Rustin
2311 N.W. Northrup
Portland, Oregon 97210

Dr. Joseph Trainer
School of Medicine
University of Oregon
3181 Sam Jackson Park Road
Portland, Oregon 97201

Pennsylvania

Dr. Harold I. Lief
Department of Psychiatry
School of Medicine
University of Pennsylvania
4025 Chestnut Street
Philadelphia, Pennsylvania 19104

Dr. Sally Schumacher
Western Psychiatric Institute & Clinic
Department of Psychology
University of Pittsburgh
Pittsburgh, Pennsylvania 15261

Dr. Alan Wabrek
School of Medicine
University of Pennsylvania
4025 Chestnut Street
Philadelphia, Pennsylvania 19104

South Dakota

Wayne A. Dahl A.C.S.W. & Donna Jean Dahl
The Dahl Center for Marital & Sexual Counseling
2421 South Third
Sioux Falls, South Dakota 57105

Texas

Dr. Edward Ridman
American Association of Marriage & Family Counselors
6211 West N. W. Highway
Dallas, Texas 75225

Virginia

Brian C. Campden-Main, M.D. &
Thelma J. Campden-Main, M.A.
The Marital & Sexual Therapy Institute
3545 Chain Bridge Road
Fairfax, Virginia 22030

Washington

Richard B. Hartley, Ph.D. & Helen Hartley
Northwest Center for Marital & Sexual Studies
1124 North Yakima
Tacoma, Washington 98403

Dr. Nat Wagner
Department of Psychology
University of Washington
Seattle, Washington 98105

Canada

Dr. Harry Brody
Department of Obstetrics & Gynecology
University of Calgary
Alberta, Canada

Anonymous 19th century German woodcuts appearing on pages 97 through 100 are from The Museum of Erotic Art, San Francisco. Reprinted by permission of Drs. Phyllis and Eberhard Kronhausen

Bibliography

Belliveau, Fred, and Richter, Lin. *Understanding Human Sexual Inadequacy.* Boston: Little, Brown, 1970. $6.95

Brecher, Ruth, and Brecher, Edward, eds. *An Analysis of Human Sexual Response.* New York: New American Library, 1966. $1.25

Hartman, William, and Fithian, Marilyn. *Treatment of Sexual Dysfunction.* Long Beach. Calif.: Center for Marital & Sexual Studies, 1972. $12.50

Hastings, Donald W. *Impotence & Frigidity.* Boston: Little, Brown, 1963. $7.95

Kaplan, Helen Singer. *The New Sex Therapy.* New York: Quadrangle Books, 1974. $17.50

Kinsey, Alfred C.; Pomeroy, Wardell; Martin, Clyde. *Sexual Behavior in the Human Male.* Philadelphia: Saunders, 1948. $10.25

Kinsey, Alfred C.; Pomeroy, Wardell; Martin, Clyde; Gebhard, Paul. *Sexual Behavior in the Human Female.* Philadelphia: Saunders, 1953. $10.25; New York: Pocket Books, 1965. $2.50

Kirsch, Irving, and Smith, Brenda. *Sex Therapy.* Chatsworth, Calif.: Books for Better Living, 1973. $1.25

Lehrman, Nat, ed. *Masters & Johnson Explained.* Chicago: Playboy Press, 1970. $1.25

Masters, William, and Johnson, Virginia. *Human Sexual Inadequacy.* Boston: Little, Brown, 1966. $13.50

———. *Human Sexual Response.* Boston: Little, Brown, 1966. $13.50

McGrady, Patrick M., Jr. *The Love Doctors.* New York: Macmillan, 1972. $7.95

McIllvenna, Ted. *When You Don't Make It.* San Francisco: Multi-Media Resource Center, 1973. $2.95

McIllvenna, Ted, and Vandervoort, Herb. *You Can Last Longer.* San Francisco: Multi-Media Resource Center, 1973. $2.95

Robbins, Jhan, and Robbins, June. *An Analysis of Human Sexuality.* New York: Signet, $1.25

Santini, Rosemary. *The Sex Doctors.* New York: Pinnacle Books, 1975. $1.95

Bookmark by Aubrey Beardsley From The Collected Drawings of Aubrey Beardsley edited by Bruce S. Harris. © 1967 by Crescent Books, Inc. Reprinted by permission of Crown Publishers, Inc.

From a Discourse on the Worship of Priapus by Richard Payne Knight 1786

Courtesan *by the seventeenth century Dutch painter, Jacob Backer*
From *FILLE DE JOIE.*Copyright © *1967 by Grove Press, Inc.*
Reprinted by permission of Grove Press, Inc.

The Oldest Profession

From Babylonian Priestesses to Happy Hookers

The Prostitute

The night is growing cold now,
and my painted-on smile is fading.
How many more must I please
before the rent is paid and
there's bread on the table . . .
Then I think, just one more,
I'd like a ribbon for my hair.

Funny, how people think they know us.
Girls of the night, the kind ones say.
Some people just call us hookers.
and then there are those who pass by
and point at them "hoor" ladies.

Sometimes, in a darkened room,
a generous Joe pitches an extra
twenty on the bed and says,
"Howdja get started in this kinda life,
kid?" And I just lay back on the pillow,
stare at the ceiling and answer quietly,
"Oh, I guess I just like to Fuck."

— *Phillistene*

In addition to being the oldest profession, prostitution has always been inextricably involved with the affairs of mankind. Although it would appear that prostitution is a subject requiring no definition, the fact is that it most certainly does. To some, the word "whore" refers strictly to a female who indulges in sexual relations for profit. To others the word is equated with promiscuity, but not necessarily with commercialism. In its broadest sense, the word can refer to anyone, male or female, who sells any aspect of self, sexual or otherwise. We are discussing prostitution in the most commonly accepted sense— sex for profit.

As an illustration of the diverse attitudes toward prostitution, there is the old story about the man who approached a woman at a party and asked her if she would bed down with him for a million dollars.

"Of course I would," she replied smiling and with no hesitation. "Who wouldn't?"

To which the man rejoined, "Would you be willing to sleep with me for five dollars?"

The woman tossed him an indignant sneer and snapped, "What do you think I am? A whore?"

"We've already established that fact," he said. "Now we're merely haggling over the price."

In antiquity, prostitution was regarded with a multitude of widely varied attitudes. More than one ancient civilization maintained temples to goddesses of love and fertility which were attended by priestesses whose sacred duties included prostitution. Every Babylonian woman was required to sacrifice her virginity to the goddess Mylitta. The ancient Jews, on the other hand, condemned to death any daughter of Israel who prostituted herself, though they tolerated the presence of foreign concubines and harlots.

The history of prostitution is as colorful as that of civilization itself. Alternately, throughout the ages, the prostitute has known the depths of degradation and despair, and the pinnacle of glory. There were women from the upper strata of whoredom, notably the empress Theodora, who attained a throne and great political power as a result of their proficiency in the bed of commercial virtue. There have even been prostitutes who eventually attained the golden crown of sainthood.

Typical of these latter-day Magdalenes was Mary the Egyptian, who lived during the reign of the

Roman Emperor Claudius. At the age of twelve she went to Alexandria, where for seventeen years she earned her livelihood as a common prostitute. Finally, deciding to make a pilgrimage to Jerusalem in order to worship at the true cross, she pleaded with some sailors to take her with them on their next voyage to the holy land. When they told her the price of passage she said, "Brothers, I have nothing to give. Take my body in payment."

The sailors accepted her offer and liberally enjoyed the use of her body during the trip. When Mary arrived in Jerusalem and went to the door of the church, she was repelled by an invisible force. She tried several times to enter, but on each attempt she was prevented from crossing the threshold. Weeping profusely, she took a vow of chastity and begged for the protection of the Virgin Mary. The plea was apparently effective, for she was finally able to enter the church and offer her devotions. After this she crossed the Jordan River and did forty-seven years penance in the burning sands of the desert, which returned her to grace. She became the patron saint of courtesans, and the abandonment of her body to the sailors was represented on stained glass windows in a number of European churches centuries later.

Then, from the sublime to the most base, there is the derivation of the word *fornication*. Taken from the Latin word *fornix*, it means "arch" and referred to a specific recess in buildings where the lowest class of Roman streetwalkers plied their trade for the equivalent of pennies per customer.

Whenever the climate of opinion and the times were favorable, prostitution flourished openly. In his monumental *Histoire de la Prostitution*, Paul Lacroix compared the European attitude toward prostitution to the classic view of the Jews: they were perpetually persecuted on all levels by church, state, and society, yet all classes were happy to deal with them and indeed, found it almost impossible to live without them.

The Florentine humanist, Poggio Bracciolini, in his *Liber Facetiarum* wrote a number of delightful tales about prostitutes. Tale CXIII concerns a whore who complained about a barber's malpractice.

There is a tribunal in Florence called the Court of Morals, which deals mostly with matters concerning whores, and which seeks to protect them from being molested in the city. A whore once appeared before this court, claiming injury by, and damages against a barber. She had engaged him to shave her lower parts, but his razor had cut her cunt so badly that for many days it was unable to admit any men therein. On these grounds she claimed damages equivalent to the fees which she had lost. I wonder, what should be the decision of the court?*

Despite a more or less continuous campaign against prostitution, predominantly Catholic countries in general were always more tolerant in their attitude toward the ladies of the oldest profession than the Protestant nations. The reason behind Catholicism's more liberal attitude was based upon an opinion of no less a person than St. Augustine, who asserted, "Remove prostitutes from human affairs and you would pollute the world with lust." St. Thomas Aquinas thought along the same lines, saying, "Prostitution in towns is like the sewer in a palace; take away the sewers and the palace becomes an impure and stinking place."

Although the support was offered in a decidedly left-handed manner, the message was clear. Both church fathers recognized in prostitution the element of an erotic safety valve.

Such weighty arguments on behalf of prostitution

Eighteenth century engraving after a painting by Boucher illustrating a novel, La Courtisane Amoureuse
From FILLE DE JOIE Copyright © 1967 by Grove Press, Inc. Reprinted by permission of Grove Press, Inc.

* Translation copyright © 1968 by Bernhardt J. Hurwood.

notwithstanding, vigorous campaigns to stamp it out have always been waged with ardor and enthusiasm. All too often, however, the motives of the abolitionists were less than admirable.

The beautiful, talented, and witty courtesan who has survived all assaults will probably always exist, regardless of what nation or era in which she lives. So will the stereotyped "common whore" of the streets. There has to be a deep, fundamental reason for the existence of prostitution. All of the old excuses lumped together do not provide the answer. The ritual of religious motive, except for a few isolated instances outside the Western world, has long been defunct. The position of the church fathers no longer holds water, especially in modern times. Most people today can find willing sexual partners without having to pay cash on the line, but there will always be those who prefer uncomplicated sexual relations on a pay-as-you-go basis, with no emotional involvements.

While obvious reasons for prostitution have shifted from century to century, there have always been cohesive factors that were valid in their time. One such element, which has existed from the earliest of times and to a certain extent still does today, is the attitude that divorces sexual pleasure from marriage and family life. Happily this is vanishing rapidly, but it was a prime cause of prostitution in the days when "decent" women were not supposed to experience sexual pleasure.

Toward the end of the last century, a literate prostitute named Hedwig Hard wrote a penetrating autobiography, pin-pointing this attitude with precision. She told of a regular client who was married to a beautiful woman, and who had two children and an established niche in society. There appeared to be no marital discord in his life, so Hedwig asked him one day why he wasted his time seeking her company when he had such a charming wife at home. He answered by saying, "All her beauty and culture brings nothing to my heart. She is cold, cold as ice, proper, and above all, phlegmatic. Pampered and spoiled, she lives only for herself; we are two good comrades, and nothing more.

"If, for instance, I come back from the club in the evening and go to her bed, perhaps a little excited, she becomes nervous and she thinks it improper to wake her. If I kiss her, she defends herself and tells me that I smell horribly of cigars and wine. And if perhaps I attempt more, she jumps out of bed, bristles up as though I were assaulting her, and

Eighteenth century book illustration depicting elegant courtesan and her wealthy lover.
From FILLE DE JOIE Copyright © 1967 by Grove Press, Inc. Reprinted by permission of Grove Press, Inc.

threatens to throw herself out of the window if I touch her. So, for the sake of peace, I leave her alone and come to you."

Even though there may be married women today who find sex repugnant and thereby drive their husbands into the arms of other women, they are hardly making a major contribution to the maintenance of prostitution. Husbands are not forced to seek a sexual outlet in the embraces of prostitutes. There are simply too many sympathetic women around who are willing and able to be bed partners when called upon. As a pragmatic woman executive remarked recently, "I don't know why so many men spend so much time beating around the bush. If they want it, all they have to do is ask."

The traditional folk picture of the father taking his virgin son to the friendly neighborhood brothel for his initiation into the mysteries of Venus is about as up-to-date as the buggy whip. For that matter, so is the friendly neighborhood brothel. Brothels exist, but they are either assembly line operations or beyond the reach of all but the most affluent. Despite this, prostitution continues to flourish and always will. One of the chief factors is the law of supply and

Anonymous drawing circa 1820 depicting ancient temple prostitution

demand. Today, more than ever, many prostitutes openly admit that they enjoy their work and enter the profession voluntarily; many intelligent and educated woman find it the quickest and easiest way to get enough money to establish themselves in a straight business, or pay for an education, sometimes even to support a husband while he finishes school.

Although they are rare, there is even a fair number of so-called "whores with hearts of gold," a perfect example of which is this true first-hand story.

It was 1946. Our ship was loading nitrate in the port of Tocopilla, Chile, which nestles at the foot of the Andes. While plying her trade one night in a sleazy cabaret filled with sailors, pimps, drug pushers, and dozens of her colleagues, a pretty dark-haired brunette discovered in one of the lavatories the radio operator of our rusty Liberty Ship. He was so sick and drunk he could not stand up. Knowing that he was my shipmate, she came over and said in broken English, "I no do business tonight. I go sleep with my sister. We put him in my bed." Together we dragged his dead weight back to the shabby little cubicle containing the bed which was the chief tool of her trade. She undressed him, washed his face, folded his clothes, put them on a chair next to the bed, and

placed a basin alongside in case he got sick during the night. Then she left.

Late the next day when he returned to the ship he told us that she not only came to see him in the wee hours of the morning, she climbed into bed with him and gave him the fuck of his life. When dawn came and he discovered that his wallet was missing, she took him out, bought him breakfast, and gave him enough cash to pay the boatman who ran the harbor launch.

Which brings to mind another true story. I once asked a beautiful girl working in an old-style Galveston whorehouse the old cliché question, "How did a nice girl like you get into this business?" She hestitated a moment, came up with a transparently phony story, then detecting my skeptical expression, blushed and said, "To tell the truth, I love it. I like the hours, the living conditions, and the clothes I can buy. I make more money than I ever knew existed. And, besides, I just plain like sex."

Unfortunately not all whores are that well adjusted. The chief of the Los Angeles Vice Squad told me how he once asked a girl why she stayed with the pimp who mistreated her and took all her money. She answered, "Because it's nice to wake up in the morning and find out that there's at least one guy who cares that you're alive."

THE SIGN by Antoine Wiertz (1806-1865). The artist's rendition of the prostitutes' classic gesture to entice customers.

The Courtesan in History

Sign outside an ancient Roman lupanar with the inscription "To the sisters four"

From FILLE DE JOIE. Copyright © 1967 by Grove Press, Inc. Reprinted by permission of Grove Press, Inc.

The courtesan, who distinguishes herself from the others of the sisterhood, her poor relations, by her wit, luxury, and elegance, makes her appearance from the most remote times, with her audacious pride, her vain show, her unbridled ambition, and her natural perfidy.

If prostitution began in the world on the day when certain creatures sold themselves, this market, like all markets, has been submitted to a multitude of conventions. Those whom debauchery left miserable have received a contemptuous name; but the favored of fortune have, on the contrary, been baptized with a name almost aristocratic.

The courtesans are one of the signs of wealth, one of the manifestations of the outlay, the ornaments of a great city, the end toward which the secret desires of men tend, a social force. However, even when self-interest is the leading issue, there can be, there often is, love in the illegitimate connections of the sexes. When a woman gives herself in obeying the desires of her heart and the allurements of the flesh, it is voluptuousness and not prostitution *(prostitutum)* which, taken in its etymologic sense, extends to all species of obscene traffic.

Be that as it may, a courtesan, by definition, is a woman of pleasure. Pleasure is an art with its rules, its inspirations, its unexpected discoveries, and its caprices. The poet employs words, the painter colors, the musician notes, the sculptor marble, the courtesan employs her body: the instrument differs, that is all.

The witty remark of a whore about Venetians

When I was at the baths at Petrioli, I was told by a man of erudition, of a whore's witty remark which is not unworthy of being included in the society of our other tales. There lived in Venice, he said, a public prostitute, who was patronized by men of many nations. Someone asked her one day the nationality of those men provided with the largest virile member. Unhesitatingly the woman replied that it was the Venetians. "Their pricks are so long," she said, "that though they are often away in distant lands beyond the seas, they are still able to connect with their wives and produce children." Thus he jibed at the Venetian wives, who are left under the protection of others, while the husbands travel.

Tale CCXLII, *The Facetiae* of Poggio Bracciolini. Translation copyright © 1968 by Bernhardt J. Hurwood.

Likewise, her royalty asserts itself from the origin of history. The left-hand queens have exercised a greater political influence than the right-hand queens. The character of the courtesan and her methods of action have modified themselves according to the spirit of the times, but her rôle has always been preponderantly that of the ruler. And this is so much the case that men can be said to have their "hearts on their pillows."

The courtesans, who formerly eagerly devoured men's money, have disappeared from the *demi-monde* where they lorded it; for the rest, there is no longer any *demi-monde*. The elegant and gallant women no longer have lovers exclusively as paymasters; they have friends whose principal mission is to clear the way toward the realization of their ambitious desires. They aspire less to direct wealth than to conquering weighty situations out of the pride in commanding, success, and glory. Having lost in sensibility and sensuality what they have gained in intellectual powers, they have remained miraculously perverse.

It is less through the intimacies of sex—their accentuated beauty having become more charming thanks to the practice of sports—that they count on to subjugate, than by the bewitching roguishness of their embellished minds. Nourished on the rarest of literature and philosophies; if not holding baccalaureates or doctorates, at least highly learned; smitten with the splendors of art; musicians, painters, armed almost always with a position which assures their independence; cuirassed against the prejudices of former times and its principles; scorning everything that is *coco* or *pompier* [conventional]; they appear since the war not only as creatures of the élite but determined to seize in their small redoubtable hands all the good of the earth.

For the man who loves them they have a scornful compassion.

Young girls, for whom marriage has become problematic by reason of the difficulties of existence, have flung one last glance on their elders, the old maids overwhelmed with years and descending body and soul into the grave. What a spectacle! Here it is no more a matter of pleasant ways, of possible irony, but sad reflections to which has succeeded this audacious resolution which possesses all the authority of a principle: "To live her life!"

Herodotus relates that formerly there were women whose sole occupation was war and who had reduced the men to the rôle of the domestic. These Amazons, in order that they be distinguished from other women, had the custom of cutting off the left breast. Today, what good would this be? The "bosom" is an ornament which is no longer worn. But does the heart in this hoyden bosom still beat? Oh! without a doubt. It is no less true that a distinguished, educated young woman who renounces marrying a man of her rank because smitten with independence, with well-being, a young woman, I say, who, renouncing marriage and motherhood, gives chase to protectors and accords her favors in order to acquire a more or less brilliant position, would not be able to detach herself from the category of courtesans. She is, on the contrary, the most finished specimen of them.

One can better compare her only to those hetaerae of Greece who had preferences for this one, aversions for that one, and belonged only to those who knew how to please them. It must be said that these hetaerae, through their wit, culture, and exquisite elegance of manners, were able to walk side by side with the most eminent men of Corinth and Athens.

In truth, would not one believe to have come back again to the finest days of the age of Pericles?

The lives and loves of the courtesans, straitly bound to that of humanity, appear to the observer as the most exact expression of the manners of different periods. Besides, laws, which all derive from the psychology of peoples, are established on the various understandings of love and marriage. If love formerly was considered as an individual sentiment, transient, or a debauchery, marriage on the contrary had to be durable because the family is the true social cell. But life always had its basis in passion.

Title page of an eighteenth century London guidebook to prostitutes and brothels
From FILLE DE JOIE. Copyright © 1967 by Grove Press, Inc. Reprinted by permission of Grove Press, Inc.

Fencers and other revelers in a fifteenth century bordello. Woodcut by the fifteenth century Master of Bandrollen.
From FILLE DE JOIE. Copyright © 1967 by Grove Press, Inc. Reprinted by permission of Grove Press, Inc.

Miss Chudleigh dressed as Iphegenia at a diplomatic ball. She was actually the Duchess of Kingston, and a renowned eighteenth century whore.
From FILLE DE JOIE Copyright © 1967 by Grove Press, Inc. Reprinted by permission of Grove Press, Inc.

The Unexpurgated Story of Cinderella

From *Fleshpots of Antiquity* by A. Frichet.

Rhodopis was not an Egyptian by birth. A native of Thrace, she showed herself possessed of an insatiable amorous ardor, as if the fires of the sun had burned in her blood. If we believe Ctesias, whose testimony Athenaeus invokes, Rhodopis knew all the artifices to aid in inflaming and satisfying the passions.

This girl had been the companion in slavery of Aesop, the fabulist, in the house of Iadmon. She was brought into Egypt by Zanthes of Samos, who at her expense followed a rather vile profession, since he had bought her in order that she exercise the position of courtesan to the profit of her master. She succeeded wonderfully well; her renown attracted a crowd of lovers to her, among whom was Charaxus of Mytilene, brother of the celebrated Sappho. This Charaxus was so taken with this charming slave that he gave a considerable sum for her ransom.

Rhodopis, having become free, did not leave Egypt, where her beauty and talents procured immense riches for her.

Handsome Charaxus, to whom she owed her liberty and the beginning of her opulence, allowed her to establish herself in the city of Naucratis, where he came to see her on each voyage he made to Egypt to sell wine. Rhodopis loved him enough to be faithful to him so long as he stayed at Naucratis, where love held him more than the interests of his business.

And now, here is where legend intervenes:

During one of the absences of Charaxus the beautiful courtesan was bathing in the Nile; she had deposited her clothing on one of the banks. An eagle passes, swoops down on her slipper, carries it off in its talons, and in passing over Memphis, lets it fall at the feet of the Pharaoh Amasis who was then holding court there for the assembled people. The Pharaoh adored little feet, and the slipper was to tiny that he continued the trial in hand for a week. At the same time he had it published in all his kingdom that the owner of the miraculous slipper had to make herself known.

The noise of this publication reached Rhodopis who, having recognized her slipper from the description the crier had given of it, left for Memphis and presented herself before the Pharaoh with one foot shod and the other bare. If the slipper alone had turned the head of Amasis, it was quite another thing when he saw the foot; but whether through caprice or calculation, Rhodopis refused to make the happiness of the monarch if this monarch did not take her for his wife. Amasis, who was in love, submitted to everything that Rhodopis wished, and the courtesan, having become queen, consecrated the fortune she had acquired in practicing her first profession to raising a pyramid. This pyramid, each stone of which is the price of a caress, is seven hundred feet in breadth by three hundred and fifty feet in height.

Illustrations by Edgar Degas for the De Maupassant story "MADAME TELLIER'S BROTHEL"

The Brothel Tokens of Ancient Rome

by Phillip Peck

Spintriae, *or Roman brothel tokens. Thirteen sexual positions are illustrated here along with their numbered reverses.*

*P*ictured on these pages are *spintriae* (Latin word meaning unnatural lust, or prostitute)—the famous brothel tokens of ancient Rome, supposedly used to buy a quick lay or a night of sex. They bear the uninhibited distinction of being the world's only coin or token to show, literally and explicitly, the sex act, in all its variety. The tokens are no larger than a quarter, and each shows a naked couple enjoying sex on an ornamented couch, with rich drapery sometimes in the back-

ground. The series illustrates at least 13 different positions of copulation or fellatio; and no doubt others will be discovered by the diligent archaeologist. The set probably comprised 16 scenes, because on the back of each is a number, from 1 to 16 inclusive, with no one being rarer or commoner than the others.

What do the numbers mean? Were there only 16 whores in the brothel—no more, no less? Were there 16 classes of prostitute, each with a different price? Not likely! Upon such questions founders the brothel token theory, popular with scholars of the nineteenth century, especially Rostovtseff, who stated:

The *spintriae* presumably had fixed values, corresponding to the different categories of prostitutes, whose rates, as we know, were officially controlled. The prostitute herself, or if she was attached to a brothel the whoremaster, would present the token to one of the Imperial cashiers and receive the appropriate sum in cash. It is even more probable that, once the tax on prostitution had been instituted, which each month amounted to the fee charged one customer, the *spintriae* served for the payment of that tax . . .

This is all very interesting—and true, regarding the taxation and regulation of prostitutes. But 16 different rates boggles the imagination. Much more likely they were gambling tokens. The more opulent brothels customarily ran casinos on the side. Our playing cards have a one-to-thirteen sequence: ace through ten, plus jack, queen, king. What little evidence survives suggests the possibility that Rome had some games of chance that utilized a one-to-sixteen sequence. Or possibly they were the ancient equivalent of the poker chip. In that case, these tokens would have only passed from customer to croupier; and the sex scenes served to advertise the other attractions of the establishment.

To explore another angle, Professor Buttrey has recently published an interesting paper in which he demonstrates that the *spintriae* are linked with another numbered series of tokens featuring the portraits of emperor Augustus, his wife Livia, and his successor Tiberius. The very same stamps for the

Wall mural from a Pompeiian lupanar
From FILLE DE JOIE Copyright © 1967 by Grove Press, Inc.
Reprinted by permission of Grove Press, Inc.

Illustration by Edgar Degas for the De Maupassant story
"MADAME TELLIER'S BROTHEL"

The story goes that once, while sacrificing, he took an erotic fancy to the acolyte who carried the incense casket, and could hardly wait for the ceremony to end before hurrying him and his brother, the sacred trumpeter, out of the temple and sexually assaulting them both. When they protested at this dastardly crime, he had their legs broken.

But having found seclusion at last, and no longer feeling himself under public scrutiny, he rapidly succumbed to all the vicious passions which he had for a long time tried, not very successfully, to disguise. I shall give a faithful account of these from the start . . . Being invited to dinner by Cestius Gallus, a lecherous old spendthrift whom [emperor] Ausustus had dishonorably removed from the Senate, and whom he himself had reprimanded

numbers were also used on the backs of the Imperial series. This important discovery enables us to date the *spintriae* to the latter part of the reign of emperor Tiberius (14—37 A.D.). One rare reverse replaces the number with AUG (*i.e.* Augustus, or emperor) and is used for both the *spintriae* and the Imperial tokens. Buttrey suggests that AUG on the reverse may identify the naked, copulating male in the *spintriae* scenes as being the emperor Tiberius himself.

Tiberius was a suspicious, cruel tyrant who made himself very unpopular. Spies and informers had a field day, causing many innocent Romans to be tortured or killed without trial. Fear gripped the city; and after Tiberius' furtive, abrupt retirement to Capri in 26 A.D., wild rumors swept Rome about his secret life there. The gossip was that Tiberius sought seclusion to indulge his evil sexual desires. The ancient historian Suetonius says of his cruelty and lechery:

Illustration by Edgar Degas for the De Maupassant story
"MADAME TELLIER'S BROTHEL"

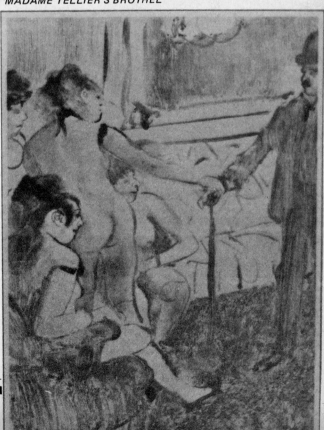

for his ill-living only a few days previously, Tiberius accepted on condition that the dinner should be the usual orgy, with all the waitresses naked.

On retiring to Capri he made himself a private sporting-house, where sexual extravagances were practiced for his secret pleasure. Bevies of girls and young men, whom he had collected from all over the Empire as adepts in perverted practices, and known as *spintriae*, would perform before him in groups of three, to excite his waning passions. A number of small rooms were furnished with the most lascivious pictures and statuary obtainable; also certain erotic manuals were obtained from Egypt—the *spintriae* would know from these exactly what was expected of them. He furthermore devised little nooks of lechery in the woods and glades ... Imagine training little boys, whom he called his "minnows," to chase him

while he went swimming and get between his legs to lick and nibble him. Or having babies not yet weaned from their mother's breast suck his penis ...

With such a background of hatred and innuendo existing at the same time these tokens were made, the *spintriae* may well have been a satire on the reputed habits of a "dirty old man"— emperor Tiberius.

Whatever their true purpose was, these fascinating tokens stand today as mute but graphic reminders of the licentious decadence of ancient Rome under the Caesars. They were in circulation during the reigns of infamous Caligula and Nero. Through chance burial and rediscovery, a few have survived. Today collectors prize them for their rarity, but even more for their unusually candid view of that notorious early Imperial era, nearly two thousand years ago.

 # *Coyote*

Certainly one of the most significant things going on today is the work of *Coyote*, the pioneering San-Francisco-based hookers' organization that is working towards the decriminalization of prostitution. Margo St. James, the organization's founder, explained that particular aim before the 1974 elections by saying, "We use the word 'decriminalization' rather than legalization or regulation because that just makes the government the pimp. Really, who wants Ronald Reagan as a pimp?" Ms. St. James also observed, "The whore has many political and economical enemies, the politicians and men of power who patronize her, keep her jailed—both figuratively and literally, without voice, without alternatives."

Should you be interested in *Coyote* and its work, see the following:

Coyote Calls For Volunteers

Coyote is an organization of prostitutes, ex-prostitutes and friends of prostitutes whose long-range goal is the decriminalization of prostitution. Recent accomplishments include halting the quarantine of all women arrested on prostitution charges and the opening of a free clinic by the Dept. of Public Health for loose women. A court monitoring project is ongoing and law suits have been filed.

Coyote needs volunteer help in its advocacy and community education efforts. We need people to do part-time office work, letter writing, typing, telephone contact work, court monitoring, OR interviewing, counselling and participation in rap groups. Call 441-8118 or write PO Box 26354, SF 94126

Coyote does not live on Love alone!
— MEMBERSHIP FORM —

Animal _____
Name _____
Address _____
City _____ Zip _____
Phone number(s) _____
☐ Change of Address

MEMBERSHIP RATES
(Membership dues include newsletter)

☐ $3   Student-Senior Citizen
☐ $5   General
☐ $25   Contributing
☐ $50   Participating
☐ $100 Sustaining

☐ $3   1 year subscription to Coyote Calls

Amount Enclosed $ _____

Please make check or m/o payable to COYOTE and return form to P.O. Box 26354, San Francisco, California 94126

Getting It On at the Hooker's Ball

(Reprinted from the *Berkeley Barb*, November 1-7, 1974.)
by Jennifer L. Thompson

"The Arc de Triomphe? It's here, soldier!" Nineteenth century French cartoon. From Erotic Illustrations *by Gordon Grimley. Copyright © 1974 by Gordon Grimley. Reproduced by permissiion of Grove Press, Inc.*

*D*ecadence and bare asses ran rampant at the First Annual Hooker's Ball. Leotarded whores, panama'd pimps, and transvestites festooned with feathers, glitter, and satin, dominated the $25-a-head "celebrity" Foreplay Party preceding the ball. Several less canny sports lost their wallets.

Barb founder Max Scherr embarked on his film career that evening, shooting a documentary of Margo St. James' First Annual Hooker's Ball and Foreplay Party. "You camera people have got to stop giving all your attention to the queens. This is a hookers' ball," complained a working woman.

"Choo, choo, choo," one queen chugged, gliding past the liver pâté to the champagne bar. The dress she wore was hot pink with black sequin sleeves. A slit revealed a shapely thigh and calf as the turbaned woman swished her black satin scarves to the delight of goggle-eyed observers. A blond mustache added a piquant touch to an otherwise homely face. "I'm doing security, Honey, they know when there's trouble you get a drag queen," *Barb* was told.

About two dozen transvestites, identifiable by slipping misshapen bosoms, volunteered for the show. Two make-

Les Cousines de la Colonel by Felicien Rops

believe ladies performed exotic dances while balancing two feet of feathered head gear on their pointed little heads.

One blushing bride greeted friends by flashing a chalk white penis which those adept in figuring out social nuances immediately shook with barely a bat of the five-inch eyelash. Once this exchange was completed petticoats dropped modestly to the floor.

Hookers kept a low profile, for good reason. I asked a friend of mine from the hall of justice whether or not he thought the vice squad would send a few of its fellows to the event. "Heh, heh, heh," he nervously chuckled, glancing furtively over his shoulder. "I've seen a number of familiar faces here tonight."

One pimp dressed in the traditional white suit, four-inch shoes, and broad-brimmed leather panama, first tried to tell *Barb* he was an actor. The man was enjoying himself. He led a kick line of working women and queens. He flashed smiles at every lady who would receive them.

One of the pimp's ladies spotted a shaved head on a woman's body. "Who's that," she asked. "Betty Dodson," *Barb* answered. Both she and her take-care-of-business man exclaimed, "Far-out," and sauntered over to meet the infamous erotic artist.

At least 300 people sardined themselves into two small rooms for the Foreplay Party. The rooms in the Longshoreman's Hall are reminiscent of a church or school's social lounge. Crepe paper streamers hung from the ceilings. Glitter fell on the vinyl tiles. Metal stack-up chairs were strewn about both rooms for those who could restrain themselves to one area. Posters advertising HUMP (Hookers United Mostly for Profit) disguised institutional cinder block walls.

One young man came dressed as a vampire letter carrier. His companion wore black tights and leotards capped with a silver mink stole. "This is better than I ever imagined," the fellow told *Barb*. He got his official uniform from a supply store in Oakland. The store asked what the uniform was for. The man told them it was for the Hooker's Ball, at which point the salesperson said, "We're not supposed to sell these

Eighteenth century illustration from John Cleland's Fanny Hill.
From FILLE DE JOIE. Copyright © 1967 by Grove Press, Inc. Reprinted by permission of Grove Press, Inc.

James in the political message segment of the Foreplay Party, reported that now Ted Kennedy is not running for President he will be able to take certain positions which should make Joan very happy.

And right on cue, Vaughn Meader, the impersonator who became rich and famous in the early '60s imitating John F. Kennedy, blasted from the past, New England accent untarnished. Meader, who is now doing skin flicks with Linda Lovelace, came attired in a lion tamer's outfit. Completing the gent's costume were two young ladies, bodies painted yellow and black in leopard fashion. G-strings girded their loins, pasties their breasts, and pipe cleaners protruded from their noses and heads.

Quite a spectacle! But on to the Ball where the hoi polloi quadrupled to fill the longshoreman's geodesic hall to the rafters. At least one thousand friends of hookers came to ball with the hookers, regardless of the $10 admission fee. Those who couldn't afford the price of admission were admitted free.

outfits for unofficial use, but for the Hooker's Ball we'll do it."

Margo St. James floated throughout the crowd during the evening, beaming and looking every inch a madam in a satin burgundy dress that would grace any house along the Barbary coast.

Towards the end of the Foreplay Party, St. James said a few words about *Coyote*'s efforts to decriminalize prostitution and the incredible amount of tax dollars vice squad arrests cost San Franciscans, and mentioned her favorite slogan, "No Hippo-Critters allowed." St. James singled out for praise two black hookers in leotards who had been particularly helpful organizing the ball and doing other work for *Coyote*.

It was the queens, however, who stole the show. "Once again it was proven," a harlot reported, "that men end up on top."

As far as Paul Krassner's stance on the issue, Krassner, the editor and Zen bastard of *The Realist* who joined St.

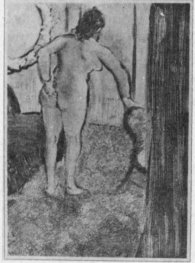

Illustration by Edgar Degas for the De Maupassant story "MADAME TELLIER'S BROTHEL"

Harriette Wilson, famous upper class London whore of the early nineteenth century.
From FILLE DE JOIE. Copyright © 1967 by Grove Press, Inc. Reprinted by permission of Grove Press, Inc.

True to promise, the Ball was the "social event of the year" for heterosexuals, bisexuals, trisexuals, transsexuals, asexuals, and I guess that about covers it.

The balconies were filled with TV and film cameras shooting the writhing mass below. Dr. Hook and the Medicine Show opened the show with a song Shel Silverstein wrote about hookers.

There was a Big Bar and a small bar. There was a table about twenty feet long where *Coyote* T-shirts, buttons, and other memorabilia were sold. The dance floor seemed to go on for miles. The stage formed a wall above the heads of dancers.

Coyote yells pervaded the air as the parade of costumes moved about the exposition-sized hall. Even Mardi Gras was never like this. The belly dancers and bands were good entertainment, while the greatest entertainment of all was provided by the people who came to ball with the hookers. A good ball was had by all.

The Nightless City
or the History of the
Yoshiwara Yūkwaku
by J. E. DE BECKER

不夜城 （吉原遊廓） J・E・デベッカー著

Cover of 1971 reprint of THE NIGHTLESS CITY. Charles E. Tuttle Company, Rutland, Vermont, and Tokyo, Japan.

Translation of parents' consent for their daughter to become a prostitute in pre-twentieth century Japan (From THE NIGHTLESS CITY)

Name of the girl.........................

Age.....................

This.........................(name) residing at.....................

daughter of.....................you....................., owner of.....................

brothel, agree to take into your employ for.................years at the

price of.................ryō.

.................ryō you retain as "mizu-kin".................ryō,

the balance, I have received.

I guarantee that the girl will not cause you trouble while in your

employ.

She is of the.................sect, her ancestral temple being the

.................in....................street.

Parents' name .... (SEAL.)

Guarantor .... (SEAL.)

Landlord .... (SEAL.)

.............................Name of "teishu."

.............................″joroya.″

.........................being now prepared to practice as a prostitute, I am very much obliged to you for your kind consent to my request to guarantee the agreement. Under these circumstances, I promise that I will respect and observe the said agreement and not cause you any trouble whatsoever. When it is necessary to sign and seal papers filed with the proper authorities in connection with the practice of prostitution, I beg that you will kindly sign and seal the same, and that you will, when necessary, sign and seal the documents *re* additional loans as attorney for..............., and kindly guarantee the repayment of the said loans. I further request that you will look after her in all matters affecting her interests while engaged in the business of prostitution. If you act as above, the principal party will never act contrary to your directions, and.............too will raise no objections.

In witness whereof, I have hereby drawn up this letter of request and signed and sealed the same hereunder.

Dated.............................

(Signature)..............................

Standard request by prospective prostitute to brothel keeper in pre-twentieth century Japan. From The Nightless City, or The History of the Yoshiwara Yukwaku *by J. E. De Becker, published in Yokohama anonymously in 1899.*

Map of the Yoshiwara, Tokyo's celebrated red light district as it existed in 1899 (From THE NIGHTLESS CITY)

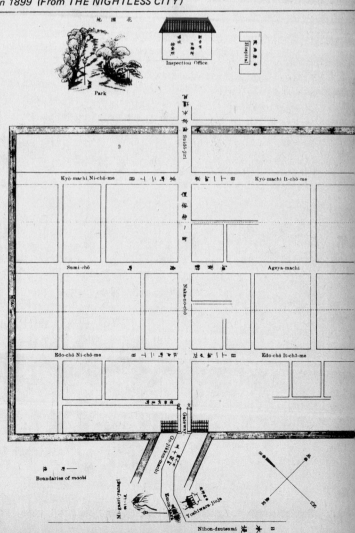

Everleigh, who with her sister Ada, comprised the most famous team of madams in the history of Chicago. A celebrated nude statue from their original house is now in possession of The Gaslight Club in Chicago. Its buttocks were used by thousands of customers to light matches.
From FILLE DE JOIE. Copyright © 1967 by Grove Press, Inc. Reprinted by permission of Grove Press, Inc.

Best-Known Bordellos

Anonymous eighteenth century French engraving

*I*n the United States, prostitution is legal only in certain counties in the state of Nevada . . . To avoid confusion in Las Vegas (where it is not legal), the police issue working show girls special i.d. cards so that if they are stopped walking along the streets while in their full stage make-up between shows they will not be mistaken for members of the oldest profession.

The following is a guide to the best-known legal bordellos in the country.

STARLIGHT GUEST RANCH
East on Highway 50 from Carson City, Lyon County.

Located in trailers behind a chain-link fence (press bell for admittance), this house is open 24 hours with 6 to 9 nice young girls available at most times. No liquor available. The prices are $10.00 for a straight lay. $15.00 for a half/half. If you are interested ask about other specialties. Telephone number (702) 882-9812.

MOONLIGHT GUEST RANCH
East on Highway 50 from Carson City, Lyon County.

This purple building located behind a chain-link fence is open 24 hours. No liquor available. There are from 5 to 7 young girls for your pleasure to choose from. A $10.00 bill should get you laid. Telephone number (702) 882-9901.

KIT KAT GUEST RANCH
East on Highway 50 from Carson City, Lyon County.

Located in a permanent red building at the bottom of the hill, this house is open 24 hours. Press bell on chain-link fence for admittance. There are 5 to 8 girls on duty at any one time with the prices starting at $10.00. No liquor available. Telephone number (702) 882-9975.

SAGEBRUSH GUEST RANCH
East on Highway 50 from Carson City, Lyon County.

This house is one of the hardest to find. The easiest method is to use your odometer, from the center of Dayton to the turnoff is 5.2 miles, turn to your left, the road is red gravel. In the daytime you can see the sign "Six Mile Canyon Road." There are from 5 to 6 girls available, with the prices starting at $10.00 for a straight lay. No liquor available. Telephone number (702) 882-9999.

TOWN HOUSE GUEST RANCH
Wabuska on Highway 95 Alt., Lyon County.

Located in a permanent building just off the highway on the south side of the railroad tracks. Open from 10:00 a.m. to 3:00 a.m., 7 days a week. There are 4 to 7 young women available, with the prices starting at $10.00 for a straight lay,

$15.00 for a half/half. As a special attraction, this house has a Mirror Room; except for the floor this room is completely covered with mirrors. The price starts at $25.00, but you will get more than your money's worth. Telephone (702) 463-3150.

GREEN FRONT
Hawthorn, Mineral County

Located just 2 blocks off Highway 95, this house has 2 to 3 women available, with liquor served at the bar. This house has no set hours of operation and no telephone number.

LUCKY STRIKE
Mina, Mineral County.

Follow the directions in the map for this house, as there is only one street crossing the tracks. This house is located in a permanent building, open from 12 noon to 2:00 a.m. Liquor is available at the bar as are other beverages. There are 3 to 4 girls to choose from with as many as 6 in the summer months. Rates start at $10.00. There are films available for viewing with the girl upon occasion. Telephone number (702) 573-9991.

SILVER PRINCESS
Basalt, Junction of Highway 6 and end of Highway 10, Mineral County.

This house is located in trailers at the end of Highway 10. Open 2:00 p.m. to 4:00 a.m. Monday thru Friday and 2:00 p.m. to 5:00 a.m. on Saturdays, Sundays 3:00 p.m. to 12:00 midnight. No liquor available. There are 3 to 5 women with the ages running from 21 to 40 available. The prices start at $10.00 for a straight lay. No telephone service in this part of the country.

BOBBY'S BUCKEYE BAR
East 1 Mile on Highway 6 from Downtown Tonopah, Nye County.

Permanent building with attached trailers. Open from 2:00 p.m. to 2:00 a.m. Liquor and other beverages available at a very nice bar. The number of girls varies but 4 to 5 to choose from at any one time is average. The prices start at $10.00 for a straight lay. $15.00 for a half/half. Telephone number (702) 482-6274.

COTTONTAIL RANCH
Highway 95 at Junction of Nevada 3, Nye County.

Now open 24 hours, with 4 to 7 young women to choose from. Liquor and other beverages available at a small bar. Movies, *etc.* available at a reasonable price. Prices for the girls start at $10.00 for a straight lay, but remember you get what you pay for. (This house is currently involved in a civil rights investigation, charged with refusing a black patron via the public accommodations law.) Telephone number 702 and ask operator for Lida Junction No. 2.

FRAN'S STAR RANCH
3 miles North of Beatty on Highway 95, Nye County.

This house has recently changed owners and name (was VICKIE STAR RANCH). The house, a modest wooden build-

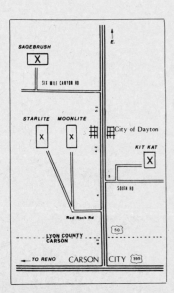

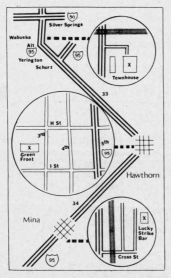

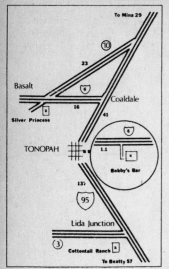
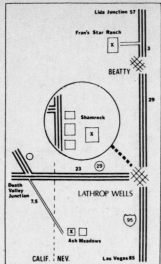
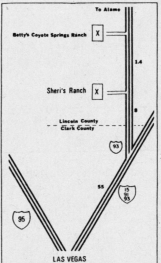
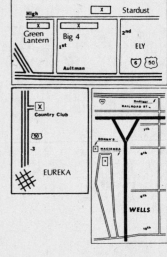

ing ¼ mile off the highway, can be seen from the highway. There is a sign at the entrance. Now open 24 hours, but liquor still not available. There is an airstrip for daylight landings in front of the house, but construction work is underway to make it available for night landings. The Beatty Airport, located 3 miles south of town, is also available. There are 4 to 6 young girls available with the prices starting at $10.00, depending on your special wants. Telephone number (702) 553-9986.

ASH MEADOWS SKY RANCH
7½ miles from Death Valley Junction, Nye County.

Now reopened and under new owners and managers, this house has 6 to 10 very young girls to serve you, with the prices the same as in most of the state. Open 24 hours. The girls are located in a separate building which has been redecorated for your pleasure, especially the Chinese Basket Room. Across the patio and swimming pool are the bar and restaurant. Equipped with a pool table, slots, etc., this house also has a separate 20-unit motel, camper facilities, horses, with a 9-hole golf course and trap shooting range under construction. Airstrip information: lighted, all weather, elevation 2,215 feet, 3,300-foot-long runway. Radio frequency 122.8 monitored 24 hours a day. Both aviation and auto gas available. 18 minutes by air from Las Vegas. The map indicates the easiest way to this house with good pavement most of the way, the remaining ¾ mile being worked on. Telephone (702) 372-9993.

SHAMROCK
Located in the Crossroads of Lathrop Well, Nye County.

Housed in a permanent building partially surrounded by shrubbery. Open from 4:00 p.m. to around 3:00 a.m. No liquor available. There are 2 to 5 women available, with prices starting around $10.00. No telephone number listed.

SHERI'S RANCH
Highway 93, 63 miles north of Las Vegas, Lincoln County.

It's just over an hour's drive to Sheri's Ranch from Las Vegas. As prostitution is illegal in Clark County (Las Vegas), this house is located 8 miles inside the Lincoln County Line.

Taxi fare from Las Vegas, including waiting time and return is about $50.00. You can also charter a plane, as this house has a private airstrip which is the only lighted strip in the county. Airstrip information: elevation 2,500 feet. Runway length 2,700 feet. Buzz for night landings and light will be turned on.

This house started out a few years ago in a trailer but now is housed in many permanent buildings. Equipped with a full service bar, including a pool table. Also for your enjoyment a swimming pool for parties, and horses. Movies and similar entertainment also available. Prices start at a modest $10.00. There are 14 to 16 young girls available, with 8 to 10 to choose from at any one time. Open 24 hours. There is no telephone service in this part of the country, but this house has an answering service in Las Vegas (702) 385-4131.

BETTY'S COYOTE SPRINGS RANCH
Highway 95, 64 miles north of Las Vegas, Lincoln County.

Just a short 1¼ mile north of Sheri's Ranch, this house specializes in its VIP treatment of clients. The main salon is beautifully decorated and carpeted to complement the beautiful young girls, of which there are 8 to 10 to choose from, and there is no rush for you to make a choice. Open 24 hours. The prices are the same as most in the state. Liquor and other beverages available. No telephone number.

STARLIGHT
Ely, White Pine County.

Located at 190 High Street. This house is open 24 hours, and is clean. Liquor and other beverages are sold at the bar. There are 5 girls available, with the prices starting around $10.00 for a straight lay. Specialties like movies sometimes available. Telephone number (702) 289-4330.

BIG 4
First and High Streets.

Don't let this old building scare you away. Open 24 hours. Liquor served at the long bar. There are 6 to 8 young women for your pleasure, with the prices starting at $10.00 which is a house minimum for a straight lay. Telephone number (702) 289-2446.

GREEN LANTERN
Ely, White Pine County.

95 High Street. Open 24 hours. This building burned down last fall but is now operating temporarily out of house trailers. Bar serves liquor and other drinks. There are between 4 to 6 girls available, with the prices starting at $10.00 which is also the house minimum. Telephone number (702) 289-4382.

COUNTRY CLUB
¼ mile east of Eureka on Highway 50, Eureka County.

TEMPORARILY CLOSED. This house is in a permanent building with attached trailers. The house is in a very rundown condition, broken sign, etc. Phone number (702) 237-9903.

DONNA'S
Wells, Elko County.

Permanent building open 24 hours. Liquor and beer available at the bar. The address is 685 8th Street (see map). There are 5 to 7 girls available for your pleasure from 12:00 noon to 2:00 a.m., at other times 2 or 3 girls are still awake. A $10.00 bill will get you laid by one of the swinging young girls who are in abundance at this house. Telephone (702) 752-9959.

HACIENDA
Wells, Elko County.

Permanent building open 24 hours. For admittance ring bell on side of door. The address is 619 8th Street. 5 to 6 girls on duty from noon to 2:00 a.m., at other times 2 to 3 girls. Rates start at $10.00. Liquor and other beverages are available. Telephone number (702) 752-9914.

TONI'S CLASSY INN
Elko, Elko County.

Permanent building located at 357 Douglas Street. Open 24 hours with liquor available at the bar. 5 to 6 girls available during the day and early evening, at other times 2 to 3. Rates start at $10.00 for a straight lay and up. Telephone number (702) 738-9529.

SUE'S BAR
Elko, Elko County.

Permanent building located at 319 Douglas Street, but the entrance is around the corner at S. 3rd Street. Liquor is available, and this house is open 24 hours a day. There are 5 girls available most of the time, and the prices start at $10.00, depending on what you want. Telephone number (702) 738-9391.

PAT'S M & L
Elko, Elko County.

Permanent building located at 232 S. 3rd Street, open from noon to 3:00 or 4:00 a.m. Depending on the amount of business, 3 to 4 girls is average for any one time. Prices are the same as most houses. Telephone number (702) 738-9433.

ROSE'S LUCKY STRIKE
Elko, Elko County.

This house is located at 246 S. 3rd Street in a permanent building, which is open 24 hours. Liquor and other beverages are available at the bar. 4 to 5 women on duty most of the time. $10.00 for a straight lay. Telephone number (702) 738-9433.

BETTY'S D & D
Elko, Elko County.

Open 24 hours at 103 S. 3rd Street in a permanent building. Liquor is available at the bar in the back. Ring bell for admittance. 4 to 5 girls around at all times to serve you. Rates start at $10.00 for a straight lay. Telephone number (702) 738-9496.

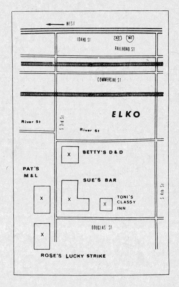

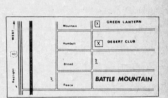

DESERT CLUB
Battle Mountain, Lander County.

Permanent building open 24 hours. (Ring bell before 2:00 p.m. and after 2:00 a.m.) Liquor is available at the bar inside the front door from 2:00 p.m. to 2:00 a.m. The number of girls varies between 4 and 7 depending on the season. A straight lay is $5.00 and up if you feel like bargaining about the price. Telephone number is (702) 635-9952.

GREEN LANTERN
Battle Mountain, Lander County.

Permanent old building open 24 hours a day. (Ring bell at door from 2:00 a.m. to noon.) There are 4 to 5 girls from which to make a choice. You can get laid for as little as $5.00 if you play it cool as to how much money you can afford to spend. Telephone number (702) 635-9948.

MY PLACE
Winnemucca, Humboldt County.

Now under new management in a permanent building. Liquor is served. The house is open from 3:00 p.m. to 3:00 a.m. on weekdays and to 5:00 a.m. on Fridays and Saturdays. The prices start at $10.00 with 4 to 5 girls on hand.

PLAYERS' CLUB
Winnemucca, Humboldt County.

Permanent building. Liquor and other beverages served. Hours are the same in all the houses in Winnemucca. There are 5 to 6 girls available with prices starting at $10.00. Telephone number (702) 623-9927.

VILLA JOY
Winnemucca, Humboldt County.

This clean house where liquor and other beverages are available has 5 or 6 young girls, with the prices starting at $10.00 for a straight lay. Telephone number (702) 623-9903.

IRENE'S
Winnemucca, Humboldt County.

This house has from 4 to 5 young girls and other women to choose from most of the time. Liquor is available at the bar. The prices start at $10.00 for a straight lay and $15.00 for a half/half. Telephone (702) 623-9939.

COZY CORNER
Winnemucca, Humboldt County.

A nice permanent building with a bar, 5 to 7 girls available at any one time. Prices start at $10.00. This house is different in that the girls are very well trained in pleasure making and you always get your money's worth. This house does not treat you in an assembly-line manner as do a few other houses in the state. You can sit and drink with the girls without being rushed to the bedroom before you are ready to go. Telephone (702) 623-9959.

LA BELLA'S
Lovelock, Pershing County.

This house is located at 140 9th Street and is open 24 hours a day, but the bar closes at 3:00 a.m. For entrance ring bell at the side of the door. There are 5 to 7 girls available for your enjoyment at any one time. The prices start at $10.00 and up depending on your pleasure. This house is very clean and quiet with very agreeable young women. Telephone (702) 273-9907.

MONTEREY BAR
Lovelock, Pershing County.

This house is located just a few blocks from La Bella's at 660 Amhurst, open from 12:00 noon to 2:00 a.m. with liquor and other beverages available. It was closed until recently but has reopened with 2 to 4 girls working the bar. Prices start at under $10.00 if you care to bargain with the girls. Telephone number (702) 273-9902.

ROADHOUSE
2.6 miles east of Lovelock on Highway 80, Pershing County.

This is the newest house to open in Nevada, and is fronted by a permanent building with trailers in back. Open from 10:00 a.m. till 5:00 a.m. Liquor and beer available at the bar, pool table, etc., There are 3 girls available, with the prices starting at $10.00. Telephone number (702) 273-9901.

MUSTANG BRIDGE RANCH
7 Miles east of Reno at the Mustang turn-off, Storey County.

Follow the red arrows after leaving the freeway until you cross the one-lane bridge. Surrounded by a fence, this plush pleasure house is the closest one to Reno (Washoe County) where prostitution is illegal. There are 20 to 30 girls available, with the house minimum starting at $10.00. Open 24 hours, you can get anything you could possibly want at the price. This house uses assembly-line style arrangements between clients and girls.

Please note that all prices are subject to change due to inflation.

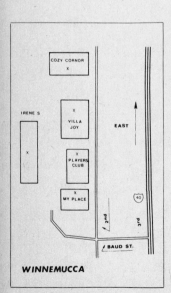

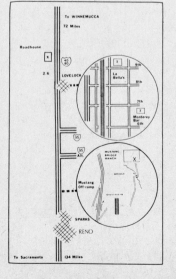

The French Aretino *by Borel Engraving, 1787*

Fun and games in a Denver whorehouse. From FILLE DE JOIE Copyright © 1967 by Grove Press, Inc. Reprinted by permission of Grove Press, Inc.

A Note on Massage Parlors

Rather than become entangled in a semantic maze as to whether or not massage parlors belong in the category of prostitution, we will allude to them here, since they are an important segment of the sexual marketplace, and contribute their fair share to the gross national product. Since there is a great deal of opening, closing, and shifting of locations, it would be impossible to provide a concise directory of parlors around the country. In The Sexual Bazaar section, however, we will include among the product ads information on some of the more established parlors currently in operation.

And then there is Xaviera. . .
but really, need we say any more about her?

Scene from the set of a motion picture, The Massage Parlor Hookers, depicting the typical waiting room in a massage parlor.
Photo by B.J. Hurwood. Reproduced courtesy of Cinemid Film Productions, Inc.

Illustration by
Edgar Degas for the
De Maupassant story
"MADAME TELLIER'S
BROTHEL"

A Brothel for Women Only

The name Mary Wilson doesn't ring bells any more, but take it from us, some of the things she advocated back in 1824—that's right, 1824—would sound avant garde today. If you don't believe it, just read on. Miss Wilson, it seems, had concocted a plan to promote "Adultery on the part of married women, and fornication on the part of old maids and widows." She addressed her plan to "the ladies of the metropolis and its environs," and it consisted of an "Eleusinian institution to which any lady of rank and fortune may subscribe, and to which she may repair *incog*; the married to commit what the world calls adultery, and the single to commit what at the tabernacle is termed fornication, or in gentler phrase, to obey the dictates of all-powerful Nature, by offering up a cheerful sacrifice to the God Priapus, the most ancient of all deities. I have purchased very extensive premises, which are situated between two great thoroughfares, and are entered from each by means of shops, devoted entirely to such trades as are exclusively resorted to by ladies. In the area between the two rows of houses I have erected a most elegant temple, in the centre of which are large saloons, entirely surrounded with boudoirs most elegantly and commodiously fitted up. In these saloons, according to their classes, are to be seen the finest men of their species I can procure, occupied in whatever amusements are adapted to their taste, and all kept in a high state of excitement by good living and idleness. The ladies will never enter the saloons even in their masks, but view their inmates from a darkened window in each boudoir. In one they will see fine, elegantly dressed young men, playing at cards, music, *etc.*—in others athletic men wrestling or bathing, in a state of perfect nudity—in short they will see such a variety of the animal, that they fail of suiting their inclinations. Having fixed upon one she should like to enjoy, the lady has only to ring for the chamber maid, call her to the window, point out the object, and he is immediately brought to the boudoir. She can enjoy him in the dark, or have a light, and keep on her mask. She can stay an hour or a night, and have one or a dozen men as she pleases, without being known to any of them. A lady of 70 or 80 years of age can at pleasure enjoy a fine robust youth of 20, and to elevate the mind to the sublimest raptures of love, every boudoir is surrounded with the most superb paintings of Aretino's Postures after Julio Romano and Ludovico Carracci, interspersed with large mirrors: also a sideboard covered with the most delicious viands and richest wines. The whole expense of the institution is defrayed by a subscription from each lady of one hundred guineas per annum, with the exception of the refreshments which are to be paid for at the time.

The greatest possible pains have been taken to preserve order and regularity and it is impossible that any discovery can take place by the intrusion of police or enraged cuckolds, as will be demonstrated to every lady before she pays her subscription, and as is more fully detailed in the private prospectus to be had of Madame de Gomez, the subdirectress at the institution, who will also furnish them with a catalogue of the most extensive collection of bawdy books in French, Italian, and English which have ever been collected, and which I have purchased at the expense of £2000 for the use of my patronesses. The different saloons have been decorated by one of the first painters of the age, with designs from Mr. Payne Knight's work on the ancient worship of Priapus, which renders them one of the most singular exhibitions in Europe. No male creature is admitted into any part of the temple but the saloons, and those only the trusty tried and approved functionaries, who are well paid for their services, and not let in to gratify curiosity. Having thus made it my study to serve my own sex in a most essential point, I trust to their liberality for encouragement in my undertaking; and am, Ladies, your most obedient Servant, *Mary Wilson . . .*"

Bibliography

Adler, Polly. *A House Is Not a Home.* New York: Rinehart, 1953.

Beck, Robert [Iceberg Slim]. *Pimp: The Story of My Life.* Los Angeles: Holloway House, 1969. $1.50

Benjamin, Harry, and Masters, R.E.L. *The Prostitute in Society.* London: Mayflower, 1966.

——. *Prostitution and Morality.* New York: Julian Press, 1964.

Bloch, Iwan. *Sexual Life in England.* London: 1958.

Bullough, V.L. *The History of Prostitution.* New York: University Books, 1964.

Cleland, John. *Fanny Hill: Memoirs of a Woman of Pleasure.* New York: G. P. Putnam's Sons, 1963.

Ellis, Albert, and Sagarin, E. *Nymphomania: A Study of the Oversexed Woman.* New York: Manor Books, 1965. 75¢

Fille de Joie. New York: Grove Press. 1967. $25.00

Fitzpatrick, William. *Tokyo After Dark.* New York: Macfadden-Bartell Corp.,1965.

Greenwald, Harold. *The Call Girl.* New York: Ballantine Books, 1960.

——. *The Elegant Prostitute.* New York: Ballantine Books, 1973. $1.95

Greenwald, Harold, and Krich, Aron, eds. *Prostitute in Literature.* New York: Ballantine Books, 1969.

Hall, Susan. *A Gentleman of Leisure: A Year in the Life of a Pimp.* New York: New American Library, 1972. $12.95

Hinkel, Ida and Unger, Madeline. *Hooker.* New York: Dell Books, 1974. $1.50

Hollander, Xaviera. *The Happy Hooker.* New York: Dell Books, 1972. $1.50

——. *Letters to the Happy Hooker.* New York: Paperback Library, 1973. $1.50

——. *Xaviera Goes Wild!* New York: Paperback Library,1974. $1.50

Hurwood, Bernhardt J. *The Girls, the Massage, and Everything.* New York: Fawcett,Gold Medal, 1973. $1.25

Lacroix, Paul. *History of Prostitution Among All the Peoples of the World, from the Most Remote Antiquity to the Present Day 2 vols.* Reprint. New York: AMS, 1975. $80.00

[Larry The Silver Fox.] *My Life with Xaviera.* New York: Warner Paperback Library, 1974. $1.50

McManus, Virginia. *Not For Love.* New York: G. P. Putnam's Sons, 1960.

Millet, Kate. *The Prostitution Papers.* New York: Avon, 1973. $1.25

Parent-Duchatelet, Alexandre Jean Baptiste. *Prostitution in Paris.* Reprint. New York: AMS, 1975. $11.00

Ralph, C. H., ed. *Women of the Streets.* London: British Social Biology Council, 1955.

Robbins, Jhan. *The Anatomy of a Prostitute.* New York: New American Library, 1972.

Saikaku, Ihara. *The Life of an Amorous Woman.* New York: UNESCO New Directions Publishing Corporation, 1963.

Sanger, William Wallace. *The History of Prostitution.* Reprint. New York: AMS, 1975. $21.50

Scott, George Ryley. *A History of Prostitution from Antiquity to the Present Day.* Reprint. New York: AMS, 1975. $15.00

Stein, L. Martha. *Friends, Lovers & Slaves.* New York: Berkley, 1973. $8.95

Winick, Charles, and Kinsic, Paul. *The Lively Commerce: Prostitution in the United States.* New York: Quadrangle, 1971. $8.95

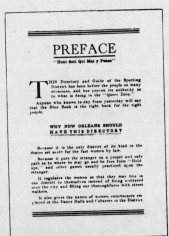

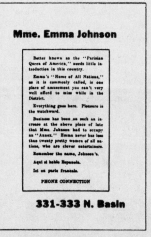

Actual pages from the famous New Orleans Bluebook *which was a guide to prostitution in that city.*
From FILLE DE JOIE Copyright © 1967 by Grove Press, Inc. Reprinted by permission of Grove Press, Inc.

Brass statue of the goddess Kali in intercourse with the corpse form of Shiva. Eighteenth century

Sex, Mysticism, Religion, and the Supernatural

Deities, Demons, Witches, and Sexy Spirits

ong, long ago, when man was very young, and the moon was still mistress of the night skies, the earth was a wondrous place filled with gods, demons, sorcerers, and djinns. Miracles were real, and magicians accomplished stupendous feats. There was no pollution, no smog, no nuclear sword of Damocles dangling over the green fields and blue seas. Best of all, there were no Kremlins or Pentagons where sleep was forbidden to enter. Although darkness provided cover for terrors and evils, it also afforded protection for lovers, who did the same things by the dying embers of fires that they do now in centrally heated apartments.

As the most intelligent of beasts, man soon learned a great deal about his environment; he built shelters and became the master of fire. He also began forming ideas about the sun, the moon, and the stars. But one mystery completely baffled him—the mystery of life itself and the knowledge that he could reproduce himself. This was the greatest miracle of all, and it stood to reason that everything surrounding this miracle was steeped in magic and the supernatural.

Recognizing himself as part of the overall tapestry of nature, man fit his own sexuality into the pattern with no difficulty. Human fertility was obviously related to the fertility of fields. Spring was a time of renewal and rebirth. Therefore, it became a season dominated by deities related to fertility. Since human fertility was related to love and lust, then logic dictated the facts. Love, fertility, sexuality, springtime—all were somehow mystically related, and over the centuries, beliefs became more complex, more interrelated, and more sophisticated.

The sex organs, looked on as objects of pride, were frequently venerated because of the powerful magic surrounding them. Consequently ancient artists, in depicting the uncovered body, depicted it as it was. Marble genitals were not smashed and replaced with sexless figleaves until guilt-ridden Europeans arrived on the scene to wield their righteous hammers.

The most universal ancient use of artificial human genitalia, however, was not primarily artistic. The chief function of these artifacts was religio-magical. It was accepted that the genitalia exerted powerful influences when called on properly. The male influenced fertility, and the female afforded protection against evil. The reasoning behind this was perfectly understandable. These were the portions of the anatomy which, when used properly, brought pleasure and ultimately recreated

life. Obviously, if they possessed such powerful forces that new life resulted, they must have salutary effect elsewhere in nature. Hence the origin of genital amulets to ward off all evil.

Among those figurines to have survived the ravages of time and Victorian outrage are the less-than-familiar *Shelah-na-gigs* of Ireland. Often hideous and threatening in appearance, many have glaring eyes, bared teeth, and bony, deathlike ribcages. What they all have in common are spread thighs and gaping vulvas of cavernous proportions. Originating in pre-Christian times, they remained popular over the centuries, eventually to adorn churches and other buildings as amulets against the evil eye and other occult perils. Of course, the Irish were not the only ones to employ such objects, and similar artifacts can be found throughout Europe.

The interrelationship of sex and religion in the ancient world was so extensive that one can elaborate on only a few of the more interesting aspects of it. A well-known illustration is the frequently quoted description by Herodotus of ancient Babylonian temple prostitution. In it he describes how women would prostitute themselves to the first man who offered them a piece of silver within the sacred precincts of the temple of Ishtar. He erroneously calls the goddess *Mylitta*, a name that probably stems from the even more ancient Akkadian *Mu'allitu*, meaning "the one who brings forth," which was one of the many titles given to the goddess.

Lesser known Babylonian texts, dating back to nearly 2000 B.C., tell of a sacred, ritual marriage between the king as the incarnate deity, and a priestess representing the fertility goddess. During the ceremony, the priestess is adorned with ornaments of gold, silver, carnelian, and ivory. Statues of the goddess were similarly decorated, the most prominent feature being a golden vulva. In one of these texts the priestess sang a love song to the king, which went as follows:

I will open my bosom,
When he shall have made love to me on the bed.
Then I shall in turn show my love for my lord!
I shall fix for him a good destiny . . .
I shall fix for him as destiny
To be the shepherd of the land.

The first peoples to look askance at sex in religious observances were the Egyptians and the Hebrews, especially the Hebrews. In the course of spreading the doctrine of monotheism they tended to downgrade the gods of their neighbors,

Shelah-na-gig carvings from ancient Irish churches illustrating the pre-Christian concept that a display of the genitalia was a powerful charm against evil.

especially those gods displaying overt sexuality. It was the Hebrew attitude toward the alleged sinfulness of others that gave Christianity its initial antisexual bias. The result was at times almost ludicrous. *The Song of Solomon*, which contains probably the most explicitly erotic passages in the Old Testament, was interpreted by Christian theologians as representing Christ's love for the church. Nothing could have been further from the truth. The sensual King Solomon, who had 700 wives and 300 concubines, is hardly likely to have anticipated either the coming of Christ or the foundation of a church by his followers. Consider the following excerpt from Chapter 8.

How beautiful are thy feet with shoes,
O prince's daughter.
The joints of thy thighs are like jewels,
the work of the hands of a cunning workman.
Thy navel is a round goblet, which wanteth not liquor;
Thy belly is like an heap of wheat set about with lilies.
Thy two breasts are like two young roses that are twins.
Thy neck is a tower of ivory, thine eyes like the fish pools in Heshbon, by the gate of Bath-rabbim;
Thy nose is as the tower of Lebanon which looketh toward Damascus.
Thine head upon thee is like Carmel, and the hair on thy head like purple.
The king is held in thy galleries.
How fair and how pleasant art thou, O love, for delights.

A fascinating aspect of pre-Christian fertility customs, or phallic worship, is the background to the celebration of Easter, and the custom of eating fish on Friday. The ancient Babylonian goddess Ishtar, mentioned earlier, was essentially the same entity to all ancient peoples, regardless of the name she was known by: Isis, Aphrodite, Venus, or Astarte. Friday was her sacred day, and the fish, one of the most universal sex symbols of all, was frequently consecrated to her on that day, and eaten by her worshippers, who afterwards practiced public phallic rites. The early Christians merely incorporated some of the spring fertility festival rites into Easter. The name itself derives from the name of the goddess Astarte.

Another transformation was that of the pagan satyr. To Romans the satyr was at best a lower-echelon supernatural creature, a carefree, sylvan exurbanite who spent all his time frolicking in the wood with nymphs, gobbling grapes, guzzling wine, and attending orgies. He was probably the prime symbol of Roman wish/fantasy-fulfillment. To early Christians, however, the satyr represented the mythology of a civilization that to them was hostile, and therefore sinful. He certainly characterized sensuality of the highest degree, and represented the antithesis of the Pauline doctrine that "The body is not for fornication, but for the Lord." So what did the Christians do to this harmless forest hedonist? They used him as the physical prototype for their devil, the archenemy of God and man, the personification of all evil.

A gathering of witches. Sixteenth century woodcut

Early woodcut showing woman disrespectful toward a lascivious devil

But before we become too involved with sex and Christianity as it developed in the West, we should go back in time and look briefly at some of the concepts in other parts of the world and their occasional links to Western culture.

Vampires and vampirelike demons have always been inextricably involved with sex. The ancient Babylonian demon, Lilitu, evolved in Hebrew folklore to become Lilith. According to Talmudic legends she was Adam's first wife, and as punishment for failing to obey him she was banished from the Garden of Eden and doomed to spend all eternity as a flying, blood-sucking demon of the night. It was she who caused men to have lascivious dreams and nocturnal emissions, and later the Christians came to regard her as the queen of the incubi and succubi (seductive demons we will discuss further on). The Greeks had a similar demon called the lamia. She had the breasts and head of a woman and the body of a winged serpent. She came into Roman lore as the strix (plural *strigae*), from whose name the Italian word *strega,* or witch, derived.

Among the Greeks and Romans, strigae, lamiae, satyrs, and sileni (highly sexed and drunken woods spirits) were continually engaging in sexual frolics, not to mention the gods and goddesses who periodically engaged in sexual liaisons with humans—all of which were accepted as part of the general state of life.

The sexual element in ancient India was immensely important as we can see today from the numerous erotic sculptures still in existence on many temples. The philosophical and religious complexities are far too complex to treat in depth here; however, a brief extract from an obscure nineteenth century book called *Annotations on the Sacred Writings of the Hindus,* by English scholar Edward Sellon, seems appropriate.

"It is a singular fact [writes Sellon], that upon this adoration of the procreative and sexual Sacti (or power) seen throughout nature, hinges the whole gist of the Hindu faith, and notwithstanding all that has been said by half-informed persons to the contrary, the puja (wor-

ship) does not appear to be prejudicial to the morals of the people [a typical Victorian apology]."

Describing the sect of the *Kauchiluas* and the *Nautch* women, Sellon writes, "On the occasions of the performance of divine worship, the women and girls deposit their Julies or Boddices [sic] in a box in charge of the Guru or priest. At the close of the rites, the male worshippers take a Julie from the box, and the female to whom it belongs, even were she his sister, becomes his partner for the evening in these lascivious orgies [again making a Victorian value judgement]. Dancing formed an important part of the ceremonial worship of most Eastern peoples. . . .And to every temple of any importance in India we find a troop of Nautch, or dancing girls.

"These women are generally procured when quite young, and are early initiated into all the mysteries of their profession. They are instructed in dancing and vocal and instrumental music, their chief employment being to chant the sacred hymns and perform nautches [dances] before the god, on the recurrence of high festivals. This is not the only service required of them, for besides being the acknowledged mistresses of the officiating priests, it is their duty to prostitute themselves in the courts of the temple to all comers, and thus raise funds for the enrichment of the place of worship to which they belong.

"Being always women of considerable personal attractions, which are heightened by all the seductions of dress, jewels, accomplishments in art, they frequently receive large sums in return for the favours they grant, and fifty, one hundred, and even two hundred rupees have been known to be paid to these syrens [sic] in one night. Nor is this very much to be wondered at as they comprise among their number perhaps some of the lovliest women in the world."

A later section of Sellon's book refers to the customs of some other sects. He writes, "Another of their sects adore Krishna and his mistress Radha united. These are the Longionijas, whose worship is perhaps the most free of all the Pujas. A third, the Radha-ballubhis, dedicate their offerings to Radha only. The followers of these last-mentioned sects have adopted the singular practice of presenting to a naked girl the oblation intended for the goddess, constituting her the living impersonation of Radha. But when a female is not to be obtained for this purpose, the votive offerings are made to an image of the Yoni, or emblem of the feminine power. These worshippers are called Yonijas in contradistinction to the Lingayats or adorers of the Krishna (Vishnu) Linga."

The devil abducting a witch. Old woodcut

Perhaps even more revealing than the observations of a foreigner is the blessing which appears at the end of the *Ananga Ranga*, an Indian love manual lesser known than the *Kama Sutra* but considered by scholars to be one of the most poetical and lyrical ever written—not surprising, since it was authored by a poet, Kalyana-Mall. To quote from the great bibliographer, Henry Spencer Ashbee, "As he [Mall] assures his readers before parting, the object of the book, which opens with praises of the gods, is not to encourage chambering and wantonness, but simply and in all sincerity to prevent the separation of husband and wife." An ancient Alex Comfort, Mall, in Ashbee's words "would save them from the monotony and satiety which usually follows possession, by varying their pleasures in every conceivable way, and supplying them with the means of being physically pure and pleasant to each other."

Here is the poet's closing blessing: "May this treatise, *Ananga Ranga*, be beloved of man and woman, as long as the Holy River Ganges springs from Shiva and his wife Gauri on his left side, as long as Lakshmi loves Vishnu, as long as Bramha is engaged in the study of the Vedas, and as long as the earth, moon, and sun endure."

Quite different from the reverent attitude toward sex found in India and the other Eastern countries within its spiritual sphere of influence, China and Japan produced an entirely unique lore in regard to sex and the supernatural.

Some of the most popular legends from China, Japan, and Korea abound with romantic tales, often with the tragic ending of physical love affairs between humans and supernatural creatures. The most common of these are fox ladies. Unlike werewolves, fox ladies appear in human form and seduce

Hell depicted in an early European woodcut

Fifteenth century woodcut depicting amorous couple being led into fleshly sin by a devil

human males. When true love enters into the relationships, they often last for years and even produce half-fox, half-human offspring. When the fox lady (or badger lady, who pops up in Japanese tales) is malicious, the unfortunate human lover inevitably dies.

Sometimes we find in Chinese tales accounts of young men who have love affairs with ghosts. Prolonged affairs of this sort are almost always fatal, although in one classic story by P'u Sung Ling, an eighteenth century author known as "the last of the immortals," there is quite another change. The hero, one Sang, has an affair with both a ghost and a fox lady at the same time. The debilitating effect on his body is too much and he commences to waste away and die. Since both the fox lady and the ghost really love Sang, they join forces and nurse him back to health. The ghost is reborn, grows up and joins the two of them and all three live happily ever after in a ménage à trois.

Not all of P'u Sung Ling's tales have such happy endings. To quote from the book *Terror by Night* by Bernhardt J. Hurwood, "In other imaginative tales by P'u Sung Ling, assorted amorous Chinese girls change into such things as wasps and crows. In the story, "Ying Ning, the Laughing Girl," the heroine is not only the daughter of a fox but a rather accomplished sorceress. At one point in the story she rids herself of an unwanted suitor by creating an illusion of the type attributed to European witches in the *Malleus Maleficarum*. She lures him to an isolated part of her garden, which he assumes to be their trysting place. Instead of seizing the girl, he is bewitched into sexually assaulting an old tree trunk that has a hole with a scorpion inside. The results prove painful and fatal."

Sexually oriented sorcery is far from dead in the Far East; even today, quite recently a university-educated Chinese woman who grew up in Kuala Lumpur, Malaysia, told us how men from Thailand are greatly feared by mothers and fathers of attractive daughters. The Thais, it seems, are endowed with arcane supernatural powers that enable them to cast spells on any woman they desire, to lure them away for as long as they wish to have them. Some never return again, but those whose lovers weary of them are de-witched. Once freed of the spells they return to hearth and home.

And on the subject of sorcery, let us return again to Europe.

Although until as late as the seventeenth century, the woods were full of self-proplaimed witches and warlocks who did a thriving business in spells, love charms, potions, and curses, there were many times more who were burned for the crime of witchcraft because it was one of the easiest accusations to "prove" in court. This fact of life made it terribly easy for anyone with an axe to grind to permanently get rid of anyone they chose, for reasons ranging from political ambition and religious prejudice to sheer vengefulness. This was especially true of many victims of the Inquisition, not only in Spain, but throughout Europe.

Despite the presence of some bigoted scoundrels in the hierarchy of the church, the underlying motive behind all these persecutions was to stamp out heresy and to eliminate remaining vestiges of paganism.

For several centuries, one of the greatest problems confronting the church was the eradication of out-and-out phallic worship. It should be mentioned at this point that one of the Latin names applied by the ancient Romans to the penis was *fascinum*. The word was used primarily to describe phallic amulets, and from it we have derived our modern words *fascinate* and *fascination*. One of the surviving proofs that Christians continued to pay homage to the *fascinum* is found in an eighth century ecclesiastical edict: "If anyone has performed incantation to the *fascinum*, or any incantation whatsoever, except anyone who chants the creed or the Lord's prayer, let him do penance on bread and water during three Lents."

The persistence of the practice was such that 500 years later the Synod of Mans decreed severe punishment for any person". . . who has sinned to the *fascinum*, or has performed any other incantations . . .''

Drawing of the witches' Sabbat inspired by the writings of Pierre de Lancre.
From The Encyclopedia of Witchcraft and Demonology *by Rossell Hope Robbins.* © *1959 by Crown Publishers, Inc. Reprinted by permission of Crown Publishers, Inc.*

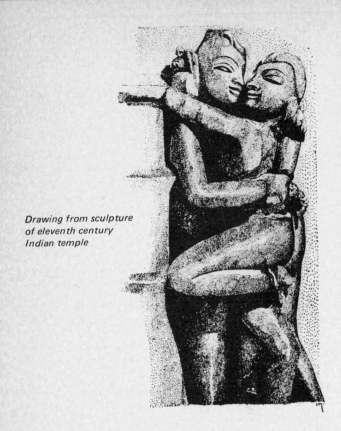

Drawing from sculpture
of eleventh century
Indian temple

Sometimes churchmen themselves were the sinners. In the *Chronicle of Lanercost* we read of what happened during Easter week in 1282 at Inverkeithing, known today as County Fife, Scotland. A parish priest by the name of John put up a wooden image of the pagan god Priapus in the town square. Then he led all the young girls of the town in a dance around the statue while he himself carried a large wooden phallus. He then "accompanied their songs with movements in accordance, and urged them on to licentious actions by his no less licentious language." For this Father John got himself into hot water with his bishop but defended himself on the grounds that he was only acting in accordance with local customs.

In France ancient phallic rites adapted to Christianity amid similar strains. Especially intriguing was the de facto conversion of the god Priapus from pagan deity to Christian saint. "In the south of France, Provence, Languedoc, and the Lyonnais," wrote Thomas Wright over a century ago, "he was worshipped under the title of St. Foutin. This name is said to be a mere corruption of Fontinum or Photinus, the first Bishop of Lyons, to whom, perhaps through giving a vulgar interpretation to the name, people had transferred the distinguishing attribute of Priapus. This was a large phallus of wood, which was an object of reverence to the women, especially to those who were barren, who scraped the wooden member and, having steeped the scrapings in water, they drank the latter as a remedy against their barrenness, or administered it to their husbands in the belief that it would make them vigorous."

Other phallic saints were worshipped elsewhere in France, Belgium, and Italy. In certain areas it was customary for brides to offer their virginity to the saint with the wooden phallus. It was a convenient way to avoid embarrassing explanations to a husband expecting a virgin. How could a pious man argue against his wife's devotion to a saint?

Another phallic custom that lasted well into the nineteenth century was the baking and eating of phallic cakes on feast days, especially during the Easter season. In the village of Saintes, folk observed the *Fête des Pinnes*, or Feast of the Penis, every Palm Sunday. Carrying the little phallic cakes along with their palm branches, the women and children would march to church. There the priest blessed the cakes, after which they were stored away for the rest of the year.

Probably one of the most offbeat objects ever to find its way into the church was the so-called holy prepuce. Its history is filled with mystery and contradiction. Despite the renunciation by the early church fathers of old Jewish customs, among them circumcision, the church continued to celebrate the Feast of Circumcision. According to *The Holy Prepuce and the Miracles*, "Having done away with the actual ceremony it would seem inconsistent that the church would continue to take its celebration into consideration at any time. The strange events which occurred in connection with the Feast of Circumcision may perhaps seem a trifle peculiar on the surface, but when we consider the frantic quest for holy relics that swept Europe in the middle ages, a glimmering of understanding appears."

Thus, during the thirteenth or fourteenth century, the abbey of Coulombs in the diocese of Chartres came to possess a valuable relic of tremendous importance. Although the monks never revealed how this relic came into their possession, nor from whose beatified body it had been snipped, it was generally believed to have arrived via strictly miraculous means. The Holy Prepuce, as it was called, was revered by all who came near it, for it had the power to render sterile women

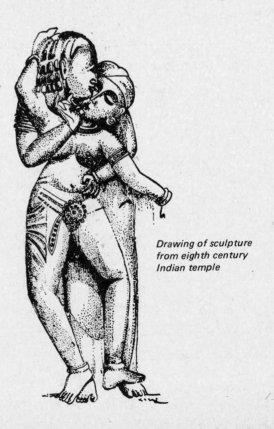

Drawing of sculpture
from eighth century
Indian temple

Drawing of sculpture from tenth century Indian temple

covered by the thief. "Thirty years later it was discovered by a priest on the property of a wealthy lady. Not knowing that the box he had contained a number of sacred relics, the honest father took it at once to the owner of the land on which he had found it. Upon being opened, it was found to contain part of the anatomy of St. Valentine, the lower jaw of St. Martha, with one tooth still in its socket, and a small packet inscribed with the name of the Savior. Noticing a most fragrant aroma that was permeating the atmosphere, the lady picked up the little packet, assuming it to contain some aromatic balm. The moment she touched it her hand stiffened and swelled perceptibly. A further investigation proved that she was holding none other than the miraculous holy prepuce stolen from the church of St. John Lateran."

In 1458 a French theologian, Nicolaus Jaquier, wrote one of the most significant early treatises on witchcraft. He traced its expansion to followers of sects hostile to Christianity, claiming that they gathered together on special occasions for what he called a *synagoga diabolica*. They would then venerate Satan in the form of a buck, copulating with him and with one another. Afterwards, declared Jaquier, they would also receive from their diabolical deity magic enabling them to cause insanity, disease, and death, not to mention impotence in men and barrenness in women.

Such pressures prompted Pope Innocent VIII to issue his famous bull against witchcraft, *Summis desiderantes affectibus*, on December 9, 1484, which said in part: ". . . Many persons of both sexes, unmindful of their own salvation and straying from the Catholic Faith, have abandoned themselves to devils, incubi, and succubi, and by their incantations, spells, conjurations, and other accursed charms and crafts, enormities and horrid offenses, having slain infants yet in the mother's

fruitful. The mere possession of so efficacious a relic did wonders for the reputation of the abbey and for more reasons than one. Not only did the Holy Prepuce cure sterility, its merest touch assured women of an easy delivery.

In time its reputation spread beyond the borders of France. King Henry VIII of England insisted on borrowing it so that his Queen, Catherine of Aragon, might avail herself of its special powers. Unfortunately, it was not returned immediately. In fact, it took twenty-five years to find its way back to Coulombs, during which time there was an alarming increase of sterility. Happily, it was eventually delivered back into the hands of its rightful guardians where, as far as we know, it is still serving the community as a contra-contraceptive.

The abbey of Coulombs was not the only repository of a holy prepuce. Others claiming to have one were the Cathedral of Puy in Velay, the Collegio church in Antwerp, the Abbey of Our Saviour of Charroux, and the church of St. John Lateran in Rome. Like the monks of Coulombs, the established authorities of St. John Lateran never revealed to the world how they gained possession of their holy prepuce, but they were always emphatic in their assertion that it was the only authentic one. Its existence, however, was infinitely more precarious than any other. During the periodic sacks of Rome by Gothic, Vandal, and even Christian incursions, it was stolen and carried off. But it always found its way back to its holy sanctuary, and the sacrilegious thieves were invariably punished by terrible fates.

In *The Holy Prepuce and the Miracles*, we are told of one particular theft in which the casket containing the relic along with several others was buried outside Rome and never re-

Drawing of sculpture from ninth century Kashmiri temple at Avantipur

womb, as also the offspring of cattle, have blasted the produce of the earth, the grapes of the vine, the fruits of trees, nay, men and women, beasts of burden, herd beasts, as well as animals of other kinds, vineyards, orchards, meadows, pasturelands, corn, wheat, and all other cereals. . . . These wretches furthermore inflict . . . terrible and piteous pains and sore diseases, both internal and external. They hinder men from performing the sexual act and women from conceiving, whence husbands cannot know their wives, nor wives receive their husbands. Over and above this, they blasphemously renounce that Faith which is theirs by the Sacrament of Baptism, and at the instigation of the Enemy of Mankind they do not shrink from committing and perpetrating the foulest abominations and filthy excesses to the deadly peril of their own souls, whereby they outrage the Divine Majesty and are a cause of scandal and danger to very many.''

The pope also announced in his bull his appointment of two inquisitors of the German Dominican order, James Sprenger and Henry Kramer. Obediently putting their talents together, this fearsome pair wrote the *Malleus Malificarum*, or *Hammer against Witches*, an appalling handbook combining sexual fantasy, sadism, and legal-theological mumbo-jumbo. One of the most towering monuments to ignorance ever written, it was nevertheless destined to be wielded by Catholic and

Fifteenth century woodcut depicting a devil making love to a woman From The Encyclopedia of Witchcraft and Demonology by *Rossell Hope Robbins.* © *1959 by Crown Publishers, Inc. Reprinted by permission of Crown Publishers, Inc.*

Pretty young witch annointing herself with oil, drawing inspired by the writings of the demonologist Pierre de Lancre.
From The Encyclopedia of Witchcraft and Demonology *by Rossell Hope Robbins.* © *1959 by Crown Publishers, Inc. Reprinted by permission of Crown Publishers, Inc.*

Protestant alike, until common sense swept superstition away and began replacing it with reason.

Reflecting the authors' pathological hatred of women and utter repugnance to sexuality, the book reads like a fanatical misogynist's Krafft-Ebing. Broken into three parts, it first defines and describes witches; second, tells how witchcraft functions and how to deal with it; and finally, how to conduct witch trials.

Like the unforgettable general in *Dr. Strangelove*, Sprenger and Kramer asserted in all seriousness that witches ''prevent the flow of vital essences to the members'' by somehow closing the seminal ducts and impeding ejaculation. They go on to explain how witches deprive men of their penises.

They cited the example of a young man from Ratisbon (today known as Regensburg, Bavaria), who terminated a love affair with a young woman, unaware that she was a witch. Soon afterwards he was horrified to discover that by means of some glamor he had been deprived of his genitals. Heading for the nearest tavern, he began to drown his sorrows in wine and poured out his tale to a sympathetic female drinking companion. After he demonstrated the effectiveness of his emasculation-by-enchantment the woman recommended that he approach the suspected witch directly and try to reason with her, but failing that, to employ violence. When, after a few minutes talking to the ''witch,'' he realized that his approach was getting him nowhere, he whipped out a towel, looping it around her neck, and began to strangle her, threatening that she would die if she didn't restore his penis and testicles at once. As her face began to turn black, she conceded defeat, and thrust her hand between his thighs. As for the young man, the learned inquisitors related that afterwards he ''plainly felt, before he had verified it by looking or touching, that his member had been restored to him by the mere touch of the witch.''

The most fantastic "case" offered by the *Malleus Malificarum*, however, concerns a youth who had been similarly deprived of his penis through the machinations of the neighborhood witch. This one was apparently perfectly willing to return it without a struggle, for when he asked her for it, she merely told him to climb a certain tree where he would find it in the midst of a rather large collection of such organs temporarily housed in a bird's nest. Delighted with what he saw when he got there, he reached out for the largest one in sight, but was restrained by the honorable witch, who regretfully told him he could not have it because it belonged to the parish priest. Sprenger and Kramer explained this extraordinary occurrence by revealing that witches sometimes collect male organs in great numbers, as many as twenty or thirty members, and put them in a bird's nest, or shut them up in a box, "where they move themselves like living members and eat oats and corn."

With ideas such as these firmly implanted in the minds of those who wielded power, a new dark age descended on Europe. Not only did it place deadly weapons in the hands of madmen and fools, it enabled ruthless despots and power-hungry politicians to use them for their own selfish purposes. A case in point is the fate of the Knights Templars.

Founded during the Crusades as a religious order devoted to military service on behalf of the Cross, the Templars were granted many privileges, including secret initiation rites and immunity from taxation. Despite their original vows of chastity and poverty, the Templars went into the money-lending business and before long acquired large tracts of French real estate, causing the crown, as they grew rich and powerful, to cast envious eyes in their direction. The kings of France, always living beyond their means, found the Templars to be a ready source of cash. The Templars, having technically still to keep their sex lives free of women, took to homosexuality, feeling that if they had to indulge, it was best to keep it discreetly within the order.

Early in the fourteenth century, King Phillip IV began collecting all the scandal he could about the Templars, and was especially generous to those informers who gave him tidbits about sodomy, Satanism, and other sinful or heretical practices. When he had assembled enough alleged evidence to make a case, he presented it to Pope Clement V (a Frenchman himself, who had outraged Rome by establishing the papacy in Avignon, thereby initiating the so-called Babylonian Exile of the Popes).

Illustration from a fifteenth century French edition of the Malleus Maleficarum
From The Encyclopedia of Witchcraft and Demonology by *Rossell Hope Robbins. © 1959 by Crown Publishers, Inc. Reprinted by permission of Crown Publishers, Inc.*

Mid-nineteenth century illustration of sleeping man being assaulted by a succubus
From The Encyclopedia of Witchcraft and Demonology by *Rossell Hope Robbins. © 1959 by Crown Publishers, Inc. Reprinted by permission of Crown Publishers, Inc.*

An inquisition was called in conjunction with the French monarchy, but it was a farce, because the king held all the trumps and Clement rubber-stamped his wishes. Despite complete confessions extracted from the Templars under unspeakable tortures, the Council of Vienne summoned by the pope never officially concluded that the Templars were guilty of heresy. Nevertheless, the order was abolished and all the members convicted of crimes by the secular court. Every last man of them was burned at the stake. The pope tried to transfer the Templars' considerable assets to another order he favored, but the wily King Phillip got there first and confiscated everything.

One of the most ludicrous aspects of witchcraft was the ecclesiastical controversy over incubi and succubi. An incubus was said to be a demon in male form whose chief activity was to come in the night to sleeping women and force them into copulation. A succubus was merely the female manifestation of the same demon, who chose as "victims" members of the male sex. Fantastic as it may seem, theologians and scholars of the highest repute entered into the debate. Part of the problem stemmed from St. Augustine, who had written that "they had corporeal immortality and passions like human beings." In 1494 Bartolomeo de Spina asserted that "some are formed from the odor and sperm of men and women in intercourse." And a contemporary, one William the Good, wrote: "That there exist such beings as are commonly called incubi and succubi, and that they indulge in their burning lusts, and that children, as it is freely acknowledged, can be born from them, is attested by the unimpeachable and unshakable witness of many men and women, who have been filled with foul imaginings by them, and endured their lecherous assaults and lewdness."

One of these unimpeachable witnesses was St. Thomas Aquinas, who had written that incubi took semen from men and deposited it in the bodies of women. Another, Caesarius of Heisterbach, believed that they collected semen emitted during masturbation or erotic dreams, and from it manufactured bodies for themselves. Two sixteenth century experts, one of whom was a physician, emphasized that incubi always went out of their way to obtain the best semen available, explaining that they only dealt with robust, ardent young men, who produced semen that was "abundant, very thick, very warm, rich in spirits and free from serosity." Then, in the words of Ludovico Maria Sinistrari, who summed up their assertions: "The incubus copulates with women of a like constitution, taking care that both shall enjoy more than normal orgasm, for the greater the venereal excitement the more abundant the semen."

Sinistrari, Professor of Philosophy at Pavia, and consultant to the Supreme Tribunal of the Holy Inquisition, had ideas of his own as to the true nature of incubi and succubi—unique

Facsimile of the title page of a seventeenth century edition of the Maleficarum. *From* The Encyclopedia of Witchcraft and Demonology *by Rossell Hope Robbins. © 1959 by Crown Publishers, Inc. Reprinted by permission of Crown Publishers, Inc.*

ones, it must be said, that differed from all other authorities. He believed them to be only mildly evil spirits who were basically lustful, but of a higher order of life than human beings. They were, he said, not even beyond the reach of Christian redemption, because unlike true demons, they could not be exorcised.

Regardless of the arguments about their true nature, incubi and succubi were believed to attend witches Sabbats and to copulate freely with both male and female participants. Merlin, King Arthur's legendary magician, was said to have been the result of a union between an incubus and a witch. Indeed, rumors circulated that incubi figured prominently in the ancestry of William the Conqueror and Martin Luther. About Luther, the church made no comment.

The lascivious creatures of the night were a particular threat to convents and monasteries, who were relentlessly plagued with nocturnal assaults on their inmates. Virtuous widows and wives, especially those whose husbands were away on long journeys, were also vulnerable to incubus attacks, and single young men with pretty fiancées were far from immune. To complicate matters, these troublesome spirits had the habit of assuming the appearances of individuals well known to the victims. Often as not they appeared in the guise of men with spotless reputations. What was a woman to do when an incubus looking exactly like her confessor crept into her bed: worse yet, one who bore an uncanny resemblance to her father, best friend's husband, or favorite uncle? Sinistrari's theories notwithstanding, such things, including otherwise embarrassing pregnancies, were understood and accepted as the work of the devil (with God's permission, of course). For as it was written in the *Malleus Malificarum*, such sufferers were, at best, victims of supernatural rape. After all, only witches and their ilk voluntarily entered into sexual relations with such "unclean spirits."

The witch hunters, although they never quite succeeded in stamping out witchcraft, provided future psychiatrists and novelists with the raw material for centuries of nightmares. In addition to the horrors concomitant with witchcraft came those attending the beliefs in vampirism, lycanthropy, incui, and succubi, all of which had their roots hopelessly tangled in religio-sexual mythology, superstition, and guilt.

Sorcery is a recurrent phenomenon in human history, as its contemporary manifestations attest, and it is always found amalgamated with sex. The universality of this age-old relationship explains the fascination it has exerted on theologians, historians, jurists, anthropologists, and psychologists, who have applied their combined energies to the study of the subject. In Western culture the classic eruption of witchcraft lasted from around the thirteenth century to the end of the eighteenth, and also involved important religious and political elements. That these factors were all cemented together by superstition, hypocrisy, and viciousness is just a testimony to the basic nature of the human animal.

The old fairytale version of the witch as an old hag living in a cluttered hut in the forest is not a total fiction. There were many such women who were witches not as members of a coven, and not out of choice, but out of absolute necessity. Medieval times were little brighter than the Dark Ages as far as the poor were concerned. Living at the bottom of the social

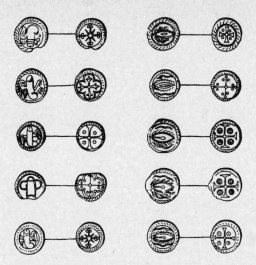

Genital ornaments from the old Church of San Fedele in Como, Italy

scale in a feudal system, the poor were de facto slaves.

Women (usually premature widows), forced while they were still young and attractive to surrender their bodies to the barons who legally ruled their lives, were liable to be left to fend for themselves if they lived to grow old and ugly. Those who were disfigured by disease early in life faced a similar dismal future. If they established themselves as witches they were at least able to earn a pittance by concocting love potions, simple medications, and harmless spells. Sometimes when they were not totally lacking in physical charm (and there are numerous accounts of young, pretty witches), they earned additional incomes by prostitution or by dealing in commodities not unlike modern moonshine or drugs to help their wretched neighbors ease the pain of everyday life.

During the eleventh, twelfth, and early thirteenth centuries, the church recognized that witchcraft of sorts existed, but usually dealt with it leniently. During this period, however, the doctrine of Manicheism began to spread, and this was a heresy that could not be overlooked. Coming to Europe from the Middle East and North Africa via Bulgaria, it inspired a number of sects such as the Albigensians, and also the Cathars, of whom anthropologist Arne Ruenberg wrote: "The visible world was to them created by Satan, the apostate son of God, while the souls of mankind were regarded as belonging to the Kingdom of Heaven, from which they had descended to earth . . ."

The Cathars and other Manichean sects taught that the pope was the Antichrist and the Catholic church a center of blasphemy. Although they appealed to the disillusioned and gained many followers, they were no match for the power of the church, as was soon found by thirteen noted Bulgars living in the diocese of Orleans. In the year 1022 this group, whose life-style could be compared to present-day hippie communes, was accused of sodomy and heresy. After a rapid one-sided trial, all were burned at the stake as heretics. In time, the French word for Bulgar, *Bougre*, came to be used as a synonym for heretic in general. Gradually that meaning fell out of popular usage and the secondary meaning, sodomite, replaced it. Eventually the English picked it up and mispronounced it as

bugger, an example of the familiar process of using a foreign term to disguise native frailties.

When heretical sects were not slaughtered during local European crusades aimed at them, they went underground. In so doing they assimilated pre-Christian supersititious beliefs and practices and in time came to be regarded by the Church as out-and-out Satanists. By the middle of the thirteenth century, the Vatican was ready for total war. Since the visible world was at once the battleground and the eventual prize, it boiled down to a mortal struggle between the opposing forces of God and Satan—at least, in the eyes of the Church. The tragic twist was that many of the alleged opponents were innocent victims of error, ignorance, and sometimes deliberate viciousness.

Probably no other aspect of witchcraft has caused more controversy than the Sabbat. Judging by early writings it began as little more than an after-dark picnic, attended by Manichean-like cultists, possibly along with a sprinkling of left-over pagans. To carry the theory a little further, the proceedings were little more sinister than an extension of Christian rites because all the celebrants were doing was paying homage to Satan as lord of the visible world. As a cheerful gathering with a certain amount of ritual thrown in, there was plenty of eating and drinking—especially drinking and it is likely that some of those attending sneaked off in to the bushes for more private rites of their own.

In some parts of Europe the celebration was probably a carry over from the old Roman Saturnalia, with open phallic rites observed. We are told of huge French Sabbats in the early part of the fifteenth century, where participants drank drugged wine and danced nude around a gigantic phallus representing the potency of God.

Obviously for such a momentous occasion as the Sabbat, certain preparations were necessary. Over and over we read of the unguents, or sorcerer's grease, which had to be compounded from a hair-raising pharmacopoeia, then smeared over the naked body. This lubricant, which might have doubled for sexual assistance later on, was a vital aid to transvection or flying through the air. Powerful potions were concocted and swallowed, most of which are recognized today as containing

Robin Goodfellow, a seventeenth century priapic hobgoblin, from an illustration to a popular ballad of the period

Robin Goodfellow depicted as a devil presiding over a gathering of witches

drugs guaranteed to produce delirium or hallucinations. Some witches who confessed to having flown to the Sabbat may well have been thoroughly convinced that they were telling the truth. The expression "fly by night" stems back to these times.

Virtually every narrative describing a Sabbat tells how the devil himself attended, sometimes disguised as some animal but eventually in a more or less human form, so that he might have sexual relations with his followers. This indicates that someone had to perform the Satanic role. But was it a man or a woman? The question arises out of a curious similarity that occurs in virtually every contemporary narrative. Invariably the women confessing their sexual relations with Satan complain that his penis was ice cold, and that penetration was extremely painful. We read confession after confession (each separated from the other by time, distance, and language), in which the common denominator is this outsized penis, sometimes "about a yard and a half long," "long thick as one's arm," or something similar but always causing great pain to the female.

This would indicate an artificial phallus, possibly carved out of marble, bone, or something equally retentive of cold. Judging from some descriptions, it might even have been a large animal horn. A woman in disguise could easily have wielded it. It stands to reason that no man could maintain an erection long enough to copulate with scores of frenzied followers. And even if by some superhuman means he could, his partners would not experience such sensations as pain and extreme cold.

Every manner of sexual excess emerges from these narratives against surreal backgrounds of smoking cauldrons, frenzied dancing, cacophonous music, agonized shrieks, howls, and screams. Writing of the confession of a young witch, Jeannet d'Abaide, Thomas Wright says:"She had seen at the Sabbat men and women in promiscuous intercourse, and how the devil arranged them in couples, in the most unusual conjugations—the daughter with the father, the daughter-in-law with the father-in-law, the penitent and the confessor, without distinction of age, quality, or relationship, so that she confessed to having been known an infinity of times by a cousin of her

mother, and by an infinite number of others." He goes on to explain that the girl claimed to have been deflowered by the devil at the age of thirteen. He then reports that Jeanet and the other witches, "suffered extremely when he (the devil) had intercourse with them, in consequence of his member being covered with scales like those of a fish, that when extended it was a yard long, but that it was usually twisted."

Whether witches' Sabbats actually took place as orgiastic convocations of Satanists and their fellow travelers or whether they were mere figments of the twisted imaginations of inquisitors and other witch-hunters is difficult to say with absolute certainty. Certainly, the methods of torture these humorless zealots employed were effective enough to extract any confessions they chose from their victims. Knowing what we do today about the pathology of sex, we can unequivocally state that the majority of witch-hunters, Catholic and Protestant alike, were merely expressing their own warped sexuality as they tormented and systematically destroyed their hapless victims.

The witchcraft enjoying a renaissance today is certainly inspired to some extent by the brand that flourished in the fifteenth, sixteenth, and seventeenth centuries. Some represents a disillusionment with contemporary organized religion, some is merely a rationale to indulge in sexual excesses in the guise of unorthodox religion. The modern element of sex and drugs adds a degree of sophistication, yet some peculiar wrinkles have been added. The popularity of William Blatty's novel, *The Exorcist*, and its film version, has brought about a rash of possessions, some of which are regarded even by present-day theologians (although with extreme caution) as the real thing.

The sexually oriented contemporary witchcraft has some intriguing facets. In *Sex and the Occult*, author Gordon Wellesley quotes a British journalist, identified as T.K., who succeeded in getting himself initiated into an English coven in 1966. After describing the paraphernalia and the surroundings, all of which resembled the set and props from a Hammer Films horror picture, T.K., who was initiated in the nude, bound, and blindfolded, was finally untied and permitted to see again. He wrote, "First my companion, then I, were made to lie on our backs on the white sheet, with our heads towards the altar. Olive oil was smeared on my body. Then one of the young

Bas relief depicting ancient Christian Agape, or love feast

girls who had introduced me, and who was figuring as the "Queen," came forward, bent over me, kissed my lips, my navel, and touched my penis with her lips. She was completely naked. Then a knife was pressed against my chest and I was told it would be better to fall on it now than to reveal ever the secrets of witchcraft. I had to swear fidelity to the Great God of Evil. Then we all got dressed and went out to the local pub for a drink."

One of the sexiest and most charming contemporary witches on the scene today is the willowy, flame-haired Gay-Darlene Bidart, author of *The Naked Witch*. Her comments on sex and witchcarft are lighthearted and pithy, for example: "Hot love affairs, in which your body has burned with seemingly unquenchable fires of desire, and you've felt yourself writhing miserably like a damned soul without satisfaction, could only have been instigated by diabolical elements. In these cases, you've often found yourself making love in odd places, such as on top of Volkswagens in deserted garages (you couldn't even wait to climb into the back of the car)! Outstandingly diabolical affairs, however, are always characterized by copulation before a fire, particularly in the presence of copperware. In a house or apartment, no matter where you *start* entangling loins, you will always move in the direction of a stove."

She also offers practical advice, such as:

Release cosmic energy with outdoor exchange of carnal knowledge.

6:00 a.m. spell: Arise, kneel, and lick your lover's phallus to deliver him from devils that depress his desire for you.

9:00 a.m. spell: Flog your naked lover with flamingo feathers to remove temporary impotence.

Dance your nipples over a man's heart and grind your pelvis in a circular motion to invoke divine union.

Unhappily, however, not all practitioners of witchcraft are as lighthearted as Gay-Darlene Bidart. Some can be downright frightening.

Although the *Rosemary's Baby* variety of witchcraft is virtually nonexistent now, it cannot be dismissed altogether. The bloody Moors killings in Great Britain, and the more recent Sharon Tate murders in California, offer grisly testimony to that. Certainly there is nothing surprising about the current manifestation of witchcraft. Not only is there a general occult fad, but we have a growing relaxation of sexual rigidity, a youthful drug culture, and the increasing unfortunate awareness of a bleak future for mankind in general. Since *homo sapiens* has traditionally called on supernatural and magical forces to help him in the past, he is presently following an old predisposition to help him cope with the future.

Unquestionably the most horrifying byproduct of a twisted religious antisexual attitude lies in the case of the *Skoptsi*. A Russian religious sect, first discovered by authorities in the eighteenth century, the *Skoptsi* (whose name is taken from the Russian word for eunuch) were a fanatical religious sect whose concepts of purity were so extreme that they demanded total and absolute sexual abstinence. They believed that Adam and Eve had been created sexless, and that genitalia and female

Depictions of alleged idols worshiped by the Knights Templars at the time of their political strife with the king of France and the pope

breasts were abominations created by the forces of evil to drive mankind into a state of sin. It was said that in the course of their religious meetings they would work themselves into hysterical frenzies, and then mutilate one another with swords, knives, razors, and hot pokers.

As time passed, they enjoyed periods of freedom followed by periods of severe persecution. They continued to practice voluntary castration and breast amputation, but in order to prevent their ranks from thinning down, they relaxed their severe rules to allow the faithful to have a child or two before submitting to the operation. Some writers assert that they managed to survive and reproduce not by procreating but by kidnapping children of others. Whatever the truth of these reports, they apparently managed to perpetuate themselves underground and spread to other sections of Europe and even to America.

Moreover, it is alleged that they are still one of the most powerful secret Christian sects in existence—not in the West, but in the Soviet Union. Former Soviet Premier Georgi Malenkov was said to have been castrated as a youth, and to have risen in the ranks both of the *Skoptsi* and the Communist Party. The story was printed in the *New York Daily News* on August 20, 1953, under the byline of the late Lee Mortimer. Referring to the *Skoptsi* by name, Mortimer declared that **Soviet eunuchs, all *Skoptsi*, had held for years "a virtual monopoly on public offices in the Urals and Russian Asia."** A former correspondent in the U.S.S.R., T. L. Cummings, Jr. went so far as to accuse the *Skoptsi* of poisoning Stalin as part of a plot to take over the Soviet Union.

It all sounds a bit farfetched. Unquestionably the *Skoptsi* did exist at one time as a wild and fanatical group. There are a few of them around today, but they are considerably subdued. It hardly seems likely that they are the masters of the Russian Communist hierarchy.

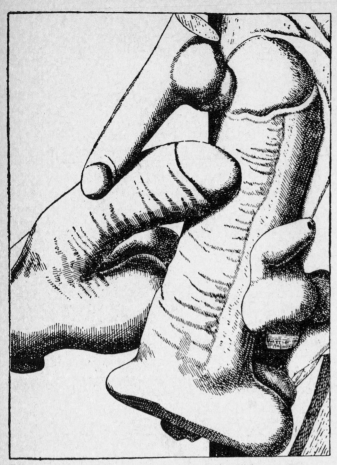

Eighteenth century phallic offerings used during religious festivals in the Kingdom of Naples

Ancient Roman portable shrine dedicated to Priapus

Happily there are no other religious sects of any consequence among us which impose such drastic measures on their followers. There are still too many who regard virginity as a virtue, and sex education as a Communist plot, just as there are still too many Communists around who regard sexual freedom as some kind of Western conspiracy. As for the established churches, there appear to be definite signs of progress. Protestant ministers are giving valuable abortion counsel, and though there are few who will admit it openly, certainly Catholic priests have even dispensed birth control advice in the confessional.

Perhaps the millenium is not quite around the corner, but there is every sign that the churches are losing their age-old mania about sex.

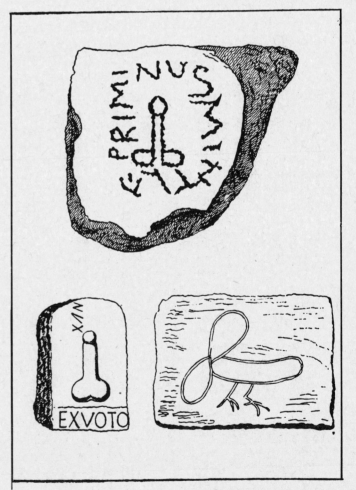

Phallic artifacts from Scotland indicating pre-Christian influences

Bibliography

Alexander, Hartley Burr. *The Mythology of All the Races.* Boston: 1916.

Bauer, W. W. *Potions, Remedies and Old Wives Tales.* Garden City, N.Y.: Doubleday, 1969.

Baring-Gould. *The Book of Werewolves.* London: 1865.

Baroja, Julio Caro. *The World of the Witches.* Chicago: University of Chicago Press, 1965. $9.50 (cloth), $3.45 (paper)

Bayley, Harold. *The Lost Language of Symbolism.* London: 1913.

Bidart, Gay-Darlene. *The Naked Witch.* New York: Pinnacle Books, 1975. $1.75

Gay-Darlene Bidart, author of The Naked Witch

Bois, Jules. *Le Satanisme et la magie.* Paris: 1895.

Bonaparte, Marie. *The Life and Works of Edgar Allan Poe.* London: 1949.

Bond, John. *An Essay on the Incubus or Nightmare.* London: 1753.

Bouguet, Henri. *Discours des sorciers.* Paris: 1603.

Bovet, Richard. *Pandaemonium, or the Devil's Cloister, Being a Further Blow to Modern Sadducism, Proving the Existence of Witches and Spirits.* London: 1684.

Brown, Sanger. *The Sex Worship and Symbolism of Primitive Races: An Interpretation.* Reprint. New York: AMS. $10.00

Calmet, Augustin. *The Phantom World.* Translated by Henry Christmas. London: 1850.

Carus, P. *The History of the Devil.* Chicago; 1900.

Cohen, Chapman. *Religion and Sex: Studies in the Pathology of Religious Development.* London: 1919. Reprint. New York: AMS, 1975. $14.50

Delassus, Jules. *Les incubes et les succubes.* Paris: 1897.

De Rachewiltz. *Black Eros.* Translated by Peter Whigham. Secaucus, N.J.: Lyle Stuart, 1964.

Dulaure, Jacques Antoine. *The Gods of Generation: A History of Phallic Cults among the Ancients and Moderns.* Translated by Adolph Frederick Niemoeller. Reprint. New York: AMS, Press Inc., 1975. $15.00

Dunlap, Knight. *Mysticism, Freudianism and Scientific Psychology.* St. Louis: 1920.

Givry, Grilot de. *Witchcraft, Magic & Alchemy.* Translated by J. Courtenay Locke. London: George G. Harrap. 1931.

Goldberg, B. Z. *The Story of Sex in Religion.* New York: Grove Press, 1962. 75¢

Goldsmith, E. E. *Life Symbols as Related to Sex Symbolism.* New York: 1924.

Haining, Peter. *Anatomy of Witchcraft.* New York: Taplinger, 1972. $6.95

——. *The Warlock's Book.* New York: University Books, 1971. $6.00

Hill, Douglas. *Magic and Superstition.* New York: Hamlyn Publishing Group, 1968.

Howard, Clifford. *Sex and Religion: A Study of Their Relationship and Its Bearing upon Civilization.* London: 1925. Reprint. New York: AMS, 1975. $10.50

——. *Sex Worship.* Chicago: 1909.

Hugel, Friedrich. *The Mystical Element in Religion.* New York: 1923.

Hurwood, Bernhardt J. *Terror By Night.* New York: Lancer, 1963. 50¢

Huxley, Aldous. *The Devils of Loudon.* New York: Harper & Row, 1971. $1.50

Jameson, Eric. *The Natural History of Quackery.* Springfield, Ill.: C. C. Thomas, 1961.

Copyright © 1971 by Thomas Nelson (Australia) Ltd. Reprinted by Taplinger Publishing Company, 1971 ($4.95)

Jones, Ernest. *Nightmare, Witches and Devils.* New York: 1931.

King, Teri. *Your Astrological Guide to Sex & Love.* 12 vol. New York: Pinnacle Books, 1974. 95¢

Knight, Richard Payne. *A Discourse on the Worship of Priapus.* London: 1786.

Lea, Henry Charles. *Materials Toward a History of Witchcraft.* New York: 1957.

——. *The Witch Persecutions in Transalpine Europe.* Philadelphia: 1942.

Leary, T.; Metzner, Ralph; Alpert, Richard. *The Psychedelic Experience.* New York: University Books, 1964. $6.00

Leuba, J. H. *Psychology of Religious Mysticism.* London: 1925.

Maple, Eric. *The Dark World of Witches.* Indianapolis, Indiana: Pegasus, 1970. $1.95

——. *Magic, Medicine and Quackery.* London: Robert Hale, 1968. o/p

Martello, Leo Louis. *Witchcraft: The Old Religion.* New York: Penthouse Book Club, 1975. $7.95

Meares, Ainslie. *Strange Places and Simple Truths.* London: Souvenir Press, 1969

Nemecek, Ottakar. *Virginity, Pre-Nupital Rites and Ritual.* New York: Philosophical Library, 1958.

Pascale, Marc de. *A Book of Spells.* New York: Taplinger, 1971. $4.95

Patai, Raphael. *Sex and Family in the Bible and the Middle East.* Garden City, N.Y.: Doubleday, Dolphin. 95¢.

Pico della Mirandola. *Libro detto Strega o delle Illusioni del Demonio.* Translated by Leandro delli Alberto. Venice, Italy: 1556.

Radford, E. *Encyclopedia of Superstitions.* New York: Greenwood, 1949. $11.50

Robbins, Rossell Hope. *The Encyclopedia of Witchcraft and Demonology.* New York: Crown Publishers, 1959. $11.00

Schroeder, T. A. *Heavenly Bridegrooms.* New York: 1918.

——. *Revivals, Sex and Holy Ghost.* Boston: 1919.

Scot, Reginald. *Discovery of Witchcraft.* New York: Dover, 1972. $3.50

Sellon, Edward. *Annotations on the Sacred Writings of the Hindus.* London: 1865.

Sinistrari, Ludovico Maria. *De Daemonialitate et Incubis et Succubis.* Paris: 1875.

Spence, Lewis. *An Encyclopedia of Occultism.* New York: University Books, 1960. $15.00. Reprinted. New York: Citadel Press, 1974. $5.95

Stone, L. A. *Story of Phallicism.* New York: 1927.

Underwood, Peter. *Into the Occult.* New York: Drake, 1973. $5.95

Wellesley, Gordon. *Sex and the Occult.* New York: Bell, 1972.

Westropp, H. M., and Wake, C. S. *Ancient Symbol Worship.* New York: 1875.

Wright, Thomas. *The Worship of the Generative Powers During the Middle Ages in Western Europe.* London: 1866.

Sexuality Around the World

There is an old adage that if you want something badly enough you will find it. Long before the days of guidebooks and volumes of advice about how to find sexual adventure on unfamiliar turf, those endowed with a strong enough sex drive, imagination, and determination rarely failed to find what they were seeking. Certain groups, such as swingers, have an advantage because they maintain a fairly active underground grapevine. The same advantage applies to devotées of exotic sex and experienced patrons of the oldest profession.

The first prerequisite for individuals with open minds and a firm desire for sexual action is to drop all inhibitions and be prepared to ask direct questions. There is not a taxi driver in any major city who cannot direct you to action of some sort. Of course, the disadvantage of getting your information that way is the high probability of getting ripped off. This is not to imply that you will be waylaid by the taxi drivers themselves, but there is a strong possibility that they will send you somewhere that is tourist-oriented and bound to part you from a hefty chunk of cash—of which the taxi driver will get a substantial commission. Concierges of hotels are better sources, and in certain instances, bellhops. A degree of caution is required when dealing with the latter, because they, too, are in the commission business. However, if you build the proper rapport and are a fair amateur psychologist, bellhops can be goldmines of valuable information.

If you are in a city that happens to be a seaport, find out where the merchant seamen hang out. Investing in a few drinks for a thirsty sailor or two can lead you to adventures in places not found in any guidebooks. To a lesser degree, you will do well to seek out hangouts for international flight crews. Resort areas throughout the world are ripe for the sexually adventuresome. Almost any of the Club Méditerranée operations are sexual paradises for those so inclined.

In cities where sexpapers of the *Screw* genre are published—notably Amsterdam, where one can buy *Suck* (available in English)—it is considerably easier to find one's way around. Denmark and Sweden are so wide open that anyone who can read needs no outside assistance. London, Paris, Hamburg, West Berlin, and Rome are similarly filled with readily available sources. Norway and Iceland are sexual deserts by comparison to the rest of Europe. Tokyo, however, is another story. Although, as you will see, there is an immense amount of sexual diversion available in Tokyo, and in other cities in Japan, a certain problem exists. The Japanese are very image conscious and do not care to have foreigners get the idea that they encourage sexual adventure. But here is an important key. What we in the United States would call a "blue" movie, for example, the Japanese would call "pink." Consequently, if you see any establishment in Japan displaying the English word "pink," you will know at once that sex is involved.

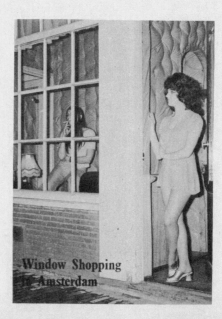

Postcard showing red light district in Amsterdam

Window Shopping in Amsterdam

*D*espite efforts of certain members of the local citizenry in one place or another, Europe remains the happiest hunting ground for the horny. There is one monumental source for the sexual adventurer in Europe that is so complete and accurate that it can truly be called definitive. The book is *Mankoff's Lusty Europe* by Allan H. Mankoff (hardcover, Viking Press, $10.00. Paperback, Pocket Books, revised and updated. $1.95). Mankoff, presently executive editor of *Penthouse* in London, spent five years researching the book, during which time he managed to travel over 100,000 miles, interview approximately 7,500 people, and check out 3,128 neighborhoods and establishments in seventeen countries and fifty-one cities. Its publication in 1972 resulted in accolades and tears of joy in all the media, from *Vogue* to *The San Francisco Ball*. Leo Lerman in *Vogue* said, "... this is your book, and if you do go anywhere, you can't do without it."

Just to whet your appetite, here are some of the subjects Mankoff covers, not only in great detail, but with wit and style:

A sensuous journey through Europe's "pleasure underground"

Mankoff's Lusty Europe

Allan H. Mankoff

"Delightful, delicious, wicked... Don't miss it."—*Swing*

Lovers' Hotels

Bordellos for Men

Bordellas for Women

Lovers' Restaurants

Group Sex Houses

Discotheques (public & private)

Sexual Saunas

Mixed Saunas

Nude Skiing

Romantic Cafés

Wine Bars (great for single girls)

Women's Lib Activities

Sexual Seances

Mateswap Houses

Call Girls

Madams

Street Scenes

Nude Restaurants

Homosexual Rendezvous (bars, clubs, hotels, *spectacles*)

Transvestite Couturier

Pregnant Pubs

Jazz Clubs

Boites

Master/Slave Marriage Bureau

Sex Museums in Police Stations

Drugs

Section for "The Woman on Her Own"

Boutiques

Street Markets

Student Rendezvous

Lesbian Discotheques

Nudist Camps

Call-boy Service for Women

Sex Shows (hard and soft core)

Assisted Showers

Intro Bureaux

Dansants (where girl asks boy)

Virgins (to rent or to wed)

Birth Control and V.D. Clinics

Ghosts

Discipline (equipment and practitioners)

Sex Shops

Romantic Parks (gardens, zoos, vistas, restaurants, hotels, lovers' leaps)

Even "Jack the Kisser"

Here are a few examples of the text:

"According to a brochure for 'Sex Weekend in Copenhagen' there will be dancing, and drinks will be served by topless waitresses while having group sex. Dexterous, these Danes."

"No city can touch Paris's encyclopedic versatility. Paris nights continue to offer the warmest and most diversified welcome for the sensual traveler. For the French don't really give a sou what you do. As long as you don't care what they do. And *that* is the essence of Paris."

"On your way to the airport, in the southwest portion of the city [Barcelona], you'll observe dozens of high-rise apartments, just completed or still in the process of construction. In the midst of these, 'virgin' prostitutes wait at sundown near the intersection of Calle del Capitan Martin Busutil and the Gran Avenida de la Victoria, and in adjacent streets like Calle de los Caballeros. Gentlemen on their way out of the Barcelona Tennis Club and anyone else in the area may be offered a fast fellatio alfresco at 150 pesetas [*less than $3.00 at the current rate of exchange. Ed.*]—in the car or the bushes. If you prefer dancing, in the same neighborhood is Cabana Tio Tom where barmaids gather, after they have finished work, from clubs all over the city. Rousing native pop groups. Best action after 3:30 a.m." *

*From MANKOFF'S LUSTY EUROPE, by Allan H. Mankoff. Copyright © 1972 by Allan H. Mankoff. Reprinted by permission of The Viking Press, Inc.

SEX NACHRICHTEN 2. — DM
DEUTCHE SEX ILLUSTRIERTE 2.50 DM
Both are illustrated newspapers published in Hamburg. The address for both is 2 Hamburg 4—Postfach 102, Germany. They include feature stories, personal ads, cartoons, and general sex information. To fully appreciate them, though, you must read German, or get someone to translate for you if you find something intriguing.

MONIKA DÜLK VERLAG
Berlin 201, Postfach 182, Germany.
Publishes a series of detailed illustrated maps in full color and explicit symbols telling you almost everything you want to know about where to find sexual entertainment in the following cities: Berlin, Düsseldorf, Frankfurt, Hamburg, Hannover, Paris, Stuttgart, Vienna, and Zurich.

Happily, Mankoff is still going strong. In a recent postcard from Moscow he revealed, "Just accomplished first streak across Red Square. Turned Blue."

If you are a true bon vivant, we advise you to get two copies of *Mankoff's Lusty Europe*. The hardover for your permanent library, and the paperback (in England available from Granada, Mayflower Books) to carry around and facilitate your peregrinations through the erogenous zones of Europe.

Although *Mankoff's Lusty Europe* is an absolute necessity for anyone looking for action in Europe, there are a number of locally produced papers, magazines, booklets, maps, and guides which can be quite helpful. Here are a few random examples of what sort of material you should look for.

No mention of Germany can be complete without the story of Beate Uhse. In her private life, Beate Uhse is a pert, blonde mother of three. Publicly, she is the head of the world's largest chain of sex-supermarkets, devoting sophisticated marketing techniques to the multifaceted arts, crafts, chemistry, engineering, and literature of sex. Beate, whose first name translates into English as "Blessed," began her career as a girl ferry pilot for the Luftwaffe during the Second World War. Immediately after the outbreak of peace she observed an alarming epidemic of pregnancies that seemed to be directly proportional to the influx of Allied occupation troops. Having determined that she would now serve the fatherland with both feet on the ground, she plunged enthusiastically into an enterprise destined to make her eventually one of the richest social

Luxury in a Polynesian setting.
Photo by Dave Gardner and Bob Palagye.
Courtesy Tahitia, 829 Third Avenue, New York, N.Y.

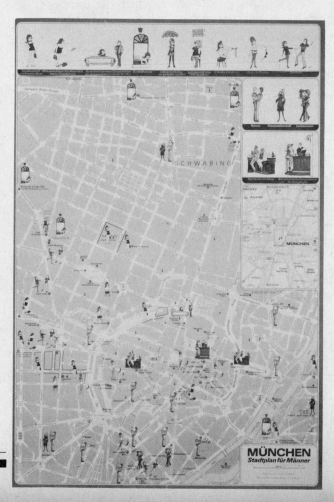

The cover of the current one hundred page catalogue from Beate Uhse

The back cover of the Beate Uhse catalogue, showing the various locations of her stores in Western Germany

sexually explicit publications such as those produced by Tuppy Owens, *e.g., Sexual Paradise*, *The Sex Maniac's Diaries* and *Calendars*, *Penthouse*, *Penthouse-Forum*, and other magazines of the *Playboy* genre, always remember that the English reserve presents a formidable barrier between the foreigner and British subjects. From the earliest of times the English have been a lusty people, but in general, your opportunities for sexual involvements depend strictly on an "invitation only" basis.

Italy has to be the most complex country in Europe, and it would be a good idea to thoroughly read Barzini's *The Italians* to get an overview. Sex has played a dominant role in Italian life since before the days of the Roman Empire. Italian charm and ebullience is real, but Italy is a land that has produced Fellini, so in matters sexual always remember there are contra-

rejects in post-war Europe. By applying hard-sell methods to a real problem, she became a Teutonic Margaret Sanger—but with a difference. Beate was not a crusader, she was out to make a profit. Not only did she succeed in satisfying her customers with the contraceptive information she sold, she became the demographers' darling, doing her bit to stave off the population explosion. Today a multimillionaire, Beate Uhse conducts an operation that is a veritable Sears and Roebuck of sex, with countless satisfied customers. She may well be the world's largest consumer of plain brown wrappers in history.

The most sensational, slick color porno magazine available internationally in multilingual editions is *Private*, published by Private Press AB, Fack S-104 62 Stockholm 17, Sweden. There are photographs that would make *Playboy* etc. look like kindergarten reading, as well as features, guide material, reader participation columns—in short, the works.

While we are on the subject of Sweden, here, according to Norman Jackson, author of the upcoming book, *Sexy Europe*, are the two best sex cabarets in Stockholm.

The Funny Girl Cabaret
Tegnergatan 8
Phone: 10 59 62
The Funny Girl's shows include live sex, nonstop, plus music, comedy, food and drink.

Cabaret Chat Noir
Dobelnsgatan 4, 111 40 Stockholm
Phone: 08/20 93 54
Like the Funny Girl, the Chat Noir has an intimate decor, armchairs, intimate bar, and an "incredibly daring sex circus."

Wherever you go in Europe, and whatever your plans, it is a good idea to bone up on the realities of sexual mores well in advance. In England, for example, despite the availability of

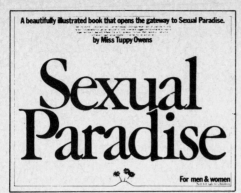

Cover of
Tuppy Owens'
Sexual Paradise
published in Great Britain by Miss Owens' own company Cand Haven Limited

"Grandmother and child" — *East German cartoon*

dictions around every corner. Illusion and reality have a way of blending and shifting there. It is so easy to fall in love with Italy itself that your sexual energy can easily be spent in areas that do not seem on the surface to have anything whatever to do with sex. When there, however, do read *Playmen*. When this magazine was first published, the Vatican trembled, not out of fear but in righteous indignation. But *Playmen* survived. In any event, whatever your proclivities, after spending some time in Italy you will be seduced emotionally.

In Eastern Europe, despite rigid official policies that are anti-sex-for-fun, the human spirit cannot be repressed. Prostitution exists in the closet, and the leaders of socialist countries are very adept at using sex as a political tool. Many a secret has been wheedled out in the bedroom. A significant footnote to sexual attitudes in Eastern Europe lies in the fact that officialdom there frequently accuses "decadent Western morality" of being a dangerous influence that can undermine society, using terms identical to those used by the extreme right in America vis-a-vis alleged Communist sex fiends employing the wiles and proclivities of Venus to destroy America.

Politically as well as geographically on the opposite end of the spectrum from the East of Europe is Spain. As Mankoff illustrates in detail, there is a great deal of sexual activity going on there, but it is very foolish for foreigners to try going too far, not only in Spain but in any country with a Hispanic culture. The old church influence is still very strong, and sex is equated with sin. There are whores, and there are ladies. Never confuse the two; that advice goes for women as well as for men. The American or other European female who behaves in as open a fashion as she might at home can get into serious difficulties by inadvertently creating false impressions. In general, foreigners in Hispanic countries will be better off providing their own companions, or if alone and male, seeking out prostitutes. Woman alone can find all the willing sexual partners they desire, but the strict double standard can lead to problems, and they are always better off finding playmates who are similarly strangers to the country.

Following is an excerpt from a letter sent to us from Lisbon by Norman Jackson when he was researching his forthcoming book on a man's guide to Europe.

"Tamila Club is a wide-open, good-natured, good-willed hooker joint. Living room ambiance, quiet jazzy combo, prices within reason. An honest house, something that is

not always the case in the prostitution milieu. I met a darling Portuguese whore here, Aline. She offered me a free piece because I am a journalist, and was referred by a close friend of hers. She said that it is not rare for pros in Lisbon to do it free if they like a guy and he doesn't happen to have the bread. Anyway, if there is such a thing as a wholesome hooker joint, Tamila Club in Lisbon is it."

Tamila Club
68-B, Avenida Duque de Loule
Lisbon, Portugal
Phone: 73 41 17
Hours: 6:00 p.m. to 3:00 a.m.

In pre-Castro Cuba there were, especially in Havana and its environs, numerous *posadas* or discreet hotels, where especially on Tuesday afternoons, lovers met for brief, passionate rendezvous. The concept, of course, was not unknown elsewhere in Latin America, and today there are some interesting

"I'll never agree to your divorcing your husband. To me marriage is sacred." — *Polish cartoon*

*An old
French
postcard*

new wrinkles being applied. One is the Hotel Valdivia in Santiago, Chile.

If you happen to have extravagant fantasies, and you want to experience them in real life, make a note of this place just in case you ever happen to pass through Santiago, and you have time for a memorable, offbeat dalliance. The Hotel Valdivia is run by one Señor Guillermo Mella. Rooms are inexpensive, running from $5.00 to $10.00. Music is piped into all suites, multilingual waitresses of amiable disposition handle room service, and amorous couples are assured of discretion from the moment they arrive via a specially designed back entrance. There you park your car in a partitioned stall and are greeted by a dignified, white-uniformed matron, who leads you down beside a waterfall, rock-garden-lined corridor to the fantasy chamber of your choice.

Are you in a neanderthal mood? For you there is a cave, complete with stalagtites, stalagmites, cowhide and fur rugs, and a huge bed eighty feet from the entrance. For nature buffs there is a miniature forest. A psychedelic room is decorated in glaring oranges and reds. A round room has no corners and is equipped with a monumental circular bed that has translucent chiffon panels. Nostalgia buffs may like the automobile room, which features a 1939 DKW convertible as its principal play-pen. Surrounded by assorted racing photographs, auto parts, and flashing strobes, an illusion of speedy tearing around is readily created. Commented the hotel's architect, Daniel Zamudio, "Everyone likes to remember the things he did with girls in cars." A quick survey of our female friends indicated a

similar feeling of nostalgia. The Polynesian room features a hammock ten feet in length. For bondage freaks there is a cage room, complete with bars, and for super hedonists, the Arabian room has a low bed surrounded by 1,001 pillows and mirrors galore.

Mexico, being right next door, has always been a favorite playground. Again, prostitution is the big thing, and for those who are interested in venturing south of the border with some advance information, read on.

LA FRONTERA. $3.50.

This long overdue book on the bordellos of the Mexican-American border is now available. Hours of work and thousands of miles of driving are condensed into this handy guidebook. All the towns on the frontier, from the Pacific Ocean to the Gulf of Mexico are discussed, with maps showing exact locations of each establishment. An informative introduction, written by a man with years of Latin American whorehouse experience, provides a practical and philosophical guide for the vacationer looking for a relaxing and safe time with the playmates of Mexico.

This guidebook is an excellent investment for a weekend trip or a lengthy holiday. You will learn how a man can have a half a dozen girls in one night at reasonable prices or take an exceptional senorita to bed for an entire night. *La Frontera* will expose you to the third world culture through firsthand experience. Available from: Mission Publications, P.O. Box 426, Union City, California 94587.

British Goods at Auction *by
Thomas Rowlandson, London,
eighteenth century*

The pasha in his harem
*by Thomas Rowlandson,
London, eighteenth
century*

The Hague, Holland . . . and

An Afternoon with Monique Von Cleef

Your Pain Is Her Pleasure

by Ken Gaul

Photograph of Ken Gaul and two silver models by John Stevens used as publicity for the first New York Erotic Film Festival

No catalogue of sexual superstars would be in any way complete without a recognition of the fascinating, extraordinary, and wonderfully unique Monique.

While in Amsterdam attending the first Wet Dream Erotic Film Festival, I met Monique Von Cleef. I had heard of her before. She once ran a "House of Pain" (as the media labeled it) in Newark, New Jersey, and serviced an enormous clientele (including doctors, attorneys, politicians, and noted entertainers), some of whom paid hundreds of dollars for an hour of her unique discipline. She was busted, however, and deported back to Holland; lawyers waged her case all the way to the Supreme Court, though, and she was exonerated *post facto*. So just meeting her was an interesting experience.

Al Goldstein of *Screw* magazine, who was at the festival, was going to visit her house in the Hague, and he invited me along. So with some trepidation and utmost fascination, I went . . . and walked into one of the most bizarre experiences of my life!

Arriving at Monique's place, I sat and partook of Al's interview, shooting some photos along the way and getting mellowed right out behind some excellent Middle Eastern herbs. Al's initial work done, she invited us to stay and witness a session with one of her "slaves" who was scheduled to arrive shortly. One of Monique's "assistants"—a tasty Dutch lass named Femka—arrived shortly and the "slave" followed soon after. What Monique had not bothered to tell me, though, was that the slave she was going to put through his paces was a member in good standing of the church.

Now, being an ex-Catholic, I can only say this revelation made me absolutely fucking crazy. The man, though, was quite humble and eagerly apologetic, being absolutely everything you'd ever thought closet-crazy would be. Al continued his interview with the good man, and by this time I'm getting comatose from too much smoke and cognac. So the man excused himself to prepare for his "sessions," and Monique asked us if we would like some coffee. Sure, say I, and Monique claps for her "French maid" to bring it with haste.

So I'm lying back on the floor resting, and as I look up half-grogged I see black high heels, black stockings, black garter belt, black mini-maid outfit, white apron, and a dainty little maid's cap sitting on top of a nicely coiffed head. Waking up a bit more, and looking more closely, I notice probably the ugliest pair of French legs I've ever seen, very hairy arms, and a cheap looking wig sitting atop the holy countenance of, you guessed it, Monique's "slave."

Rousing us all out of our reclining positions, Monique bade us follow her upstairs to "the Room." On entering, one just stood for several minutes and said nothing, observing—whips, chains, handcuffs, hoods (getting excited?), cats-of-nine tails, a boxing ring, and a set of stocks. After some preliminary locking of Al in the stocks for a photo-session whipping, and me in stocks for same (with Monique not sparing the rod at all), beautiful Femka removed all of her clothing, revealing yards of lusciousness, which Al proceeded to suck and I proceeded to fuck. Then it was the "slave's" turn to react to Monique's cue.

"Suck her, you disgrace to the church. Eat her, get aroused, feel shame at your holy transgressions. Now get the hell in those stocks." Locked in the stocks in his French maid outfit, this messenger of God looked absolutely pathetic, and I was tempted to start hurling my own vicious curses at him—not knowing proper etiquette in a situation such as this, however, I held my tongue.

Femka, however, moved in, and quite soon there was a clerical bulge in his brief French panties. Extracting a surprisingly unatrophied stiff member, she proceeded to stroke it in unison with (I swear) his ear-piercing litany of release. I'm standing off to the side taking all of this in, in absolute stunned disbelief. So the chanting continued at full volume, Femka stroking madly and Monique hurling abuse and whipping his bare ass after having dropped the French panties to his ankles, till finally, in a blast that would have put the Mormon Tabernacle Choir to shame, French Frills ejaculated and self-polluted himself in a shameful manner.

Downstairs later, as Al and I were about to leave (with Femka) Monique bade us her good-byes. "Fascinating, Monique." "Thanks for inviting us over." "Call me when you're in New York." "Loved the burnt sienna wallpaper in 'The Room.'" I mean, what the hell *do* you say? From out of

the shadows, though, strode God's messenger and embraced Al and me. It was sort of like we had witnessed his release, his shame, his *apologia* for having transgressed upon human freedom, sensuality, and life-affirming pleasure in his role of an anti-life clergyman. So he hugged us and kissed us on the cheek—and he tapped humble feelings in me. He was so sorry for what he knew he was, and he seemed to be trying to apologize and assume the sins of every religious charlatan (a redundancy) who hides behind piety and basic human fear, and preaches a doctrine of love of an almighty via absolute fear of the beyond. I had difficulty dealing with being enraged, and at the same time, I was touched.

I saw Monique von Cleef, though, in an incredible role. She was closer to "an almighty force" than he'd ever be. Her role was a psychiatrist, social worker, mother, guru, counterforce vehicle. She never hurts anybody physically, really. She just provides the illusion—for which people gladly pay.

I left her home with an abiding respect—and with a question in my mind about where her "clients" would go for their outlet if she weren't around.

Photograph by Ken Gaul

The East

Humorous phallic figure from the Philippines. Copyright © 1968 by Drs. Phyllis and Eberhard Kronhausen

*I*ndia, despite its rich treasurehouse of ancient erotic art and literature, is singularly lacking in any special action for the contemporary visitor. Indian public officials have frequently remarked that if anyone were to attempt producing works of a similar nature to those of bygone centuries, they would be put in jail.

Thailand, on the other hand, offers a veritable banquet of sexual delights, found most particularly in Bangkok. One needs no special advance information other than that in Bangkok exist the most elaborate massage parlors in the world, where a man or a woman can go for anything from a straight, expert massage to an orgy of ancient Roman proportions.

Most fascinating, however, is what was going on in Saigon during the period of U.S. military involvement. Here are extracts from a protracted diary-letter sent by a personal friend who was a correspondent there at the time. If some of the statements appear overly sexist, one must remember that this is a reflection of reality in a military situation, as it has been throughout history—and in this case it is definitely part of history, like it or not.

Letters from Vietnam

Saigon

Dear Bern,

Next week I am invited to Vung Tau, an hour or so south of here on the shore—a resort town. My host is an army captain who has been out here five years and really knows his way around. Also invited, a round-eye (slang for caucasian) who works for the army historical division at Military Assistance Command Vietnam Headquarters, and has the hope for some round-eyed pussy. Any round-eye who is not an absolute dog gets a mighty lot of courting around here, and it tends to go to their already not usually modest and/or cooperative heads. She gets taken to the Cercle Nautique by colonels and jazz like that. Now for me, I haven't been here as long as they have, and the slants still look pretty good to me. Some of them, that is.

Did you get my note on the 60-floor clap factory? I thought it would intrigue you. It isn't exactly 60 stories high, but if you took the bloody thing apart and stacked it up, that's what you'd get.

Lend me your ears (eyes)—over Cholon way, Saigon's largely ethnic Chinese sister city, there is what would appear to be the highest and largest building in the city, the President Hotel, said to be owned, with other extensive properties and hotels, by a Chinese woman of great wealth. On the roof are a swimming pool, gorgeous manicured garden, tiny Buddhist shrine, and the laundry. On one floor down—the 12th—is a large, barren, concrete-floored and walled billiard room with a blaring juke box smack in the middle and birdies, birdies (read chippies) all over the ever-lovin' scene. Adjacent there is a bar; next adjacent is a restaurant; and next adjacent is a bar/club/dancing.

At this time, the 11th and 10th floors are reserved for GIs on R&R, or in town overnight on duty—whatever the reason. There are a few unsuspecting civilian transients located deeper down in the building, but by and large, this is military country. What's weird is the building is largely unfinished and still being worked on.

The scene in the afternoon is not quiet—*that juke box!*—but calm, with boys and girls surveying the situation. The deal and the price are for the night, and something after nine the pressure goes on. The boys want a reasonably decent-looking chick at the lowest going price; the girls want top money, but if they hold out too long, they can wind up sleeping alone on the corridor floor. Got the picture?

Prices, I can authoritatively report, start with the real dollie-dollies, some of whom were designed by an expert, and decorated by a mad Hollywood pornographer, at a nerve-and-exchequer-numbing 9,000 pee (piasters). At 275 (official) and even at 370 (black market) to the greenback, this is some tag, not to mention 1,200 pee for room and playground. But one usually can make out, if that is the proper phrase, for around 4,000 as curfew approaches. After midnight, what is left (and there are some dogs among them), prowls the 11th and 10th floor **corridors, tapping on doors. As they make their rounds,** their more fortunate sisters, in shorties, with and without the bottom half, are being raced up and down the halls in supermarket carts by GIs clad in boots and bathtowels. Got the picture?

Consider seriously the proposition that a man has not completely seen a country until he has been laid there. A colleague living in Phnom Penh suggested that the VD rate in PP is astronomical, and since it was only two more nights until I would be back in Saigon, I decided that the Cambodian girls simply did not rate the risk. PP is no town for the single man. The bars are few and pretty sad; the Chinese hotels are all said to be cathouses but . . . infectious, again. A heritage of the French days. The dancing bars open at two and close at eight. In the afternoon and evening respectively. The bars close at ten. After seven the place rolls up the proverbial carpet.

Let me tell you about Mamma Bic, whom I met just last night. Mamma Bic is the house mother of the Green Berets, and runs what has to be one of the raunchiest dives on Tu Do street. She claims 31, looks 41, and will screw, blow, buy drinks for, and finance any broke Special Forces man who wanders her way. She claims, and my most informed friend supports, that she has lent without return at least thirty thousand dollars to these guys. In her place, if she is sitting with you, you don't buy tea for the girl you are with, you buy whiskey for Mamma Bic. Then she'll fix you up with any age, size, and technique you want. I have met a few "originals" in my life, but she heads the list. That is a story, but she doesn't want to be written up. Just roundly screwed. As I keep telling you, Vietnam is a fascinating place! I may never come home.. . .

General comment, based on considerable experience in Europe and Vietnam: with rare, rare exceptions, most whores do not fuck well; I have met only one with "heart of gold," and I think that that was highly limited; they could almost all benefit greatly from generous and frequent application of soap and water. So wither a young man's dreams.

As ever, Reg

Letters from Japan

*T*he complexities of sexuality in Japan have been the subject of many scholarly and, upon occasion, not so scholarly books and articles. Fortunately, a ranking diplomat in Tokyo volunteered to provide us with the real thing, not only as it pertains to what is going on now, but with valuable insights into the past. His anecdote about the "Supaa-Tikulaa" is a perfect beginning, and what follows speaks for itself.

Dear Bern,

One tale has come back to me which might be of interest. It is, in its essentials, true. In 1953 an American GI in Tokyo, an acquaintance of mine, was going after a girl whose private person he wished to possess in the worst way.

She was an American Nisei and possessed in an extreme degree the worst prejudice of American girls, *viz.*, a prejudice against getting laid, more prevalent then than now. In the best American tradition, however, she allowed my friend a few liberties, including some digital exploration, but nothing involving in any way the portion of his body to which he attached more importance.

He was beginning to suffer terribly. He went to one of the Pinkku Shoppu in Shimbashi. At that time, just after the occupation, Japan was less preoccupied with apparent morality than now. Pornographic books were widely available, dirty shows proliferated, and there were many shops which sold sex aids of various kinds, in addition to routine pornography. For reasons lost in mystery, the general sphere of literature described as "blue" in English is "pink" (pronounced pinkku in Japanese) and a Pinkku Shoppu was a place which sold goods appealing to prurient interests and sexual deviances of one kind or another.

My friend consulted with the proprietor. He prescribed a "hottu kureemu" (hot cream) to get things on the right track, and he suggested a Bandy-dandy Supaa-Tikulaa (super-tickler) to give her the habit right away. The Supaa-Tikulaa was displayed to us in our barracks before the trial heat. It was indeed an impressive object, executed in many colors, with knobs, feathers, and little feelers (all in rubber) wandering in various carefully calculated directions.

The hottu kureemu succeeded immediately. The girl was corrupted on the spot, and my friend was hauled almost by force to the nearest short-time hotel as soon as his finger, dipped discreetly in the magic potion, had reached a spot where its work could best be done. Once in the hotel room, her caution returned, but she insisted in any case upon absolute darkness. My friend managed

Page of typical sex ads from contemporary Japanese magazine featuring "Friends of the night," "Electric blowfish," "Playthings for women," "Really hairy porno films," and "secret pink pictures"

with considerable difficulty to slip on the Supaa Tikulaa and to accomplish his low ambitions at last.

The girl loved it. In fact, she couldn't get along without it. My friend was kept very busy indeed all night along, and by morning he had some raw spots brought about by abrasion with the Supaa Tikulaa. He had been required, however, to promise replay as soon as he went off duty the following afternoon. The girl was waiting for him in a taxi as soon as he left the barracks, and he passed another feverish night. There was no need for hottu kureemu. Although she insisted upon keeping the room dark and was very modest about looking at him or touching his body, she insisted upon being screwed often, strongly, and long. She had been a virgin when it all started, at least in the sense that my friend was the first to have screwed her properly—if his technique was proper or at least conventional. And, of course, she had no idea that her pleasure was due at least in part to equipment other than the basic chassis.

At last the truth came out. My friend was getting tired and irritable. Simple fatigue, in addition to a severe case of saddle sores, was wearing him down. He tried to fob off the girl with excuses and claims about being assigned to extra duty, but she shattered each stratagem and claimed her reward every night. Then he forgot it. He left the Supaa Tikulaa in his footlocker—where, indeed, a buddy saw it when he was borrowing a pack of cigarettes. We all waited for our friend's return. He came

back at last, shambling with fatigue. "What did she say?" "How did it go?" we asked.

"I can't describe it, It's too horrible . . . she was so pissed. I did everything but screw her hanging from the light fixture upside down . . she almost drowned me in the tub. I swear, it was the greatest performance of my life. I feel like I've been sucked dry. And what did she say? *"Never forget that goddamed thing again."* With that he slumped on his bunk. A week later, he requested, and received, an immediate transfer to Korea.

As ever, John

Tokyo

Dear Bern,

There used to be some good ads in the old days like, "Cherry Bar—all girls guaranteed part-time virgins" and "one hour extra for only one hundred yen before 11:00 a.m." and "even senior colonels come here," etc. But now the English language papers don't run that kind of ad any more, and the bars don't care, because the real profits in the skin trade are realizable from Japanese, not foreigners. In fact, there is a minor market for American broads for service as hostesses and singers in bars which cater primarily or exclusively to Japanese. Every once in a while the consulate here has a case of a girl who was recruited in Baton Rouge or somewhere to sing in a Japanese night club and has arrived to discover that they don't much care about her vocal chords and is all upset over the whole thing and wants to break her contract. Of course, they paid her way here, and they own her end-to-end for the next ten years, if she lasts that long. An unenforcable and illegal contract, of course, but the girls get upset.

Now, all the funny ads are in Japanese, like "Brief respite, 3500 yen; all night, 4800 yen," and so on.

Ad for Climax Sex-porn shop, Toei Promenade, 19 Kabuki-Cho, Shinjuku-Ku, Tokyo, Japan

Looking for new members — The queen is waiting for you. . . The club where you can be both happy and have peace of heart. ONLY HIGH CLASS PEOPLE! THE QUEEN OF THE S/M WORLD. Call: (03) 881-8385 RIBEI CLUB

I don't know if you've heard of the rosary. This used to be available at whorehouses in Japan. Buddhist rosaries consist of a relatively small number—a dozen or so—of fairly large, round wooden beads, with a tassel at one end. The girl would insert the rosary into the man's backside bead by bead, as part of the foreplay. Then, the man screws her in a more or less conventional fashion. Finally at the supreme moment, the man says he is on his way and the girl hauls on the tassel, removing the rosary all in a rush. Friends who have tried it say that every man should experience it once, but not many wish to try it twice. "One of the problems is, you don't know whether you are coming or going," I was told. Japan is an interesting country.

Just for fun I am sending an item from Bunny Books called *Ajia no Mitsu-e*, or *Erotic Pictures of Asia*. The content is nothing all that unusual (although the fifteenth century Persian item below captioned: "I know this is a camel, you dummy, but buggers can't be choosers" has some charm. The main interest lies in the excision by airbrush or a bar or block or rectangle of censorship, of the organs most central to the process being undertaken. Whatever the guy on page 176 is doing, it is not clear what he is doing it *with* (see below, right). This shows the fussiness which has come over the Japanese in the past six or seven years. *Genesis* and all its competitors arrive with the main parts blacked out, a job for bored housewives employed part time to wield a Magic Marker in the customs houses.

We went to Shimoda, a sea resort about 150 miles southwest of Tokyo, which is at the tip of a peninsula sticking into the Black Current, a stream of warm sea water from the South China Sea, more or less like the Gulf Stream, but better. So, even if Tokyo is cold, Shimoda is reasonably pleasant.

In pre-Meiji, pre-modern Japan, Shimoda belonged to the shoguns. There are high hills next to the sea and an excellent port, which made it a good place for keeping a cold eye on coastal traffic. When Commodore Perry came swaggering in with his Black Ships, the Japanese met him at Shimoda. He was an obtuse, stubborn man with lots of powerful guns, so the Japanese agreed to a treaty, which was signed at Ryosenji Temple in Shimoda. Signing treaties in a religious establishment seems odd to us, but Buddhist temples in old Japan were often the only public facilities. Temples were, and are, frequently owned by individual families, who charged fees for lodging (there were few hotels outside the biggest cities), food, and other services which were not necessarily religious.

Well, Perry did his thing in 1854 and sailed away. A while later, when it had been decided that this was a good, or at least an historical thing, the Ryosenji Temple began to solicit the tourist trade. Memorial tablets and explanatory boards were put up, and a portrait of Perry, copied from a contemporary print and looking as if he were monumentally constipated on hardtack and salt pork, was erected. The tourists came, of course, but not enough of them.

boilerplate
10 Most Popular Sex Aids at IDEA A.B.C.

1) **Doll for Ecstasy:** ¥3,300 ~ ¥4,000 A doll operated by remote control that undulates from left to right in a female permitting multi-orgasms.	6) **Love Chocolates, Lip Cream, etc.:** ¥600 ~ ¥1,000 Safe aphrodisiac candy and salves, to prolong life's most joyous act for both male and female.
2) **Passion Turtle:** ¥2,500 This special turtle opens a new realm of euphoria in coitsus for both sexes.	7) **Necktie Novelties:** ¥1,200 For the man in search of new, de-lightful sexual positions, the tie de-sign features 48 positions for coitus and two ancient Japanese *ukiyo-e* positions as a bonus on the backside.
3) **Kokeshi Doll** ¥800 ~ ¥1,500 See this phallus-shaped doll and no imagination is needed to visualize its many uses.	
4) **Erotic Gold & Silver Ball-Bells:** ¥5,000 & ¥6,000, respectively When inserted into the female these balls make a highly pleasing erotic sound for both partners during coi-tus.	8) **Cassette Tape:** ¥2,400 **Cartridge Tape:** ¥4,800 Listen to words and sounds of the most ecstatic moment of love-making.
	9) **Jelly-Fish of Passion:** ¥1,200 ~ 2,000 Attached to the male organ during coitus, a female floats on an euphoric cloud. Her well of love running over. In addition, there are more than 10 attachments to be used by men.
5) **Vulva Vibrator:** ¥1,500 ~ ¥2,500 This represents one of the greatest inventions since sliced bread afford-ing females the opportunity to drift from blissful orgasm to orgasm.	10) **Wireless Wire Tap:** ¥15,000 Small wireless microphone, capable of listening to at a point 100 meters distant. Sensitivity is excellent. No explanation is needed for the many possible uses for this sophisticated electronic mite.

Make your life most enjoyable with these divices.

The Ryosenji Temple authorities had an inspired idea. "Why not commemmorate Commodore Perry with a pornographic museum?" All agreed that this was a highly appropriate proposal. It had little or nothing to do with Commodore Perry (whose sexual activities in Japan are not, as far as I know, a matter of record) but the Izu Peninsula, which includes Shimoda, has a long and fertile history as a center of phallicism. Even now, several local towns have annual festivals at which huge wooden dicks carved to the last intimate detail are car-ried on thrones through the streets by sobbing maidens, or at least women. Many temples on the peninsula have absolute forests of pricks in their sanctuaries, and a few liberated ones feature discreetly haired snatches as well. But these places are mostly distant and inaccessible, and the hypocrisy about such matters which infests modern Japan inhibits frankness.

Shimoda, however, is an extremely accessible place, with hundreds of **thousands** of visitors every year. The Perry Commemorative Museum has been an enormous success. It does not amount to much. There is a series of SM (to borrow a Japanese term) paintings, of a long and complicated traditional tale about a girl who has a pretty hard time but finally makes good. There are also a lot of gadgets more or less involved with sex, including some Indian gadgets, an absolutely super ginseng, and a big collection of phallic images.

Lastly, there is the whole topic of Asian sex hangups which are as acute as our own, but usually backwards. The Indians, in particular, believe that women are more sexy than men and are a kind of bottomless sump of eroticism, attractive to the low-minded male but some-how involving him in uncleanliness every time he dips in. And the male is very explicitly draining off a little of his masculine substance every time he knocks one off. So the whole strategy is to have your ass and keep your semen, too. This idea has spread to China and Japan as well. A very good and thoughtful book on the psychol-ogy of this is *The Twice Born* by Morris Carstairs, a Scottish psychiatrist raised in India who went back for anthropological research—published in England and I believe in the U.S. about fifteen years ago. It is a first-class book in a field which is awash with crap. The Chinese and Japanese aspects are discussed accessibly in Joseph Needham's mammoth *Science and Civilization in China* (look up under Taoism in the indexes) and to a much lesser extent in Sir George Sansome's *Japan: A Short Cultural History*.

As ever, John

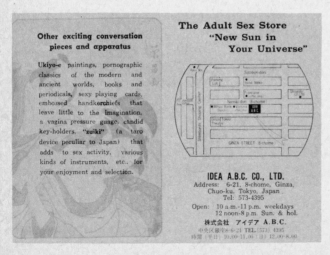

Other exciting conversation pieces and apparatus

Ukiyo-e paintings, pornographic classics of the modern and ancient worlds, books and periodicals, sexy playing cards, embossed handkerchiefs that leave little to the imagination, a vagina pressure guage, candid key-holders, "**zuiki**" (a taro device peculiar to Japan) that adds to sex activity, various kinds of instruments, etc., for your enjoyment and selection.

The Adult Sex Store "New Sun in Your Universe"

IDEA A.B.C. CO., LTD.
Address: 6-21, 8-chome, Ginza, Chuo-ku, Tokyo, Japan
Tel: 573-4395
Open: 10 a.m.-11 p.m. weekdays
12 noon-8 p.m. Sun. & hol.
株式会社 アイデア A.B.C.
中央区銀座8-6-21 TEL (573) 4395
時間〔平日〕10.00-11.00〔日〕12.00-8.00

Woodblock print in the style of Shusui Kyoto, circa 1770

The Tibetan Shoden is said to bring great joy.

The preserved radish in the bottle was found in 1910 and donated to the shrine.

The vase is self-explanatory.

Lucky dolls. These are fertility dolls, essentially, except that the monkeys are for the cure of skin diseases and smallpox. The phallic doll at the right wards off evil spirits and devils.

Lucky underwear. When worn, this is believed to ward off evil spirits, not unlike phallic/sexual amulets in Western culture.

The Harikata (literally, sex tools) are ancient sexual stimulating devices used by high-born court ladies, who were prohibited by tradition from overtly enjoying themselves sexually as men did.

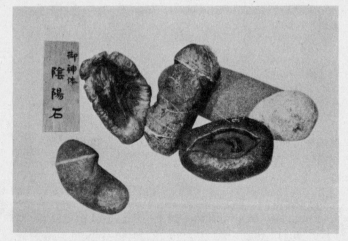

The "natural stones," probably not found in this particular set of shapes, represent the yin and the yang.

Tengu and Okame are classic masks. Tengu is a prideful woman, nose-in-the-air-type. Okame is symbolically ugly. The long nose in Japan is said to indicate a long penis. The mask with the long nose is of a guardian spirit with obvious sexual prowess. A Tengu seen grabbing his nose is doing so for sexual reasons. The figure of two women in the middle is cleverly fashioned in the shape of cock and balls. The Okame at the right is obviously enjoying the gigantic phallus; but notice that her cheeks are breasts.

Japanese key ring, alleged for mysterious reasons to promote safe driving

The New Sword *Painting attributed to Toba-Sojo, sixteenth century*

Sex and the Eight Hundred Million

By Shirley Craig

Rubbing from ancient Chinese stone depicting punishment by the penis of a horse. Courtesy of Drs. Phyllis and Eberhard Kronhausen

The following, by Shirley Craig, who worked with Shirley MacLaine on her documentary film, The Other Half of the Sky: A China Memoir, *pretty well sums up the situation there as it is today.*

The People's Republic of China: 800 million people comprising over one quarter of the world's population. As a nation of people, it would seem that since their massive Liberation in 1949, and subsequent Cultural Revolution in 1968, they have come a long way from the once semi-Feudal system dominated by strongarm tyrants and overpowering landlords. Today China is a land of workers, peasants, and soldiers.

In order to begin to be able to comprehend their attitudes on sex and love, it is important to understand the structure of the cultural environment in which these 800 million people live today, as compared to their "bitter past." Their history is filled with barbaric, almost inhuman customs, such as footbinding—crippling and imprisoning women to virtual slavery; the execution by exposure of superfluous female children; the selling of unwanted children in order to feed other members of the family; the betrothal of young people who never see each other before the day of their wedding; stoning widows to death for remarrying and other horrendous abuses legitimized in the confines of "wedlock"; the infamous Bund river in Shanghai alongside which the "Flower Kingdom" of prostitutes, opium dens, deprivation and decadence flourished; and the constant battle against starvation, and to maintain some kind of roof over their heads and clothes on their backs.

Today China has emancipated itself from the oppressive rule of its elders and has established a new order for its men and women. Terms like the "new society," "a new breed of human beings," "the hope for the future world," are often used to describe this massive collection of people. But their attitudes toward sex differ from the rest of civilization.

Our attitudes about anything and perhaps sex in particular, come as a result of social conditioning and the approaches we have to ourselves and our environment. Outside the communist world, and particularly in Western society, "individualism" is the major thrust of our way of life, and that "individualism" is something that is brought to our sex mores. But in China, there is almost no sign of "individualism." The Chinese work collectively for the good of the state, putting the social reconstruction of China first. In return, the state puts them first, providing them with every practical need for survival in life, housing, food, education, medical care, etc., seemingly taking away that ultimate responsibility of "self." The highest honor any single Chinese man, woman, or child can receive is to be considered a hard-working, politically conscious, well-respected member of the community. And frankly, it seems that there is little time for anything else.

Life is structured within a very limited framework. From the time you rise out of bed in the morning until you get back into it at night, no energy is wasted. Leisure time, other than that supplied by the Revolution Committee (the local self-governing committee which administers to every need of the community), is frowned upon. The message is *constantly* to work hard for social reconstruction, and every ounce of human energy, emotional and physical, is put into that monumental task.

Some people have said that their whole philosophy toward sex and love is a self-denying, masochistic, almost inhuman one, dominated by the supreme importance of the state and the total insignificance of the individual. Perhaps that is true. But when one sees the thousands of smiling contented faces, certainly the question of its truth arises.

Chinese women talk seemingly openly and freely about their husbands, their attitudes towards love and sex and "women's liberation." It is mind-boggling to realize that there are very few attitudes in China today toward sex per se.

"What was the major thing that attracted you to your husband? Was it his brown eyes, his sense of humor, the fact that he was good-looking, had broad shoulders, was a doctor, a farmer . . .?" the American women in the film would ask. And the answer would always be: "Political ideology." One interpreter explained that her husband's higher political consciousness was what made her decide to marry him. "It would be no good if we did not speak the same political language." The state acknowledges "higher political consciousness" as one of the finest qualities in a worker.

The state also recommends that the young postpone marriage or any thoughts of "young love" until their late twenties. Their early and most creative years of physical and mental development should be put to use for the betterment of the state. So marriage is decreed for a woman from twenty-six years and over, and for a man twenty-eight years and over. Sex before marriage, we were told, is virtually nonexistent. In answer to the question: "What would happen if a young girl became pregnant outside of wedlock?" the answer was, "We have had no such case in this district." Divorce and adultery are also virtually unheard of, and where problems in marriages

do exist, the leader of the local Revolution Committee steps in and sorts them out. Birth control is efficiently dispensed, but to married couples only. And more than two children is frowned upon. "One is too few, two is just enough, three is more than enough, four is wrong, and five is very wrong."

Masturbation is discouraged at an early age. Young boys are reprimanded for "playing with themselves" and told that it is unhealthy and unnecessary. As for women and masturbation . . . this seemed a complete mystery that most women do not desire to solve. Homosexuality wasn't discussed, and open displays of affection are rarely seen. Occasionally young children are seen walking in the streets holding hands, but there are certainly no overt gestures from adults of kissing or hugging in public.

From the forty-seven hours of film that were brought back from China, it was obvious there is a reluctance to speak about sex. Perhaps out of embarrassment, ignorance, or just because they do not put the same emphasis on it as we do here in the Western world. The Chinese were far more interested and proud to explain that that week they had increased their rice production by five barrels or the factory had doubled its produce, rather than whether or not they got into oral sex or did anything other than the missionary position.

Marriage is something that everybody does, and children, it seems, are something everybody has. When asked what would happen if a young woman didn't want to marry and have children, the women would giggle in embarrassed astonishment. "Did such cases exist in the United States?" was the reply.

China has few overtly discussed attitudes about sexuality, but that is not to say they don't enjoy good and healthy sex lives. It just isn't as important as feeding 800 million people every day, or working on that ever-continuing Revolution of Social Reconstruction.

Anonymous eighteenth century Chinese painting of young woman masturbating with a tree

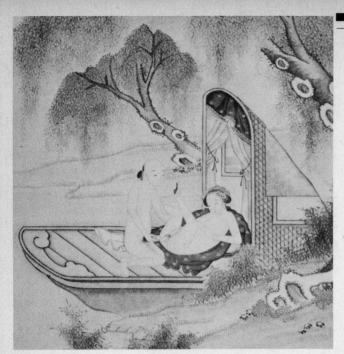

Romantic detail from a Chinese Ming scroll.
Copyright © Drs. Phyllis & Eberhard Kronhausen 1968

Endnote

Admittedly, we have devoted a disproportionate amount of space to arbitrarily selected parts of the world. It has been a matter of necessity dictated by limitations of space. Australia, for example, for years was very strict on the importation of sexually oriented materials, but today is producing newspapers of the *Screw* genre. It is the scene of a flourishing American-style massage parlor business, and was recently the location of a high-quality soft-core film spoofing sex, *Alvin Purple*, which for a long time outgrossed *The Godfather* at Australian boxoffices.

To present a properly comprehensive survey of sexuality in Africa alone would require an encyclopedia. The emerging African nations are undergoing immense cultural changes today. But despite this, old tribal attitudes and customs still prevail and are dying slowly. It would be unfair to make generalizations because the range is so wide from one ethnic group to another. In some tribes, for example, adultery was regarded with such abhorrence that adulterers and adulteresses were punished by slow, painful death. In others there was great sexual freedom. In areas that have had contact with Europeans and Americans over the centuries, many Western ideas have been adopted. Prostitution, of course, is a practice that has been widely accepted. So has sexuality in art. Since the first Europeans set foot on African soil in the fifteenth century, Africans have been subjected to severe culture shock, sexually and otherwise, by having alien ideas forced upon them. Vestiges of this still remain, but fortunately, Africans are highly sophisticated, and until the Judeao-Christian attitudes toward sex and sin were introduced to them, they had minimal sex problems. Sex had its place in nature and was accepted for what it was.

Moslem culture encompasses more than the Mideast, and anyone who has studied it or observed it firsthand knows that sex and sensuality play important roles. There is no better source of information on sex in Islam than in the writings of **Sir Richard F. Burton,** *e.g.,* his unexpurgated translation of *The Thousand and One Nights, The Perfumed Garden,* etc. A word of caution for visitors to Moslem countries. The world situation being what it is, and the political attitudes toward Americans in particular being what they are, travelers in these countries are advised to abstain completely until they return to more familiar territory. Islam does not look kindly upon foreigners who dally with its daughters. Prostitution, of course, is the great common denominator.

It is also wise not to bruise oneself jumping to conclusions about Israel. There is a tendency to think of it as essentially a European enclave in the Mideast. But remember that the majority of the population, Jews and Arabs alike, come from areas in which Islamic tradition is dominant, a fact which strongly influences attitudes. There is also a rigid minority of Orthodox Jews, whose attitudes are puritanical and strict.

As for those parts of the world that we have not mentioned specifically, consult the bibliography, for it fills in the gaps and can provide you with sources of information for anything in which you may be interested.

Typical page of sex adverts taken from an Australian newspaper, featuring massage parlors, and striptease and topless shows

Bibliography

Berndt, Ronald M., and Catherine H. *Sexual Behavior in Western Amhem Land.* New York: Viking Fund Publications in Anthropology, 1951.

Bryant, A. *The England of Charles H.* London: Longmans, Greene, 1934.

Bryk, Felix. *Voodoo-Eros: Ethnological Studies in the Sex Life of the African Aborigines.* New York: United Book Guild; 1964.

Cabanes, A. *The Erotikon.* Falstaff Press, 1933.

Day, Beth. *Sexual Life Between Blacks and Whites.* New York: World Publishing, 1972. $8.95

Edwardes, Allen. *Erotica Judaica.* New York: Julian Press.

——. *The Jewel in the Lotus.* New York: Julian Press. $6.50

——. *The Rape of India.* New York: Julian Press.

Edwardes, Allen, and Masters, R. E. L. *Cradle of Erotica.* New York: Julian Press. $5.95

Flugel, J. C. *Man, Morals and Society.* Duckworth, 1954.

Forberg, Frederick Charles. *Manual of Classical Erotology.* New York: Grove Press, 1966. Original privately printed by Julian Smithson, M.A. and Friends, London.

Giese, Hans, and Schmidt, Gunter. *Studenten Sexualitat: Vehalten und Einstellung.* Hamburg: Rowohlt Verlag 1968.

Heard, G. *Morals Since 1900.* Drakers, 1950.

Kiefer, O. *Sexual Life in Ancient Rome.* London: Routledge, 1934.

Kolbanovsky, V. *Love, Marriage and Family in the Socialist Society.* Moscow: State Publishing House, 1951.

Levy, Howard. *Oriental Sex Manners.* London: New English Library, 1971.

Licht, H. *Sexual Life in Ancient Greece.* London: Routledge, 1931.

Linner, Birgitta. *Sex and Society in Sweden.* New York: Harper & Row, 1972. $2.95

Malinowski, Bronislaw. *The Sexual Life of Savages in North-Western Melanesia.* New York: Halcyon House, 1941.

Mankoff, Allan H. *Mankoff's Lusty Europe.* Reprint. New York: Pocket Books, 1975. $1.95

Mantegazza, Paolo. Translated by Samuel Putnam. *Sexual Relations of Mankind.* New York: Eugenics Publishing Co., 1935.

Marshall, Donald S. *Ralivavae: An Expedition to the Most Fascinating and Mysterious Island in Polynesia.* Garden City: N.Y.: Doubleday, 1961.

Marshall, Donald S., and Suggs, Robert C., eds. *Human Sexual Behavior: Variations in the Ethno-Graphic Spectrum.* New York: Basic Books, 1971.

Mead, Margaret. *Sex and Temperament in Three Primitive Societies.* New York: 1935.

Nemecek, Dr. Ottokar. *Virginity, Pre-Nuptial Rites and Rituals.* New York: Philosophical Library Inc., 1958.

Neubert, R. *Questions of Sex.* Moscow: State Publishing House, 1960.

O'Curry, E. *Manners and Customs of the Ancient Irish.* Williams & Norgate, 1873.

Reade, R. S. *Registrum Librorum Eroticorum.* London: 1936.

Rogers, J. *Sex and Race: Negro-Caucasian Mixing in All Ages and All Lands.* 2 vols. New York: 1940-1944.

Riencourt, Amaury de. *Sex and Power in History.* New York: David McKay, 1974. $12.95

Rougemont, D. de. *Love in the Western World.* New York: Harcourt, Brace, 1940.

Schapera, Isaac. *Married Life in an African Tribe.* New York: Sheridan House, 1941.

Stafford, Peter. *Sexual Behavior in the Communist World.* New York: Julian Press, 1967. $8.50

Suggs, Robert. *Marquesan Sexual Behavior.* New York: Harcourt, Brace & World, 1966.

Taylor, G. Rattray. *Sex in History.* New York: Ballantine Books, 1954.

The Perfumed Garden. Translated by Sir Richard Burton. (Many editions available.)

Unwin, J. D. *Sex and Culture.* Oxford: Oxford University Press, 1934.

Verrier, Elwin. *The Muria and Their Ghotul.* Bombay: Oxford University Press, Geoffrey Cumberlege, 1947.

Westermarck, E. A. *Origin and Development of the Moral Ideas.* New York: Macmillan, 1906.

Wright, T. *A History of Domestic Manners and Sentiments.* Chapman & Hall, 1862.

Reproduced by permission of New English Library

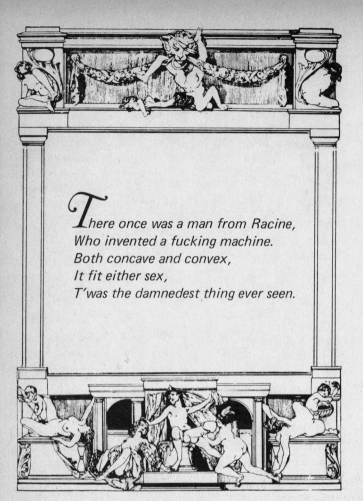

There once was a man from Racine,
Who invented a fucking machine.
Both concave and convex,
It fit either sex,
T'was the damnedest thing ever seen.

The Sexual Bazaar Bizarre ?

*O*nce upon a time fanciful devices such as the mythical machine immortalized in this old limerick existed only in the imaginations of those whose predilections led their fancies down the exotic pathways of sexuality. There were, of course, exceptions. Throughout history enterprising individuals contrived truly incredible sexual contraptions that catered to the fantasies of jaded debauchees whose financial status allowed them to indulge in their wildest whims. There was Dr. Graham's Celestial Bed and the fabled Berkeley Horse. In the realm of pure fantasy, artist Tomi Ungerer has let his imagination run rampant, and undoubtedly the maddest mechanism ever to be constructed in recent times was the bicycle used in the X-rated film *It Happened in Hollywood*, produced by Jim Buckley and directed by Peter Locke (released by Milky Way Productions).

Today, between modern technology, sophisticated marketing techniques, and a worldwide quest for new ways to enhance sexual pleasure, a whole new multi-million-dollar industry has mushroomed. To some it presages a beginning of the end, parallel to the decline of the Roman Empire. To others, it is the dawn of a new era of sensual delight.

Whatever the case, the fact remains that today, just as "you don't have to be Jewish to enjoy Levy's Rye Bread," you don't have to be a millionaire to avail yourself of the myriad sexual exotica currently available in the international sexual bazaar. Furthermore, thanks to a general lowering of postal barriers, if you can't go directly to your local friendly neighborhood sex boutique, the availability of catalogues and explicit ads in a wide variety of publications brings whatever you may want within reach of your mailbox. If your intention is merely to browse, there is enough variety here to provide you with spicy conversation pieces *ad infinitum*. If you are planning a shopping spree, however, remember the age-old adage: *Caveat Emptor*—let the buyer beware. You are on your own.

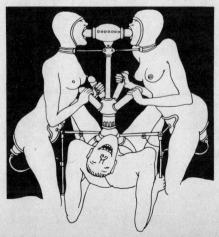

From under the desk of Eric Bakalinsky

Dear Editor:

An upper division sociology class at University of California, Berkeley, making a comprehensive study of personal, classified ads in underground publications worldwide since 1960, spontaneously nominated and unanimously conferred the title "most creative classified ad in an underground newspaper" to the ad I placed in the *Berkeley Barb:*

Miscegenation with a lively dromedary was the hump that broke the camel's back. I can dig it, but it takes more than that to break me. So I, a 25-year-old handsome Virgo with vivacious tongue, seek lusting wench and/or woman next door for wholesome wantonness and inordinate joy. I love all races, but not racists or camel drivers.

*T*he great philosopher, Voltaire, once engaged in a serious discussion with an English friend on the subject of sodomy. After exploring the subject from all aspects, the Englishman observed that he would like to delve into the matter more deeply and increase his knowledge by means of firsthand experience. "By all means, my friend," Voltaire encouraged. Some weeks later when the two men met again, the subject came up once more. Revealing that he had indeed fulfilled his intention and personally engaged in the act, the Englishman observed that he had found it so interesting that he was giving serious consideration to trying it again. Upon this Voltaire smiled, raised a warning finger, and declared, "Ah no, my friend. Once, a philosopher; twice, a sodomite."

From Sixty Erotic Engravings From Juliette. *Copyright © 1969 Grove Press, Inc. Reprinted by permission of Grove Press, Inc.*

The Mons Veneris
Golf and Country Club

Golfers & Flubbers

Throw away your old bags, bring your balls, and join our new club!

COME!

Bring your own sticks!

GREAT EATING!

Ask anyone who's tried it.

UNIQUE!

A new delight in each of our 18 holes.

NEW THRILLS!

As you play over luxurious mounds surrounded by rich shrubbery.

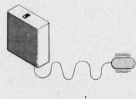

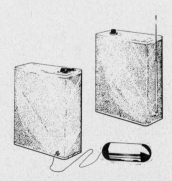

Sex Boutiques

*A*lthough many people prefer to purchase their sexual devices via the mail order route, there are a number of sex boutiques around the country in which customers can browse and buy over the counter. Because so many of them come and go, a comprehensive country-wide listing of them would be impractical and unfair to the reader. There are, however, three major boutiques that are well established, and which do, in addition to their retail operation, an extensive mail order business. We have thoroughly investigated each and can offer accurate, first-hand information.

THE INTERNATIONAL LOVE BOUTIQUE
7046 Hollywood Boulevard
Hollywood, California
(213) 466-7046

This is without question the most elegant, pleasantly appointed, and friendly sex boutique in the United States. Owners Bernice Fisher and Terri Richmond are charming, helpful, and expert at putting all visitors at ease. There is never any high pressure; everyone who enters the portals is treated more like a guest than a potential customer. The boutique's array of merchandise includes the entire range of sex aids, novelties, toys, games, art—both original and in reproduction. A feature which makes The International Love Boutique totally unique is their museum of sex located on the lower level of the store. If you are not in the Los Angeles area, you may write for their color, illustrated catalogue. They accept American Express, BankAmericard, Master Charge, but no C.O.D.'s. For rush charge mail orders of $10.00 or more call Eve Adams from noon to 9:00 p.m. Los Angeles time.

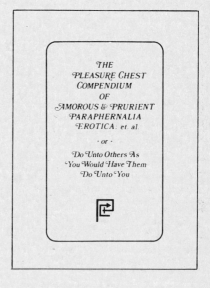

THE PLEASURE CHEST
COMPENDIUM
OF
AMOROUS & PRURIENT
PARAPHERNALIA
EROTICA: et. al.
- or -
Do Unto Others As
You Would Have Them
Do Unto You

THE PLEASURE CHEST in New York carries a full line of sexually oriented products. The atmosphere is dim and sensuous. The personnel are courteous and businesslike, and they do not discourage browsers. They, too, publish a well-appointed catalogue which sells for $3.00. Rapidly becoming a chain operation, they have a number of locations at the following addresses:

230 Columbus Avenue
New York, N.Y. 10023
(212) 724-7291

248 East Fiftieth Street
New York, N.Y. 10022
(212) 838-8417

120 Eleventh Avenue
(mail order only)
New York, N.Y. 10011
(212) 242-4372

152 Seventh Avenue South
New York, N.Y. 10014
(212) 242-4372

New shops are opening in Los Angeles, Miami, Philadelphia, and Toronto. Consult local phone directories and newspapers for exact locations.

Display at International Love Boutique. Photo by B. J. Hurwood

Bernice Fisher, co-owner, International Love Boutique. Photo by B. J. Hurwood

Dutch ashtray depicting bestiality

LOVECRAFT LTD.
108 Yorkville Avenue
Toronto, Canada
(416) 923-7331

Lovecraft is another elegant shop with a decor similar to The International Love Boutique in Los Angeles. Lovecraft publishes a catalogue that is tasteful and attractive. It is also free. Merchandise may be charged on Chargex, BankAmericard, Barclay Card, or Master Charge. Checks and money orders should be made out to MIA Sales. No C.O.D.'s.

The following is provided without comment as we have not checked it out in person:

ONLY SEXY THINGS   (Catalogue $3.00)
Coral Reef Shopping Center
14983 South Dixie Highway
Miami, Florida 33158
(305) 251-6384

A foolish young woman named Alice,

Used dynamite for a phallus.

They found her vagina in North Carolina,

And part of her anus in Dallas.

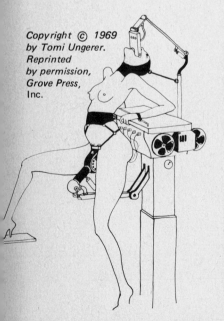

Copyright © 1969
by Tomi Ungerer.
Reprinted
by permission,
Grove Press,
Inc.

Mail Order Companies

The following is a list of some of the major mail-order companies . . . Catalogues and brochures are available.

Advanced Products
P.O. Box 239
Gary, Indiana 4049

Basic Health Aids
P.O. Box 517
New York, N.Y. 10013

Better Rubber Products
P.O. Box 437
New York, N.Y. 10013

Calston Industries
P.O. Box 5030
Sherman Oaks, California 91413

Century Products
6915 S. Vernon
Chicago, Illinois 60637

Diverse Industries, Inc.
7422 Melrose
Hollywood, California 90046

Erik Imports
2326 Cotner Avenue
Los Angeles, California 90064

Evelyn Rainbird, Ltd.
P.O. Box 548
F.D.R. Station
New York, N.Y. 10022

Fabrico
1512 N.E. 29th Street
Ocala, Florida 32670

House of Dawn
210 5th Avenue
New York, N.Y. 10010

Inter X-Company
31-07 21st Street
Long Island City, N.Y. 11106

John Amslow & Associates
Suite 10
P.O. Box 2369
Culver City, California 90230

Linda Products
P.O. Box 69985
Los Angeles, California 90069

Lone Wolf
6311 Yucca Street
Hollywood, California 90028

Majestic Distributors
120 13th Street
Brooklyn, New York 11215

Maxon Products
P.O. Box 40518
San Francisco, California 94140

Product Promotions East
120 11th Avenue
New York, N.Y. 10011

Ruthe's 69 Club
Suite 1056
6311 Yucca Street
Hollywood, California 90028

Select Items
1236 La Cienega Boulevard
Los Angeles, California 90035

Speciality
Box 4447
North Hollywood, California 91607

Synergistic Mail Corp.
G.P.O. Box 2345
New York, N.Y. 10001

Ultima Sales Company
6913 Melrose Avenue
Los Angeles, California 90038

United Sales, Inc.
4731 West Jefferson Boulevard
Los Angeles, California 90016

Universal Specialties
P.O. Box 69977
West Hollywood, California 90069

Life-sized sex doll with appropriate openings top and bottom on display at International Love Boutique. Photo by B. J. Hurwood

"I regret to say that we of the FBI are powerless to act in case of oral-genital intimacy, unless it has in some way obstructed interstate commerce."
J. EDGAR HOOVER

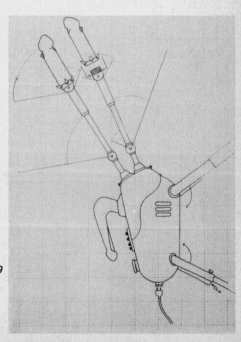

Copyright © 1969 by Tomi Ungerer. Reprinted by permission, Grove Press, Inc.

$\mathcal{B}$y and large the merchandise sold in the sexual bazaar is expensive. Consequently, if you intend to purchase anything through the mail from anyone other than the big, well-established boutiques that do mail order business as well as retail, it is a good idea to deal with firms from which you can reasonably expect to get satisfaction. Unfortunately Ralph Nader, Consumers' Union, *et al* do not offer any help in this area. There are, however, two sources of consumer information that are reliable.

Jerkin' Jerry's Sex Fair
c/o Downstairs Mail Service
167 West 21st Street
New York, N.Y. 10011

This is a newsletter on sex product information that tells you where to obtain free catalogues and other pertinent information. $1.00 per issue or $5.00 for six issues.

Sexsense
P.O. Box 432 Old Chelsea Station
New York, N.Y. 10011

This, too, is a newsletter which keeps you up to date on sex products, quality, costs, and where to get them. Twenty-four issues cost $18.50. Eleven issues $9.95.

$\mathcal{A}$ds

The ads that follow offer you an idea of what sort of merchandise is available and at what price. Though prices may vary slightly from dealer to dealer they generally remain within a close range. In short, here is a representative cross section of the sexual bazaar.

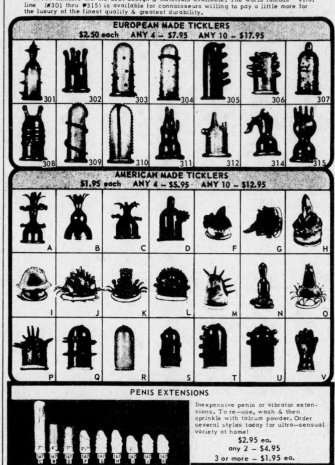

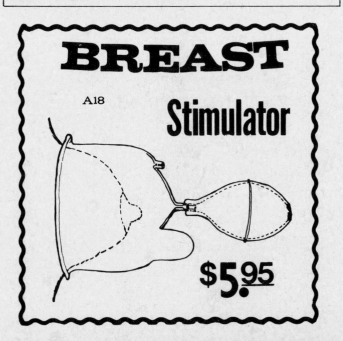

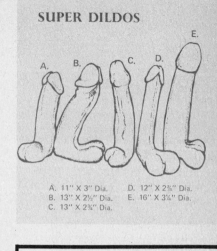

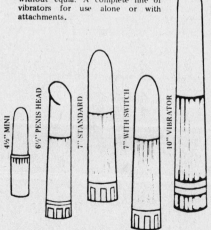

-167-

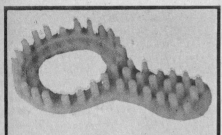

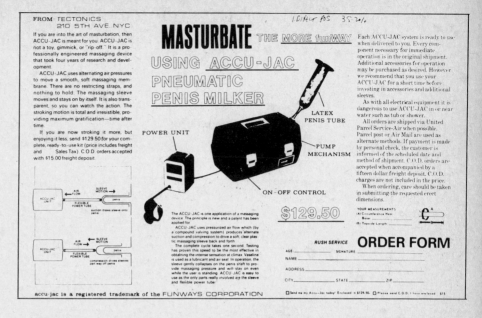

-169-

Massage Parlors

Just as there are sex products for sale, so, thanks to the myriads of massage parlors around the nation, are there fleshly services for sale in infinite variety. What you see here is a sampling of massage parlor ads arbitrarily selected. In some parts of the country these ads appear in the straight papers, while in other parts their exposure is limited to the sexpapers. Depending upon where you happen to be, consult the appropriate paper for the most up-to-date information.

And Now For the Sexual Bizarre (Bazaar?)

At one time such terms as "sexual deviation" and "perversion" were applied to just about anything other than the missionary position, and in some quarters, still are. What is considered deviate in one society is the norm in another, and since it is not our intention to split hairs or make value judgments here, we aren't going to launch into semantic controversies over words. Thanks mainly to the late Richard von Krafft-Ebing, the label "perversion" became attached to anything that didn't turn him on.

There is unending controversy among psychiatrists and psychologists as to what is or isn't "deviate" behavior. It can be ludicrous sometimes, because it is hard to convince even the most sexually liberated person that such tendencies as coprophilia (preoccupation with acts of excretion) and necrophilia (sexual activities involving corpses) are not "deviations." On the other hand, there have been a few classic cases of necrophilia that developed into a socially accepted direction. I quote from the book, *Deviation: A Study of Abnormal Love*, by D. Gunther Wilde (out of print).

"The most celebrated necrophiliac in the world was the poet Edgar Allen Poe. Unlike the Bertrands and the Ardissons who thicken psychiatrists' case history books, Poe never committed an overt act of necrophilia. Instead, he channeled his longings into his writings. When he was still in his teens, Poe wrote a short couplet which accurately describes necrophilia long before the term was even coined.

I could not love except where death
Was mingling his with beauty's breath.

"Certainly, anyone who is even slightly familiar with Poe's works will recognize at once the continuous morbid preoccupation with death. All of Poe's heroines are pale, consumptive brunettes, with large, dark eyes. The

The Great
Red Kangaroo
*by Mel Ramos.
Private European
Collection*

love which the hero bears for them is always tragic and transcends the grave.

"What very few people realize is that the description given by Poe to all these tragic heroines actually recreates his own mother."

Vampirism and cannibalism speak for themselves. Fetishism is sexual preoccupation for particular objects or parts of the body. How often have you heard a man say, "I'm a tit man," "I'm an ass man," or "I'm a leg man"? Happily, now, in the day of the liberated woman, we hear women stating similar preferences, all of which makes the pairing process much easier. Bestiality refers to those who prefer having their sex with animals. The voyeur likes to peek and/or watch sexual activity, even ordinary disrobing: and the exhibitionist, sometimes called a "flasher," likes to show what he has. We say "he" because female exhibitionists are more subtle than male flashers and tend to display their charms with less crudity than their male counterparts—but not always.

Love
and Death.
*Goya print
depicting
necrophilia*

The Squid *Bizarre bestiality as depicted by the eighteenth century Japanese master, Hokusai*

Nineteenth century
illustration
depicting
vampirism

Fifteenth century
woodcut
depicting
flagellants
flogging
themselves
as penance

The nymphomaniac is a rare bird and exists mainly in the fantasies of men who think she is a desirable partner. She is actually a pathetic, frigid woman who cannot reach an orgasm and takes it out on every man she encounters in bed. Beware, because nymphomaniacs make lousy lovers! The satyr, or male counterpart of the nymphomaniac, is suffering from a pathological condition. He can achieve ejaculation after ejaculation, but he derives no sexual satisfaction. Although some satyrs maintain almost perpetual erections, beware. They, too, are lousy lovers because psychologically they are incapable of giving, and all their sexual activity is directed toward taking. The transvestite, or cross-dresser, is really a fetishist, and he or she is not necessarily homosexual.

Sado-masochism is virtually universal and infinite in its variety. Sadism being that end of the spectrum related to inflicting pain, and masochism on the receiving end. The words were coined by Krafft-Ebing, sadism coming from the Marquis de Sade and his works, masochism from the Chevalier Leopold von Sacher-Masoch and his works.

In the words of De Sade himself. ''Now since there can be no doubt that pain affects us more strongly than pleasure, when this sensation is produced in others, our very being will vibrate more vigorously with the resulting shocks.''

And as Sacher-Masoch so aptly remarked, ''I have no desire to be mistreated by one who loves me too much, but by one who loves me too little. I find jealousy dreadfully painful, yet I am in ecstasy if a woman arouses me to jealousy, deceives me, and mistreats me. . . . To me, love for a woman is to fear her. Most women prefer men who are their superiors. I desire a woman who is superior to me . . . the cruel woman who is my ideal, is for me the implement with which I terrorise myself.''

Breeding Bull Penis Cane
"TOROAN MAKILLA"

An Ideal Gift for the man born under the sign of "Taurus"

HERE IS A CANE THAT'S TRULY DIFFERENT! A FULL LENGTH WALKING CANE 35" LONG WITH RUBBER TIP, RUGGED FOR STROLLING AND THE GREATEST CONVERSATIONAL TROPHY PIECE FOR YOUR DEN AS WELL!

THIS CANE IS THE PENIS OF A SELECT LARGE BREEDING BULL, CURED, STRETCHED AND AGED UNTIL IT RESEMBLES OLD KNARLED MOUNTAIN MAHOGANY, BY AN ANCIENT, CAREFULLY GUARDED BASQUE FORMULA HANDED DOWN GENERATION TO GENERATION.

DURING THE 16th CENTURY, MILITARY OFFICERS IN AUSTRIA AND GERMANY CARRIED SWAGGER STICKS MADE OF THE PENIS OF A BULL. THESE ORIGINAL STICKS WERE NOT STIFF ENOUGH TO SUPPORT WEIGHT SO WERE USED AS QUIRTS, OR WHIP HANDLES. OFTEN THESE STICKS WERE EQUIPPED WITH A METAL FERRULE CONTAINING CHALK FOR MARKING CATTLE AT THE AUCTION.

TODAY, A METAL ROD THROUGH THE PENIS MAKES POSSIBLE THE CURVED HANDLE, AND A TRULY STURDY WALKING STICK. THIS ANCIENT ART OF STRETCHING, DRYING, AND AGING LONGER THAN A 4 MONTHS PERIOD IS ALMOST EXTINCT.

ONLY A FEW ARE NOW PRODUCED EACH YEAR THROUGHOUT THE WORLD.

Complete with Brief History on Parchment suitable for framing.

A most rare, unique and authentic walking stick like no other you have ever seen.

SEXY CUNT*RY GIRL
I DIG DOGS!
THE BIGGER THE BETTER SO
I got the world's largest breed to satisfy me. For a sample set of photos of "Wolfy" and me, **Send three dollars to:**

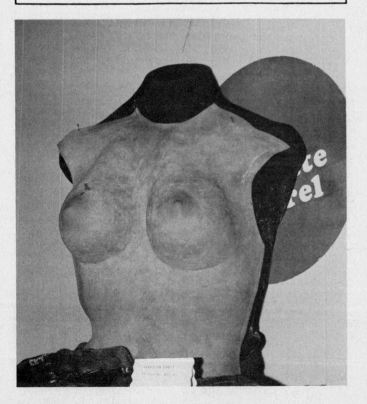

Rubber body form worn by transvestites featured at International Love Boutique. Photo by B. J. Hurwood

HE ASKED ME TO EAT HIM AND I DID

The Peculiar Vice

Perhaps it was the cold climate which originally aroused in Englishmen a desire for whipping. Nowhere else in the world do we find such a deep affection for the rod.

One of the most celebrated English writers to comment on the aphrodisiac qualities of flagellation was Christopher Marlowe, who said:

> When Francus comes to solace with his whore,
> He sends for rods and strips himself stark naked;
> For his lust sleeps, and will not rise before,
> By whipping of the wench it be awakened.
> I envy him not, but I wish I had the power,
> To make myself his wench but one half-hour.

We find an account of similar goings-on in real life as reported by Ned Ward, the first well-known London gossip columnist, in his popular *London Spy*. Telling of his visit with a friend one night at "Widow's Coffee House," he describes the arrival of an old lecher who enters and asks whether there are any rods in the place. Ward then explains the old man's intentions by commenting, "This unnatural beast gives money to those strumpets which you see, and they down with his breeches and scourge his privities till they have laid his Leachery (sic). He all the time begs their mercy like an offender at a whipping post, and beseeches their forbearance; but the more importunate he seems for their favorable usage, the severer vapulation they are to exercise upon him, till they find by his beastly extasie (sic) when to withhold their weapons."

Possibly one of the best explanations for this British leaning towards flagellation comes not from any behavioral scientist, but from the pen of an anonymous Victorian gentleman, who described vividly his reminiscences of school days. Explaining to his correspondent that in the old school boys and girls were birched frequently in each other's presence, the writer grew eloquent. With a clear recollection of the events involving those frequent scenes of physical punishment, he wrote:

In the school mentioned above, the female who always assisted the mistress was evidentially most fond of seeing the operation, though she liked us all, and was herself a great favourite with the boys. But it was always with a giggle and a joke that she told several boys almost every morning that they were not to get up until *Missus* had "paid them a visit," or after seeing them in bed telling them that they were to keep awake until Missus should have a "little conversation with them," that moreover she might be expected every moment with a couple of tremendous rods. This girl put us up to a great deal, and I fear, developed our puberty far too precociously; she had a very large breast, and she arranged her dress so that while being horsed* we had our hands completely slipped into, and feeling her bubbies; and the rocking and plunging used repeatedly to bring on emission. Many of the boys used to try to get whipped merely to experience this sensation. Although forty years have elapsed since all this, yet the remembrance is as vivid as if it had occurred only yesterday.

*To be placed over the back of another person while being flogged; in this case, over the girl's back.

During the Georgian and Victorian eras, any woman who displayed a natural talent for administering the rod had a bright and rosy future. One noted whipper named Mrs. Collett acquired such a solid reputation that she boasted no less a personage than King George IV among her customers. Her niece, Mrs. Mitchell, was so impressed with her aunt's prosperity that she carried on the family business successfully until she died.

The undisputed queen of the "governesses" was Mrs. Theresa Berkeley, who has been described as such a perfect mistress of her profession that she became immensely wealthy during her lifetime. One writer said of her, "She possessed the first requisite of a courtezan (sic), viz., lewdness, for without a woman is positively lecherous she cannot long keep up the affectation of it, and it will soon be perceived that she moves her hands or her buttocks to the tune of pounds, shillings, and pence."

Theresa Berkeley's greatest claim to fame, however, was not for her talent as a madam, great as it was, but as an inventor. The machine which earned her such a mighty reputation was a device known as the Berkeley Horse. It was developed for the purpose of flogging a victim with the maximum efficiency. Essentially it was an open-bottomed folding chair that resembled an adjustable ladder. The victim could be strapped down, with head, buttocks, and gentials exposed, and attacked from a variety of angles.

Another of Mrs. Berkeley's favorite devices was a hook and pulley attached to the ceiling on the second floor of her house. On this apparatus the client could be suspended, swung, spun, or whipped, with the greatest of ease. As a rule, whenever such exotic methods of punishment were used, the jaded appetites of the victims were more readily satiated.

There could be no more fitting conclusion to a discussion of flagellation than the final lines of *The Rodiad*. Probably written by a schoolmaster in praise of his vice, the poem's anonymous writer was a versifier of no mean talent, whose prime motive was to reiterate that "the schoolmaster's joy is to flog."

> Delightful sport! Whose never failing charm
> Makes young blood tingle and keeps old blood warm
> From you I have no fancy to repair
> To where unbuttoned cherubs haunt the air;
> Rather, methinks I would with better grace
> Present myself at some inferior place
> There offer, without salary, to pursue,
> The business that on earth I best could do—
> Purpose to scourge the diabolic flesh;
> Forever tortured and forever fresh;
> Cut up with red-hot wire adulterous Queens
> Man-burning Bishops, sodomizing deans;
> Punish with endless pain a moment's crime,
> And whip the wicked out of Space and Time;
> Nor if the "Eternal Schoolmaster" is stern
> And dooms me to correction in my turn,
> Shall I complain. When better hope is passed.
> Flog and be flogged—is no bad fate at last.

Sado-Masochism

Since sado-masochism is one of the most popular sexual activities in the world today, what may seem to be an excessive quantity of material related to it follows. If anything here turns you on, then you should find a goldmine of information. If not, skim over and seek greener pastures in other sections.

Available from the International Love Boutique, 7046 Hollywood Boulevard, Hollywood, California 90028

Bondage group from Sex Museum at International Love Boutique. Photo by B. J. Hurwood

Available from Unique Products, Ltd.

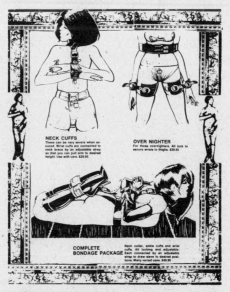

Bondage figure in cage from Sex Museum at International Love Boutique. Photo by B. J. Hurwood

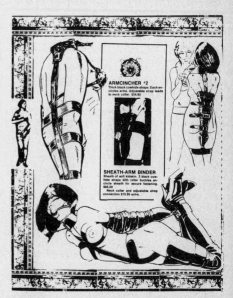

Display case of S/M gear at International Love Boutique. Photo by B. J. Hurwood

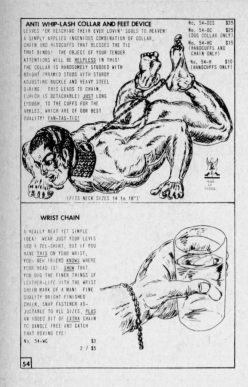

Japanese bondage story illustration employing traditional theme of the male abuser a blind Buddhist monk

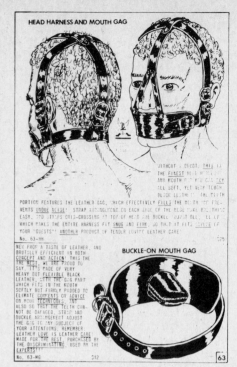

Silent Rules of Bondage

There are certain rules and principles that all devoted bondage enthusiasts stick to. They are little-known rules that are never mentioned, but which both participants go by. An experienced bondage fan knows how far he can go with his slave without harm and knows what *not* to do and for how long a person can be tied in different items.

It is imperative that a beginner also knows, so that he or she does not cause harm, either inflicting or receiving.

Bondage is becoming more popular all the time. More people are realizing and looking for the enjoyments bondage can bring. Because of this new influx of beginners, I feel it is a must to emphasize that bondage is for pleasure, not pain.

The things you may read about someone being tied in an outlandish position for overnight are written only for fantasizing and reading enjoyment.

Yes! It *is* part of the game to tell your slave—"You're going to be gagged, blindfolded, *etc. etc.* for hours or even overnight." This is part of the excitement—the tantalizing idea and feeling that this might happen! But remember, a human being cannot withstand severe bondage for any length of time.

Hold it. Yes, I know. Some of you oldtimers at bondage are saying, "We've had overnight sessions." True, but if a person is to be tied down overnight the way it should start is thus: Subject tied up good at first, gags and all. Pretend he or she will have to spend the night this way. (Don't leave the room!) Before retiring, take blindfold and gag off slave. *Never, never* leave a gag on overnight! An hour is the maximum a gag should be kept on anyone. Leaving a blindfold on overnight is really up to both parties. I personally think that if a blindfold is put on, it should be done loosely so that after you leave, slave can wiggle it off. Now for overnight subjects, legs should *not* be forced up behind them or into any position that can cause cramping after a while. Legs should be tied straight out, either to bed posts or whatever. Hands should not be tied behind back for the whole night. They should be positioned at the sides or cuffed together at wrists. Hasp cuffs are good for this, as they lock.

A rope, chain or strap should lead from the wrist cuffs to the foot of the bed so subject cannot lift arms upward. Bed straps should be put around upper torso to guarantee slave can't get off bed or bend.

Some devotees would use a locking neck strap attached to front of bed, leaving the feet and top of body secured, so he has no way of reaching top or bottom. This is debatable (using neck strap), as you want to take all precautions that your slave will not hurt himself the eight or so hours he is tied alone. An overnighter should be made as comfortable as possible. No matter how comfortably you tie him, he will still be sore in the morning. Spike-heeled shoes or boots tied on to feet will be just enough to make him uncomfortable but not painful. A couple of rubber or leather straps around shoulders and arms should be O.K.

Never use a single glove arm blind for more than an hour maximum—preferably thirty minutes.

If you are going to use a gag, never leave the room. Always check to make sure the subject is breathing normally. If there is the slightest irregularity take it off, saying, "I'm going to take this off for a couple of minutes so you can answer some questions." You can put it back on again after a short while. But take it off again at a shorter interval of time.

If you're going to use a mask, do so with extreme care. Some people might not think they have claustrophobia but learn fast that they do when a mask blocks out all their senses.

Glossary of Bizarre Terms

Animal training/bestiality: Training of animals to participate in sexual acts . . . both oral and copulation. Animals most frequently trained are dogs, horses, and pigs.

B & D: Bondage and discipline. Bondage means to tie up or to restrain in some manner. Discipline means the use of physical and/or psychological punishment in order to correct or train another person.

Coprophagia/coprolalia: Desire to eat feces, often in order to experience sexual pleasure.

Cross-dresser: A person who enjoys dressing up in the clothing of the opposite sex. Usually a male who dresses as a woman and wears makeup and wigs of a woman.

Dominant/submissive: The dominant person in an S&M type relationship is the sadist who uses bondage, discipline, humiliation, etc., to give sexual gratification to the submissive party, and in turn is gratified himself. The submissive person in an S&M relationship achieves sexual satisfaction by being disciplined, bound, humiliated, etc.

Enema: Injection of fluid into the rectum. Fluid puts pressure on man's prostate gland and sometimes causes orgasm. Often used in S&M type relationship.

English culture/art: Sexual relations involving bondage and discipline to achieve sexual stimulation.

Exhibitionism: Attaining sexual gratification by exhibiting and attracting attention to the genitals; also by performing sexual acts in front of others.

Fetishism: The compulsive use of some object in attaining sexual satisfaction. Foot fetish—the worship of feet. Kissing the feet for sexual gratification. Use of toes to massage and give sexual gratification. Frequently submissive persons perform those acts. Leather fetish—similar to lingerie fetish. People can get turned on by wearing, feeling, touching leather.

Lingerie fetish—some people achieve sexual satisfaction by touching, smelling, wearing, etc., a woman's lingerie.

High heel fetish—a turn-on from wearing high heels or watching others wear them.

Greek culture/art: Copulation between a man's penis and the anal opening of another person of either sex.

Mistress/slave: A type of relationship in which the dominant person orders the submissive person to perform tasks for her . . . such as household duties and running errands.

Pony: Similar to a slave. A person dominated by a mistress.

Orgy: Webster defines an orgy as wild, drunken, or licentious festivities. Among swingers, an orgy is generally a swinging party involving five or more people where all kinds of sex are enjoyed.

S&M: Sadism and Masochism.

Sadism—Sexual gratification gained through causing physical pain and/or humiliation. Masochism—the condition in which sexual gratification depends on suffering, physical pain and humiliation.

Trans-sexual: A person who has undergone surgery to have his/her reproductive organs changed to resemble those of the opposite sex.

T.V.: Abbreviation of term transvestite. A transvestite is a male who enjoys dressing up as a female and acting as a female.

Voyeur: Person who attains sexual gratification by looking at sexual objects or situations (i.e. others performing sex acts).

Water sports: The practice of urinating on another to achieve or give sexual gratification. Used sometimes in S&M type relationship.

From: *Swingers Dictionary* by Linda Lee, *Club Contact Swingers Directory* Vol. II., The Continental Spectator, New York. Reprinted with permission.

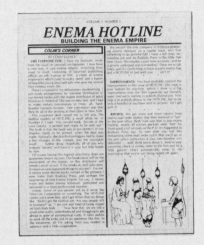

Enema Hotline

BUILDING THE ENEMA EMPIRE

The Enema Hotline is published monthly by Roxbury Press; 256 So. Robertson Boulevard; Beverly Hills, California 90211. Annual subscription rate $20.00. Sample copy $2.00.

This three or four page newsletter gives you the up-to-date news on what's happening; it's a place where enema fans can advertise, or find out who is advertising.

Roxbury Press also publishes fiction books—"fast-paced mystery adventures loaded with enemas of every variety." *House of Enemas* by James T. Flood—newsstand price $5.00—*Hotline* subscribers $4.00 and *Secrets of the Love Enema*—$5.00 newsstand price—*Hotline* subscribers $4.00. For more information on publications or *Hotline* subscription, write to the above address.

Fetish Times

The only newspaper that deals with every kind of *fetish* that the imagination can summon. Published once a month by B & D Co. Box 7109, Van Nuys, California 91406. This paper is available either through subscription or off the newsstand and priced at $1.00 a copy or 12 issues for $9.89 plus postage.

The Transvestite World Directory

The Transvestite World Directory is a special once-a-year edition of *The Transvestite* magazine. Individual copies cost $5.00 and are available on request from Empathy Press; Box 12466; Seattle, Washington, 98111. (Publisher is "Cathy" Charles Slavik.)

The directory lists meeting places for TV and TS groups. It is a magazine where Transvestites can share their views and opinions with other Transvestites, and like *The Transvestite* (published approximately four times a year), there is ample space for classified advertisements. A subscription to *The Transvestite* is available by sending $12.00 (for four issues) to Empathy Press at the above address. Subscribers to *The Transvestite* also receive a newsletter listing all the new member/subscribers and their photos and personal listings.

USE THE COUPON BELOW TO SUBSCRIBE TO THE TRANSVESTITE MAGAZINE

Send to: Empathy Press, Box 12466, Seattle, Wash. 98111

Dear Cathy:

Yes; I want to become a subscriber to *The Transvestite*. I am enclosing a check for $12.00 for the next (4) issues. (If you desire to have your magazine come by First Class enclose $15.00). I understand, also that as a subscriber to *The Transvestite* I will receive a newsletter listing all the new member/subscribers and their photos and personal listings. Below I have placed my listing that I want printed in the Newsletter and Magazine.

Name _____ Age _____ Amount Enclosed;

Address _____ _____

City _____ State _____

Zip _____ If this is a renewal, check this box ☐ and state your subscription code #
Empathy Press, Box 12466, Seattle, Washington 98111.
Magazines are sent in PLAIN, UNMARKED ENVELOPES.

Books, Catalogues, and Brochures

Books, Catalogues, and Brochures dealing with the Sexually Bizarre . . . everything your imagination can fantasize are available from:

P.O. Box "C" Gracie Station
New York, N.Y. 10028
(Publishers of the *Adventures of Sweet Gwendoline* by John Willie)

Antoinette Enterprises
6311 Yucca Street
Hollywood, California 90028
(Bondage films)

A Taste of Leather
ATOL Limited
Box 5009 VI
San Francisco, California 94101

Baron Von Olsen
1230 Grant Avenue
P.O. Box 370 B
San Francisco, California 94133

Photo Talents
Box 1195 G.P.O.
Evanston, Illinois 60204

Photo Talents has available over 20,000 original sexy photographs for sale. They are still one of the largest sources of pinup and lingerie photographs, as well as bondage, nudes, S&M, *etc.* Complete photo listing are available on request and a subscription to the *Photo Talent Newsletter* is available for $8.00 per year.

As well as hot tips on how to please your lover, the newsletter provides you with reviews of all the latest books, films, and action around the U.S.

Bob Anthony Studios
701 7th Avenue
Suite 1010
New York, N.Y. 10036

Calston Industries
P.O. Box 5034 F
Sherman Oaks, California 91403
(Bondage by the pound)

Candor Books Inc.
P.O. Box 748
Madison Square Station
New York, N.Y. 10010

Centurians
Box AE-000
Westminster, California 92683

Elmer Batters
P.O. Box 1707
San Pedro, California 90733
(Publishers of *Leg Art Magazine—*
The Royal Order of the Garter)

Hangin' Tree Ranch
P.O. Box 81988
San Diego, California 92138

Hollywood Showcase
P.O. Box 35334
Los Angeles, California 90035
(Animals as sex partners)

P.M. Products
Room 936A
152 West 42nd Street
New York, N.Y. 10036

Select Items
1236 S. La Cienega Boulevard
Los Angeles, California 90035
(Best books on bestiality)

Unique Imports
P.O. Box 1460
Studio City, California 91604

Visual Adventures
P.O. Box 5818
Cleveland, Ohio 44101

Selected Reading

NOTE: Literally hundreds of books and pamphlets were written on the subject of flagellation and sado-masochism during the eighteenth and nineteenth centuries in England, most of which are available (if in existence) through rare book dealers. Many surviving copies can be found in the Henry Spencer Ashbee collection in the British Museum. Here is a brief sampling of titles.

Whipping Tom Brought to Light and Exposed to capital View: In an account of several late Adventures of the pretended Whipping Spirit. 1671.

The Merry Order of St. Bridget: Personal recollections of the use of the Rod. by Margaret Anderson. London, 1792.

Madame Birchini's Dance. by George Peacock. London, n.d.

Experimental Lecture, by Colonel Spanker, on the Exciting and Voluptuous pleasures to be derived from crushing and humiliating the spirit of a beautiful and modest young lady; as derived by him in the assembly room of the Society of Aristocratic Flagellants. London, n.d. (end of nineteenth century).

The Mysteries of Verbena House: or, Miss Bellasis birched for thieving. By "Etonensis." London, 1882.

Curiosities of Flagellation. Anon. n.d. London, late nineteenth century.

Bibliography

Bergler, Edmund. *The Basis of Neurosis, Oral Regression and Psychic Masochism.* New York: Grune & Stratton, 1949.

———. *Principles of Self Damage.* London: P. Owen, 1959.

Bloch, Iwan. *Marquis de Sade's Anthropologia Sexualis of 600 Perversions, 120 Days of Sodom; or, The School for Libertinage, and the Sex Life of the French Age of Debauchery; from Private Archives of the French Government.* 1934. Reprint. New York: AMS, 1975. $22.50

Bloch, Iwan. *Marquis de Sade; The Man and His Age.* Translated by James Bruce. 1931. Reprint. New York: AMS, 1975. $15.00

———. *Strange Sexual Practices.* Translated by Keene Wallis. New York: Anthropological Press.

Braun, Walter. *The Cruel and the Meek: Aspects of Sadism and Masochism: Being Pages from a Sexologist's Notebook.* Translated by N. Meyer. Secaucus, N.J.: Lyle Stuart, 1967.

Caprio, Frank S. *Variations in Sexual Behavior.* New York: Grove Press, Black Cat, 1962. 95¢; New York: Citadel Press, 1967.

Cleugh, James. *The Marquis and the Chevalier.* New York: Duell, Sloan & Pearce, 1952.

Eisler, Robert. *Man Into Wolf: An Anthropological Interpretation of Sadism, Masochism and Lycanthropy.* London: Routledge & Kegan Paul, 1951.

Eulenberg, Albert. *Algolagnia: The Psychology, Neurology and Physiology of Sadistic Love and Masochism.* Translated by Harold Kent. New York: Era Press, 1934.

Greene, Gerald, and Greene, Caroline. *S-M: The Last Taboo.* New York: Grove Press, 1973. $10.00 (cloth), $2.95 (paper)

Kraff-Ebing, Richard von. *Lehebuch der Psychiatrie Auf Klinicher Grund-Inge.* Germany: 1879.

———. *Uber Gesunde und Kranke Neruen.* Germany: 1903.

———. *Psychopathia Sexualis.* Germany: 1886.

Panken, Shirley. *The Joy of Suffering.* New York: Grove Press, 1974.

Podolsky, Edward. *Sexual Masochism: The Sexual Pleasure of Pain.* New York: Epic, 1961.

Reik, Theodor. *Masochism in Modern Man.* Translated by Margaret Beigel and Gertrude Kurth. New York: Farrar & Rinehart, 1941.

Spirit of Seventy-Sex Catalogue. New York: Philharmonic Press. $8.85. Available by mail: Philharmonic Press, Dept. VV3, 516 5th Avenue, New York, N.Y. 10017.

Stekel, Wilhem. *Sadism & Masochism.* Translated by Louise Brink. New York: H. Liveright, 1929.

Sex in the Visual Arts

From Antiquity to the 19th Century

Warrior, Bronze Age, drawing found in Sweden.

Sexuality in art has been with us since the first caveman took sharpened stone in hand and began scratching lines on rock. As you will see, sex and eroticism, as depicted in art throughout history, has run the gamut from the gross to sublime. We offer no judgments here; it is up to individuals to establish their own values. What we do offer is an overview of what has been done and what is currently being done.

Virtually all of the masters have, at one time or another during their careers, produced works of art that would be rated "X" by contemporary, self-appointed arbiters of what is or is not "moral." Happily, long after these short-sighted individuals have turned to dust, the works of Da Vinci, Rembrandt, their predecessors, and spiritual descendants will survive. Perhaps one day, even those who cry out against all artistic representations of sexuality will stop employing double-think and apply true logic. If God created man in his own image, then nothing involving pictorial or other representation of the human body can possibly be regarded as anything less than divine.

Here and in the following pages we offer a panoramic view of erotic art by sculptors and painters ranging from the obscure to the celebrated, ancient to modern. It is fascinating to see how styles and techniques vary, from the realistic to the stylized, fanciful, and grotesque. It is also extremely significant to observe in a number of these works the basic common denominator: interpersonal sexual interaction as depicted by the individual artist which provides us with a continuum proving the eternal link that binds all humans together from the dawn of time.

Ithyphallic cave drawing from prehistoric times, found in Altamira, Spain.

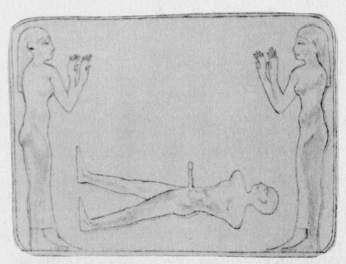

Detail from sarcophagus of Taho. Isis and Nephthys call upon the support of spiritual forces.

Isis and Anubis reviving the phallus of the mummy from the tomb of Phtahnefer.

Pompeian painting in the Museo Nazionale at Naples.

Erotic oil lamp from ancient Rome.

Grotesque bronze phallic lamp, found at Pompeii.

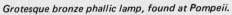

Ancient Roman pottery fragments found at Arezzo, Italy.

The Breasts. *Detail of marble by Andrea del Verrocchio (1435-1488), goldsmith, sculptor, and master of Da Vinci. This work is also attributed by some to Donatello (1386-1466).*

Grotesque caricature of Pope Julius II, attributed to Rabelais (1494?-1553).

Bathing Nymph with Watching Faun. *By Raphael (1483-1520), the Italian master whose work marked the culmination of the Renaissance, also the architect in charge of the building of St. Peter's in Rome. One of the giants of the Baroque.*

The Wife and the Fool. *Woodcut by Peter Flötner (ca. 1493-1546), German painter, sculptor, and designer.*

Drawing by Andrea del Sarto (1486-1531), important Florentine Renaissance artist, known chiefly for his religious works.

Detail from painting by Sandro Botticelli (1446-1510), one of the leading Florentines in the second phase of the Italian Renaissance.

At Cross Purposes. By Lucas Cranach, the Elder (1472-1553), artist of the South German Renaissance school, creator of numerous religious and mythological works, and woodcuts.

Figure on a beam of Montreuil-Bellay Castle in France, 15th century.

Lot and His Daughter. Painting by Hans Baldung, known as Grien (1476-1545), leading artist of the South West German Renaissance, renowned for his drawings and woodcuts.

The Holy Family. Painting by Michelangelo (1475-1564).

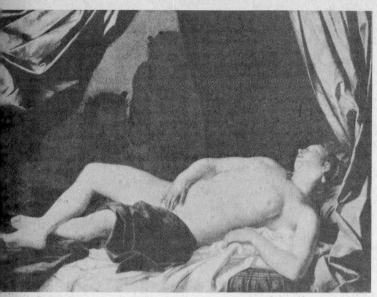

The Curious Faun. *Painting by Titian (1477-1576), one of the greatest Italian masters, whose career marked the peak of the Venetian Renaissance.*

Neptune and Nymph. *Painting by Barend van Orley (1495-1542), best known for his religious portraits, tapestry designs, and stained glass windows.*

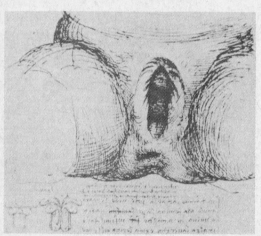

Vulva. *Drawing by Leonardo Da Vinci made in 1503.*

Painting by Giulio Romano (1493-1546), associate of Raphael, architect, painter, and designer. This is one of a series from which engravings were made by Marcantonio Raimondi to illustrate the infamous Aretino's Postures.

The Joyous Kiss. *Engraving by Giulio Bonasone (1498?-1574?), distinguished Bolognese painter and engraver.*

Love Feast. *Detail of painting by Pieter Pourbous (1510?-1584), Flemish artist best known for his portraits.*

Tarquin and Lucretia. *Engraving by Enéa Vico (1520-1563). Bibliothèque Nationale, Paris.*

Lovers. *Painting by Paolo Farinato (1524-1606), Veronese architect, engraver, and painter best known for his frescoes in the churches of Verona.*

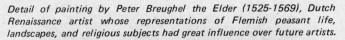

Detail of painting by Peter Breughel the Elder (1525-1569), Dutch Renaissance artist whose representations of Flemish peasant life, landscapes, and religious subjects had great influence over future artists.

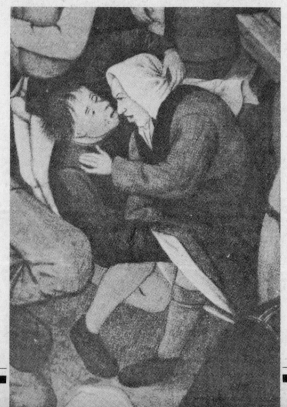

The Rustic Lovers. *By Peter Aertzen, known as Lange Pier (1508-1575), Dutch painter of church scenes and peasant life.*

Mars and Venus. *Painting by Paolo Veronese (1528-1588), important artist of the late Venetian Renaissance.*

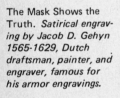

The Mask Shows the Truth. *Satirical engraving by Jacob D. Gehyn 1565-1629, Dutch draftsman, painter, and engraver, famous for his armor engravings.*

Jupiter and Callisto. *Painting by Hans von Aachen (1552-1615), Court Painter to Emperor Rudolph II, known best for his mythological scenes and portraits.*

The Toilette of Venus. *Copper engraving by Annibale Carracci (1560-1609), founder of the Roman School of Baroque Painting.*

The Hermit and the Sleeping Angelica. *Painting by Peter Paul Rubens (1577-1640), the master whose work marked the peak of Flemish painting.*

Before. *Satirical copper engraving by William Hogarth (1697-1764).*

After. *Satirical copper engraving by William Hogarth (1697-1764), the companion study to* Before.

Satyr and Nymph. *Drawing by Jean Boucher (1700-17 ?), elder brother of François Boucher, painter and etcher.*

The Ecstasy of St. Teresa. *Marble by Lorenzo Bernini (1598-1680), genius of the Baroque, who influenced all of European art in the future.*

The French Bed. *One of Rembrandt's (1606-1669) lesser known etchings.*

The Moment of Generation. *Engraving by Jean Pierre Houel (1735-1813), French animal and landscape painter, student of Casanova.*

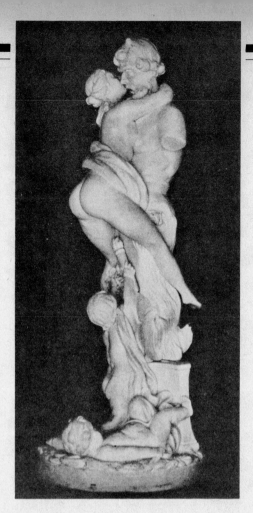

The Lovesick Nymph and the Garden God. *Porcelain by Etienne M. Falconet (1716-1791), sculptor of the late French Baroque.*

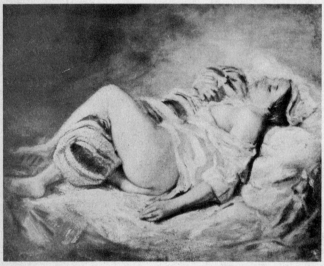

Love Dream. *Painting by Honoré Fragonard (1732-1806), one of the most important painters of the late French Rococo.*

Rapture. *Painting by François Boucher (1703-1770).*

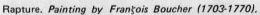

Doves. *Pastel by François Boucher (1703-1770), the leading artist of the French Rococo.*

Fashionable Contrasts: or, The Duchess's Little Shoe Yielding to the Magnitude of the Duke's Foot. *Engraving by James Gillray, 18th-century satirical artist.*

The Love Feast. *Watercolor by Thomas Rowlandson (1757-1827), who is remembered chiefly as a caricaturist and humorist. Rowlandson might have become a fine artist had it not been for his extravagant lifestyle. No less a giant in the art world, Sir Joshua Reynolds, compared him to the master, Rubens.*

The Lover's Hour. *Painting by Jean Baptiste Huet (1740-1810), French painter of animals and landscapes, strongly influenced by Boucher and Watteau. Also associated with the royal tapestry manufacturies of Gobelin and Beauvais.*

The Turkish Bath. *Painting (tondo) by Jean Auguste Ingres (1780-1867), student of David and equally influenced by Raphael. For seven years, director of the French School in Rome. Commander of the Legion of Honour.*

The King of Kings. *By Dominique Vivant Denon (1747-1825), artist, archaeologist, and diplomat.*

Painting by Achille Deveria (1800-1857), one of the leading French erotic artists of the period.

Dalliance. *Steel engraving by Nicholas Eustache Maurin (1799-1880), well known as a portrait painter and lithographer.*

Gynecee. *Woodcut by D. Chodowiecki, from Letters of the Right Honourable Lady M-y M-y M-e, etc. (1781).*

The Discreet Jewels. *Lithograph by François Souchon (1786-1857), pupil of David, painter of historical subjects and landscapes, and director of the painting school of Lille until his death.*

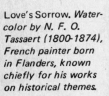

Love's Sorrow. *Watercolor by N. F. O. Tassaert (1800-1874), French painter born in Flanders, known chiefly for his works on historical themes.*

The Loving Couple. *Pastel by Jean François Millet (1914-1875), co-founder of the Barbizon School of Painting, best known for his* The Man with the Hoe.

The Nocturnal Visit. *By Antoine Wiertz (1806-1865), Belgian painter of the bizarre and symbolic, often on an extremely large scale.*

The Treacherous Reflection. *By Franz Xaver Winterhalter (1806-1873), German portraitist who specialized in personalities of high society.*

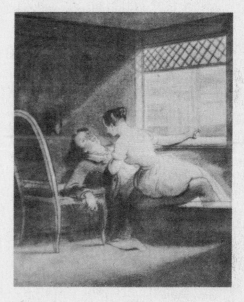

In the Lodge. *Watercolor by Honoré Daumier (1808-1879), French painter best known for his satirical lithographs.*

Who Will Buy the Love Gods? *Painting by the German artist Wilhelm von Kaulbach, (1805-1874) known for his murals, historical and mythological works.*

Drawing by Mihaly Zichy (1827-1906), Hungarian painter and illustrator. Zichy was official court painter to Czar Alexander II of Russia. This is one of a limited edition of his collected works published posthumously in Leipzig in 1911. Reproduced by Permission of Grove Press.

The Bathers. *Painting by Auguste Renoir (1841-1919), the most outstanding of the French Impressionists.*

The Rape. *Bronze by Auguste Rodin (1840-1917), the leading French sculptor of the 19th century.*

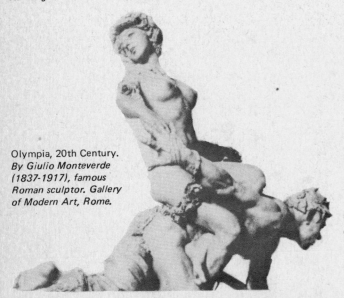

Olympia, 20th Century. *By Giulio Monteverde (1837-1917), famous Roman sculptor. Gallery of Modern Art, Rome.*

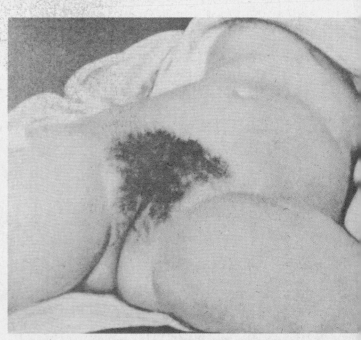

Female Torso. *Painting by Gustave Courbet (1819-1877), leading 19th-century French realist.*

Dreams. *Painting by Giulio Aristide Sartorio (1861-1932), Rome. He was known not only for his paintings and as an engraver, but also as a writer and architect.*

Original woodcut illustrating Chansons pour Elle *(1939) by Aristide Maillol (1861-1944), who was born in France, where he worked as a sculptor and painter. Bibliotheque Nationale, Paris.*

Venus Callipyge. *Drawing by Gustav Klimpt (1862-1918), Viennese impressionist who later became co-founder of the Vienna School of Secessionists.*

Phallic Fantasy. *Drawing by Henri de Toulouse-Lautrec (1864-1901).*

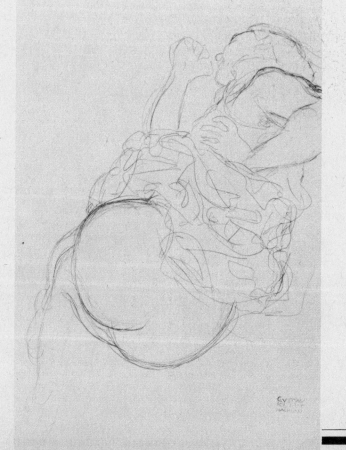

Drawing by the Marquis Franz von Bayros (1866-1924), who was quite conceivably one of the finest erotic artists of all time. Von Bayros devoted most of his career to illustration. His opulent fantasies and rich imagery are wholly unique, and his influence on contemporary eroticists is very significant.

Mutual Friends. *Painting by Albert Marquet (1875-1947), who was born in Bordeaux, France. He was a lithographer and illustrator.*

The Mortar. *Drawing by Otto Greiner (1869-1916), German painter, pastelist, and lithographer who was also known for his writings.*

Illustration for Lysistrata by Norman Lindsay (1879-   ), Australian artist.

The Embrace. *Early painting by Pablo Picasso (1881-1973).*

Dalliance *(1926). By Eric Gill (1882-1940), English engraver, sculptor, typographer, and writer. Although a great bulk of his work reflects religious themes, it also contains a rich, underlying quality of eroticism, representing his desire to draw what was "natural and normal."*

Powerless Greed. *Painting by Otto Dix (1891-1969),
who worked mainly in graphics, oil, and tempera.*

Two Friends. *Watercolor by Egon Schiele (1890-1918), a German
expressionist. His untimely death at age twenty-eight deprived the art
world of a potential 20th-century master.*

Maidens Together. *By Jules Pacsin (1885-1930), an important erotic
artist of the early 20th century. Pacsin has been compared to Boucher
and other 18th-century engravers and painters, except for the fact
his work contained a great deal of acid satire. He committed suicide
on the first day of his one-man show in Paris.*

In Expectation. *Painting by Wilhelm Kohlhoff (1893-   ), painter
and lithographer, noted for his landscapes of Prussia and paintings on
porcelain.*

The Cock in the Cornfield. *Drawing from* Ecce Homo *by George Crosz
(1893-1959), the brilliant German expressionist whose work was a
devastating mirror image of the world as he saw it in pre-Nazi Germany.
Condemned by the Nazis as "degenerate," Grosz escaped to the U.S.A.
and spent the remainder of his life in New York.*

Caricature of King Edward VII of England, by Jean Beber, 1901.

These three drawings are from a limited series by Salvador Dali (1904-) entitled Les Métamorphoses Érotiques. In each instance the artist took an old drawing from a children's textbook and caused the image to metamorphose into eroticism.

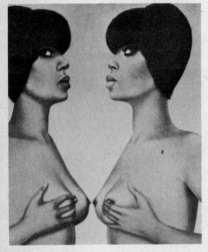

The Pleasing Physique. Detail of oil painting by Felix Labisse (1905-), a contemporary French surrealist born in France, where he still lives and works as an illustrator.

Drawing by Martin Van Maele (d. 1926), a Belgian satirical artist, about whose private life very little is known. His work is placed on the same level as such masters of erotica as Rowlandson, Deveria, Rops, and Beardsley. Van Maele's particular forte was in the realm of imaginative sexual fantasy.

Leda and the Swan. *Drawing by Gilles Rimbault, 1969, contemporary French artist.*

The Probe of Night. *Painting by Kazimierz Mikulski, National Museum, Cracow, Poland.*

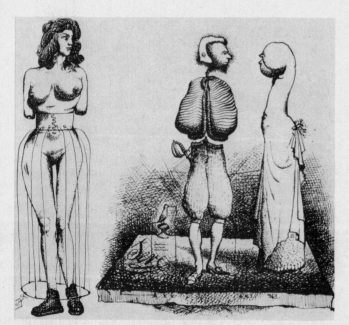

Crinoline *(left) and* The Amorous Bodies *(right). Drawings by F. Starowieyski, 1963.*

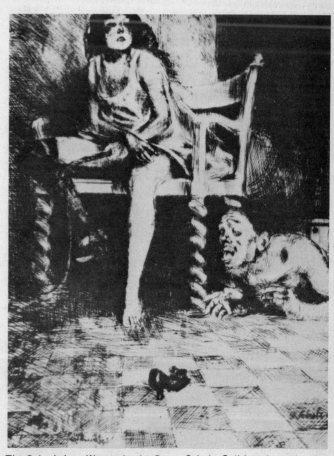

The Submission. *Watercolor by Bruno Schulz, Polish artist and writer, who died in the Warsaw Ghetto uprising during World War II.*

The International Museum of Erotic Art

540 Powell Street, San Francisco, California 94108 • Open seven days a week, from 11:00 a.m. to 11:00 p.m.

"The enjoyment of erotic art has for far too long been the exclusive prerogative of the wealthy and privileged classes, as for that matter has sexual freedom in general. It is high time that we extend these privileges to the average citizen, regardless of class, educational background, or economic position." So write Drs. Phyllis and Eberhard Kronhausen in the introduction to the catalogue for their museum's art collection.

This renowned collection of erotic art, probably the largest and finest in the world outside the Vatican, was gathered by the Kronhausens, the husband and wife psychologist team who searched out art and artists in almost every corner of the globe for over a period of fifteen years. First presented to the public at the First International Exhibition of Erotic Art in Lund, a well-known university town in Southern Sweden, similar exhibitions followed in Stockholm and Aarhus, the second largest city of Denmark, as well as three smaller (and unfortunately censored) exhibitions in Germany. After over a quarter of a million Europeans had viewed their collection, the Kronhausens decided to bring it to the United States for Americans to share.

After the decision to import their collection was made, it took over two years of litigation against the United States government before the Kronhausens won the right to import their art works. United States customs officials seized the one thousand photographs mailed, representing almost every aspect of their collection, and declared the collection "obscene" and in danger of being seized and destroyed. The fact that the collection contained erotic works from such world-famous artists as Picasso, Dali, and centuries-old Japanese and Chinese "pillow books," did not deter government officials.

Even though the Kronhausens finally won the victory to import their art works into the United States, another battle of much greater significance developed immediately. Museum director after museum director turned them down. Although in fairness, there were some directors who would have liked to have had the exhibition housed in their institutions, their trustees or board members tended to represent more conservative attitudes. However, not ones to easily give up, the Kronhausens teamed up with the National Sex Forum, the educational branch of the Genesis Church and Ecumenical Center in San Francisco, and the latter leased a three-story turn of the century building and turned it into the First International Museum of Erotic Art, the only erotic art museum that has ever existed in the world.

The museum houses the Kronhausen Collection as a permanent exhibition, as well as sponsoring periodic one-man or group shows of contemporary erotic artists.

The museum has its own shop, which sells posters, print reproductions of some of the art work, both Oriental and Western, as well as a catalogue priced at $2.95 containing over one hundred reproductions from the exhibit. The following are examples of some of the artists' work included in the Kronhausen Collection reproduced with the express permission of Drs. Phyllis and Eberhard Kronhausen. For those who unfortunately are not able to visit San Francisco and the museum a more extensive representation of their entire collection is contained in their two encyclopedic volumes, *Erotic Art* and *Erotic Art II* (published by Grove Press).

Chimu pottery. Pre-Colombian Peru.

Chimu pottery. Pre-Colombian Peru.

Phallic Contest. *Scroll, 17th century, Kyosai.*

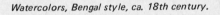

Indian watercolor, early 17th century, used as book illustration.

Watercolors, Bengal style, ca. 18th century.

A scene from a painted scroll by Jichosai, an 18th-century master of satire.

A scene from a painted scroll, Hokusai school, ca. 1830.

Watercolor by Johan Tobias Sergel (1740-1814); Sweden.

Parody of Sumo wrestling, manuscript from late 19th century.

Drawing by Nicolaus Vadasz (1884-1927), Hungary and France.

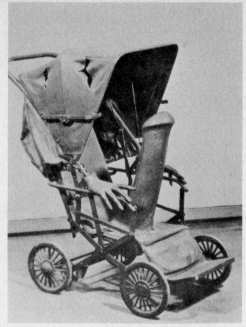

Rolling into the Future Without Love or Sorrow
object by Peter Alvermann, Germany.

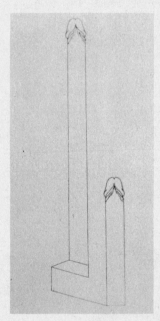

*Untitled ink drawing
by Carl Magnus,
Sweden.*

Diana and Actaeon
Pencil by Pierre Klossowski.

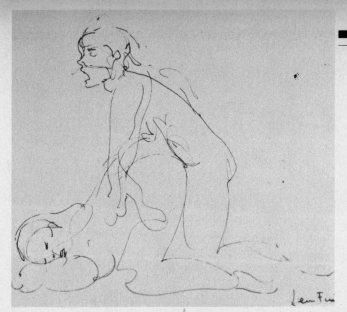

Drawing by Leonor Fini, Trieste and France.

Chinese ink by Karel Appel, Holland.

Ink drawing by André Masson.

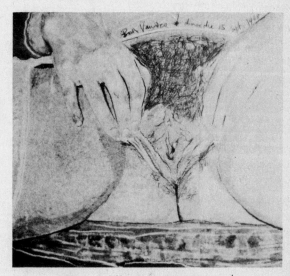

From the series Les Offrandes, collage impregné
by Boris Vansier, Switzerland, of Russian origin.

Pencil sketch by Hans Bellmer.

Noah's Ark watercolor by Kerstin Apelman Oberg, Sweden.

Silkscreen from On 1st deck of playing cards *by Bob Stanley, U.S.*

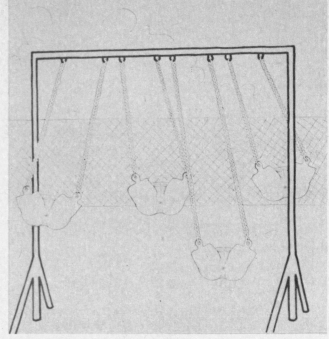

Swing in Central Park. *Kiki Kogelnik, U.S.*

Offset print from copperplate, by Mario Tauzin.

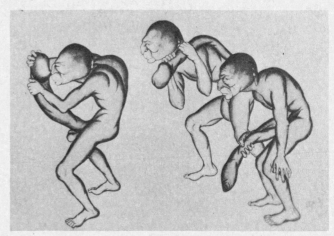

Elsje, Holland. Pastel.

Women With a Giant Penis Leaning on a Station Wagon, ink, *Claes Oldenburg.*

Ramon Alejandro, Cuba and France. Ink.

Frank Cierciorka, U.S. Pencil.

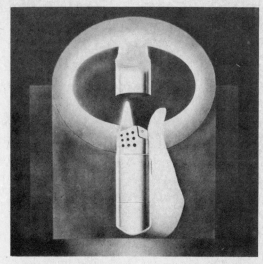

Alfred Beloch, Germany. Painting on cardboard with colors used for correction of printer's plates.

William Copley, U.S. Oil.

Luna 8, hydrocal; Luna 9, hydrocal; Luna 6, hydrocal. *Richard Etts, U.S. Photographs courtesy Robert Rosinek, Gallery of Erotic Art.*

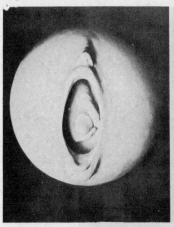 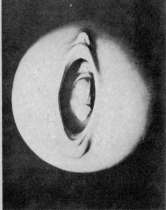

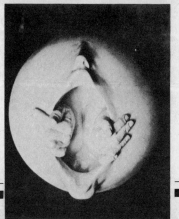

The Woman Eating Monster. *Frederic Pardo. Oil on wood.*

Contemporary Artists

The artists whose works appear in the following pages comprise a selected group with whom we have had contact, either directly or through their respective galleries. Due to spatial limitations we have been reluctantly forced to present only a small number of artists, who represent only a tip of the iceberg in the world of erotic art. Today there is a burgeoning international erotic art movement that is unparalleled in history. Whereas in the past artists who employed the erotic motif did so only in a fraction of their work, today there are thousands who have taken a stand and are devoting themselves exclusively to the depiction of sexuality in art. As you read the personal statements of those who chose to speak out, you will see that there is a general growth of confidence in the ranks and a strengthening of purpose. Wherever possible, we have included information as to where and how the artists may be contacted by serious collectors who may wish to purchase or commission original works. You will also note that we have excluded portraits of those artists who were either camera-shy or unprepared to provide self-portraits.

SUSAN BEECHER

"I became a potter about ten years ago . . . and I must admit that I love the whole sensuous quality that is involved when one throws a pot . . . the water, texture of the clay, and the movement of the wheel are wonderful! There came a time when I began to search for something new in my work as well as in my life. The whole sexual revolution was running rampant in the outside world and so it finally occurred to me that I wanted to mirror this in my work .,. . I began putting little people on my pots . . . I spoke to many friends about their sexual feelings, experiences, longings, and happenings . . . I added these to what was happening with myself and I had more than enough situations for my pots . . . and three years later the little people on my pots are still going strong.

"I believe that erotica is definitely therapeutic for the artist as well as for the artist's audience . . . somehow people have to come to terms with their own feelings and beliefs when they are faced with a sexual scene . . . I believe that the world is still full of hatred because it is full of sexual repression.

"The last thing I think I should talk about is humor. I think somehow that one needs to have a pretty good sense of humor in order to survive this world with one's mind intact . .,. and that humor just makes living more fun . . . and I feel that I try to incorporate humor and fun into my pieces. After all, having little people fucking away on bowls and plates is rather funny!"

Susan Beecher lives and works in New York.

GERARD BERINGER

A French artist about whom very little is known, but who upon hearing about the CATALOGUE sent us samples of his work. They arrived too late for us to contact the artist, but we felt he deserved a place in the Directory of Contemporary Erotic Artists. He lives and works in Paris.

Self portraits in crayon (0.57 m. x 0.75 m.) Photo by Daniel Lattard.

For Picasso *(12" high, 18" diameter). Clay pottery. Photograph by Mark Lindenaur.*

Searching *(14" high). Clay pottery. Photograph by Mark Lindenaur.*

The artist with two panels, vertical (12½' x 12½'). 1973. Charcoal on paper.

JUDITH BERNSTEIN

"Art is a fantasmagoria—coming from the artist's innermost secrets and creating a body of work that is an architectural environment of the mind.

"Since 1969 I have been drawing large-scale phallic/screws, nine feet high and thirty feet long. Each drawing contains a massive force of energy that creates its individual icon. These architectural scale charcoal drawings are fetishistic in character. My work is an image of the seventies ... an image reflecting a sexually aware age on a widespread basis ... an age of ambiguity and an age when women are demanding equality on all levels. The phallus and all it stands for is not exclusively a male image."

The artist lives and works in New York City.

ARNE BESSER

Besser was born in Illinois in 1935, and studied in New Mexico and California. In California at the Art Center School he worked under Lorser Feidelsson and James A. Tyler. He has worked as an illustrator for the American Historical Society, New York, and New York's Columbia Medical School as well as having been extensively exhibited throughout the United States. His most recent one-man show was held in 1972 at the Louis K. Meisel Gallery, and his art was part of the group exhibition at the Baltimore Museum of Art in Maryland, earlier this year.

Mr. Besser presently lives and works in New York.

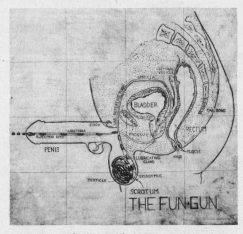

The Fun Gun *(55" x 60"). 1967. Acrylic and forty-five caliber bullets on canvas.*

Reba *(60" x 48"). 1975. Oil on canvas. Courtesy of Louis K. Meisel Gallery.*

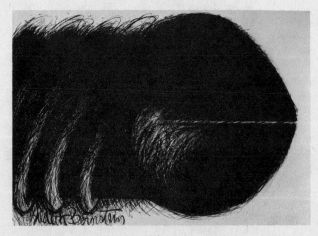

Horizontal *(108" x 150"). 1973. Charcoal on paper.*

Untitled *(70" x 52"). 1972. Oil on canvas. From the collection of Morton Neuman. Courtesy of the Louis K. Meisel Gallery. Photograph by Eric Pollitzer.*

HERB
BROWN

The artist in front of one of his collages. Photograph
by Charles Alaimo.

Herb Brown lives in New York City, was born in Lynn, Massachusetts in 1923, and attended the Boston Museum School.

Brown says: "I guess Henry Miller turned my head around and made me wonder why artists weren't dealing with sex. The major body of work seemed to be pre-Christian and extra-Christian—on the other hand there were areas of art that were erotically inclined, notably Rubens. And for me, one of the great euphemisms, Rodin's *The Kiss.* So I said to art, 'that's a lotta crap. Let's get it up front.' For a long time expressionism was my way of making a picture. I disliked abstract expressionism because I didn't understand it. Well, whatta you know, my first erotic painting in 1958 turned out to be an almost abstract expressionist work no more up front than Rodin's! I guess my socio-cultural background was showing. Many paintings later, while the image became more apparent I still maintained the expressionist form and continued to deal with the formal values of picture making. I chose subjects that were in the immediate vicinity—self-portraits, city-scapes, still lifes—so it wasn't surprising when about a year after I painted the first erotic picture my wife became pregnant. From 1958 to 1966 I continued painting erotic family groups, and all the things four kids can get into.

"Then there was the issue of giving the erotic pictures titles. Certain ones derived titles from what was suggested by the posters I painted over. Others at first I called *Love I, Love II,* etc. It felt awkward and not in keeping with the power of the paintings. Then I changed them to *Fucking I,* etc., but this seemed like an overreaction. I ran out of ideas and opted for the latter because it came closer in both feeling and meaning."

Party *(60" x 90").*
Collage. Photo by
Charles Alaimo.

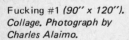
Fucking #1 *(90" x 120").*
Collage. Photograph by
Charles Alaimo.

Hilo Chen. *Photo courtesy
Louis K. Meisel Gallery.*

HILO CHEN

Hilo Chen was born in Taipei, Taiwan in 1942, but moved to Paris, France in 1968 where he lived for one year before moving to New York City. In the years 1962 to 1966 he was exhibited extensively in Taiwan. He held his first United States exhibition in Connecticut in 1966. His first one man show in New York was in 1974 at the Louis K. Meisel Gallery, where he is now permanently represented.

Beach 33 *(36" x 60").* 1975. Oil on canvas. Courtesy of Louis K. Meisel Gallery. Photograph by Gerard Murrell.

Beach 28 *(36" x 60").* 1975. Oil on canvas. From the collection of Mr. and Mrs. N. Buksbaum. Courtesy of Louis K. Meisel Gallery. Photograph by Gerard Murrell.

LYN CHEVLI

"I am a woman who loves life, and since one of the fundamental elements of my life is sexuality, it provides a natural source for me to draw from in my work as an artist. I work primarily in bronze, but have done work in silver and steel. I also work in pen and ink, and write. Beauty, humor, and honesty excite me, so this is the focus of my work. I dislike pornography on the grounds that it is dull and I hate to be bored, but I do not believe in censorship of any kind. Quality is important to me, so I despair of current tastes in art which I think are largely phony and lacking in courage. To me the "sexual revolution" is pure mythology, but hopefully the work of artists dealing with erotica will change prevailing attitudes, starting with those of museum directors."

Lyn Chevli lives and works in Laguna Beach, California.

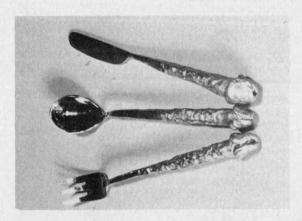

Bronze Table
Setting (7"). 1971.

Bird of Paradise, #1
(4"). 1970. Bronze.

JOHN DeANDREA

John DeAndrea was born in Denver, Colorado where he studied at the University of Colorado. His work has been extensively exhibited throughout the world. He is represented by O.K. Harris Works of Art in New York City which held one-man exhibitions for him in 1970, 1971, and 1973. He works and still lives in Denver, Colorado and is considered to be one of the country's foremost neo-realists.

Woman Sitting, Legs Apart. *1972. Fiberglass and polyester. From the Benedek Collection, New York. Courtesy of the O.K. Harris Works of Art. Photograph by Eric Pollitzer.*

Man and Woman Leaping (Life-size) 1971. Polyester and fiberglass. From the collection of Gallerie Fey and Nothelfer, Berlin. Courtesy of the O.K. Harris Works of Art.

DONNA MAE DIEHL

Donna Mae Diehl lives and works in La Jolla, California. Her principal study was at the Art Center Workshop in La Jolla, where she has had a number of successful shows. Although she has worked in abstract expressionism, in 1971 she turned her talents to erotic drawings in black and white. Strongly influenced by the work of von Bayros and Zichy, critic Michael Dormer said, "Her work has a potent charm, and one can almost hear the enthusiastic whispery applause from the likes of the ghosts of George Grosz, Heinrich Klee, and Aubrey Beardsley." The majority of her work presently rests in the hands of private collectors. She represents herself and may be contacted care of P. O. Box 659, La Jolla, California 92037.

Pen and ink. 1972.

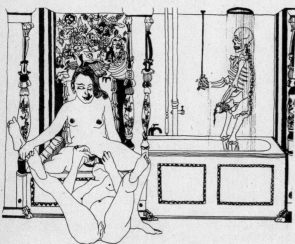

Pen and ink. 1972.

BETTY DODSON

Little more need be said about Betty Dodson, except that she is considered to be one of the leading women erotic artists, as well as crusader for the women's liberation movement. One of her most recent art exhibitions was held at the International Museum of Erotic Art in San Francisco.

Ms. Dodson presently lives and works in New York.

The Female Orgy (60"x 80"). 1970. Oil on canvas. Private collection.

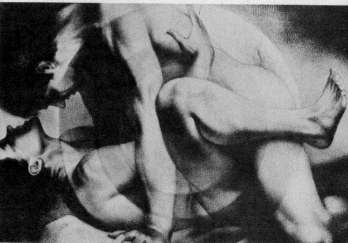

Pen and ink drawing.

J. DON EATON

J. Don Eaton is a sculptor and jeweler who crafts and sells his work from a shop on 4 Princess Street, Sausalito, California. He is a very private person, believes his work should speak for itself, and does not discuss any details of his personal life. His jewelry lies within the price range of the general public, but the sculpture seen here is strictly geared to the museum and private collectors market. *The Lotus on the Opal* consists of 24k gold figures on a bed of Australian opal, with an 18k white-gold background (selling price: $4,000.00). *The Mountain Climbers* are 14k gold figures on a large opal (selling price: $11,000.00)

Bed. *Australian opal, 24k gold figures, 18k white-gold background.*

Mountain climbers. *14k gold figures on an opal.*

Photo by Melissa Melas. Print by Camera Man, New York City.

DANA GREENE

"The only way we can show people what they *don't feel* is by making them feel something they never felt before. Because *Erotic forms (all natural forms)* evoke a physical response—we can get people to *turn on* by making them more aware. Actually we are teaching them to *see* the erotic forms all around them. Hopefully, people will begin to feel more at home with their sensuality. This will lead to more satisfying sexual feelings between men and women. When people learn to become more in touch with themselves and their feelings, they will become more in touch with nature and all living things. Ultimately, we will all be able to come together and then we will understand what it means to be at one with one's self and all living things—eternally."

Ms. Greene lives and works in New York.

Untitled *(8"). 1971. Bronze. Foundry, Joel Meisner & Co. Inc. Photograph by Will Faller.*

Untitled (6½" x 9½"). 1975. Plaster. Mold maker, Gino. Photograph by Camera Man, New York City.

DAVID GREGORY

David Gregory was born in Albany, New York and was educated at the School of Visual Arts in New York as well as the Camden Arts Center in London, England. He works in a wide variety of media from block printing and silkscreen to etching, painting, sculpture, and photography. His most recent one-man exhibition was held at the Gallery 10 in New York City in 1971.

Mr. Gregory currently lives and works in New York.

Hand and Breast. *1971. Etching. Courtesy of Gallery 10.*

Hand of Lust. *1970. Etching. Courtesy of Gallery 10.*

DONALD GROVER

Donald Grover majored in art history and received his masters in weaving at Kent State University. He has exhibited at Kent State and Bonwit Teller in New York. He also writes for *Craft Horizons* on fiber. Grover says, "I think fiber is the most sensitive medium for translating into sensuous images." The two works represented here are from his Great American Condom series, multi-knit fiber (mohair, angora, wool, and lurex).

Mr. Grover presently lives and works in New York.

The Great American Condom Series.
Knit Condoms.
Photograph by Will Faller.

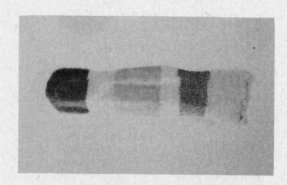

Photograph of artist with his work, entitled Sanke Lady.

LUIS JIMENEZ

"Essentially I am working with what I consider to be contemporary icons. In my work I try to deal with basic human experiences common to us all—sex, birth, and death."

Mr. Jimenez lives and works in New Mexico.

Birth *(8' 3")*. *Fiberglass, epoxy, metal, neon. Courtesy of O.K. Harris Works of Art.*

Erotic Rodeo Queen *(27½" x 39½")*. *1974. Colored pencil. Courtesy of O.K. Harris Works of Art.*

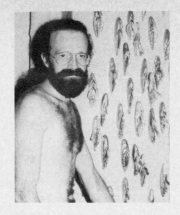

DOUG JOHNS

New-York-born sculptor Doug Johns, who lives and works in a loft on West 29th Street, is rapidly gaining a reputation as one of the most innovative erotic artists in his field.

He says: "Sex has always been a hidden, taboo thing in our society, and was beyond my experience until the last few years. I think this has been the case with most people. So now my passion in life is making myself and the people around me aware that our genitals are beautiful. This, I believe, is helping to shatter the visual walls that have imprisoned us all. I began by depicting fantasies, for example, auto-fellatio, auto-cunnilingus, group sex, and I found that in order to make them visually accurate I had to venture into areas that no other artists had before, with the exception perhaps of Da Vinci. In my studies I had approximately one hundred and fifty people pose for me, and I found that the human flower, both male and female, is not standardized like a daisy, but each is highly unique, original, and very complex, and far more beautiful than anyone has imagined."

Doug Johns' work is available at Erotics, 117 Christopher St., New York, N.Y., 10014.

Cockheads. *Acrylic cast from wax.*

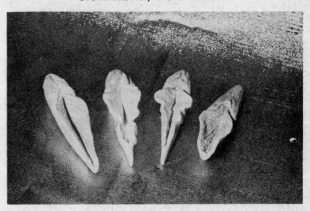

Portraits of Women. *Acrylic cast from wax.*

JOHN KACERE

John Kacere was born in Iowa in 1920, where he studied at the University receiving a M.F.A. He has taught at several universities including University of Manitoba, Canada; Parson's School of Design, New York; and Cooper Union, New York. His most recent one man show was held at the O.K. Harris Gallery in New York City, although his art has been displayed in many one-man and group shows across the United States and the world.

Mr. Kacere presently lives and works in New York.

Photograph of artist wearing silk dress of own design.

KAREN KATZ

Karen has a Masters in Fine Arts from Yale, lives and works in a New York Soho loft. Her principal medium is fabric appliqué and quilting. She is in great demand by record companies to produce her unique, flamboyant art for album covers, and also designs costumes for celebrities, among them magician Doug Henning, star of *The Magic Show*. Ms. Katz has exhibited at the Museum of Contemporary Crafts in New York. Her work has appeared in various publications, including *New York* magazine. In addition to designing clothes and record and book covers, she has also created a series of photographic tapestries as well as handbags, pillows, quilts, and a variety of other kinds of soft sculpture. In fact, as Karen says, "anything that looks like fun."

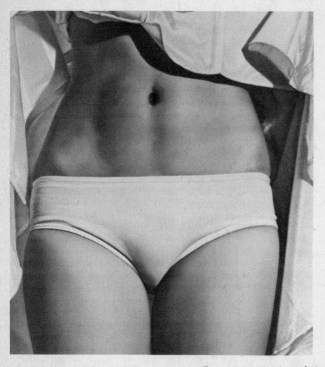

Torso (68½" x 77"). 1972. Oil on canvas. From the collection of the Galerie de Gestto, West Germany, Courtesy of the O.K. Harris Works of Art. Photograph by Eric Pollitzer.

Silk and fabric appliqué.

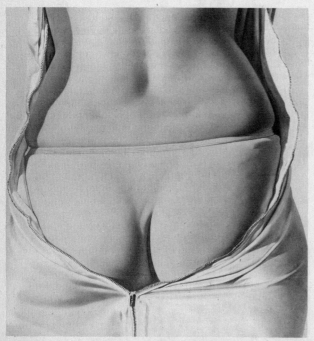

Light Purple Panties; Silken Zippered Slip (70½" x 78½"). 1971. Oil on canvas. From the collection of the J.B. Speed Museum, Louisville. Courtesy of the O.K. Harris Works of Art. Photography by Eric Pollitzer.

SUSAN KUTOSH

"I was born in Elizabeth, New Jersey, and raised in Schenectady, New York. I have also lived in Tuscon, Arizona; Toledo, Ohio; Boston, Massachusetts; and am presently residing and dancing in New York City. In 1971 I received my Bachelor of Fine Arts Degree in painting from Carnegie Mellon University, and my Master of Arts Degree in painting from Kent State University in 1973. My education was completed after I ceased the martydom of marriage and motherhood and opted for responsibility toward my art. Exhibitions of some significance include a one-woman show at Kent State University Gallery 1, October 1973, and a one-woman show at the Press Club, 300 Sixth Avenue Building, Pittsburgh, Pennsylvania, June 1973. At this time I am engaged in a series of pieces on Marilyn Monroe."

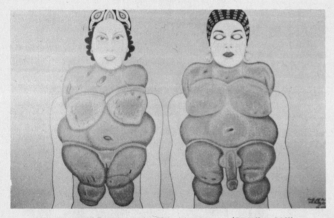

Double Self-Portrait with Fertility Image *(37½" x 60")*. *1974. Oil on canvas.*

Me, Marcie and Other Women *(Left half of painting only) (5' x 14')*. *1973. Oil on canvas.*

Despite the growing acceptance of erotic art as a legitimate means of creative expression by serious painters and sculptors, the more conservative quarters of the art community tend to shy away from any works of art that lean toward explicit depiction of sexuality in any way. This is especially true of most major museums and galleries.

Fortunately, there is a decided trend away from this attitude thanks to the efforts of such crusaders as the Kronhausens, whose personal collection is housed, as we have pointed out, in the Museum of Erotic Art at 540 Powell Street, San Francisco, California. Because those farsighted individuals who recognize the importance and significance of contemporary erotic art are exerting a significant effort to make erotic art available to the general public, it is now emerging from the exclusive realm of the wealthy private collector.

As is the case with all relatively small, close knit, minority groups, those who deal in fine erotic art tend to cooperate with one another in order to advance their mutual cause. Should you be interested in purchasing works of art by any of the artists represented here, or indeed others who for reasons beyond our control we were not able to include, if you contact any of the galleries or dealers mentioned here, you will in all probability be furnished with the information you desire.

EROTICS
117 Christopher Street
New York, New York 10014

GALLERY 10
138 West 10th Street
New York, New York 10014

JACQUES BARUCH GALLERY
900 N. Michigan Avenue
Suite 605
Chicago, Illinois 60611

LOUIS K. MEISEL GALLERY
141 Prince Street
New York, New York 10012

O. K. HARRIS WORKS OF ART
469 West Broadway
New York, New York 10012

SIDNEY JANIS GALLERY
6 West 57th Street
New York, New York 10019

WARREN BENEDEK GALLERY
360 West Broadway
New York, New York 10012

NOTE: A special mention should be made of the following:

J-N HERLIN, INC.
108 West 28th Street
New York, New York 10001

Mr. Herlin is a dealer in twentieth century art books, and though he does not specialize in erotic art *per se*, his knowledge of the field is extensive, and his personal contacts with many fine artists place him in a unique position to provide interested parties not only with fine books but original art as well.

SHELLEY LOWELL

"My art uses sex organs but I do not consider it erotic art. In fact, I consider my art to be anti-erotic. It is not intended to arouse sexually.

"Through my art, I want to free a society chained in sexual taboos. I want man and woman to transcend the superficial 'physicality' of their bodies so that they can make deeper and more meaningful relationships on an interpersonal level without sex organs coming between them.

"My art is adamant clichés and witticisms about social moves intended to shock and stimulate society into questioning its attitudes to result in truer and healthier relationships between man and woman."

Ms. Lowell lives and works in New York.

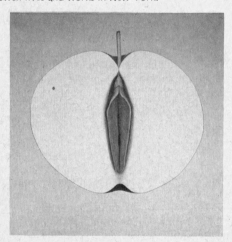

Rediscovery (48" x 48"). 1972. Acrylic on canvas.

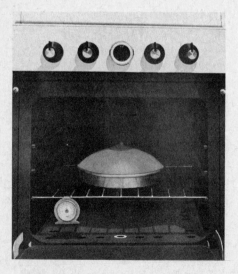

Don't Make Any Noise, the Cake Will Fall (30" x 32"). 1973. Acrylic on canvas.

MALCOLM LUBER

Malcolm Luber is thirty-six years old, has a Bachelor of Fine Arts degree from Hunter College, New York, a Master of Arts from Hunter College, New York, and a Ph.D. from New York University. He has been a freelance artist and designer, has had numerous exhibitions in New York and Connecticut, has taught fine arts at East New York Junior High School, New York; Canarsie High School, New York; and is currently Assistant Professor of Fine Arts at the South Central Community College in New Haven, Connecticut.

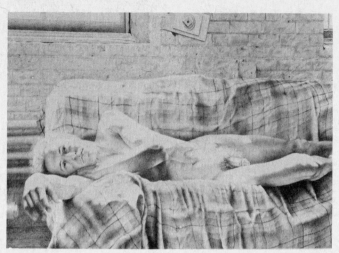

Untitled (42" x 60"). 1974. Pencil on paper. Courtesy of Louis K. Meisel Gallery.

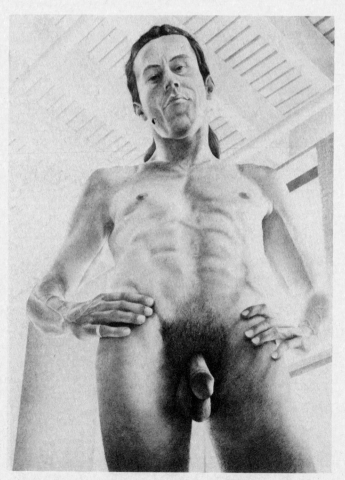

Untitled (60" x 42"). 1974. Pencil on paper. Courtesy of Louis K. Meisel Gallery.

PHOEBE McKAY

SHIRLEY FREY McCONAHAY

Phoebe McKay was born and raised in Greenwich Village, New York City. The daughter of artists, she can't remember when she didn't draw. She explains, "My subject has always been people, and I prefer to work from the living model. A successful drawing is not just an arrangement of forms, but an impression of a subject which should linger in the mind, almost as the memory of the reality itself. When I draw a nude, I try to recreate the person. My drawings are sensual, sexual because human beings are, much as they still like to deny it, even in this more relaxed age."

Phoebe tries to draw as often as possible and will travel to any out-of-the-way Soho loft where a few people have gathered for a session of "life drawing." "But," she says, "private sessions are always best."

Originals and reproductions of Ms. McKay's work are available at Erotics, 117 Christopher Street, New York, New York 10014.

"I was born and raised in Indiana, went to school in Kentucky, moved to Connecticut, to California, back to Connecticut, and now to North Carolina. Academically I am a historian. I taught American History for three years at Santa Monica City College, took off for two years to write a book on sex and violence (doing my research at the Kinsey Institute), and then taught Psychology of Human Sexual Behavior at the University of Bridgeport. Throughout those years I started painting and macraméing until 1973, when I came to the decision that my creative energies needed to be channeled full time into art. I enjoy creating sensual and organic works that can be used by others (masks, swings, hammocks) or works that communicate from my nonverbal side to other right hemispheres—a cunt securely holding a woman surrounded by seaweed, tiny people trying to manipulate huge screws and nuts, eggs and sperm containing tiny people loving, fighting, and killing. Altogether, a trip through my studio can be a head/body/emotional experience."

Pen and ink 1974.

Artist and Body Mask #1. *Photo by Clark Broadbent.*

Pen and ink. 1974.

Cunt Swing.

Photo by
Federico Gadsky.

Self-portrait
by the artist.

JOAN MELNICK

Born on Staten Island, thirty-three years ago, she became interested in art at an early age. She studied at the Fashion Institute of Technology and State University of New York at New Paltz, where she received a Masters in Art Education.

She is presently teaching painting and drawing at Lehman College. Her interest in erotic art began several years ago while exploring organic forms for her paintings and etchings. She feels that eroticism exists in all organic forms and has extended this into her work with a desire to share this awareness with others. Her work can be seen at the Levitan I & II Gallery, New York City, and at the Ponce Gallery in Mexico City.

GEORGE NORTH MORRIS

"For several years, I have been developing a personal iconography which combines my previous abstract experience with the most dangerous kind of content, human physical love. Dangerous primarily because of ancient cultural phobias; ultimately because the market for sexually oriented art is limited.

"I see my work as the twentieth century equivalent of the bedroom walls of Pompeii, the lushness of Boucher and Fragonard, and the wedding-gift Shunga prints of the Japanese. My aim is to combine esthetic and human relationships in about equal proportions without secretive symbols, fetid expressionism, or smart aleck comedy.

"In this verbal culture of ours, visual expression has always been far too pleasurable. Add the element of sexuality, and the mixture is dynamite.

"Traditionally sexual intercourse takes place at night with the lights out. We mustn't look at what is going on. Consequently we have no real understanding of the beauty of this most intimate human contact. My painting deals with this beauty."

Untitled. Colored pencil. 1975.

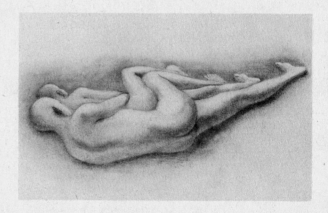

Untitled. Pen and ink. 1975.

Pencil sketches.

Self Portrait (25" x 36"). 1974.
Acrylic on paper. Courtesy of
Louis K. Meisel Gallery.

Self-portrait
by the artist.
Pen and ink.

JERRY OTT

Jerry Ott was born in Albert Lea, Minnesota and studied at the Mankato State College. His work has been widely exhibited around the world with successful exhibitions in Sweden, Germany, Japan, Denmark, and Canada as well as extensively throughout the United States. At present he is represented by the Louis K. Meisel Gallery in New York City which held a one-man exhibition in 1973.

Mr. Ott presently lives and works in Minnesota.

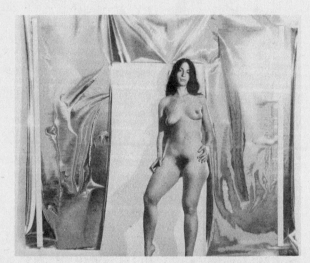

Judy/Mylar/Icon #2 (78" x 96"). 1973. Acrylic on canvas. Courtesy of the Louis K. Meisel Gallery. Photograph by Robert E. Mates and Paul Katz.

Two Models/Mylar/Plane (72" x 96"). 1973. Acrylic on canvas. From the collection of Mr. & Mrs. Z. Solomon. Courtesy of Louis K. Meisel Gallery. Photograph by Robert E. Mates and Paul Katz.

DAVID PARIS

"As a baby I was creative with whatever was at hand. As I grew into childhood I naturally turned to art as a solace. I only drew war pictures until I one day discovered that by tracing the outline of a paper doll a naked girl would appear. So happy was I with this bevy of little beauties to keep me company that I thereupon decided to devote myself to that calling, come what may.

"Years passed, and I entered my first art class and puberty at the same time. Both were a delightful shock. My calling was more enjoyable than I had hoped. And would become better yet as I became a sculptor. Now I could feel as well as look.

"Several art schools later sprinkled with the inclusion in some insignificant group shows, I decided there was something missing in my life—money. I could no longer make it on charm alone. So I got married and went into the engineering field. I stuck to both long after I knew that neither was for me. After years of making esthetic petrochemical plants I returned to art and became a full-time artist.

"Sex today is frequently portrayed as competitive, aggressive, as a display of power, or—at the other extreme—with cool esthetic detachment. While some people can identify with these attitudes, I think most people would prefer to think of sex as a warm, human, honest expression of basic feelings. I have tried to make my lithographs reflect these feelings. For it is my belief that when people can identify with a picture it will become a meaningful part of their lives. And to me that's what art is all about."

Pen and ink
lithographs.

MEL RAMOS

Ramos was born in Sacramento, California where he received a Master of Arts at the Sacramento State College in 1958. He has taught in high schools and colleges throughout the United States and has extensively lectured on art. He is one of the leading neo-realists whose art has been viewed by many thousands of people in galleries and musuems throughout the world, as well as having been included in many books and articles on art.

ROBIN RAY

Robin Ray is the son of a commerical artist and has lived in London all his life. He is a painter by training; an illustrator by inclination; a creative director of an advertising agency by experience; and a sculptor by preference. His striking black and while illustrations for a limited edition of *The Story of O* are prized by collectors. His style ranges from Beardsley-like fantasy to photographically detailed illustration. One of the keystones of Ray's work is his imaginative sense of humor. He is currently in partnership with Tuppy Owens' Cand Haven Ltd. as designer of all publications. His ambition is to work full time at erotic drawings and sculptures, preferably on private assignments.

You Get More Salami with Modigliani *(14" x 20"). 1974. Watercolor on paper. From the collection of Francisco Antonio Sierra. Courtesy of Louis K. Meisel Gallery.*

A/C *(30" x 24"). 1972. Lithograph. Courtesy of the Louis K. Meisel Gallery. Photograph by Gerard Murrell.*

Photograph by
Tom Di Nardo.

FRANK ROOT

EDWARD SAMUELS

A Philadelphia artist and perfector of the "vinyl linear relief," Root is renowned for the imagination imbued in his erotic sculptures. Shows of his work cause flaming tempers, arguments between the genders, critical doubletalk, conspicious sidestepping, and sexual comment manifesting itself in the form of critical opinion.

First he studied music, even finally playing the drums with Roy Eldridge, Red Rodney, Sarah Vaughan, Eddie Condon, Red Garland, Al Grey, Nina Simone, and Slam Stewart. He was also a part of Lenny Bruce's backup trio.

While in elementary school, Root picked up a charcoal pencil and drew a self-portrait. "It scared the hell out of me. It resembled me so closely, I dropped the pencil and swore never to draw anything again."

Winner of several international-display awards, he created the setting for the Philadelphia Museum of Art's Bicentennial Crystal Ball.

Root has appeared in the film *The Erotic Memoirs of a Male Chauvinist Pig,* and has a part in *Black Mass.*

Root's relief of John Barrymore adorns the MGM Grand Hotel in Las Vegas; images of John Wayne, Sydney Greenstreet, and others hang in offices of theater owners and posh nightclubs in Philadelphia. Several of the latter even had "Frank Root" rooms: black, recessed spaces filled with fantastic tiny lights, creating an undescribable spatial sensation. And some of his art has been purchased by such personaltiies as Carol Channing, Bill Blass, and Norman Norrel.

Despite the demand for these commercial images, Root claims to be a "tits and ass" man, true to the Lenny Bruce self-description. "After making a really erotic piece, designed to arouse and force a powerful mood on the viewer, likenesses are easy."

His work is available through the Louis K. Meisel Gallery in New York, and while sometimes blatantly erotic, it is always expertly crafted and sure to arouse strong opinions.

Ed Samuels is one of the foremost erotic artists and sculptors living and working in New York. He has had many one-man shows all around the United States and a special exhibition at the International Museum of Erotic Art in San Francisco in 1973. His sculpture includes some very fine pieces of erotic jewelry.

Ed says: "The most pleasurable experiences are making visual for others those things with which I feel a desire to become one. The sharing is not just with others but with myself as well, because to surprise myself is what's most gratifying."

Photo by Anders Homquist.

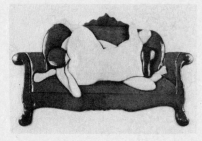

The Red Couch
(48" x 36"). Vinyl.

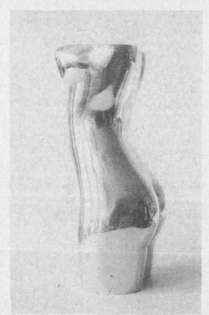

Torso Box (2¼") 1975.
14 Karat gold. Photo by
Anders Holmquist.

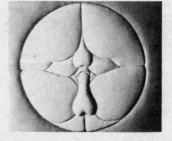

The White Ball
(48" x 48"). Vinyl.

*Photograph by
Ed Seeman.*

*Photo by
Susan Weiley.*

JUNE SEEMAN

Born on New York City's upper West Side and influenced by her artist-mother, June Seeman began painting while she was still a child. During her teens her work was frequently exhibited in Woodstock and Provincetown. She attended Sarah Lawrence College and later graduated from the Yale School of Design where she studied with Josef Albers, a giant of the optical art movement.

Her artistic range extends from illustrations for children's books (*Serendipity Tales* by Elizabeth J. Hodes, Atheneum) to her current erotic drawings.

Although erotic imagery has been a continual thread woven through Ms. Seeman's most recent work, her etchings also follow a stream of consciousness in which both the artist and the viewer can discover a multiplicity of images both harmonious and incongruous to her basic themes. The greater license in total expression in the arts today has afforded Ms. Seeman a new freedom to develop her erotic imagery from bud to flower.

She now lives in New York with her film-maker husband, Ed Seeman. Her drawings were recently displayed in a retrospective at the Green Mountain Gallery, and her etchings are currently available at Brentano's branches throughout the country.

JOAN SEMMEL

Joan Semmel is one of the foremost women erotic artists. She studied at the Cooper Union Art School, the Pratt Institute, and Yale Summer School until 1963, when she moved to Madrid, Spain, traveling and painting extensively throughout Europe and South America. She has had many successful one-woman shows in such cities as Barcelona, Madrid, Montevideo, Buenos Aires, Valencia, finally returning to the United States in 1970. Since arriving back in New York, she has had many significant exhibitions in galleries and has been widely written about in such magazines as *New York, Viva, Changes, Village Voice, Art-Rite, The Nation, etc.* Joan now continues to live and work in New York City.

Editor of *A New Eros, Sexual Imagery in Woman's Art* to be published in 1976, by Hacker Art Books.

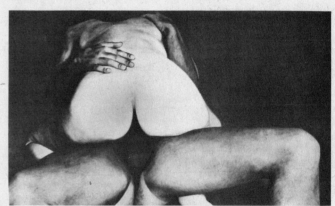

Untitled painting. (48" x 80").

Pen and ink.

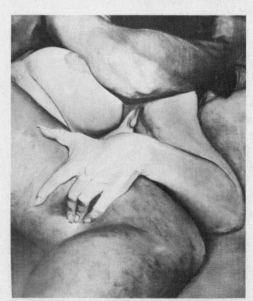

*Untitled
painting.*

Pen and ink.

FRANCINE SHAPOLSKY

Ms. Shapolsky studied at the Albert Pells School of Art in New York. She lives and works in New York. She became convinced that erotic art was her medium after seeing the work of Betty Dodson, and has continued in the milieu ever since. Her painting and drawings are rich in fantasy, and show an influence of the sixteenth century French grotesque. The word she feels provides the most all-encompassing feeling in her art is *metamorphosis.*

Pen and ink.

Pen and ink.

PAUL SIMON

Brooklyn born, Paul Simon was educated at Brooklyn College studying under Ad Reinhardt, Jimmy Ernst, and Milton Brown. He is presently an assistant professor of art at Mattatuck Community College in Waterbury, Connecticut. He helped form the "Daggett Street Ten," a group of studio artists who produce a vast mixed media multi-art presentation. Some of his recent exhibitions have been at the Artist Gallery in Connecticut, and at the New Haven Showcase of the Arts, a group exhibition. He works primarily in wood and masonite.

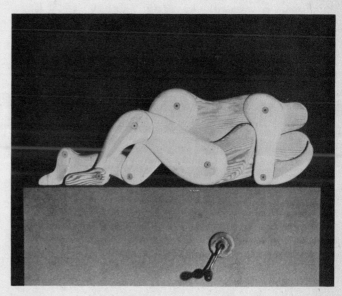

Phugue Toy (Lovers III) *(4½" wide, 5' high, 14" diameter). Wood and masonite.*

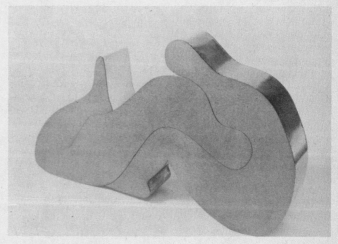

Lovers 2 *(46" x 26¼" x 7¼") Masonite, aluminum, and polystyrene.*

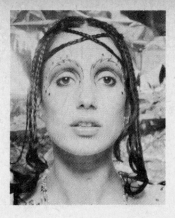

*Photo by
Jon Stevens.*

DOLLY SISSO

Dolly Sisso, also known as Spiral Galaxy, was born in Fez, Morocco, and was raised in Israel. There she became an artist, rapidly gaining recognition as one of the front runners in the avant garde. Next she became a model and in a short time was one of Israel's top fashion models, during which time her assignments took her to Japan, Germany, France, England, and New York. Coming to the United States in 1973, she became associated with Jon Stevens, modeling for many of his silver nudes, in which guise she became the symbol for the Eros '75 erotic festival. She is currently living and working in New York, where she continues to pursue both her art and modeling careers. She is also writing a book on yoga, and has plans to develop a line of cosmetics and photo makeup.

Watercolor from the Series of Cosmic Orgasms *(12" x 9").*

*Watercolor
from the
Series of
Cosmic Orgasms
(12" x 9").*

*Photo by
Dale Wolff.*

MARCIA LEE SMITH

Born and educated in Cincinnati, she received her B.S. in Art in 1965 and went on to study for her M.F.A. at the Pratt Institute. She has had many successful one-woman shows in New York and the rest of the country, the most recent of which was held at the Gallery 10 in New York City.

Ms. Smith lives and works in New York.

Lithograph.

Lithograph.

NANCY SPERO

Nancy Spero is a feminist artist who lives and works in New York. She has a B.F.A. from the Art Institute of Chicago, and she studied in Paris at the Atelier Andre L'Hote and the Ecole de Beaux-Arts. She has had one-woman shows at the A.I.R. Gallery, New York; Douglass College; Rutgers University; the Mombaccus Art Center, New Paltz, N.Y.; Williams College; The University of California at San Diego; and the Galerie Breteau, Paris. She has also participated in group shows throughout the United States and in Hamburg, Lausanne, Madrid, and Paris. An activist and public speaker in addition to being an artist, Ms. Spero has taught and lectured extensively in such places as The Art Institute of Chicago; Queens College, New York; The Boston Visual Arts Union; and The School of Visual Arts, New York.

*Photograph by
Susan Weiley.*

JESSICA STANLEY

Philadelphia-based cartoonist and illustrator, she is not exclusively a specialist in erotic art. But the experience of drawing sexy magazine cartoons allowed her a freedom of imagination that occasionally blossoms into a fantasy piece or sensuous design. Jessica's tight rendering and flair for lush drawing has placed her in local demand. She has not only appeared as a model, having been featured on two *Cavalier* magazine covers, but has collaborated on photographic layouts behind the camera.

Pencil drawing.

Normal Love *(9¾" x 8¼"). 1974.
Gouache collage and printing on paper.*

"I came in for backache, doctor, not heartache".*Watercolor.*

Screw Corporate Art *(9¾" x 8¼"). 1974.
Gouache collage and printing on paper.*

CHARLES STARK

ANITA STECKEL

"My main concern has been to orchestrate into painterly clarity the tumultuous masses and lights which combine in a figure. I do not see parts of the body as static, precisely definable objects, but rather as when watching the shifting skies of a storm, one sees that continuous rearrangement of cloud clusters and transluscencies combine in all their movements to give a singular character to the storm.

"So it is also with the tumbling meats of a bird's behind. A multitude of movements, changing lights, and quaking topographies, contours going slack and swelling out, come together to reveal a singular identity.

"In trying to get this all together I have come to be characterized as an erotic painter. It's here to be sure, but perhaps storm-resolver painter would be closer."

Of Anita Steckel's art, *Off Our Backs* magazine said: "Breakthrough genuis, revolutionary, masterpiece." She has the singular distinction of being the first woman artist to ever have an all-male nude show. She was chosen by *Ms* Magazine as one of ten American women artists from all over America in their first "found women" section and was chosen to design the official Feminist Party poster. Ms. Steckel founded an organization of women artists to fight puritanism and sexism in the visual fine arts—the "Fight Censorship" group—and wrote a position paper relating to their cause which has since been published in the *Village Voice* wherein she says: "If the erect penis is not wholesome enough to go into museums—it should not be considered wholesome enough to go into women."

Ms. Steckel presently lives and works in New York.

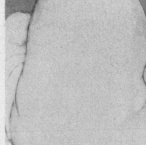

Untitled
(8¾" x 11¾").
1969. Acrylic on masonite.

Giant Woman on New York *(3' x 4')*. Collage paint and pencil on found art photo.

Untitled *(7¾" x 4-7/8")*. 1973. Ink and watercolor.

Mona Takes the Brush *(3' x 4')*. 1974. Collage paint and pencil on found art photo.

*Photo by
Caren Golden.*

JON STEVENS

JOYCE FARMER SUTTON

Jon Stevens is an artist whose medium is the camera. He began his career as a jazz drummer, surfing instructor, and model, and graduated to photography when he found that appearing before the lens did not satisfy his creative instincts. A pioneer in the technique of producing rich, erotic images of nude bodies covered in silver and gold, Stevens' work has appeared in a number of major publications around the world ranging from *Screw* to France's prestigious *Zoom*. A glittering figure himself, frequently seen in public clad in outré, multicolored costumes and erotic jewelry, Stevens is a living personification of his own work.

Mr. Stevens lives and works in New York.

"Born in California in 1938, I attended the Art Center School in Los Angeles before retiring at age nineteen to be the complete housewife and mother for six years. In 1971 I earned a B.A. in classical languages at the University of California and became "radicalized" politically and personally, deciding to change the world. I began as a pregnancy and birth control counselor, helping women make their own decisions regarding this ageless problem, and eventually wrote, with Chin Lyvely, a comic-style book regarding the subject called *Abortion Eve*, currently used by a number of counseling agencies.

"I consider myself a gadfly, working toward helping everyone's self-reliance, teaching people not to be afraid of their minds and bodies. I work mainly with and for women, since I have a vested interest. I feel strongly that too much has been communicated in the past about women by "experts" who are not women and often have very little understanding of us and our potential.

"Chin and I have published two alternate-media comics exploring women through menstrual periods, lesbianism, sexual fantasies, etc: *Tits and Clits* and *Pandora's Box*. Currently, I am working on more cartoons, cartoon strips, and graphic designs for both alternate-media and regular publications."

Photography.

*Black and
white print.
1974.*

If you can't be
with the one you love,
then love the one
you're with!

*photo by
Charles M. Monquin.*

RICHARD VORSE

"Concerning erotic art: one of the first acts of a boy with clay in his hands is to reproduce his cock. One of the first monuments erected by primitive societies: the phallus. I can remember modeling cocks with my childhood friends long before art became a preoccupation. Great joke then, significant in hindsight.

"Glad of erotic movement . . . public acceptance . .,. enables me to 'wax eloquent.' On the subject of erotica, feelings, nuances, instead of producing commercial porn—a previous attitude.

"Porn, shown of bodies, is at present being thoroughly attended to. Erotic art on the other hand—the communication of more sophisticated attitudes, inner feelings—has really just begun."

Mr. Vorse currents lives and works in New York.

Pewter figures. Photograph by Charles M. Monquin.

*Original wax mold before casting.
Photograph by Charles M. Monquin.*

XINA

"Childhood loving village countryside mother sewing, patchwork grandmother weaving growingknittingcrochetembroidery color art life living leaving learning design FIT NYC Provincetown artists New York love expression. . .BANANAS. . .CUCUMBERS. . .CARROTS. . . ZUCCHINI. . ."

Xina works and lives in New York.

Lady with Banana #1. Fabric collage and artificial fruit.

Picnic Basket.

Bibliography

Anand, Mulk Raj. *Kama Kala. some notes on the philosophical basis of Hindu erotic sculpture.* Geneva, New York: Nagel, 1958.

Arwas, Victor. *Felicien Rops.* New York: St. Martin's Press, 1972. $10.00.

Banach, A. *Les Enfers Domaine Polonais.* Paris: Jean-Jacques Pauvert, 1966.

Beardsley, Aubrey. *The Collected Drawings of Aubrey Beardsley.* New York: Bounty Books, 1967. $8.98.

Becker, Raymond de. *The Other Face of Love.* New York: Bell Publishing, 1969. *Being Without Clothes.* New York: Aperture Books, 1970. $10.00.

Bowie, Theodore, *et al. Studies in Erotic Art.* New York: Basic Books, 1970.

Danielou, Alain. *L'Erotisme Divinise.* Paris: Editions Buchet/Chastel, 1962.

Doucet, Jerome. *Peintres Et Graveurs Libertins du XVIIe Siecle.* Paris: A. Mericant, 1913.

Emde-Boas Starkenstern, Magda van. *Pornografie en Beeldende Kunst.* Gravenhage: MVSH, 1966.

Fouchet, Max Pol. *The Erotic Sculpture of India.* New York: Criterion Books, 1959.

Fuchs, Eduard. *Geschichte der ertoischen Kunst.* (3 vols). Munich: A. Langen, 1922-26.

——. *Die Grossen Meister de Erotik: ein Beitrag zum Problem des Schopferischen in der Kunst.* Munich: A. Langen, 1930.

Gabor, Mark. *The Pinup: A Modest History.* New York: Universe Books, 1972. $6.95.

Gerdts, William H. *The Great American Nude: A History in Art.* New York: Praeger, $25.00.

Gerhard, Poul. *Pornography in Fine Art from Ancient Times up to the Present.* Los Angeles: Elysium, 1969.

Gichner, Lawrence Ernest. *Erotic Aspects of Hindu Sculpture.* Washington, D.C.: 1949.

Ginsburg, Ralph. *Les enfers: panorama de l'erotisme: domaine de langu anglaise.* Paris: J-J Pauvert. English edition. *An Unhurried View of Eotica.* New York: Grove Press, 1959.

Gorsen, Peter. *Das Prinzip Obszon: Kunts, Pornographie und Gessellschaft.* Hamburg: Rowohlt, 1969.

Grimley, Gordon. *Erotic Illustrations.* New York: Bell Books, 1974. $10.00.

Grosz, George. *Ecce Homo.* New York: Brussel & Brussel, Inc., 1965. $2.95.

Karwath, Cary von. *Die Erotik in der Kunst: ala Manuskript nur fur Subskribenten Gedruckt.* Vienna and Leipzig: C. W. Stern, 1908.

Kahmen, Volker. *Erotic Art Today.* New York: New York Graphic Society, 1971. $14.50.

Kronhausen, Phyllis, and Kronhausen, Eberhard. *Erotic Art.* New York: Grove Press, 1968. Reprint. New York: Crown Press.

——. *Erotic Art II.* New York: Grove Press, 1970.

——. *A Gallery of Erotic Art.* New York: Bantam Books, 1974. $2.95.

Lewandowski, Herbert. *Das Sexual problem in der modernen Literature und Kunst: Versuch einer Analyse und Psychopathologie des Kunstlerischen Schaffens und der Kulturentwicklung seit 1800.* Dresden: Paul Aretz, 1929.

Marcade, Jean. *Eros Kalos: Essay on Erotic Elements in Greek Art.* Geneva, N.Y.: Nagel, 1962.

——. *Roma Amor: Essay on Erotic Elements in Etruscan and Roman Art.* Geneva, N.Y.: Nagel, 1961.

Moen, Arve. *Edvard Munch: Woman and Eros.* Oslo: Forlaget Norsk Kunstreproduksjon, 1957.

Parque, La Jeune. *Histoire de L'Erotisme.* Paris, 1969.

Peckham, Morse. *Art and Pornography. An Experiment in Explanation.* New York: Basic Books, 1969.

Ungerer, Tomi. *Fornicon.* New York: Grove Press, 1969. $25.00.

Rabenait, Arthur Maria. *Mimus Eroticus.* 15 vols. Hamburg: Verlag fur Kulturforschung, 1965-67.

Rowlandson, Thomas. *The Amorous Illustrations of Thomas Rowlandson.* New York: Cythera Press, 1969. $25.00.

——. *The Forbidden Erotica of Thomas Rowlandson.* Los Angeles: The Hogarth Guild, 1970. $22.50.

Salmon, Andre. *L'Erotisme dans l'Art Contemporain.* Paris: Librarie des Arts Decoratifs, 1932.

Le secret dans l'Image. Rome: Les Presses des Arts Graphiques Danesi, Editions aux Camellias, 1946.

Scutt, R. W. B., and Gotch, Christopher. *Art, Sex and Symbol: The Mystery of Tattooing.* Cranbury, N.J.: Barnes, 1975. $15.00.

Smith, Bradley. *Erotic Art of the Masters.* Secaucus, N.J.: Lyle Stuart, 1974. $24.95.

Van Maele, Martin. *The Satryical Drawings of Martin Van Maele.* New York: Cythera Press, 1970. $25.00.

Von Bayros, The Marquis. *The Erotic Drawins of The Marquis von Bayros.* New York: Cytheria Press.

Waas, Emil. *Erotische Graphik von der Antike bie heute.* Bonn: Verlag der Europaischen Bucherei, H. M. Hieronimi, 1966.

Zichy, Mihaly. *The Erotic Drawings of Mihaly Zichy.* New York: Grove Press, 1969. $25.00.

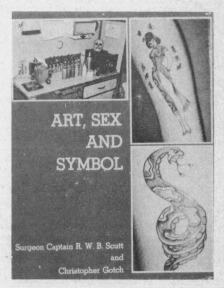

Tattooing is an ancient art form. This book, published by A. S. Barnes in the United States, is the most comprehensive illustrated history of the subject with emphasis on the sexual motif. (see bibliography).

A Peep at the Parisot with Q in the corner. Etching by George Cruikshank. Reproduced by permission of The Metropolitan Museum of Art, Harris Brisbane Dick Fund, 1917

Sex in the Performing Arts

History does not record when homo sapiens first conceived the idea of performing for the sake of entertainment. The earliest forms of performing *per se* were either ritual, celebration, or a means of recording deeds and events of historical importance. The performances, of course, were primarily dances and religious ceremonies which consisted of oral narratives and songs. Over the centuries, as man and his world became more sophisticated, these evolved into more complicated and varied forms, until eventually there was a natural move toward a recognition of the intrinsic value of music, drama, and dance for their primary entertainment qualities. Sex, always one of the basic concerns of humanity, entered the picture from the very beginning—and even today primitive peoples engage in sexually oriented performances, such as fertility dances.

Ancient drama reached its zenith during the Golden Age of Greece. The plays of Aristophanes, notably *The Frogs, The Wasps,* and *Lysistrata* have explicitly sexual themes. This is especially true of *Lysistrata*, in which the women of Troy and Athens band together during the Trojan war and refuse all sexual relations with their husbands and lovers, thereby forcing them to make peace. In Sophocles' *Oedipus Rex* and *Electra* the theme of incest is so powerfully treated that the names of the plays themselves have become basic terms in modern sexual psychopathology. A detailed study of the performing arts of any given period provides us with a vital and accurate statement of the social, sexual, and political attitudes of that time. They reflect customs, acceptable behavior, social causes, and most importantly, sexual standards. Indeed, throughout history, and to this day, if we were to remove the element of sex—expressed either as explicit sexuality or subtle suggestiveness—from the performing arts they would wither into a bland mass of oleaginous goo.

During the Middle Ages love and sex were incorporated into the performances of wandering minstrels and troubadours, and, of course, by court jesters and others whose talents were employed by royalty and the wealthy aristocracy. However, for our purposes we have arbitrarily chosen to begin our discussion at that time when theater became a medium of entertainment for the masses.

Theater

*A*side from the classics of Greece and Rome, sex as an integral element of formal theater did not really come into its own until the time of William Shakespeare. The bard was constantly concerned with the inherent drama growing out of lust, passion, and love. But his creativity was restricted by potential harassment from the lord chamberlain, who was the official crown censor. Consequently Shakespeare often resorted to euphemisms and gimmicks to disguise explicit sexuality, yet his devices were never so subtle as to leave any doubt in the mind of the audience as to what he was portraying on stage. When he referred to coital embrace as "the beast with two backs" no one hearing the line required a diagram. And when Malvolio, *Twelfth Night*, (Act II; Scene 5) describes a certain lady's handwriting, he says, "By my life, this is mylady's hand: these be her very C's, her U's, and her T's; and thus makes she her great P's. It is, in contempt of question; her hand." Eric Partridge's book *Shakespeare's Bawdy* remains the most comprehensive study of the sexual references in Shakespearean plays yet available.

In seventeenth century France, Molière is an outstanding example of one whose plays reflected the bedroom hypocrisies in the court of Louis XIV. During the same century there was a veritable explosion of sexuality in the theater of Restoration England, largely as a reaction to the puritan repression under the austere days of Cromwell. A prime example is *Sodom: or the Quintessence of Debauchery*. It is one of those rare gems of the theater, a classic pornographic satire in perfect iambic pentameter that parodies the style of Dryden. Written by John Wilmot, second Earl of Rochester, it was a barb aimed at the court of King Charles II, in which Rochester himself was regarded as one of the most controversial courtiers. To quote from *The Golden Age of Erotica* by Bernhardt J. Hurwood, "Rochester has been recognized by authorities as one of England's great poets . . . [he] spoke out clearly and concisely, with a witty impudence and an elegant style. It must be pointed out that Rochester never wrote his so-called obscenities to arouse his readers sexually. His purpose was to satirize, to lampoon, and to ridicule. . . . The *dramatis personae* of *Sodom* contains the most outrageous gang of sexual miscreants in the history of literature—at least as far as nomenclature is concerned."

During this period, sex was even more of an integral part of theater than it is today. The principal ingredients of most plays were subjects such as love intrigue, adultery, seduction, and rape. The best-qualified female actresses were whores, and as such were recruited from the *demi monde* of London. A Victorian writer said of the period, in horrified tones, that Restoration theater "not only fostered lewdness by depicting it in glowing and attractive colors, but its actors spread abroad the corruption it was their personal business to delineate. Their personal character corresponded, in too many instances, with the parts which they performed, and they reenacted in private the debaucheries which they presented on stage."

Sodom

DRAMATIS PERSONAE

BOLLOXINION, *King of Sodom.*
CUNTIGRATIA, *Queen.*
PRICKET, *Prince.*
SWIVIA, *Princess.*
BUGGERANTHOS, *General of the Army.*
POCKENELLO, *Prince, Collonel and Favourite of the King.*
BORASTUS, *Buggermaster-general.*
PINE and TWELY, *Two Pimps of Honour.*
FUCKADILLA,
OFFICINA,   *Maids of Honour.*
CUNTICULA,
CLYTORIS,
FLUX, *Physician to the King.*
VERTUOSO, *Merkin and Dildoe-maker to the Royal Family.*

With Boys, Rogues, Pimps and other Attendants.

Theaters became playhouses to such an extent that the so-called Orange girls, who peddled food and drink among the audiences, not only exchanged ribaldries but also arranged for assignations with anxious gallants after the performances. The king himself took such full advantage of the opportunities available that his queen, Katherine of Braganza, soon learned never to enter the royal apartment without sending forth ample warning of her impending arrival.

It was during this period that the music hall was born. The song and comedy was Rabelaisian and lusty, and ribald sketches concerned with the physical aspects of love were immensely popular.

By the eighteenth century, such unrestrained frolicking was so rampant in the theater, both on stage and between the acts, that the "green rooms"—nominally lounges for actors—became the locales for notorious orgies in which the most enthusiastic participants were members of the aristocracy.

By the time the Victorian Era had arrived, along with its strict double standard, all stops had been pulled out. Illustrative of what was popular at the time was a book of songs published by one William West called *The Blowmen's Cabinet of Choice Songs: A beautiful, bothering, laughter-provoking collection of spiflicating, flabbergasting, smutty ditties. . . .* containing such numbers as *Oh, Miss Tabitha Ticklecock, My Woman Is a Rummy Whore, The Randy Dinner,* and *The Invisible Tool.* Some other representative collections bore titles such as *The Cockchaser, The Cuckold's Vocalist,* and a classic (!) *Cythera's Hymnal: or, Flakes from the Foreskin, a Collection of Songs, Poems, Nursery Rhymes, Quiddities, etc. . . etc.*

In 1879 a group of enterprising and waggish Oxford scholars produced a spoof on Christmas pantomimes entitled *Harlequin Prince Cherrytop and the Good Fairy Fairfuck.* The plot dealt with a spell cast over the poor prince by the Demon Masturbation. The good fairy comes along and tries to coax him into the joys of wedlock with his fiancée, Princess Shovituppa, while shielding him from the pitfalls of involvement with Bubo, King of Ruperia, whose courtiers symbolize venereal disease in all its varied forms. All in all, a facetious put-on with a strong "moral."

One of the most popular and unique forms of theatrical entertainment in the 1850s and '60s were a series of nightly improvisations in the form of divorce trials, or more accurately Crim. Con. trials. Crim. Con. was the popular euphemism for adultery, *i.e.* Criminal Conversation, and according to the laws of the time, before divorce proceedings could be initiated, a Crim. Con. trial had to be held in which the injured party (usually the husband) sued his wife's lover for damages. In these performances, out of work actors and lawyers staged mock trials in which all the damaging evidence was reenacted before enthusiastic audiences.

Despite the theater's reputation as a cesspool of wickedness, more and more women began attending, and in consequence the more explicit aspects of sex submerged to be replaced by subtlety, wit, and sophistication. This general tone continued into the twentieth century, and though sex farces and serious dramas dealing with sexual problems continued to score high points at the box office, it was not until the late sixties that the pendulum began swinging back to explicit sex. With the opening of *Hair* in 1968, full nudity came to Broadway; *The Killing of Sister George,* with its powerful lesbian theme, provoked storms of controversy in 1969; the off-Broadway play *Ché!* was closed for alleged obscenity; and *Oh! Calcutta,* which was not particularly sexy but completely naked, packed them in at top prices.

More recently the exuberant naked celebration of sexuality is expressed in explicit language put to music in *Let My People Come,* the first all-sexual musical. It has been playing continuously in New York for almost a year, after having received excellent reviews from even the most legitimate of the New York theater critics.

Although as yet we are not witnessing explicit sex acts on the legitimate stage, it would be amiss not to mention the incredibly powerful and important scene from Peter Schaffer's *Equus,* in which one of the leading characters achieves orgasm through his god-like worship of horses while riding an imaginary "horse/man" on stage.

From the sexual musical Let My People Come, *reprinted with the permission of the producers*

Cinema

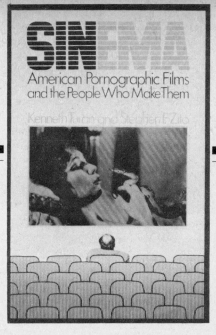

"The Cinema, that Temple of Sex, with its Goddesses, its Guardians and its Victims." □—Jean Cocteau

Sex has been an integral part of the motion picture from the earliest days of hand-cranked cameras and explosive nitrocellulose film. The sexual element has followed a parallel line with the theater insofar as subject matter is concerned. The significant changes have been in actual treatment of the content. In the days before explicit language and hard-core depiction of sexual acts, the implications were always present, except for the so-called stag films which were cheaply produced, poor-quality shorts created strictly for private viewing. Of the stag films, the majority were live-action, although a few imaginative individuals produced some fairly entertaining animated cartoons. Notable among these cartoons is an underground classic called *Everready*, concerning the exploits of a Candide-like innocent who fell into one absurd sexual disaster after another—the most memorable being a scene in which he pounces on a sirenlike female lying on a rock, who has in her vagina an oversized lobster which seizes his penis and runs off with it, resulting in one of the most hilariously absurd chase sequences in film history.

As for the early theatrical productions, especially those of the late Cecil B. De Mille, the orgies and seminudity attained epic proportions, but because these films represented the expenditure of millions of dollars and dealt with historical themes, they were regarded by the film-going public as morally acceptable. Besides, these were produced in the days of the legendary flamboyant press agents who were able to sell anything to anyone. On another level, many of the early Busby Berkley musical extravaganzas included a variety of crotch shots that titilated the masses while succeeding in passing the majority of censors unchallenged.

During the thirties, forties, and fifties the key to sexuality was in subject matter. Prostitution, adultery, and violent sexual passions were inherent in plots, but before a couple went into the bedroom there was always a discreet fade-out. Even married couples could never be seen sharing a bed. However, the biggest taboo was language. When Clark Gable uttered the word "damn" in *Gone With the Wind*, shock waves were felt throughout the world. The heavy overtones of sex were omnipresent in *Streetcar Named Desire*, but never spelled out. To this day, relatively few people in the general audience are aware that the original concept of *Who's Afraid of Virginia Woolf* concerned a male homosexual relationship.

To quote from *Sinema*, by Kenneth Turan and Stephen F. Zito, "The Nudie-Cutie was born in 1959, the year Russ Meyer, a one-time army combat cameraman and cheesecake photographer raised $24,000 and made *The Immoral Mr. Teas*, the most important and notorious erotic film released in the United States until *I Am Curious (Yellow)* was put on the market by Grove Press in 1968."

I Am Curious (Yellow) is a fascinating story in itself. Barney Rossett, president of Grove Press, was extremely courageous in undertaking the release of *I Am Curious*, since it contained explicit sex scenes never before shown on the silver screen in America. At first, it seemed highly improbable that he would be able to obtain the rights to the picture, because he was not known to the Swedish producers. However, he had published Drs. Phyllis and Eberhard Kronhausen (internationally recognized authors, collectors of erotica, and champions of sexual freedom) and thanks to their efforts on his behalf, he was able to get the distribution rights to the film, and the rest is history.

It should be noted that before and after the acceptance of explicit sex on the screen, virtually every horror and violence film ever made, especially those dealing with vampirism, appealed to the audiences deep-rooted sadomasochistic instincts. The subtleties vanished when Andy Warhol and Paul Morrissey unleashed their versions of *Frankenstein* and *Dracula*. Mel Brooks's *Young Frankenstein* also gave sex a prime showcase, but in his case, as with all of his films, it was done with zany enthusiasm aimed strictly at producing gales of merriment. On the subject of the satirical approach to sex, Woody Allen must be mentioned for his *Everything You've Ever Wanted to Know about Sex* and *Sleeper*, both of which broadly parody the profundity of modern ideas about sexuality.

In the sixties and early seventies the major producers began making cautious steps forward, confident that the rating system would enable them to get off the hook in the mass market. Their chief advantage was the availability of large budgets and stars of universal name value. Some pictures were of the highest quality on all levels; others were merely slick exploitations. But whatever the level of their artistic integrity, most of them proved to be box office successes. Representative of this period are Anthony Newley's *Can Hieronymus Merkin Ever Forget Mercy Humppe and Find True Happiness*; Roger Vadim's *Barbarella*; *The Valley of the Dolls*; Fellini's *Satyricon*; *Bob and Carol and Ted and Alice*; *Klute*; *Myra Breckenridge*; and *Last Tango in Paris*—in which the producers took

Actual flyer circulated by a porno film producer on college campuses to recruit cast members

advantage of the rash of hard core X-ers to charge an outrageous $5.00 at the box office.

Tom Jones captivated audiences by recreating the bawdy spirit of the eighteenth century, as did a later British import, *Mistress Pamela. Blow-Up* integrated exciting sexuality within the context of a story basically about the career of a photographer. *Alfie* dealt with the sexual misadventures of a born loser, and the Australian farce *Alvin Purple* explicitly spoofed sex therapy, pornographic films, and general social hypocrisy. *Joe*, the low-budget film about violence which launched the career of actor Peter Boyle, showed frontal nudity and became a runaway smash; and John Avildsen's *Save the Tiger*, a serious comment on the sad state of morality in the business world, incorporated explicit scenes of kinky sex, some of which had to be edited out in the final cut. *Fritz The Cat* emerged as the first X-rated full-length animated cartoon feature. Ken Russell's *The Devils* dealt with an actual episode in history involving sex and scandal in the church. Although *Clockwork Orange* contained only a brief sequence of explicit sex—in speeded up action at that—it was attacked more for this than for the explicit violence, which is evidence of the way a censor's mind works.

Women in Love and *The Fox* had serious sexual themes, and both provoked controversy amidst high critical acclaim. *Carnal Knowledge*, a perfectly valid film, was actually declared obscene in Georgia and required a United States Supreme Court decision to remove the stigma inflicted by a minority of bigots, *Emanuelle*, a lushly and sensually photographed French film about sophisticated sexual gambits among the diplomatic set, and Warren Beatty's *Shampoo*, which is a veritable cavalcade of the exploits of a Beverly Hills hairdresser, were both released with X-ratings. While each concentrates very heavily on the sexual proclivities of the characters, there is no explicit heterosexual sex—all such scenes being handled "discreetly" by simulated sexual behavior.

A picture worthy of special mention is *Don't Look Now*, a brilliant drama with a complex supernatural theme, starring Donald Sutherland and Julie Christie. It contained a love scene done with exquisite taste, that has been called by many the most erotic sequence ever depicted on the screen. While on the subject of the supernatural, we cannot overlook *The Exorcist* which presented some of the most shocking depictions of sexuality, both visually and in dialogue, ever filmed.

And then there are the hard-core flicks.

Before the major breakthrough made by *Deep Throat*, underground film-makers were grinding out "quick and dirties" by the mile, in terms of total footage shot. Most of these were undistinguished "loops" destined for the 25¢ peep show trade. To be sure, feature length hard-core films were made and exhibited in theaters specializing in porno film. Some of the pioneer films of the genre were produced and shown by the management of the Sutter Theater in San Francisco, and one of the first porno queens, who achieved notoriety as "Aqua Vulva," later scored a first by starring in a porno-soap opera videotape epic called *The Continuing Saga of Carol and Ferd.* A woman with higher ambitions, who for over a year was the live-in lover of Lenny Bruce, Aqua Vulva eventually earned her Ph.D from a major university and now is a professor of cinema.

There have been so many hard-core features produced since *Deep Throat* that it would be impossible to list them all. Several, however, deserve mention, because each in its own way was significant. *The Devil and Miss Jones* had a serious theme dealing with a woman who committed suicide and was returned to earth to experience all the sexual excesses she had never known during her lifetime—and made a star out of Georgina Spelvin. *Behind The Green Door*, an elaborate Mitchell Brothers production, elevated Marilyn Chambers (the Ivory Snow girl) to stardom. Danny Stone's *High Rise* contained a fine blend of comedy and production values, and had what is considered to be the most excellent lesbian love scene in the entire porno genre. *It Happened in Hollywood*, directed by Peter Locke, was so wildly hilarious despite technical flaws, it was highly entertaining.

Devil in Miss Jones

"With *The Devil In Miss Jones* the porno feature approaches an art form. . .a breathtaking erotic odyssey."—*Variety*

"Stands head and shoulders above Deep Throat."—*Judith Christ, New York Magazine*

Scene from the Australian box office runaway hit *Alvin Purple*. *Reprinted by permission of BI JAY films*

Andrea True, star of Illusions of a Lady. *Reprinted by permission of the producers, Mastermind, Ltd.*

Other pornos, such as Jonas Middleton's *Illusions of a Lady*, had strong plot lines, and despite uneven acting were visually worth seeing and indicative of a rising directional talent. *Angel Number Nine*, in 1974, was of special interest because it was the first porno written, produced, directed, and photographed by a woman, Roberta Findlay.

Sandwiched in among the others there have been a number of unusual specialized sex films. There was *Porno Pop*, produced by the Drs. Kronhausen, a full-length montage of hilariously funny, vintage porno strips—some of the hand-cranked variety dating back to the nineteen-hundreds—which was accompanied by an original Dixieland score with humorous lyrics. GLIDE in San Francisco produced a number of sex education and entertainment shorts. Among their more famous productions were *Orange*, a highly erotic series of images containing extreme sexual symbolism revolving around the peeling and eating of an orange in extreme closeup, and *Love Toads*, a delightful stop-action film of two calico bean-bag toads making love.

The Kronhausens' most recent film, *The Hottest Show in Town*, a sex circus comedy, involves the goings-on in an X-rated, adult circus. The Kronhausens frankly admit it is purely sex entertainment, "deliberately without any pretense at educational or scientific merit, except that which incidentally accompanies almost any type of entertainment." But therein,

they maintain, lies exactly its purpose and the point they are trying to make, namely that "Sex does not need any 'redeeming' social value or excuse; it is quite enough of a positive value in itself."

Although many of the people involved in porno films are predestined to perpetual obscurity in the straight film-making world, most aspire to social acceptance in it. Others, by virtue of what they have done, have made it already. Gerard Damiano, who directed *Deep Throat, Devil and Miss Jones*, and *Memories within Miss Aggie*, has become a household name. Robert Sumner, of Mayure Pictures, Inc. as both a distributor, exhibitor, and producer has established himself as a leading crusader for freedom of expression. On numerous occasions he has placed his neck on the chopping block on behalf of the entire industry. Harry Reems, who has written a best-selling autobiography, *Here Comes Harry Reems*, has done everything from Shakespeare to television commercials and has been called by no less a star than Angela Lansbury, "the bravest actor in America." Reems is a perfect example of a contra stereotype. Far from being a ravening sex maniac stud, he is a charming nonegotistical, articulate actor, who is totally heterosexual and an expert on antiques. Other porno actors and actresses who have succeeded in becoming known to the general public are Tina Russell, Marc Stevens (Mr. 10½), Darby Lloyd Raines, and Andrea True.

Linda Lovelace and Harry Reems in a scene from "Deep Throat"

One of "The Flying Fucks" from the Milky Way Productions X-rated farce, It Happened in Hollywood, directed by Peter Locke and produced by Jim Buckley

One of the most talented film-makers in the porno field is Eduardo Cemano, whose comments follow and serve as an appropriate summation.

"I am a serious film-maker, an artist and not a pornographer. It is obvious that such words as 'prurient' and 'patently offensive' will be debated forever with regard to their specific meaning. I love sex, and I think it is beautiful and I don't believe that being lustful (which is another word for prurience) should be punishable by law. I cannot attest to being an expert in literary, political or scientific values, but . . . I am an artist, I have been one all my life. How can it be left to the Courts to prove that my work has no 'serious artistic value.'

"The history of art is filled with names of great painters and sculptors who have explored sexual subject matter and have depicted the various acts of lovemaking with varying degrees of explicitness. During the past two years, I have made three features in which I explored sexual choreography, comedy, and satire: 'The Healers' 'Fongalulu' (now playing in Paris under the title of 'Sweet Love and Madame Zenobia,' which was named the Best Erotic Film at the Cannes Film Festival.

"My films are highly moralistic. They are antiviolence. And they affirm that love and only love can bring ultimate sexual happiness. They are never abusive to women. They philosophically denounce any degradation of the sexual act.

"Perhaps my films are, at present, offensive to some. But I can remember the furor over an incidental momentary nude scene in Hair, and the fights over a bit of pubic hair spotted in Antonioni's Blow-Up.

"Off Broadway expanded the boundaries of liberation for Broadway. We in the film underground are expanding the boundaries of adult movie making. But we are being crucified for it. Our low budgets allow us to take bigger risks than the

From the film Porno Pop *produced by Drs. Phyllis and Eberhard Kronhausen. Reprinted by permission*

Actor and author of his autobiography 10½, Marc Stevens

Advertisement for the original release of Fongaluli, produced and directed by Eduardo Cemano, now breaking box office records in France under the title Sweet Love

'majors.' We are the scientists of public interest, and the public responded with millions of dollars that proved that the masses had interests that were not being gratified by conventional movies. The proof that we are influential can be seen in the growing freedom in language and nudity in today's so called 'Hollywood' films. We are continually developing new audiences for sexually mature film-making, and we were succeeding in raising the artistic level of sex films until the Supreme Court responded loudly to the artistically ignorant. Unless the Supreme Court responds to the many intelligent voices that have come to the defense of creative freedom in our country, we can assume that the sexual liberation movement in film has been stopped. If the most powerful men in the film industry can so misinterpret our position in the evolution of film-making and in the acceptance of erotic art in general, then our only hope lies in the reeducation of the public."

From the film Porno Pop produced by Drs. Phyllis and Eberhard Kronhausen. Reprinted by permission

"CEMANO CAPTURES THE ANTICIPATION, WONDER, PAIN, ECSTACY, TORTURE AND RAPTURE—THAT EXPRESS THE SEXUAL ACT. A SUREFIRE AUDIENCE-GRABBER. LOVELACE, CHAMBERS AND SPELVIN, WILL JUST HAVE TO MAKE ROOM FOR TINA RUSSELL." —Bob Salmaggi

EDUARDO CEMANO'S

Madame Zenobia

Starring TINA RUSSELL

UNANIMOUSLY HAILED AS THE BEST EROTIC FILM AT THE CANNES FILM FESTIVAL

SHE MAKES HEAVEN & EARTH COME TOGETHER

COLOR • ADULTS ONLY

This is the story of a beautiful young widow, who is unable to find sexual gratification with her newly acquired fiancé, due to her continuous love affair with the "spirit" of her late husband. Madame Zenobia, a beautiful, black medium employs her occult powers to solve the heroine's problems, bringing the film to a bizarre and shocking climax.

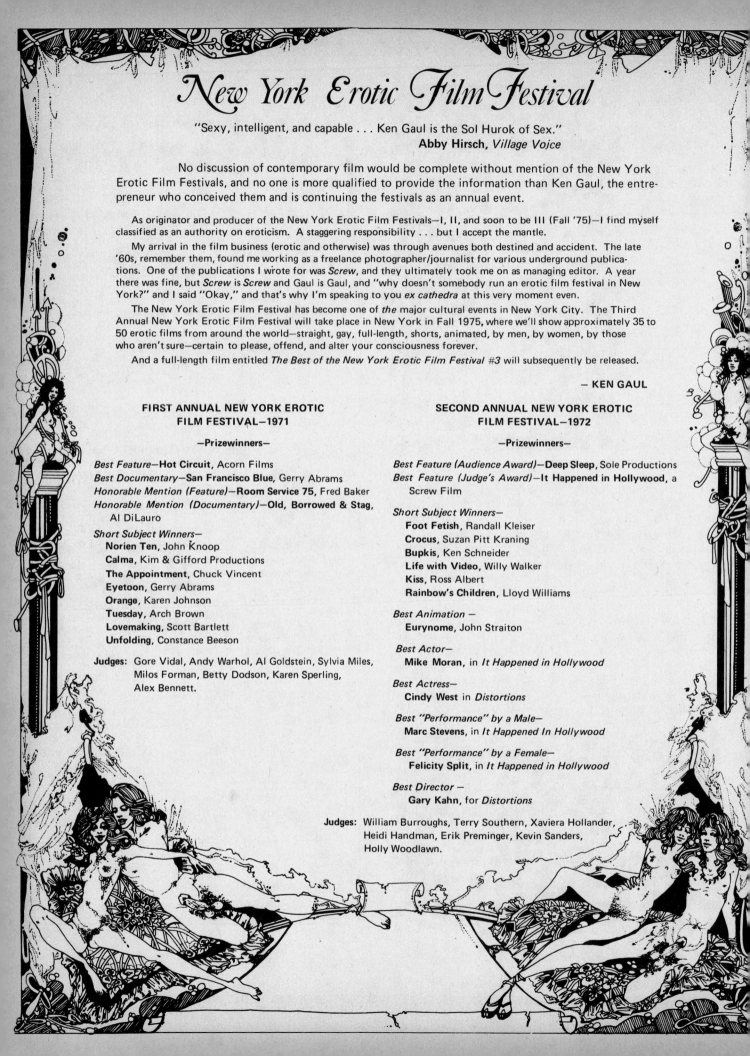

New York Erotic Film Festival

"Sexy, intelligent, and capable . . . Ken Gaul is the Sol Hurok of Sex."
Abby Hirsch, *Village Voice*

No discussion of contemporary film would be complete without mention of the New York Erotic Film Festivals, and no one is more qualified to provide the information than Ken Gaul, the entrepreneur who conceived them and is continuing the festivals as an annual event.

As originator and producer of the New York Erotic Film Festivals—I, II, and soon to be III (Fall '75)—I find myself classified as an authority on eroticism. A staggering responsibility . . . but I accept the mantle.

My arrival in the film business (erotic and otherwise) was through avenues both destined and accident. The late '60s, remember them, found me working as a freelance photographer/journalist for various underground publications. One of the publications I wrote for was *Screw*, and they ultimately took me on as managing editor. A year there was fine, but *Screw* is *Screw* and Gaul is Gaul, and "why doesn't somebody run an erotic film festival in New York?" and I said "Okay," and that's why I'm speaking to you *ex cathedra* at this very moment even.

The New York Erotic Film Festival has become one of *the* major cultural events in New York City. The Third Annual New York Erotic Film Festival will take place in New York in Fall 1975, where we'll show approximately 35 to 50 erotic films from around the world—straight, gay, full-length, shorts, animated, by men, by women, by those who aren't sure—certain to please, offend, and alter your consciousness forever.

And a full-length film entitled *The Best of the New York Erotic Film Festival #3* will subsequently be released.

— KEN GAUL

FIRST ANNUAL NEW YORK EROTIC FILM FESTIVAL—1971

—Prizewinners—

Best Feature—**Hot Circuit**, Acorn Films
Best Documentary—**San Francisco Blue**, Gerry Abrams
Honorable Mention (Feature)—**Room Service 75**, Fred Baker
Honorable Mention (Documentary)—**Old, Borrowed & Stag**, Al DiLauro
Short Subject Winners—
  Norien Ten, John Knoop
  Calma, Kim & Gifford Productions
  The Appointment, Chuck Vincent
  Eyetoon, Gerry Abrams
  Orange, Karen Johnson
  Tuesday, Arch Brown
  Lovemaking, Scott Bartlett
  Unfolding, Constance Beeson

Judges: Gore Vidal, Andy Warhol, Al Goldstein, Sylvia Miles, Milos Forman, Betty Dodson, Karen Sperling, Alex Bennett.

SECOND ANNUAL NEW YORK EROTIC FILM FESTIVAL—1972

—Prizewinners—

Best Feature (Audience Award)—**Deep Sleep**, Sole Productions
Best Feature (Judge's Award)—**It Happened in Hollywood**, a Screw Film

Short Subject Winners—
  Foot Fetish, Randall Kleiser
  Crocus, Suzan Pitt Kraning
  Bupkis, Ken Schneider
  Life with Video, Willy Walker
  Kiss, Ross Albert
  Rainbow's Children, Lloyd Williams

Best Animation —
  Eurynome, John Straiton

Best Actor—
  Mike Moran, in *It Happened in Hollywood*

Best Actress—
  Cindy West in *Distortions*

Best "Performance" by a Male—
  Marc Stevens, in *It Happened In Hollywood*

Best "Performance" by a Female—
  Felicity Split, in *It Happened in Hollywood*

Best Director —
  Gary Kahn, for *Distortions*

Judges: William Burroughs, Terry Southern, Xaviera Hollander, Heidi Handman, Erik Preminger, Kevin Sanders, Holly Woodlawn.

Films and where to get them:

The film division of Grove Press publishes a 75-page catalogue listing all their films, including: *I Am Curious (Blue)*, *I Am Curious (Yellow)*, *Freedom to Love*, *Quiet Days in Clichy*. A copy of the catalogue (gratis) is available by writing to: Grove Press Film Division, 53 East 11th Street, New York, N.Y. 10003. (Exact rental and purchase costs are listed in the catalogue.)

A second reliable source for films is the Multi-Media Resource Center in San Francisco, which also published a catalogue which is available (gratis) upon request to: MMRC, 540 Powell Street, San Francisco, California 94108.

A note to the Reader: The films available from the above sources, while sexually explicit, are not "stag" films or porno loops, which are only available through mail order suppliers listed in The Sexual Bazaar.

Television

In itself, television is a relatively new medium for the performing arts, and in some ways it has been lagging behind the growing cultural sex revolution of the last five years. Possibly because the programs actually come into people's living rooms, and are exposed to a huge socially and economically diversified audience, encompassing all ages at any given time, the network powers who be feel a necessity for "censorship." But, despite this, television is beginning to realize that audiences are becoming more sophisticated, and it acknowledges that it has to grow up along with them. No longer does Mary Tyler Moore always go home to her own apartment at night, and she has been seen arriving to work the following morning after a "date" in the same clothes she was wearing the night before. It isn't exactly blatant, but the implication is there.

There is, however, virtually no explicit sex on television (see A Note On Cable T.V.), but the medium is at last being used to educate as well as to entertain.

For example, the very successful made for television movies, *Cry Rape*, and *A Case of Rape* study a woman's emotional and social turmoil after making the decision to prosecute her rapist, exposing the prevalent but archaic attitude toward the victims of rape. Another such movie, dealing with an even more sensitive subject, was *It Happened Last Summer*, the story of a divorced father's anguish in explaining to his eight-year-old son that he is a homosexual and living in a love relationship with another man. And, since current attitudes toward venereal disease have elevated it to a socially acceptable condition, there has even been a made-for-television movie portraying a marriage in which the husband contracts syphilis in an extramarital affair and transmits it to his wife.

It should also be mentioned that Dick Cavett did a special, *V.D. Blues*, which was an extensive educational program dealing with the epidemic of venereal disease.

All of these programs spark intense debates, frequently conducted by well-known personalities appearing on the leading talk and news shows.

For example, on *Not for Women Only*, Barbara Walters held a five-part discussion on sex therapy with leading psychologists and doctors in the field. Since this was a controlled discussion and the cases cited were ostensibly hypothetical, it was deemed acceptable. However, when the Drs. Kronhausen taped a ninety-minute show for David Susskind's program, the main topic also being sex therapy, they used as an example a couple whose relationship was actually suffering because of various sexual problems and dysfunctions. Though there was not any explicit sex or harsh language, because it was not about a simulated situation, but a real life problem, the program was never aired.

Drawing by Phoebe McKay

"It would just blow people's minds," television officials said. However, a point should be made here: it is a step forward that it was indeed taped at all, and it is still available to be aired when more progress has been made.

Late-night programming also offers an opportunity to air programs dealing with sexuality when parents who do not wish their children to be exposed to certain subject matter have them safely tucked away in bed. One such program was ABC's "Wide World of Entertainment"'s study on homosexuals hosted by David Frost. The program unfortunately dealt primarily with stereotypes in its attempt to be understanding of the homosexual relationship. It did not say that homosexuality is another alternative life-style just as heterosexuality is, but it did dispel some myths and is a giant step forward. Television is coming out of the closet and beginning to discuss matters it has for such a long time ignored.

Hopes for the future are that because television can reach such vast numbers of people, it will soon take full advantage of this opportunity and produce programming that deals with all kinds of sexuality, from life-styles to education to alternatives.

A Note on Cable T.V.

Although regular network and local television channels have as yet made only tentative and cautious moves towards the depiction of sex for reasons previously pointed out, cable T.V. has pulled out all the stops. One of the most daring examples of cable programming was the late, lamented *The Underground Tonight Show*, produced by Michael Luckman, who attained notoriety for teaching a course called "Pornography Uncovered, Eroticism Exposed" at the New School for Social Research in New York. On Luckman's show such subjects as masturbation and "tit-sucking" were discussed and demonstrated along with a full range of other sexually explicit subjects.

Another landmark in sexual television is *The Anton Perich Show* in New York. The twenty-nine-year-old Yugoslavian-born Perich videotapes his shows in black and white and usually on location. The presentation ranges from the straight interview, *e.g.* Marilyn Chambers interviewing Samantha McLaren, star of *The Life and Times of a Happy Hooker*, to explicit airings of sexual activities between his subjects. In a recent article about Perich in *Film International*, Alan Greenburg wrote, " 'The Anton Perich Show' has not only put cable television on the map but has helped broaden the boundaries of the timid medium as well. It is a funny and fascinating program, a weekly sixty minutes marked by a frankness so daring and true as to be bizarre, a splash of Tabasco on an otherwise bland menu of network and private video fare."

It is also significant to note that today many major hotels throughout the United States offer X-rated films on pay TV for guests who choose to enjoy their erotica in private.

The Concert *by Thomas Rowlandson*

Music

"*If Music be the food of love, play on. . . .*" said Duke Orsino in the opening line of Shakespeare's *Twelfth Night*.

Among the ancient Athenians one of the favorite instruments was the flute, which was said to have been invented by the god Pan. Women excelled in the art of flute playing, and during the Bacchic rites the music of the flute was an aural stimulus to voluptuousness. During these fêtes, which usually developed into supreme orgies, the flute girls often aroused the participants to such an extent that they stripped themselves of their jewelry, flinging rings and necklaces at the players' feet. To quote from Frichet's *Fleshpots of Antiquity*: "these women . . . soon arrived at disorder into which their imaginations led the senses. Their entire life was as a perpetual struggle with lasciviousness: by dint of seeing their own nudity and comparing it with that of their companions, they acquired a taste for it and created for themselves, without the aid of their lovers, bizarre and ardent pleasures."

The Romans, being less musically inclined, placed greater emphasis on performance in a sexual rather than musical sense. With the advent of Christianity and its deemphasis of the pleasures of sex, music and lyrics concentrated on the romantic rather than the fleshly aspects of love. Nevertheless, during medieval times the songs and ballads of troubadours inflamed many a maiden to the heights of passion.

By Elizabethan times ballads had attained a high degree of sexual sophistication. Composers and performers, faced with the real danger of prosecution for exceeding the limits of contemporary tastes, resorted to fascinating euphemisms and other devices. For example, the still-popular ballad, "Greensleeves" had specific sexual connotations. The conception for the word greensleeves grew out of the fact that when a lover tumbled his lady in the grass the friction often resulted in green stains on the sleeves of her gown, being that portion of her attire which was often not removed during the act of love. Whereas everyone today tosses off the term "orgasm" as lightly as one might brush away a fly, such explicit language in those days was regarded as indelicate, yet no one ignored the esctasy of the sexual climax itself. Consequently, in lyrics, ballads, and poems, the euphemism "death" was frequently substituted. Read any love poem or song lyric from the time of Shakespeare through the Restoration and you will find innumerable phrases such as "Ah, sweet death." We can assure you that actual death was the furthest thing from the mind of the composers, the singers, and the listeners.

As time progressed the bawdy song attained greater popularity. Many of the limericks we know today came to life in the form of bawdy songs.

With the rise in popularity of the nineteenth century English Music Hall, ribald songs became a staple for all composers and performers. An especially popular group of these songs were known as anacreontics, the name being taken from the ancient Greek poet, Anacreon, who was known for his lusty lyrics. At one time or another we have all heard sexually oriented original songs and parodies of popular tunes, such as "The Bastard King of England," allegedly written by Rudyard Kipling and "The Reaming of Dan McGrew," a parody on the famous poem of Robert Service, the first stanza of which is as follows:

> *A bunch of the boys were whooping it up*
> *In one of the Yukon halls,*
> *The kid that handled the music box*
> *Was stealthily scratching his balls*
> *The Frisco Kid has his hand on the box*
> *Of the lady that's known as Lou*
> *While there on the floor, on top of a whore*
> *Lay dangerous Dan McGrew.*

And who has not heard of the infamous song "Roll Your Leg Over," which has been sung by virtually every college student since the words were written.

Seafarers made famous the classic "Bell Bottom Trousers," and Burl Ives in the 1940s popularized the tender words and music of "The Foggy Dew." Not a single doughboy in World War I came home without having committed to memory "Hinky Dinky Parlez Vous," and in the Second World War virtually all of the Allied forces at one time or another burst into song with either the lyric "To Roll Me Over" or "Fuck 'Em All."

There has always been considerable controversy among musicologists and other authorities as to whether or not music *per se* without lyrics can be labeled happy, sad, erotic, or anything else. Regardless of this, classical music contains many works that cannot be ignored insofar as their sexual or erotic overtones are concerned. The very fact that the expression "mood music" is generic speaks for itself.

The Renaissance period produced countless works that

evoked erotic response in the listeners. The works of Michael Praetorius with their delicate orchestrations of recorder, flute, and tambourine are especially notable. Another composer of the period, Ludwig Senfl, turned out similarly sensual compositions.

The Baroque era, with its infinitely more sophisticated complexities in composition, orchestration, and structure, gave eroticism an even greater emphasis. One need only to listen to the works of Vivaldi, Telemann, Buxtehude, Fux, not to mention Scarlatti, and the immortals, Bach and Mozart, and the message is clear. What can be more conducive to romance and lovemaking than the delicate harpsichord renditions of *The Goldberg Variations*? The music written for the Elizabethan theater by Henry Purcell is rich in eroticism, as well as are many of the works of Francois Couperin, and Jean Philippe Rameau.

The world of opera is heavily laden with sexuality. Mozart's *Cosi Fan Tutte* and *Abduction from the Seraglio* deal with all manner of lighthearted sexual peccadillos. However, to go into a complete discussion of the themes of sex and suffering in all the great operas would require a book in itself.

The Romantic and modern period of classical music is peppered with sexuality and eroticism. We need only examine the works of Wagner, Mendelssohn, and others of the period. And finally in more recent times, Rimsky-Korsakov's *Scheherazade* evokes lush images of eroticism out of *The Arabian Nights*. De Falla's *El Amor Brujo* and Ravel's *Bolero* are certainly illustrative of sexuality at the heights of artistic expression.

From the first day we opened our mouths to sing, we have been singing each other "love songs," and with the advent of recording and radio there was a proliferation unknown before in history. While on one level legitimate song writers such as Cole Porter, Jerome Kern, George Gershwin, and Irving Berlin were celebrating romantic love, others—legitimate and otherwise—were grinding out music and lyrics of an overtly sexual nature. In particular, the Empress of the Blues, Bessie Smith, was known to wail "A Little Sugar in My Bowl and A Hotdog in My Roll" over a hot, battered piano on 125th Street; and it was *alleged* that Pearl Bailey made a number of X-rated recordings sold under the counter and possibly still available today.

During the forties, Frank Sinatra probably caused more closet orgasms from his crooning among young women than

French Dancer at a Morning Rehearsal *by Thomas Rowlandson, eighteenth century*

anyone before his time, despite the fact that during this period he was not specifically identified as a sex symbol.

Following in this mode, Johnny Ray in the fifties did exactly the same thing to another generation but with a little more daring. Although the removal of his socks on stage would seem a little tame today, it kindled the fires of passion that were to come.

Music was becoming more liberated and so was its explicit delineation of sexuality, as typified by the Beatles' rendition of "Why Don't We Do It in the Road." "Je t'aime," however, was banned from the American airways—it is a duet between Jane Birkin and Serge Gainsbourg who vocalize their act of love from subdued beginnings to passionate climax.

From the moment that Elvis Presley first did his sexually suggestive bump and grind in the mid-fifties, the subliminal and overt symbolism of sexuality in modern music have never been the same. Presley's pelvic action was sending shivers up the backs of millions. Music was moving into an entirely new arena, the concert halls were filled with hysterical, screaming fans applauding some of the most outrageous performances.

Since Presley, however, we have literally seen it all.

The *revolution* began with the Rolling Stones, whose early image was rebellious. Their unkempt hair, untidy clothes, and sloppy performances defied the respectable, clean-cut image that the Beatles had previously portrayed, and then dominated the rock music scene. However, in recent years the Stones have broken away from the antiestablishment protest movement of the sixties to a new era of sexual decadence, including Mick Jagger's full facial makeup, his one-piece body suits revealing pubic hair, and his microphone which is more often between his legs than at his lips.

Another rock hero was the late Jim Morrison of the group the Doors, who was arrested in front of a Florida audience in the late sixties and banned from future performances for obscenity and indecent exposure on stage.

The overt sadomasochism of Iggy Pop, who makes himself bleed by smashing a Coca-Cola bottle and grinding the crushed glass into his chest and then launching himself onto his audience, and Lou Reed, whose big hit song, "Heroin" praises the virtues of drug addiction and whose other big success, "Vicious" ("Hit me with a flower, do it by the hour"), speak for themselves. Although many think that the kinkiness of Alice Cooper, whose act included snakes, a crucifix sequence, and a grand finale magic trick which simulates his own decapitation, has refined S-M, violence and sex into a slick put-on.

One of the most outrageous performances ever put on stage was that of the late Jimi Hendrix. His guitar became a weapon as well as an electric penis. The culmination of his act was setting fire to the instrument while standing over the burning flames thrusting his body back and forth.

Janis Joplin, although she was not overtly sexual, succeeded through her performances and life style to spark a new freedom for sexual expression in other women artists.

With the emergence of David Bowie and his open bisexuality on stage, it would seem there is nothing left to be exposed. Clearly, by sharp contrast, it vividly demonstrates that we have come a long way in a very short time from the crooning days of Bing Crosby and Frank Sinatra. Where we go from here, frankly, is anybody's guess . . .

Dance

Stylized eroticism portrayed by avant-garde dancers of the roaring twenties. From the private collection of Phoebe McKay

As with all of the other performing arts, dance has been a mirror of life. In periods of history when sexual license prevailed, so did its expression in the terpsichorean mode. Although dancing about maypoles in celebration of spring was not a performance in the strict sense of the word, it was regarded by religious authorities in fifteenth and sixteenth century England as immoral and sacrilegious because of lingering overtones of pagan sexuality. One of the most directly sexual forms of dance is the traditional Middle Eastern belly dance, an art form often attempted, but rarely executed properly by dancers who have not been brought up in the Middle Eastern cultural frame of reference. The waltz, innocent as it seems to us today, and which has been traditionally performed on stage, in films, and at gala balls, when originally introduced in early nineteenth-century Vienna was soundly denounced as immoral.

Classical ballet, though not intended to be overtly sexual, has nonetheless delineated supreme sensuality by virtue of the performers' magnificent physiques and sinewy movements. It could well be argued that the celebrated Dance of the Seven Veils from the opera *Salome* was the precursor of the strip-

Dancing students rehearsing in the open air, clad in neo-classic costume, considered shocking at the time. Circa 1918. From the private collection of Phoebe McKay

tease. Though in more restrained times it was performed with the principal decorously attired in vaguely suggestive diaphanous costume, in recent performances it has culminated in total nudity, thus heightening the erotic quality inherent in the plot of the opera.

It is in the realm of modern dance that sexuality has been permitted to emerge openly and realize its greatest potential. As far back as the nineteen twenties, such avant garde performers as Isadora Duncan shocked the public, not only by her on-stage performances, but by her personal life-style as well. Paul Swan, during the same period, titillated audiences by prancing about naked except for an occasional fig leaf. The famed Ziegfeld Girls, though not given to overt sexuality in the theater, were among the leading sex symbols of their day. And how can we fail to mention an even earlier erotic dance sensation, the can-can of Toulouse Lautrec's Paris?

With the evolution of the elaborate Broadway musical, dance sequences became more and more erotic, symbolically if not explicitly. The top choreographers let their imaginations run wild and, with the aid of suggestive costuming, went as far as they could to give Venus and her devotées their full due. *West Side Story*, choreographed by Jerome Robbins, changed American dance because the sexual aggressiveness of the female dancers in relation to their male partners was clearly unmistakable. Although the choreography in the Broadway version of *Cabaret* was not especially erotic, Bob Fosse's stylization of movement in the film presented to the audience a very definite dance adaptation of overt sexual gestures—a touch that has subsequently become his trademark.

In the Broadway musical, in film, and in elaborate stage reviews, the high-kicking chorus girls, exposing their legs in precise military-like rows could not be regarded as anything but sexual. The Rockettes are still drawing large crowds at the Radio City Music Hall, following in the tradition of the Roxy.

Today one only has to look at the New York City Ballet and the works of George Balanchine and Jerome Robbins, where the former confines of classical ballet have been discarded and rechoreographed, to discover a freedom of expression which allows us to explore the full dimensions of our sexuality.

Contemporary dance companies, such as Alvin Ailey, Martha Graham, the Joffrey, and Paul Taylor are taking advantage of this new freedom to add even greater heights of sexuality to their performances both as individuals and as an ensemble.

As popular music has evolved out of the formality of classical music and its pedagogy, dance has emerged from traditional, restrained movements to a freewheeling, natural body rhythm, making it possible to incorporate jazz, and now rock with its sexual gyrations. Dance has become yet another way in which we can fully express, with unbridled joy, the sensuality of our bodies.

Daring nude dancers of the 1920s. From the private collection of Phoebe McKay

The Juggler by Thomas Rowlandson, eighteenth century

Ballerina in classical costume. 1920s. From the private collection of Phoebe McKay

Sex and the Variety Off Beat

Photomontage of a full-size replica of a figure used in A Clockwork Orange
Photo by B. J. Hurwood

Sex has always been a mainstay of the comedians' art. The more noted of the genre were Dwight Fiske, Belle Barth, B. S. Pulley, and Sophie Tucker. Today material such as Redd Foxx's "blue" humor, Shecky Green's "Jewish" humor with touches of sex, Bette Midler's infamous "Sophie Tucker" jokes, and Joan Rivers's "clean" sex stories are keeping the audiences laughing—and blushing.

Legitimate artists such as Barbra Streisand, Judy Garland, Liza Minnelli, Marlene Dietrich, and Phyllis Diller are the brunts of the many performing female impersonators appearing in New York and Las Vegas. A visit to the show "Zou Zou," at the Blue Angel Club in New York, will allow you to witness them all—the greatest lineup of stars ever seen on the stage—impersonators miming to the all-familiar past and present voices. It is possible to be taken back to the stage of the Olympia in Paris with the late Josephine Baker or to the Winter Garden in New York with Ethel Merman.

And then there are the drag queen revues, the most notorious of which are the Cockettes from San Francisco. However, the fairy godmother of all drag queen contests was Jack Doroshow, otherwise known as Fabulous Sabrina, who achieved fame by hosting a benefit drag contest for the Muscular Dystrophy Association at New York's Town Hall, sponsored by—among others—the Kennedy Family. A mention should also be made of the two pioneer drag show clubs, Finocchio's in San Francisco and Club 82 in New York. In Club 82 in New York the waiters are "butch" women dressed in tuxedos, and the performers are "queens" dressed in drag. In London, in the late '50s, Danny La Rue opened a very chic club in which he performed every night, impersonating many of the famous British and European as well as American women.

In New York it is also possible to share some off-color humor with many of the comedians and performers who brave their way through the steam and give their all at the Continental Baths on the West Side of Manhattan, or sit back and be entertained with the delights of "Giselle" or "Swan Lake" at one of the recently celebrated, and we might add, serious drag ballet companies.

Even the world of puppets and puppeteers has not been able to stay away from the three-letter word. Wayland Flowers and "Madame" interject their tête-à-têtes with some funny "rude" dialogue, and there are, of course, the Kumquats, the most daring of all puppets, with their notorious ejaculating Punchinello.

One of the more original sexually oriented acts to be performed on stage was the traditional striptease. The most famous of striptease artists was Gypsy Rose Lee, who elevated the act of taking one's clothes off on stage to an art. Her spiritual descendant was Blaze Starr who, clad only in a G-string, pasties, and the stars in her eyes, made it in the true showbiz tradition from rags to riches. However, the most indomitable stripper of them all, Sally Rand, still does her world-renowned fan dance to the bump and grind orchestrations of bored pit men, despite the fact that she is well over sixty.

Last but not least of the off-beat artists were the theatrical gypsies who tread the boards in Burlesque. Even though it was the proving ground for such diverse talents as Fred Allen, Bob Hope, and Judy Garland, it is most frequently considered to be only the theater of the broad, slightly suggestive routine, peopled by "dirty old men" lecherously eyeballing sweet and innocent young ladies. However, its dictionary definition clearly indicates that the term doesn't only apply to things of a sexual nature, but that there is something of the Burlesque to be found in almost everything: "a literary composition or dramatic representation that ridicules something, usually the serious and dignified but sometimes the trivial and commonplace, by means of grotesque exaggeration of comic imitation."

Lenny

In recent years there have been a best seller, a successful motion picture based on the play, and one documentary film about the life of Lenny Bruce. A self-martyred, tragic figure who has today become a cultural hero, he was probably one of the most misunderstood men of the fifties. Busted on numerous occasions for obscenity and for using words like "cocksucker" in public places, Bruce not only satirized sex but every other aspect of contemporary society as he saw it. Until his death from a heroin overdose in August of 1969, he fought continuously against the authorities, who victimized him for being an iconoclast who was too far ahead of his time.

Sex Magazines on the Arts

The only two entertainment magazines that are sex-oriented and deal with film are:

FILM-INTERNATIONAL,
a new publication published by Magazine Management, Inc.,
575 Madison Avenue, New York, N.Y. 10022. Monthly, $1.25.

CINEMA X,
a British magazine published by Top Sellers Limited,
145/151 Wardour Street, London, W1V 4QA, England
English price is 25p, but it is available from some dealers at
$1.25.

Bibliography

Albertson, Chris. *Bessie: The Life of Bessie Smith.* New York: Stein & Day, 1974, $7.95 (cloth), $2.95 (paper)

Anger, Kenneth. *Hollywood Babylon.* New York: Stonehill, 1974. $12.95

Baker, H. Barton. *The London Stage.* London: 1892.

Bererdt, Joachim. *Jazz Book from New Orleans to Rock and Free Jazz.* New York: Laurence Hill, 1974. $12.95

Bogart, Max. *Jazz Age.* New York: Charles Scribner's Sons, 1969. $2.65

Clarke, Mary, and Clement, Crisp. *Ballet: An Illustrated History.* New York: Universe, 1973. $15.00

Cohn, Nik. *Rock From the Beginning.* New York: Stein & Day, 1969. $2.95

Disher, Maurice. *Music Hall Parade.* London: 1939.

Duncan, Isadora. *My Life.* New York: Award Books, 1968. 95¢

Handy, W. C. *Blues: An Anthology.* New York: Macmillan, 1972. $7.95

Haskell, Molly. *From Reverence to Rape: The Treatment of Women in the Movies.* New York: Holt, Rinehart & Winston, 1974. $10.00; Baltimore: Penguin, 1974. $3.95

Houston, Penelope. *The Contemporary Cinema.* London: Penguin, Pelican, 1968.

Hunnings, Neville M. *Film Censors and the Law.* Atlantic Highlands, N.J.: Fernhill House Ltd., 1967. $14.00

Hurwood, Bernhardt J. *The Golden Age of Erotica.* Los Angeles: Sherbourne Press, 1965.

Jacobs, Lewis. *The Rise of the American Film.* New York: Harcourt Brace & Co.,1970.

Jake, Mike. *Rock: A Social History of the Music from 1945 to 1972.* New York: Quadrangle, 1973. $9.95

Jones, Le Roi. *Blues People: Negro Music in White America.* New York: Morrow, 1963. $7.95 (cloth), $1.95 (paper)

Kirskin, Lincoln. *Dance: A Short History of Classic Theatrical Training.* New York: Horizon Press, Dance Magazine Books, 1969. $6.95

Knight, Arthur, and Alpert, Hollis. *Sex in Cinema.* 3 vols. Chicago: Playboy Press. $1.75 each

Kronhausen, Phyllis, and Kronhausen, Eberhard. *Sex People. Sexual Explorers and Their Bold New World.* Chicago: Playboy Press, 1975, forthcoming.

Lawler, Lillian B. *Dance in Ancient Greece.* Seattle: University of Washington Press, 1967. $2.95

Lovelace, Linda. *Inside Linda Lovelace.* New York: Pinnacle Books, 1974. $1.75

——. *Intimate Diary of Linda Lovelace.* New York: Pinnacle Books, $1.75

Mates, Julian. *The American Musical Stage Before 1800.* New Brunswick, N.J.: Transaction Books, 1962.

McDonagh, Don. *Martha Graham: A Biography.* New York: Praeger, 1973. $10.95

Milgram, Stanley, and Shotland, R. Lance. *Television and Antisocial Behavior.* New York: Academy Press, 1973. $10.95

Parish, James. *Hollywood's Great Love Teams.* New Rochelle, N.Y.: Arlington House, 1974. $14.95

Partridge, Eric. *Shakespeare Bawdy.* New York: Dutton, 1960. $1.35

Perry, Huey. *Blaze Starr.* New York: Praeger Press, 1974. $7.95

Quinn, James. *Film and Television as an Aspect of European Culture.* New York: Humanities, 1968. $6.50

Ramsaye, Terry. *A Million and One Nights.* New York: Simon & Schuster, 1964.

Reems, Harry. *Here Comes Harry Reems.* New York: Pinnacle Books, 1975. $1.95

Rosen, Elizabeth. *Dance in Psychotherapy.* New York: Horizon Press, Dance Magazine Books, 1969. $4.95

Rotsler, William. *Contemporary Erotic Cinema.* New York: Ballantine Books, 1973. $1.50

Roxon, Lillian. *Rock Encyclopedia.* New York: Grosset & Dunlap, 1971. $3.95

Rust, Frances. *Dance in Society: An Analysis of the Relationship Between Social Dance and Society in England from the Middle Ages to the Present Day.* New York: Humanities, 1969. $9.75

Satan's Harvest Home. London: 1763.

Sex in Music. Centurion Press, 1974. $4.95

Skornia, Harry, J. *Television and Society: An Inquest and Agenda for Improvement.* New York: McGraw-Hill, 1965. $7.50 (cloth), $2.45 (paper)

Stearns, Marshall, and Stearns, Jean. *Jazz Dance.* New York: Macmillan, 1968. $9.95

Stevens, Marc. *10½.* New York: Pinnacle, Zebra Books, 1975. $1.75

Terry, Walter. *Dance in America.* New York: Harper & Row, 1971. $10.00

Titterton, W. R. *From Theater to Music Hall.* London: 1912.

Turan, Kenneth, and Zito, Stephen Z. *Sinema.* New York: Praeger Press, 1974. $8.95

Tyler, Parker. *Homosexuality in the Movies.* New York: Harper & Row, 1972. $8.50

——. *Magic, the Myth, and the Movies.* New York: Simon & Schuster, 1970. $5.95. Paper edition $1.95

——. *A Pictorial History of Sex in Films.* New York: Citadel Press, 1974. $12.00

——. *Screening the Sexes.* Garden City: Doubleday, 1973. $4.95

——. *Sex, Psyche and Etcetera in the Film.* New York, 1969. $7.50

Vogel, Amos. *Film as a Subversive Art.* New York: Random House, 1974. $15.00

Walker, Alexander. *Hollywood UK.* New York: Stein & Day, 1974. $12.50

——. *Sex in the Movies.* London: Penguin, Pelican Books, 1968.

Wing, Ruth. *Blue Book of the Screen.* New York: Gordon Press, 1973. $25.00

Worsley, T. C. *Television: The Ephemeral Art.* Chester Springs, Pa.: Dufour, 1973. $12.95

Youngblood, Gene. *Expanded Cinema.* New York: Dutton, 1970. $9.95 (cloth), $4.95 (paper)

YOU MEET THE NICEST PEOPLE AT A PUSSYCAT THEATRE!

Reproduced courtesy of Pussycat Theatres, Los Angeles.

Sex in Literature

*A*s in the visual and performing arts, sex has similarly been a predominant theme in literature from the earliest of times. In its broadest sense, literature may be defined as "the best expression of the best thought reduced to writing" (*Encyclopedia Britannica*, 11th ed.). The use of the word "best," however, implies a value judgment, and since throughout history there have been literally tons of paper bearing words and thoughts hardly deserving of any praise at all, we must broaden our horizons. The trash of one century has blossomed into the classics of another, and since our primary concern here is with the literature of sex, we will strenuously avoid donning the mantle of the critic. Instead, we will take a short excursion through the ages, focusing our attention on content, attitudes, and trends.

In the ancient cultures of the Far East, anthropomorphic deities engaged in sexual adventures that parallel the erotic temple sculptures found throughout India, Indochina, and Indonesia. The literature of China and Japan is filled with the amorous couplings, not only of humans, but of men and women with demons, ghosts, and other supernatural creatures.

In Greek and Roman mythology, the lusty passions of the gods and goddesses mirrored the full range of human sexuality. With the passage of time and the emergence of gifted and sophisticated writers, a vast body of fiction, drama, and poetry emerged, much of which dealt with sex in the most explicit and forthright manner. The lenient mores of the times resulted in the creation of works that rarely dealt with the agonizing self-examination that is so predominant today, but with physical and emotional interactions among the principal characters. Satire and burning passions flowed from the quills of Greek and Roman writers in great profusion. One need only examine the works of Aristophanes, Sophocles, Catullus, and Sappho for ample example. *The Golden Ass* of Apulieus and *The Satyricon* of Petronius are filled with sexual antics of every conceivable nature. The gossipy biographies of Suetonius are similarly embellished with sex of the most explicit quality.

Another element of the sexual content of Roman writings especially was scurrilous, scatological invective, typified by Horace, who once wrote to a nasty old woman of wealth who tried forcing her attentions on him, "What do you ask, O woman worthy of being coupled with black elephants? Why do you send me presents and letters, to me who am not a vigorous young fellow and whose sense of smell is not blunted? . . . For to scent a polyp or the unclean goat that hides under your hairy armpits, I have a finer nose than the hunting dog that smells out the hiding place of the boar. What sweats and what infectious miasmas exhale from all her withered members when she strives to satisfy an insatiable fury which deceives her exhausted lover; when her face is disgusting with moist chalk and cosmetics prepared with crocodile dung; when in her lubricious transports she breaks down her couch and bedcurtains."

After Christianity swept the Roman Empire and sent the Olympian deities into permanent forced retirement, the sexual element was submerged and channeled into works that were ostensibly religious. The sex was still there, but it was manifested in an outwardly religious fashion, just as the human body was in art. Voluminous catalogues of debauchery and sin enabled the literate to get their fair share of sex without feeling guilty about it.

During the dark ages there was little literary output of any significance. But fortunately for future generations, monk-scribes, hidden away in dank monastery cells throughout Europe, meticulously copied old Latin and Greek manuscripts, often as not totally unaware that they were preserving for posterity some of the great erotic works of ancient Greece and Rome.

With the dawn of the Renaissance and the rise of the humanist movement there emerged a great secularization of literature and the arts. Boccaccio wrote *The Decameron*, Chaucer produced his *Canterbury Tales*, and Poggio, if not inventing the ribald joke, at least wrote the first collection of them. As more time passed, other writers, Masuccio, Straparola, Basile, and numerous anonymous wits in other parts of Europe produced such classics of bawdiness as *Les Cent Nouvelles Nouvelles, Il Novellino* and *The Hun-dred Merry Tales* (often referred to as *The Shakespeare Jest Books*). Marguerite of Navarre wrote her famous *Heptameron* in the same mold, and Rabelais turned out tales of such lusty delight that his name eventually became a generic description.

The Restoration in England gave birth to a superb body of highly erotic poetry, drama, and fiction, while at the same time eminent poets and dramatists translated the erotic classics of Greece and Rome. Names like Rochester, Dryden, Herrick, Sedley, and Cowley became almost synonymous with quality erotica. At the same time, unknown printers, recognizing the financial gain to be achieved, began producing pornographic ripoffs, most of which were worthless. Occasionally these turned out to be underground classics, eventually winding up in the private collections of enthusiastic bibliophiles. At this time, many earlier works that had achieved great notoriety in their day, notably the ribald tales of Aretino, began to appear—many clandestinely printed by university students.

During the eighteenth century, as literacy increased, the novel gained in popularity. Many were devoid of sex, but it was in this century that John Cleland wrote the elegant *Fanny Hill* with nary a four-letter word, but still regarded as one of the most sexually explicit classics of Western literature. During the same century Henry Fielding wrote *Tom Jones*, a hearty novel filled with lust, passion, and humor, which bore certain resemblances to Richardson's *Mistress Pamela* of the century before. In France the Marquis de Sade wrote his immortal classics of debauchery and torture, and Restif de la Bretonne wrote his *Pornograph* and *The Memoirs of a Good-natured Libertine.*

Painting by Hendrick Goltzius (1538-1617) inspired by Ovid's Metamorphoses

Plate from an eighteenth century French edition of Fanny Hill. *Reproduced courtesy of Grove Press, Inc.*

While all this was going on, the underground was as active as it is today. Authors calling themselves by such quaint names as Peter Prickly, Philo Cunnus, Pego Borewell proliferated, while magazines began appearing that would cause Hefner and Guccione to turn pale with dismay. Among the ranks of "respectable" novelists a curious phenomenon began to occur. Thanks to their authors' literary skill and determination to be accepted by polite society, novels containing dark themes of sexual deviation were presented with the real meaning disguised under the veil of the supernatural—although this practice was more popular during the nineteenth century.

It was during the reign of Queen Victoria that the great explosion of pornography occurred. There were "confessions" of chambermaids, doctors, adventurers, and whores. Outrageous parodies of classics were ground out, pornographic epics in perfect meter, essays on sodomy, and a mind-boggling body of flagellant literature appeared by the carload. The subject of biographies—real and fictional—is worthy of a book in its own right.

If we were to judge by the rash of fictional and nonfictional biographies that keep blossoming from the presses of the world these days, we might think that the field of sexual biography was either a new phenomenon or one that was expanding by geometric progression. Not so. There are just more individuals capable of reading today, better technology, and improved marketing techniques. As a genre, however, the sexual biography is as old as writing, and the oldest is probably a series of sexually explicit cave drawings scrawled by some enthusiastic neanderthal man at the dawn of prehistory.

Certainly one of the finest ancient examples of a sexual biography, though fictionalized, is *The Satyricon*. Of the many translations, the one attributed to Oscar Wilde is certainly among the best.

The most fabulous, the most detailed, and the most incredible such biography ever published, *My Secret Life* is still available and is a must for any serious collector. The original hardcover two-volume set may be hard to come by now, but the paperback edition is still to be found. It is a true autobiography of an anonymous nineteenth century Englishman, and until now, the actual account of how it came to light has never been told. Happily, Drs. Phyllis and Eberhard Kronhausen, who unearthed this classic, told us the story. The existence of *My Secret Life* was known to a few erudite bibliophiles. None of them, however, knew where the manuscript was or who possessed it. While researching in the library of the British Museum, the Kronhausens read extensive references to the manuscript in an unpublished monograph. The paper was a number of years old, but on the chance that its author might still be alive, they decided to try to contact him. It was their hunch that because the man was writing from such an authoritative viewpoint, he must have actually seen the manuscript.

To their delight, the man was not only alive, he also had the only (then) known copy of the manuscript in his possession, and he invited them to come and read it. He was an old man who lived in retirement in a cottage in the north of England. It was in the dead of winter, and that year happened to be one of the coldest in recent memory. "The roads were so icy," recalled Dr. Eberhard Kronhausen, "we went through five sets of chains. Once when we stopped in the midst of a blizzard in the middle of nowhere, a half-frozen bird flew into the car for warmth. . . ."

In any case, the old gentleman did indeed have the manuscript, and gave the Kronhausens permission to copy it, provided they did not damage it and performed the copying operation in his home. Unfortunately the weather was not the only major problem. The only copier available at the time was a wet copying process involving a negative and positive. The undeveloped film deteriorated rapidly, so it had to be returned to London for developing. To make matters worse, the manuscript consisted of thousands of handwritten pages. Weather and primitive copying equipment notwithstanding, they succeeded in getting the job done, although a number of the later pages came out badly and could not be made into positives.

But now their troubles had only begun. The material was so explicit they were unable to get a typist to do the job; even a young, blasé homosexual who assured them that he had seen and done every-thing and was completely unflappable went into a state of nervous collapse after two weeks and left town never to be seen again, even by his friends. There was only one course of action left. Dr. Phyllis decided to do the job herself, and she did, eventually winding up with 5,000 typewritten pages and perma-nent damage to her eyesight.

The next crushing disappointment came when the publisher to whom they submitted this incredible compendium turned it down. But the crowning blow was the discovery, stimulated by the Kronhausens' detective work of another copy of the manuscript in Germany, its publication there, and its subsequent sale to Grove Press by the German publisher.

Nineteenth century America was not without its fair share of titillating reading matter. In 1810 the first American edition of *Fanny Hill* was published by one Isaiah Thomas of Worcester, Massachusetts, but being somewhat cautious, he faked the original title page with the imprint "G. Fenton, 1747." Despite the fact that Early American wives were inveterate book burners of material they considered indecent, pub-lishers kept replenishing their stocks, and collectors sharpened their ingenuity in the art of concealment. Any women who read erotica certainly never admit-ted it. It was well known that all men were beasts, and women helpless victims of their lust. John Stuart Mill said, "The gratification of man's sexual desire is a degrading slavery to a brute instinct in one of the persons, and, most commonly, in the other, helpless submission to a revolting abuse of power." Still, sex in publishing staggered on. The men read their "inde-cent books," then, upon becoming suitably inflamed, went out drinking, whoring, and carousing, after which they assuaged their guilt by donating substan-tial sums to Bible societies, cover-the-savages-with-de-corus-attire societies, and like high-minded causes.

While all this went on, a few pragmatic authors made a comfortable living. The most successful was George Thompson, who wrote under the pseudonym of Greenhorn. He wrote about "vile seducers," "fallen women," and other wretches. Some of his titles in-cluded *The G'hals of Boston: or Pen and Pencil Sketches of Celebrated Courtezans* [sic] *by One of*

'em; *The Delights of Love: or The Lady Libertine; The Bridal Chamber and its Mysteries; The Seraglios of Upper Tendom; Gay Girls of New York*; and *The Road to Ruin; or Felon's Doom.*

Many a Civil War soldier dreamed his way into liquescence over such anonymously written quickies as *Love on the Loose; Sports with Venus: or The Way to Do it; Amours of a Modest Man*; and *The Secret Services and Duties of Major Lovitt.*

On the upper strata of literature, the novels and poems of Edgar Allen Poe contained deep and under-lying themes of incest and necrophilia. And it is gen-erally recognized today that the gothic horror master-pieces of such authors as Sheridan Le Fanu, Gregory Lewis, and Matthew Gregory Lewis were rich in hid-den eroticism, notably Le Fanu's classic novel of Vampirism, *Carmilla*, which is beautifully camouflaged lesbianism.

A particular underground classic of the nineteenth century cannot go without mention here. It is *1601: Conversation as It Was by the Social Fireside in the Time of the Tudors*, by Mark Twain. Written purely for the amusement of friends, it is a perfect parody of Elizabethan English, and deals with the drawing room conversation of Elizabeth I, Shakespeare, Francis Beaumont, Ben Jonson, Sir Walter Raleigh, and sev-eral fictional characters. The language is explicit, sex-ual, and scatological, and is in the form of a scandal-ized narration by one of the queen's retainers. In ad-dition to dealing with the sexual activities of the prin-cipals, there is the added element of a mighty and mysterious fart that is eventually confessed to by Raleigh. Privately circulated for many years, it was finally published in a limited edition in 1939, and later recorded on an LP record by Richard Dyer-Ben-net in 1962.

Illustration from an un-identified edition of Casanova's Memoirs. *Reproduced courtesy of Grove Press, Inc.*

Of the twentieth century, not a great deal needs to be said here, mainly because there is ample information about what is currently available, and it is common knowledge that contemporary fiction has implicit and explicit sex as one of its dominant themes. To be sure, most of the novels of the twenties and thirties avoided explicit language. D. H. Lawrence's *Lady Chatterley's Lover* was a notable exception and was banned from the U.S. mails until 1959. Nevertheless, other authors carried on, using skillful circumvention. In 1922 the first American edition of Alexander Kuprin's *Yama: The Pit* appeared. Dealing graphically with life in a Russian whorehouse, it read like a fictionalized version of Krafft-Ebing and, naturally, was banned in Boston.

Guy Endore's *Werewolf of Paris* was based on a true case of the 1840s. Sergeant Bertrand of the French army terrified all of Paris by digging up graves and gnawing upon the flesh of corpses. Endore fashioned Bertrand into an oldstyle werewolf and embellished his escapades with an added dash of sex for spice.

A curious, little-known novel by Ben Hecht, written when he was an angry young man in his twenties, contains lurid passages revealing his own frustrations over rejections. He made such statements as "I will hunt up a vulgar woman, one who does not piously regard her vulva as an orifice to be approached with Gregorian chants. I must be careful to avoid those veteran masturbators marching heroically under the

Engraving from 1797 edition of de Sade's L'Historie de Juliette. *Reprinted as* Sixty Erotic Engravings From Juliette. *Copyright © 1969 by Grove Press, Inc. Reprinted by permission of Grove Press, Inc.*

gonfalons of virginity. It is a difficult business, finding a woman. A modest one will offend my intellect. A shameless one will harass my virility. A stupid one will be unable to appreciate my largess. An intelligent one will penetrate my impotency."

In the thirties, publishers and authors seemed somewhat more willing to take chances. Occasionally four-letter words began appearing in the works of established writers. *Butterfield 8* by John O'Hara was published in 1935, and predated Nabokov's *Lolita* in its description of a nymphet. One particularly steamy sequence goes into an early experience of the heroine, Gloria, when she is only twelve. Gustave Mirabeau's *Torture Garden*, published originally in France in 1931, dealt with extreme sadomasochism in the grand tradition of Sade, and Jules Romain's *The Body's Rapture* left nothing to the imagination insofar as lovemaking was concerned.

Thorne Smith came along like a breath of spring air with his lighthearted fantasies, beginning in 1926 with *Topper* and continuing until his death in 1934 with a series of zany farcical novels that approached sex with a wink and a belly laugh. Erskine Caldwell, especially in *Tobacco Road*, took the earthy approach, and though mild by today's standards, much of John Steinbeck's work was regarded by many with shock and dismay.

Tiffany Thayer wrote his erotic version of *The Three Musketeers*, and Kathleen Winsor's *Forever Amber*, about a Restoration sex kitten, became an instant best seller in 1944. The public was still not

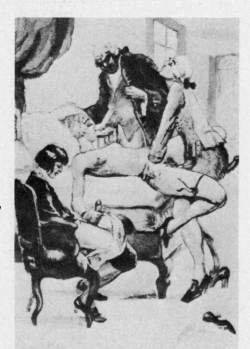

Rare illustration by "le Loup" for a limited edition of L'Anti Justine. *Reproduced courtesy of Grove Press, Inc.*

ready for what is *de rigeur* today. Edmund Wilson's *Memoirs of Hecate County*, published in 1959, was banned because of explicit sex in one story.

Kathleen Winsor gave the dreary fifties a sizzling start with *Star Money*, and it was during this period that paperback publishers began luring readers with sexy cover art. The real thing, however, still reposed between hardcovers. *The Man with the Golden Arm* by Nelson Algren pulled no punches, and Jack Kerouac's *On the Road* was a sexual romp from beginning to end.

James Michener gave his readers sex in the sunshine in *Hawaii*, and in the *Ugly American* Lederer and Burdick made American sexual relations abroad look as bad as the diplomatic variety. *Peyton Place* by Grace Metalious sent shock waves through the publishing world, and from then on frankness began an even greater upsweep.

Space simply does not permit a complete cataloguing of the profusion of novels with strong sexual themes that began flooding the literary market. One need only mention such names as Vladimir Nabokov, William Burroughs, Terry Southern, Irving Wallace, Philip Roth, Gore Vidal, Harold Robbins, and Jacqueline Susann. Henry Miller emerged from the underground and finally achieved the literary acceptance he long deserved. Mickey Spillane, who had been grinding out violence-cum-sex for years, now began adding more sex. Ian Fleming created an entire genre with his James Bond novels—and now, as the saying goes, the sky's the limit.

If we may be permitted a brief departure from our chronological order here, there are a few loose ends which must be tied up. We have said very little about poetry, which since earliest antiquity has been one of the richest repositories of erotic expression. Unfortunately, modern poets have been too unfairly ignored by the reading public, with very few exceptions, notably Walter Benton, whose *This is My Beloved* enjoyed immense success in the early 1940s largely because it was highly erotic and totally devoid of obfuscation. It was meant for a wide audience, and it touched the most erogenous zone of its readers—the mind.

We must also make mention of a phenomenon of the 50s that was nearly two decades ahead of its time—The Traveller's Companion series, published by Maurice Girodias in Paris under the imprints of Olympia Press and Obelisk Press. These modest-looking paperback novels with plain green covers were all in English but were only able to find their way into the United States and England by smuggling. They were hard core, frequently pseudonymously written, and in many cases the works of well-known, talented writers who had fallen on hard times. Until he was forced to leave Paris, Girodias frankly referred to himself as a "small outlaw publisher dwelling in obscure exile," a slight reverse exaggeration, perhaps, but not without a grain of truth. Nevertheless, during that period, Girodias published *Lolita, The Ginger Man, The Story of O, Our Lady of the Flowers, Naked Lunch*, and *Candy*, long before they gained international respectability in hard covers. It is ironic to note that the general acceptance of explicit sex in fiction was one of the factors leading to Girodias's demise as a publisher after he moved to America, but as the French so aptly put it, *c'est la vie*.

Cover reproduced by permission of William Morrow & Company.

The Sexy Slicks

Although Hugh Hefner's *Playboy* started a revolution in magazine publishing, he did not get there first. In 1773 fashionable Englishmen were treated to their first erotic periodical. It was *The Covent Garden Magazine: or Amorous Repository, Calculated solely for the Entertainment of the Polite World*. The Covent Garden section of London at the time was a favored red-light district.

Ten years later a competitor appeared, *The Rambler's Magazine: or The Annals of Gallantry, Glee, Pleasure, and the Bon Ton: Calculated for the Entertainment of the Polite World and to furnish the Man of Pleasure with a most delicious banquet of Amorous, Bacchanalian, Whimsical, Humourous, Theatrical and Polite Entertainment*. *The Rambler's Magazine* folded after only ten years, due to complaints of its being too timid and "too moral."

In March 1791, *The Bon Ton Magazine* made its debut. Specializing in scandal, sex, and erotic fiction, it also included such exotica as bizarre marriage rites around the world, female pugilism, and the inside stories of offbeat private clubs. To be sure, there were no nude color centerfolds, but *The Bon Ton* contained numerous engravings lifted from other sources.

Following in the footsteps of its predecessors, *The Ranger's Magazine* appeared in 1795. It only lasted for six months in 1796 went out of business. For some years afterward, a number of specialized publications sprang up like wild fungi; most of them were nothing more than directories of brothels and whores. Between the years of 1822 and 1827 four more *Ramblers* appeared, each one a separate entity put out under different management. All of them died.

In 1842 *The Exquisite* was born, concentrating its editorial policy on forgettable erotic fiction and accounts of scandalous, sordid Crim. Con. trials. *The Exquisite* lasted for two years. Thirty-five years later *The Pearl* burst forth, modestly proclaiming itself to be "without exception the grandest and best erotic work ever published in the English Language." Lasting into the 80s, *The Pearl* was the most successful of them all, and is available today in paperback, thanks to its twentieth century resurrection by Grove Press.

For many years afterwards there was nothing of significance in the periodical field. However, in the first decade of the twentieth century, an American magazine called *Playboy* was published. Not only did it expound a similar philosophy to its present day namesake, it bore on the cover of its first issue the drawing of a man's face bearing an uncanny resemblance to Hugh Hefner. It soon faded into obscurity.

It was with the unveiling of *Esquire* that the quality men's magazine came of age, and the rest is history. Women finally got into the act in the late 60s, when *Cosmopolitan* fell under Helen Gurley Brown's editorship. After that it was only a matter of time before *Playgirl, Viva, Foxylady, etc.* were bound to appear—male nude centerfolds and all.

All of the magazines listed here, with the exception of some British publications, can be obtained from periodical dealers in the major cities, excluding those states carrying statutes restricting freedom of the press. All of the majors are available by subscription, as are most of the runner-ups. Many of the smaller magazines try to avoid the subscription route because of the expense and complexities involved.

The Majors

Playboy — The magazine with which Hefner got there "firstest with the mostest." Major articles, fiction, and art by prominent names. 919 N. Michigan Avenue, Chicago, Illinois 60611.

Penthouse — *Playboy's* chief competition, same caliber, roster of names, but far less restrained and with a distinctly more international flavor. 909 Third Avenue, New York, N.Y. 10022.

Oui — Published by *Playboy*, originally an offshoot of the French LUI. Aimed at a younger readership, and more sexually free than its big bunnymother. 919 N. Michigan Avenue, Chicago, Illinois 60611.

Playgirl — A strong circulation contender, *Playgirl* shows the strength of the women's market in sexy slicks. 1801 Century Park East, Century City, Suite 2300, Los Angeles, California 90067

Viva — Published by *Penthouse's* Bob Guccione, and designed to be the female counterpart of *Playboy et al.* 909 Third Avenue, New York, N.Y. 10022.

Penthouse Forum — Digest-sized periodical dealing with the problems and experiences of sexuality. An outgrowth of PENTHOUSE's original forum of letters to the editors. All significant books on sex are reviewed, and massive amounts of advice are dispensed. 909 Third Avenue, New York, N.Y. 10022.

The Runner-Ups

All are essentially in either the *Playboy, Penthouse,* or *Oui* mold. Their chief lack is a budget large enough to attract name writers, although occasionally they manage. All are striving valiantly.

Gallery — 116 E. 27th Street, New York, N.Y. 10016

Genesis — 120 E. 56th Street, New York, N.Y. 10022

Swank — 18 E. 41st Street, New York, N.Y. 10017

The Others

Adam — 8060 Melrose Avenue, Los Angeles, Calif. 90046

After Dark — 10 Columbus Circle, New York, N.Y. 10019—entertainment and gay oriented.

Caper — Dugent Publishing Co. 316 Aragon Avenue, Coral Gables, Florida 33134.

Cavalcade — Challenge Publishing Co., Inc., 7950 Deering Avenue, Canoga Park, California 91304.

Cavalier — Dugent Publishing Co., 316 Aragon Avenue, Coral Gables, Florida 33134.

Climax	Challenge Publishing Co., Inc., 7950 Deering Avenue, Canoga Park, California 91304.
Daring	Candar Publishing Co., 235 Park Avenue South, New York, N.Y. 10003.
Debonair	13510 Ventura Blvd., Sherman Oaks, California 91423.
Dude	Dugent Publishing Co., 316 Aragon Avenue, Coral Gables, Florida 33134.
Fling	Relim Publishing Co., 161 E. Erie Street, Chicago, Illinois 60611.
Foxylady	Girlplay Enterprises, 676 N. La Salle Street, Chicago, Illinois 60610—another one for the ladies.
Gent	Dugent Publishing Co., 316 Aragon Avenue, Coral Gables, Florida 33134.
G.Q.	(Gentlemen's Quarterly)—488 Madison Avenue, New York, N.Y. 10022.
He and She	Countrywide Publications, Inc., 257 Park Avenue South, New York, N.Y. 10010.
Hustler	36 W. Gay Street, Columbus, Ohio 43215
Jaquar	Countrywide Publications, Inc., 257 Park Avenue South, New York, N.Y. 10010.
Night and day	Challenge Publishing Co., Inc. 7950 Deering Avenue, Canoga Park, California 91304.
Nugget	Dugent Publishing Co., 316 Aragon Avenue, Coral Gables, Florida 33134.
Nymphet	Sunway Periodicals, Inc., 21322 Lassen Street, Chatsworth, California 91311.
Wildcat	Candar Publications, 235 Park Avenue South, New York, N.Y. 10003.

Imports to Watch for

Club	(U.S. address: Fiona Press Inc., 300 E. 56th Street, Suite 27K, New York, N.Y. 10022.)

A high-quality, slightly larger sized newcomer to the U.S.A., published in England as *For Men Only*, this extremely erotic magazine is a sellout on U.S. newsstands and promises to give the biggies serious competition.

Game	(In U.S. c/o Challenge Publishing Co., Inc., 7950 Deering Avenue, Canoga Park, California 91304.) Another oversized British monthly, put out by the publishers of *Cinema X*. Knockout photo spreads, features, humor, and fiction. Well worth looking for.

The Outsiders

There are a number of magazines, not printed on slick paper, but ranging from hard core to hairy chested. Here are typical examples.

Man's World	Magazine Management, Inc., 575 Madison Avenue, New York, N.Y. 10022. Distributed everywhere in the country except New York, this is a *Playboy* doppelganger on the outside, but strictly sex and sensation between the covers.
Smut	Milky Way Productions, 116 W. 14th Street, New York, N.Y. 10011. Published by those wonderful folks who brought you *Screw*. Need we say more?
Finger	Fuck On Publishing, Inc., 8444 Wilshire Blvd., Beverly Hills, California 90211. A West Coast publication, strictly hard core, and difficult to obtain. Frequently finds itself in trouble with the fuzz.

There are dozens of others, from glossy hard cores to poorly produced ripoffs of the majors. They come and go like buses, and hardly deserve further mention.

Courtesy of Penthouse

-254-

Sexology magazine, though not a slick, was the first serious periodical dealing with the subject of sex and aimed at the lay reader. Founded by Hugo Gernsbach in 1933, the pioneering first edition carried such articles as "The New Approach to Sex Discussion," "Alcohol and Sex," "The Erogenous Zones of the Body," and "Frigidity and Impotence."

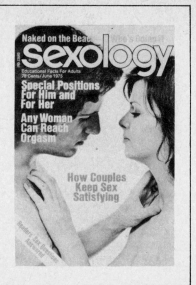

A charming young lady of Gaul,

Wore a newspaper gown to a ball.

But then it caught fire,

And burned her entire,

Front page, sports section, and all.

The Fifth Estate of Flesh

There is no resemblance between *The Police Gazette* and *Screw*, yet in its day the old P.G. was considered really hot stuff. Despite decades of sensationalist sex and scandal sheets, or the antiestablishment tabloids of the 60s such as *The East Village Other*, *Screw* was totally original, unique, and innovative. It belched forth into the world of journalism with the impact of a diarrhetic elephant in the Basilica of St. Peter's. Spawning dozens of imitators in the U.S. and abroad, *Screw* catapulted Al Goldstein and Jim Buckley into international celebrities (or villains in the eyes of some), and for better or worse established a new school of journalism.

Screw is definitely the Hertz of sexpapers. The sizes and formats of all sexpapers are virtually identical. The prices range from 75¢ and up. We are leaving out the papers specializing in swinging and fetishes or anything else covered in earlier sections.

The Berkeley Barb (2042 University Avenue, Berkeley, California 94704) In addition to sex, there is a heavy emphasis here on politics.

California Climax

The Free Thinker (Flame Publications, P.O. Box 1178, Carbondale, Illinois 62901) A newcomer, published in Carbondale, Illinois, a brave act in middle America.

The Los Angeles Free Press (5850 Hollywood Blvd., Los Angeles, California 90028) Like *The Barb*, there is a strong political content here.

The Hollywood Press (7542 Santa Monica Blvd., Los Angeles, California 90046) After sex, the biggest emphasis here is on entertainment.

The Los Angeles Star 8444 Wilshire Blvd., Los Angeles, California 90048.

Dynamite (Retire to Bedlam Ltd., 340 Jones St., Box 4229, San Francisco, California 94102) A San Francisco rag, the content indicates more caution on the part of the publisher than most other publications.

The National Ball (Jaundice Press, 17620 Sherman Way, Van Nuys, California 91406) Formerly *The San Francisco Ball*, this is a hearty survivor and one of the string of specialized sexpapers published by Jaundice Press in Van Nuys.

Pleazure (Valerie Publications, 204 W. 20th St., New York, N.Y. 10011) A New-York-based, early *Screw* imitator that has miraculously withstood the test of time, largely because of the efforts of chief cook and bottle washer, arch-smuthound Jerry Schneiderman.

Aside from the obvious hard core photos, cartoons, and steamy graffiti school of journalistic style, the chief appeal of all sexpapers rests in the personal ads, product ads, massage parlor and prostitution ads, as well as sex product information, reviews of hard core books, and all the latest X-rated films—not to mention all the latest and hottest inside stuff on the personal lives of the sexual subculture superstars.

Suggested Reading

The following is a suggested reading list that includes classics of erotica as well as obscure and not-so-obscure curiosa and arcana that would be of interest to collectors and students of the genre. We have deliberately omitted most contemporary fiction, because our principal concern here is to call attention to works less likely to be found on the best seller lists and as topics of discussion on television talk shows. In the case of many works listed, there have been so many different editions, in various languages, that they can only be obtained through rare book dealers and in special collections of the world's great libraries and museums, such as: The New York Public Library, The Library of Congress, The British Museum, The Bibliothèque Nationale in Paris, the Huntington Library in San Marino, California, and the San Francisco Public Library, whose Schmulowitz Collection of Wit and Humor contains some of the world's finest examples of obscure bawdy literature. Although virtually impenetrable by the common man, the Vatican is reputed to have one of the most extensive collections of erotic literature in the world.

Akbar del Piombo. *The Double Bellied Companion.* New York: Travellers Companion Series, 1968.

Angouleme, Marguerite de. *The Heptamerom.*

Amours of an American Adventuree in the New World and the Old. 2 vols. Enriched with fine engravings. New York: 1865.

Aretino, Pietro. *La Coregina.* Milan: 1804.

———.*Tutte le Opere di Pietro Aretino.* Milan: 1960.

———.*Works of Pietro Aretino.* Translated by Samuel Putnam. Chicago: 1926.

Autobiography of a Flea, The. n.p., n.d.

Balzac, Honore de. *Droll Stories.* Paris. (Many editions available.)

Boccaccio, Giovanni. *Amorous Fiametta.* (Many editions available.)

———.*Decameron, The.* London: 1891. (Many editions available.)

———.*Il Filocolo.* (Many editions available.)

———.*Il Filostrato.* (Many editions available.)

Book of a Thousand Nights and a Night, The. Translated by Sir Richard Burton. Paris: 1934. (Many editions available.)

Brantome, Pierre de Boudeille. *Lives of Fair and Gallant Ladies.* n.p., 1500?

Bretonne, Restif de la. *Pleasures and Follies of a Good-Natured Libertine, or the Anti Justine.* Translated. Paris: Olympia Press, n.d.

Burns, Robert. *Merry Muses of Caledonia, The.* (Many editions available.)

Casanova, Giovanni. *Memoirs.* France: 1826-38. (Many editions available.)

Cento Novelle Antiche. n.p., 1400?

Chaucer, Geoffrey. *Canterbury Tales.* New York: 1946. (Many editions available.)

Cleland, John. *Fanny Hill: or Memoirs of a Lady of Pleasure.* London: 1906. (Many editions available.)

Confessions of a Lady's Maid, The: or Boudoir Intrigue; disclosing many startling scenes and voluptuous incidents as witnessed by her in the various families of distinction with whom she lived: forming a wonderful picture of fashionable frailty, passion, and seduction. Beautifully illustrated with colored plates by an eminent French artist. London: John Dugdale, 1860.

Confessions of a Young Lady, to which is added 10 Years Life of a Courtezan, The. Illustrated with fine engravings. London: William Dugdale, Printed for the Society of Vice, 1860.

Curious and Diverting History and Adventures of a Bedstead, The; containing many singular and interesting amorous tales and narratives, particularly Lord K's rapes and seduction. Intrigues in a boarding school. London licenciousness displayed; interspersed with others, forming one of the most moving histories ever displayed to the public, of amours in high and low life. London: William Dugdale, 1840.

Defoe, Daniel. *The Fortunes and Misfortunes of the Famous Moll Flanders.* New York: 1954. (Many editions available.)

De Gourmont, Remy. *The Natural Philosophy of Love.* New York: 1922.

De Laclos, Choderlos. *Les Liaisons Dangereuses.* (Many editions available.)

Don Leon. London: William Dugdale, 1866.
    14,055 line poem in defense of sodomy, fallaciously attributed to Lord Byron.

Douglas, Norman. *Some Limericks.* n.p., n.d.

Dunbar, William. *The Twa Maryit Wemen and the Wedo.* n.p., n.d.

Egan, Beresford, and Alcock, C. Bower. *Baudelaire: Flowers of Evil*. New York: The Sylvan Press, 1947.

Festival of the Passions, The; or Voluptuous Miscellania by an Amateur. Constantinople: Abdul Mustapha, 1828.

Fielding, Henry. *The History of Tom Jones*. London: 1773. (Many editions available.)

Fiorentino, Giovanni. *50 Novelle*. n.p., n.d.

Firenzuola, Agnolo. *Ragionamenti d'Amore*. n.p., n.d.

Flaubert, Gustave. *Madame Bovary*. (Many editions available.)

Gesta Romanorum. n.p., n.d.
    Written A.D. 1000-1199.

Goncourt, Edmond, and Goncourt, Jules de. *Renee Mauperin, Gerinie Lucerteux, and Manette Salomon*. n.p., n.d.

Gramont, Comte Philibert de. *Memoirs of the Comte de Gramont*. n.p., 1713. Translated by Hamilton Anthony. London: 1911.

Hartlieb, J. *De Fide Meretricum in Suos Amatores*. Worms: 1550?

Head, Richard. *Adventures of an English Rogue*. London: 1674.

Hecht, Ben. *Fantazius Mallare: A Mysterious Oath*. Chicago: Covici-McGee, 1922.

Hoffenberg, Mason. *Sin for Breakfast*. New York: Travellers Companion Series, 1968.

Hollander, John. *Town and Country Matters: Erotica and Satirica*. Boston: David R. Godine, 1975. $6.95 (cloth), $3.95 (paper).

Hurwood, Bernhardt J., trans. *The Facetiae of Giovanni Francesco Poggio Bracciolini*. New York: Award Books, 1968. 95¢.

Joyce, James. *Ulysses*. New York: 1942. (Many editions available.)

Kainen, Ray. *A Sea of Thighs*. New York: Travellers Companion Series, 1968.

Kate Hancock: A Young Girl's Introduction to Fast Life. London: 1882.

Kin-Kou-Ki-Kuan.
    Chinese, written in the fifteenth century.

Krich, A. M., ed. *The Second Ribald Reader*. New York: Dell, 1956. 50¢.

Lascivious Gems, The; set to suit every fancy by several hands. London: William Dugdale, 1866.

Lawrence, D. H. *Lady Chatterley's Lover*. New York: Viking Press, 1959.

Love's Telltale: or the Decameron of Pleasure. London: 1865.

Lustful Turk, The. London: William Dugdale, 1860-64.

Manly, Sir Charles. *Memoirs of a Man of Pleasure: or The Amores, Intrigues, and Adventurers of Sir Charles Manly. Interspersed with curious narrative, and embellished with elegant engravings*. London: William Dugdale, 1827.

Man of Pleasure At Paris, The: or An Account of pleasures that Capital; in a series of letters, from Sr. Charles P. . . . to Lady Emily C. . . . London: John Benjamin Brooks, 1808.

Masuccio, Salternitano [Tomaso Guardati]. *Novelino*. n.p., 1476.

Memoirs of Rose Bellefille: or A Delicious Banquet of Amorous Delights! Dedicated to the Goddess of Voluptuous and her Soul Enamored Votaries. London: Paphian Press, 1828.

Miller, Henry. *Plexus*. New York: Grove, 1965. $2.95.

———. *Sexus*. New York: Grove, 1965. $2.95.

———. *Tropic of Cancer*. New York: Grove, 1961. $1.95.

Modern Rake, The: or the Life and Adventures of Sir Edward Walford, containing a curious and voluptuous history of luscious intrigues, with numerous women of fashion, his laughable faux pas, feats of gallantry, debauchery, dissipation, and concubinism! His numerous rapes, seduction and amatory scrapes. Memoirs of the beautiful courtezans with whom he lived; with some ticklerlish songs, anecdotes, poetry, etc. Enriched with many curious plates. London: J. Sudbury, 1824.

Montaigne, Michel. *Essays*. Translated. (Many editions available.)

Motley, John. *Joe Miller's Jests*. London: 1739.

My Secret Life. 2 vols. New York: Grove Press, 1966. $30.00 (boxed edition); $9.50 (large format paperback); $2.45 (abridged edition).

Mysteries of Whoredom, The, revealed in correspondence between Miss Loveman and Miss Longford, Two blooming cyprians in full trade, interspersed with interesting ancedotes, divers, interesting stories, sundry droll adventures, a variety of comic incidents, and an extensive fund of voluptuous recreation and incitement. Embellished with beautiful cuts. London: George Cannon, Printed for the Society of Vice, 1828.

New Attalantis for the Year 1762: being a select portion of secret history; containing many facts strange! but true! London: 1755.

Nicarchus *et al. The Girdle of Aphrodite.* n.p., n.d.

Nunnery Tales: or Cruising Under False Colors; A Tale of Love and Lust. London: William Dugdale, 1866.

Pallavicino, Ferrante. *The Whore's Rhetorick.* 1683. Reprint. New York: Ivan Obolensky, 1961.

Peachum, Thomas. *The Watcher and the Watched.* New York: Travellers Companion Series, 1968.

Pepys, Samuel. *Diary.* London: 1893-99.

Petronius, Arbiter. *The Satyricon.* (Many editions available.)

Petronius, Arbiter. *Trimalchio's Feast.* New York: 1913. (Many editions available.)

Pleasures of Love, The. Containing a variety of entertaining particulars and curiosities, in the cabinet of Venus. London: 1755.

Don Juan Manuel. *Count Lucanor: The Fifty Pleasant Stories of Patronio.* n.p., n.d.

P'u Sung Ling. *Strange Stories from a Chinese Studio.* C. 1600. Translated by Herbert A. Giles. Reprint. New York: Dover, n.d.

Quimme, Peter. *The Pleasure Quest of the R. S. P.* New York: Dell, 1974. $1.50.

Rabelais, Francois, *Works.* Dublin: 1738. (Many editions available.)

Randiana: or Excitable Tales; the experiences of an Erotic Philosopher. New York: 1884.

Reage, Pauline. *The Story of O.* Olympia Press: Paris. (Many editions available.)

Sacher Masoch, Leopold von. *Venus in Furs.* (Many editions available.)

Sade, Marquis de. *Juliette.* New York: Black Cat, 1968. $17.50 (cloth), $3.95 (paper).

——. *The 120 Days of Sodom and Other Writings.* New York: Black Cat, 1966. $2.45.

——. *Justine, Philosophy in the Bedroom, Eugenie de Franval, and Other Writings.* New York: Black Cat, 1965. $3.95.

Shakespeare, William. (Many editions available.)

Sins of the City of the Plains, The: or the Recollections of a Mary-Ann. With short essays on sodomy and tribadism. London: William Dugdale, 1867.

Smith, T. R., ed. *Poetica Erotica.* New York: Boni and Liveright, 1921.

Story of a Dildo, The, a Tale in Five Tableaux. Illustrated by five photograph plates. London: 1880.

Straparola, Giovanni Francesco. *The Pleasureful Nights.* n.p., 1550-3.

Victim of Lust!, The, or Scenes in the Life of Rosa Fielding. Depicting the Crimes and Follies of High Life and the Dissipation and Debauchery of the Day. With fine colored engraving. London: William Dugdale, 1867.

Voisenon, Abbe de. *Erotic Fairy Tales.* New York: Panurge Press, n.d.

Wang, Shih-chang. *Chin P'ing Mei.* n.p., C. 1500.

Yu, Li. *Jou Pu Tuan: A 17th Century Erotic Moral Novel.* New York: Black Cat, 1967. $1.95.

Zola, Emile. *Nana.* 1880. (Many editions available.)

The Thirteenth Labor of Hercules *by Bivan Denon, 1792.*

Bibliography

Armitage, Gilbert. *Banned in England.* London: 1932.

Atkins, John. *Sex in Literature: The Erotic Impulse from the Classic to the Present Day.* New York: Black Cat, 1972. $2.45

Brusendorff, Ove, and Henningsen, Poul. *A History of Eroticism.* 3 vols. New York: Lyle Stuart, 1963.

Calverton, Victor Francis. *Sex Expression in Literature.* New York: 1926.

Carrington, Charles, ed. *Weird Women (Les Diaboliques).* London and Paris: 1900.

Chambers, E. K., and Sidgwick, Frank eds. *Early English Lyrics, Amorous, Divine, Moral & Trivial.* London: 1907.

Chandos, John. *To Deprave and Corrupt.* London: Souvenir Press, 1962

Cleaton, Irene, and Cleaton, Allen. *Books and Battles: American Literature 1920-1930.* Boston: 1937.

Collingwood, R. B. *The Principles of Art.* New York: 1938.

Craig, Alec. *The Banned Books of England and Other Countries.* London: George Allen and Unwin, 1962.

Dearden, Seton. *The Arabian Knight: A Study of Sir Richard Burton.* London: 1953.

Downs, Robert B., ed. *The First Freedom: Liberty and Justice in the World of Books and Reading.* Chicago: 1960.

Ernst, Morris L., and Lindey, Alexander. *The Censor Marches On.* New York: 1940.

Farrar, James Anson. *Books Condemned to be Burnt.* London: 1892.

Fiedler, Leslie A. *Love and Death in the American Novel.* New York: 1950.

Foberg, F. C., trans. *Manual of Classical Erotology.* (De Figuris Veneris). 2 vols. Manchester: 1884.

Fryer, Peter. *Mrs. Grundy Studies in English Prudery.* New York: London House & Maxwell. 1963. $6.75

Ginzburg, Ralph. *An Unhurried View of Erotica.* New York: The Helmsman Press, 1958.

Greenwald, Harold, and Krich, Aron. *The Prostitute in Literature.* New York: Ballantine Books, 1960.

Haney, Robert W. *Comstockery in America.* Boston: 1960.

Harris, Frank. *My Life and Loves.* New York: Black Cat, 1963. $2.95

Hunt, Morton M. *The Natural History of Love.* New York: Alfred A. Knopf. 1959.

Hurwood, Bernhardt J. *The Golden Age of Erotica.* Los Angeles: Sherbourne Press.

Jackson, Holbrook. *The Fear of Books.* London: Soncino Press, 1932.

Kahane, Jack. *Memoirs of a Booklegger.* London: Michael Joseph, 1939.

Kilpatrick, James Jackson. *The Smut Peddlers.* New York: 1960.

Kronhausen, Phyllis, and Kronhausen, Eberhard. *Pornography and the Law.* New York: Ballantine Books, 1959.

Lawrence, D. H. *Pornography and Obscenity.* London: 1929.

Legman, G. *The Horn Book.* New York: University Books Inc., 1964. $12.50

———. *Love and Death: A Study in Censorship.* New York: 1949.

———. *Rationale of the Dirty Joke.* New York: Black Cat, 1968. $2.95

Lely, Gilbert. *The Marquis de Sade.* Translated by Alec Brown. New York: Black Cat, 1962. $1.95

Loth, David. *The Erotic in Literature.* New York: Macfadden Books, 1962. 60¢

Lucas, F. L. *Literature and Psychiatry.* Ann Arbor: University of Michigan Press, 1957.

Marchand, Henry L. *The Erotic History of France.* New York: 1933.

May, Geoffrey. *Social Control of Sex Expression.* New York: 1931.

Mead, Margaret. *Sex and Censorship in Contemporary Society: New World Writing.* New York: 1953.

Mordell, Albert. *The Erotic Motive in Literature.* New York: Boni and Liveright, 1919.

Orioli, Giuseppe. *Adventures of a Bookseller.* New York, 1938.

Perles, Alfred. *My Friend, Henry Miller.* New York: 1956.

Robinson, Victor, ed. *Encyclopedia Sexualis.* New York: 1936.

Rolph, C. H., ed. *Does Pornography Matter?* London: Routledge, 1961.

Schroeder, Theodore. *Freedom of the Press and "Obscene" Literature.* New York: 1906.

Staus, Ralph. *The Unspeakable Curll, Bookseller.* London: 1927.

Tabori, Paul. *The Humor and Technology of Sex.* New York: Julian Press, 1969. $12.50

Taylor, G. Rattray. *Sex in History.* New York: Ballantine Books, 1954. 75¢

Wedeck, Harry E. *Dictionary of Erotic Literature.* New York: Philsophical Library, Inc.,1962. $10.00

Bibliographies

Ashbee, Henry Spencer [Faxi, Pisanus]. *Index Librorum Prohibitorum, Centuria Librorum Abscoditorum and Catena Liborum Tacendorum.* 1885. Reprint. London: 1960.
Editions of 1877, 1879, and 1885 were privately printed and are in British Museum "Private Case."

Besterman, Theodore. *A World Bibliography of Bibliographies.* 3 vols. 3rd ed. Geneva: 1955-56.

Catalogue des ouvrages condamnés comme contraire à la morale publique et aux bonnes moeurs de ler Janvier 1814 a 31 Decembre 1872. Paris: 1873.

Clowes, William Laird, ed. *Bibliotheca Arcana seu Catalogus Librorum Penetralium, being brief notices of books that have been secretly printed, prohibited by law, seized, anathematized, burnt or bowdlerized by Spectacular Morum.* London: 1885.
Spectacular Morum is psendonym of Reverend John M. McClellan, who appears to have written preface.

Drujon, Fernand. *Catalogue des ouvrages, écrits, et dessins, de toute nature poursuivis, suprimés ou condamnés depuis le 21 Octobre 1814 jusqu'au 31 juillet 1877.* Paris: 1879.

Gay, Jules [M. le Cte D'I]. *Bibliographies des ouvrages relatif a l'amour etc.* 4 vols. 4th ed. Paris: 1894-1900.

Haight, Anne Lyon. *Banned Books.* 3rd ed. New York: 1958.

Index Librorum Prohibitorum. Rome: Typis Polyglottis Vaticanis, 1948.

Rose, Alfred [Reade, Rolf], ed. *Registrum Librorum Eroticorum Vel (sub hac specie) Dubiorum: Opus Bibliographicum Et Praepicue Bibliothecaris Destinatum.* 2 vols. London: 1936.

Deserving of special mention is the late and controversial *Eros* magazine published by Ralph Ginzburg. Printed on high quality paper and in hard covers, it was attacked by some as pornographic, while hailed by others as *"The American Heritage* of the Bedroom." Though comparatively tame by the standards of the seventies, it was a milestone, and existing copies today are a prized staple of rare book dealers, selling for as much as $150.00 each.

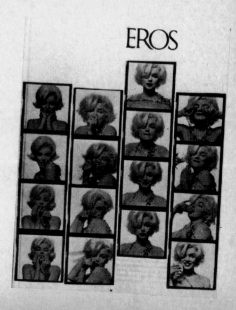

Sex and the Law

Law came into being when the first primitive men and women joined together in tribal groups. As society became more complex so did the bodies of law. Sex being one of the most universally basic aspects of human life, it quite naturally became a prime focal point for lawmakers. As societies became more complex, so did custom and taboo. What is often so hard to understand, both in the present and upon examination of the past, is why those empowered to make laws have throughout history consistently attempted to legislate those aspects of sexual behavior that relate to activities between consenting adults. No state has the moral right to interfere with the privacy of the bedroom as long as those occupying it are mutually agreeable to what transpires between them—which brings us to the first major point of this chapter. Like it or not, the human species is collectively and incurably hypocritical when it comes to sex. It always has been so and it always will be so.

Understandably, it is necessary for laws to protect innocent victims of sexual assault. No one can argue

Caught in the Act. *Painting by the nineteenth century artist, Jules Garnier. From* Pictorial History of Morals, *edited by Harry E. Wedeck. Copyright © 1963 by Philosophical Library, Inc. Reprinted with permission of the publisher.*

the validity of laws against forcible rape or any other form of sexual molestation that ultimately results in injury or death. With those exceptions, no law relating to sex should be considered moral, valid, or enforceable. Yet throughout history laws relating to sexual activities that victimize no one have been enacted, enforced, and have as a result produced social upheaval, unspeakable human suffering, and mental illness of epidemic proportions.

Incredible as it may seem, there is not a single sexual act that has not been illegal at one time or another. Examine your history books, anthropological, theological, and legal texts and you will find this statement to be absolutely valid. Despite the acceptability of homosexuality on one level in ancient Greece, there were laws against it on another [see G. Rattray Taylor's *Sex in History*]. "Thou shalt not commit adultery," says the seventh commandment, and for violating this many an ancient Jew died in disgrace. A basic tenet of canon law is that the thought can be as sinful as the deed; thus many Christians paid dearly for their indiscretions, and even their fantasies.

Laws relating to sex have often been politically motivated. When the powerful Knights Templars in France were stripped of their wealth and power, the excuse was heresy and sodomy, but the truth of the matter was that Pope Clement V and King Philip IV of France were engaged in a deadly game of chess in which the stakes were the considerable wealth and property of the order. Philip, having a geographical advantage, out-maneuvered Clement, burned the Templars, and seized the lion's share of their treasure for himself.

When Gilles de Rais, marshal of France, and protector of Jeanne d'Arc, was condemned to death for his sexual excesses, he was the richest man in France, if not in Europe. Admittedly he was a monster, responsible for the deaths of many innocent children, but because of his wealth and power, he succeeded in salvaging his estates by confessing his sins and doing public penance before being burned at the stake.

Certainly the annals of crime are bulging with cases of sex offenders who deserved to be punished for their deeds. There was Stubbe Peeter or Peter Stumpf, a sixteenth century "werewolf" of Bedburg, who in reality murdered and devoured men, women, and children, including members of his own family, and whose sexual offenses would make strong stomachs go queasy even today. One need only glance through the pages of Krafft-Ebing's *Psychopathia*

Sexualis to find a cavalcade of wretches, for the most part completely psychotic, all of whom had to be dealt with by law enforcement.

And in more modern times there were such notorious individuals as Jack the Ripper, whose specialty was murdering and disemboweling prostitutes; Haarman, "The Hanover Vampire," who lured runaway teenage boys to his quarters, where he sexually assaulted them, bit them to death, drank their blood, then ground them up and sold them as sausage on the black market in post-World War One Germany. Film buffs will certainly recall Peter Lorre in the role that made him internationally famous, as the child killer in Fritz Lang's *M*. Though fiction, the film was based on the career of Peter Kurten, known both as the Dusseldorf Vampire and the Dusseldorf Ripper. A petty criminal all his life, Kurten's ultimate sexual pleasure was derived from the sound of dripping blood. It made no difference whether his victims were male or female, young or old, and his modus operandi varied so greatly from victim to victim, that he baffled the police for nearly twenty years. Executed by beheading on July 2, 1931, his last words were to speculate whether or not he would retain consciousness long enough after losing his head to be aware of the blood spurting from his neck.

But enough of blood and gore.

One of the most curious sexual laws existed in eighteenth century Italy. It is well known that some of the great Italian tenors of the period were *castrati*, that is, men who had been castrated for the express purpose of maintaining high voices. What is not generally known is that a man who is castrated late after puberty is often quite capable of erection, sexual de-

Lust. *Engraving by Giulio Romano in the style of those for which he was imprisoned. From PICTORIAL HISTORY OF MORALS, edited by Harry E. Wedeck. Copyright © 1963 by Philosophical Library, Inc. Reprinted with permission of the publisher*

sire, and performance. He produces seminal fluid, but no sperm, and is sterile. Because of this, *castrati* who were fortunate enough to be sexually functional were widely sought after as lovers. They were romantic performers on stage and extremely safe in bed. When the church found out what was going on, political strings were pulled and laws were enacted making sexual relations with *castrati* illegal. Marriage for *castrati* was even more strongly forbidden and punishable by death.

In a fascinating Irish annulment case of the period, a certain Miss Dorothea Kinsman fell in love with her music teacher, a *castrato* named Tenducci. She was not aware of his condition and, moreover, was apparently quite satisfied with his performances both on stage and in bed. Her father, however, a strict Catholic, had other ideas. Determined to terminate the marriage, Mr. Kinsman launched legal action. During the trial, a witness related how Tenducci had once showed him the scar on his scrotum, indicating the bitter remnant of his operation. He recalled that this had happened backstage during the intermission of an operatic performance. The witness recalled how at one point Tenducci had taken a red velvet bag from one of his pockets. Being a devout man, he asked the singer if this contained a holy relic from Rome. "Oh

no," replied Tenducci. "These are my testicles. I have kept them with me in this bag ever since they were cut off."

Unquestionably, the greatest targets of legal assault in the area of sex, past and present, have been the questions of "obscenity" and censorship. In most cases the victims of the law have suffered far more than any alleged victims of alleged obscenity. To cite one example, the sixteenth-century artist Giulio Romano executed a series of engravings to illustrate a translation by Pietro Aretino of Ovid's *Aris Amoris*, or *The Art of Love*. By order of Pope Clement VII, Marcantonio Raimondi (Romano's hapless engraver) was thrown into prison, while Aretino, one of history's arch-blackmailers, continued to live the high life in his palatial palace in Venice. The book, for centuries known popularly as *Aretino's Postures,* was sold clandestinely throughout Europe, and surviving illustrations by Romano, most of which are in The British Museum, are now regarded as great works of art.

The most difficult legal problem in the matter of obscenity is one of definition. In short, the word defies definition. Some fifty years ago, an international conference on "The Suppression and Circulation and Traffic of Obscene Publications" was called in

Geneva, Switzerland. At the opening of the conference the Greek delegate called for a definition of the term. At that point Sir Archibald Bodkin, the British representative, who at home was director of public prosecutions, and himself a great and zealous pursuer of obscenity, rose and said, "There is no definition of 'indecent' or obscene in English statute law." He warned that any attempt to define the term was potentially more dangerous than the international traffic in question, and that ended matters.

In his book *The Reevaluation of Obscenity*, Havelock Ellis wrote, "Any attempt to define obscenity, once we have put aside the vague emotional terms of abuse, such as foul, filthy, lewd, disgusting, etc., in cool and precise terms cannot bring us to any crime against society. Taken in the wide sense, we may define it as that which arouses sexual love or desire. But that is what anything in nature may do for some persons at some time, and that it should be so is in accordance with the whole order established by Nature, or if you will, God."

Ellis also observed that "the censors of obscenity are too solemn to realize that they are perpetuating a joke and too unintelligent to know that the joke has serious, even tragic consequences." What could be more illustrative of this statement than his further observation that, "Even the Bible—which a few centuries earlier had been regarded throughout Christendom as a sacred book—was declared obscene by the legal officials of the nineteenth century, especially in American courts, and punishment was meted out to those who published some sections of it."

And certainly those who would seek out and wipe out what they regard as obscene might well contemplate the words of Nietzsche, who said, "One cannot do a thing a better service than to persecute it and run it into the earth."

Nevertheless, despite all attempts to apply logic and reasoning, the self-appointed protectors of public morality will continue their quixotic battles to undermine the basic principles of free speech and expression, invariably to the detriment of public interest. What could be more illustrative of this fact than the case of Los Angeles vs. *Deep Throat*. During the trial Los Angeles employed two prosecutors (as they did in the Charles Manson case and the Sirhan Sirhan trial), and spent $250,000 of the taxpayers' money. Had they won the case, which they did not, the maximum penalty that could have been exacted against the defendants was a $500 fine.

Unfortunately, what the self-appointed protectors

A gentlewoman growing big with child had two gallants, one of them with a wooden leg. The question was put: which of the two should father the child? He who had the wooden leg offer'd to decide it thus: if the child, said he, comes into the world with a wooden leg, I will father it; if not, it must be yours.

—Joe Miller, eighteenth century

of public morality do not realize is that one of their fundamental arguments—"We must protect the children"—is an admission of failure to mind their own houses. They have every right to decide what their own children may or may not read. They have no right to make decisions for other people. Once we have legislation determining what we may not read or see, it is only a matter of time before we will have further legislation telling us what we must read or see. Were that time ever to come, the final erosion of the United States Constitution will have become irreversible.

A gentleman said of a young wench who constantly ply'd about the temple (*where the legal profession assembled*) that if she had as much law in her head, as she had in her tail, she would be one of the ablest counsel in England.

—Joe Miller, eighteenth century

On September 30, 1970, the Presidential Commission on Obscenity and Pornography released its findings. After a very thorough and intensive study into whether or not *obscenity and pornography* are harmful to the public, particularly to minors, and whether or not they increase or decrease crime and other antisocial behavior, the committee—made up of leading constitutional law authorities—made many very definite recommendations.

Subsequently, much of the commission's findings, it would seem, have been lost in the streams of legislative opinions and red-tape. The following are extracts of their findings which speak for themselves:

The Commission recommends that a massive sex education effort be launched. This sex education effort should be characterized by the following: a) its purpose should be to contribute to healthy atittudes and orientations to sexual relationships so as to provide a sound foundation for our society's basic institutions of marriage and family; b) it should be aimed at achieving an acceptance of sex as a normal and natural part of life and of oneself as a sexual being; c) it should be aimed, as appropriate, to all segments of our society, adults as well as children and adolescents. The Commission feels that such a sex education program would provide a powerful positive approach to the problems of obscenity and pornography.

The Commission recommends that federal, state, and local legislation prohibiting sale, exhibition, or distribution of sexual materials to consenting adults should be repealed. The Commission believes that there is no warrant for continued governmental interference with the full freedom of adults to read, obtain, or view whatever such material they wish.

The Commission has taken cognizance of the concern of many people that the lawful distribution of explicit sexual materials to adults may have a deleterious effect upon the individual morality of American citizens and upon the moral climate in America as a whole. This concern appears to flow from a belief that exposure to explicit materials may cause moral confusion which, in turn, may induce antisocial or criminal behavior. The Commission has found *no evidence* to support such a contention. Nor is there evidence that exposure to explicit sexual materials adversely affects character or moral attitudes regarding sex and sexual conduct.

The concern about the effect of obscenity upon morality is also expressed as a concern about the impact of sexual materials upon American values and standards. Such values and standards are currently in a process of complex change, in both sexual and nonsexual areas. The open availability of increasingly explicit sexual materials is only one of these changes. The current flux in sexual values is related to a number of powerful influences, among which are the ready availability of effective methods of contraception, changes of the role of women in our society, and the increased education and mobility of our citizens. The availability of explicit sexual materials is, the Commission believes, not one of the important influences on sexual morality.

The Commission is of the view that it is exceedingly unwise for government to attempt to legislate individual moral values and standards independent of behavior, especially by restrictions upon consensual communication. This is certainly true in the absence of a clear public mandate to do so, and our studies have revealed no such mandate in the area of obscenity.

The entire 700 pages of commission findings has been published in paperback by Bantam Books/New York Times, $1.65, and in a cloth edition by Random House.

First Amendment to the Bill of Rights

Passed by Congress, September 25, 1789,
and Ratified by the States, December 15, 1791.

"Congress shall make no law respecting an establishment of religion, or prohibiting the free exercise thereof; or abridging the freedom of speech, or of the press, or the right of the people peaceably to assemble and to petition the Government for a redress of grievances."

"*W*hen man was first in the jungle he took care of himself. When he entered a societal group, controls were necessarily imposed. But our society—unlike most in the world—presupposes that freedom and liberty are in a frame of reference that make the *individual*, not government, the keeper of his tastes, beliefs, and ideas. That is the philosophy of the First Amendment and it is the article of faith that sets us apart from most nations in the world."

So said Justice Douglas in his dissenting opinion of Paris Adult Theater I, *et al*, Petitioners, vs. Lewis R. Slaton, District Attorney, Atlanta Judicial Circuit, *et al*, on June 21, 1973, which along with four other First Amendment cases brought forth the United States Supreme Court decision on Obscenity.

The complete text of the 1973 Supreme Court decision has been published in paperback by Reed/Classic Library, 1973. $2.25.

Sex and the Law and Divorce...

*A*lthough divorce is not necessarily a sex-related subject, we felt it appropriate to mention the various sexual activities that are grounds for divorce in the United States.

Every state has different divorce laws, but in every state adultery is grounds for divorce, adultery being defined as actual sexual intercourse with a person or persons other than your own husband or wife. (An interesting note: in some states fellatio and cunnilingus are not grounds for a divorce, as actual penetration has not taken place).

Sex, in the historic archaic tradition, used to be considered the "marriage right," therefore an inability (impotency) to perform sexually (on either part, male or female—a man not being able to keep or get an erection long enough to perform intercourse, or a woman who's either suffering from vaginismus—a painful spasmodic contraction of the vagina—or other physical or psychological reasons restricting her vaginal accessibility) is grounds for divorce in thirty-five states of the United States.

Sexual relations with close members of the immediate family (incest) is grounds for divorce in seven states.

Religious beliefs that inhibit sexual activity—for example, fear of becoming pregnant but refusal for religious reasons to use contraceptives and therefore not engaging in sexual intercourse—can only be used as legitimate grounds for divorce in two states of the United States.

Sodomy and buggery are legal grounds for divorce in four states. And last, venereal disease, should one partner wittingly pass the disease on to his wife or husband, is grounds for divorce in two states.

Typical statutory definition of sodomy:

"Every person who shall carnally know, or have sexual intercourse in any manner with any animal or bird, or shall carnally know any male or female by the anus (rectum) or with the mouth or tongue, or shall attempt intercourse with a dead body is guilty of Sodomy."

From The Police Gazette, *edited by Gene Smith with Jayne Barry Smith. Copyright © 1972 by H. H. Roswell. Reprinted by permission of Simon & Schuster, Inc.*

A.C.L.U. (THE AMERICAN CIVIL LIBERTIES UNION)

The A.C.L.U. is a national organization that has been working for fifty-five years to guarantee individuals the freedoms laid down under the Constitution and the Bill of Rights.

It has over a quarter of a million members, 49 statewide affiliates and 379 local chapters.

The union protects the individual and insures he is provided with his rights under the constitution. Those rights are . . . the right to freedom of expression, to due process of law, to privacy, and to equal protection of the laws.

Sex is a civil liberty; therefore if you are discriminated against for your sex in employment, housing, *etc.,* or if your constitutional rights protected by the first Amendment are violated, the A.C.L.U. can help.

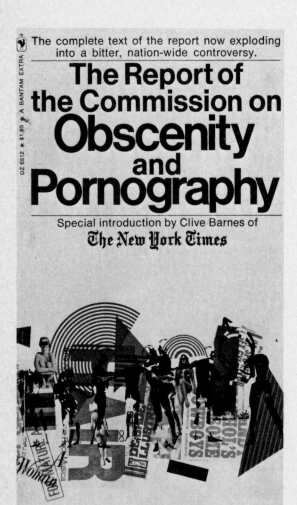

The complete text of the report now exploding into a bitter, nation-wide controversy.

The Report of the Commission on Obscenity and Pornography

Special introduction by Clive Barnes of
The New York Times

DZ 6512 ★ $1.65 ★ A BANTAM EXTRA

Pornography Outlets in Los Angeles

6 Magazine Distributors

13 Film Distributors

6 Exhibitors

5 Model Agencies

4 Magazine Producers

8 Hard-core Film Producers

3 Still Picture Photo Labs

4 Motion Picture Film Labs

Courtesy of the Department of Administrative Vice, Los Angeles Police Department.

Solution to dirty crossword puzzle appearing on page 294

Puzzle Number 8

Sex and the Law and Rape

The following is a list of rape crisis centers, where victims of rape can go for help, and groups specifically interested in the problems of rape:

CALIFORNIA
Bay Area Women Against Rape
P.O. Box 240
Berkeley, California 94701
(415) 845-RAPE

Fresno Rape Counseling Service
P.O. Box 708
Clovis, California 93612
(209) 222-RAPE

Marin Rape Crisis Center
P.O. Box 823
Kentfield, California 94904

Pomona Project Sister
107 North Gordon Avenue
Pomona, California 91767
(714) 623-6017

San Bernardino Rape Crisis Service
c/o Family Service Agency
1669 E Street
San Bernardino, California
(714) 886-4889

San Diego Rape Crisis Center
(714) 239-RAPE

San Jose Women Against Rape
Ninth and Carlos Streets
San Jose, California 95192
(408) 287-3000

Los Angeles Rape Crisis Center
235 Hill Street
Santa Monica, California 90405
(213) 653-6333

COLORADO
Denver Crisis Line
c/o Southwest Neighborhood Services Bureau
277 Clear Water Street
Denver, Colorado 80206
(303) 321-8191

CONNECTICUT
New Haven Rape Crisis Center
(203) 397-2273

Westport People Against Rape
27 Reichert Circle
Westport, Connecticut 06880
(203) 576-0397

DELAWARE
Wilmington Rape Crisis Center
P.O. Box 1507
Wilmington, Delaware 19899
(302) 658-5011

FLORIDA
Fort Lauderdale/Broward County Women Against Rape
P.O. Box 4101
Ft. Lauderdale, Florida 33304
(305) 584-RAPE

Gainesville Rape Crisis Center
P.O. Box 12888
Gainesville, Florida 32604
(904) 377-RAPE

Jacksonville Women's Rape Crisis Center
1825 Hendricks Ave.
Jacksonville, Florida 32207
(904) 384-6488

Miami Rape Treatment Center
c/o Jackson Memorial Hospital
1000 N. W. 17 Street
Miami, Florida 33136
(305) 325-RAPE

Sarasota Rape Prevention and Crisis Center
P.O. Box 74
Sarasota, Florida 33578
(813) 958-8222

Tampa Hillsborough County Stop Rape
P.O. Box 1495
Tampa, Florida 33601
(813) 254-RAPE

GEORGIA
Macon Rape Crisis Line
c/o The Woman's Center
Macon, Georgia 31201
(912) 742-8661

ILLINOIS
Chicago Legal Action for Women
c/o Loop YWCA
37 South Wabash
Chicago, Illinois 60603

Chicago Rape Crisis Center
(312) 728-1920

Chicago Women Against Rape
c/o Loop YWCA
37 South Wabash
Chicago, Illinois 60603

IOWA
Iowa City Hotline
c/o The Women's Center
3 East Market Street
Iowa City, Iowa 52240
(319) 338-4800

Iowa Rape Crisis Center
Room 65, Memorial Union
Ames, Iowa 50010
(515) 294-8437 or 292-7000

MARYLAND
Baltimore Rape Crisis Center
(301) 366-6475

MASSACHUSETTS
Boston Area Rape Crisis Center
Cambridge, Massachusetts
(617) 492-RAPE

Springfield Rape Crisis Center
Room 212
292 Worthington Street
Springfield, Massachusetts 01003
(413) 737-RAPE

MICHIGAN
Ann Arbor Women's Crisis Center
306 N. Division Street
Ann Arbor, Michigan 48108
(313) 761-WISE

Detroit Rape Crisis Line
P.O. Box 35271
Seven Oaks Station
Detroit, Michigan 48235
(313) 832-RAPE

Detroit Women Against Rape
18121 Patton
Detroit, Michigan 48219

Grand Rapids Rape Crisis Team
P.O. Box 6161, Station C
Grand Rapids, Michigan 49506
(616) 456-3535

Kalamazoo Rape Crisis Center
Kalamazoo, Michigan
(616) 345-3036

Ypsilanti Rape Relief
Ypsilanti, Michigan
(313) 485-3222

MINNESOTA
Minneapolis Rape Crisis Center
(612) 374-4357

NEBRASKA
Omaha Rape Advisors
Omaha, Nebraska
(402) 345-RAPE

NEW JERSEY
Camden Women Against Rape
c/o Contact
Camden, New Jersey
(609) 667-3000

New Jersey Task Force Against Rape
P.O. Box 2163
Princeton, New Jersey 08540

NEW MEXICO
Albuquerque Rape Crisis Center
c/o The Women's Center
824 Las Lomas N.E.
Albuquerque, New Mexico 87106
(505) 277-3393

NEW YORK
New York Women Against Rape
c/o The Women's Center
243 West 20th Street
New York, N.Y. 10011
(212) 675-7720

Woodstock Women's Project
c/o Family
Rock City Road
Woodstock, New York 12448
(914) 679-2485

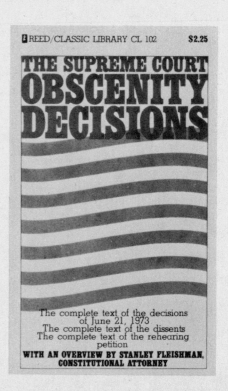

REED/CLASSIC LIBRARY CL 102 $2.25

THE SUPREME COURT OBSCENITY DECISIONS

The complete text of the decisions
of June 21, 1973
The complete text of the dissents
The complete text of the rehearing
petition
**WITH AN OVERVIEW BY STANLEY FLEISHMAN,
CONSTITUTIONAL ATTORNEY**

Rape Prevention Hotline
(516) 822-1190

NORTH CAROLINA
Chapel Hill Rape Crisis Center
c/o Switchboard
408 Rosemary Street
Chapel Hill, North Carolina
(919) 929-7177

OHIO
Columbus Rape Crisis Center
c/o Women Against Rape
P.O. Box 4442
Trivillage Station
Columbus, Ohio 43212
(614) 221-4447

Dayton Women Against Rape Collective
Women's Center
1309 North Main Street
Dayton, Ohio 45405
(513) 223-2462

OHIO (KENT)
Rape Crisis Project
c/o Center for Peaceful Change
Kent State University
Kent, Ohio 44242
(216) 672-HELP

OKLAHOMA
Oklahoma City Rape Crisis Center
c/o YWCA
320 Park Avenue
Oklahoma City, Oklahoma 73102
(405) 232-7681 Ext. 60

OREGON
Eugene Rape Crisis Center
171 Washington Street
Eugene, Oregon 97401
(503) 343-9986

Portland Rape Relief Hotline
Portland, Oregon
(503) 235-5333

PENNSYLVANIA
Philadelphia Women Organized Against Rape
P.O. Box 17374
Philadelphia, Pennsylvania 19105
(215) 823-7997

Chester County (Pennsylvania) Rape Crisis Council
P.O. Box 738
West Chester, Pennsylvania 19380
(215) 692-RAPE

TENNESSEE
Memphis Crisis Line
c/o People Against Rape
P.O. Box 12224
Memphis, Tennessee 38112
(615) CRISIS-3

Nashville Rape Prevention & Crisis Center
P.O. Box 12531
Acklen Station
Nashville, Tennessee 37212
(615) 297-9587

TEXAS
Dallas Rape Crisis Line
c/o Women Against Rape
P.O. Box 12701
Dallas, Texas 75225
(214) 341-9400

San Antonio Rape Crisis Line
P.O. Box 28061
San Antonio, Texas 78228
(512) 433-1251

VIRGINIA
Roanoke Rape Crisis Line
3515 Williamson Road
Roanoke, Virginia 24012
(703) 366-6030

WASHINGTON
Seattle Rape Relief
(206) 632-4795

WISCONSIN
Madison Rape Crisis Center
P.O. Box 1312
Madison, Wisconsin 53701
(608) 251-RAPE

Milwaukee Women's Crisis Line
c/o Women's Coalition
2211 East Kenwood Boulevard
Milwaukee, Wisconsin 53211
(414) 964-7535

WASHINGTON, D.C.
Washington D.C. Rape Crisis Center
P.O. Box 21005
Washington, D.C. 20009
(202) 333-RAPE

RAPE FILE
A special report on rape, rapists, and victims—a series
of articles reprinted in pamphlet form from *Viva* magazine, November 1974.

Sex and the Law by State

The statutes covered in the following chart relate to acts between *consenting adults*. The information contained is the most up to date presently available. In the following states penal code revisions have been completed, but not yet enacted by the legislatures: Alabama, Alaska, Indiana, Iowa, Maine, Maryland, Michigan, Missouri, Nebraska, New Jersey, Oklahoma, South Carolina, South Dakota, Tennessee, Vermont, and Washington. Revision is underway in Arizona, but has not yet been completed. Revisions have been authorized in the District of Columbia and North Carolina, but work has not yet begun. Revisions were completed but aborted in Idaho and Massachusetts. No revisions are planned in Mississippi, Nevada, Rhode Island, and Wyoming.

It should be noted that the age at which one becomes a "consenting adult" not only varies from state to state, but also within the individual states, by sex, and depending upon the sexual act in question. This makes the law very convenient for the prosecutors and very thorny for everyone else.

STATE	ADULTERY	COHABITATION	FORNICATION	SODOMY	PUBLIC LEWDNESS OR INDECENCY
ALABAMA	max. 6 months and/or max. $100	max. 6 months and/or max. $100		2-10 yrs	max. 12 months and/or max. $500
ALASKA	max. 3 months and/or max. $200	max. 2 yrs and/or $500		1-10 yrs	3-12 months or max. $500
ARIZONA	max. 3 yrs	max. 3 yrs		1-20 yrs	1-5 yrs
ARKANSAS		$20-100		1-21 yrs	
CALIFORNIA (as of Jan 1 1976)					max. 6 months or max. $500
COLORADO					
CONNECTICUT	max. 12 months max. $1,000				max. 6 months, or max. $1,000
DELAWARE	max. 1 yrs and/or max. $500			2-20 yrs	fine fixed by court not to exceed $500
DISTRICT OF COLUMBIA	max. 1 yr and/or max. $500		max. 6 months and/or max. $300		max. 90 days and max. $250
FLORIDA	max. 12 months and/or max. $1,000	max. 60 days and/or max. $500	max. 60 days and/or max. $500	max. 60 days and/or max. $500	max. 60 days and/or max. $500
GEORGIA	max. 12 months and/or max. $1,000		max. 12 months and/or max. $1,000	1-20 yrs	max 12 months and/or max. $1,000
HAWAII	max. 12 months and/or max. $100 for men; max. 4 months, and/or max. $30 for women		max. 3 months and/or max. $50	max. 20 yrs and/or max. $1,000	max. 1 yr and/or. max. $1,000
IDAHO	max 3 yrs and/or max. $1,000	max. 6 months and/or max. $300	max. 6 months and/or max. $300	minimum 5 yrs	max. 6 months and/or max. $300
ILLINOIS	max. 1 yr and/or max. $1,000				max. 1 yr and/or max. $1,000
IOWA	max. 3 yrs and/or max. $300	max. 6 months and/or max. $200		max. 10 yrs	max. 6 months and/or max. $200

STATE	ADULTERY	COHABITATION	FORNICATION	SODOMY	PUBLIC LEWDNESS OR INDECENCY
KANSAS	max. 1 month and/or max. $500			*max. 6 months and/or max. $1,000	max. 6 months and/or max. $1,000
KENTUCKY					At the court's discretion.
LOUISIANA				max. $100 or max. $500	max. $1,000 or max. 1 yr.
MAINE	up to 5 yrs or up to $1,000	up to 5 yrs or up to $300	max. 60 days and max. $100	1-10 yrs	max. 6 months or max. $25
MARYLAND	$10			max. 10 yrs or max. $1,000	max. 60 days or max. $50
MASSACHUSETTS	max. 3 yrs or max. $500	max. 3 yrs or max. $300	max. 3 months or max. $30	max. 5 yrs or max. $1,000	max. 3 yrs or max. $300
MICHIGAN	max 4 yrs or max. $2,000	max. 1 yr max. $500	max. 5 yrs max. $2,500	max. 5 yrs or max. $2,500	max. 1 yr or max. $500
MINNESOTA	max. 1 yr or max. $1,000		max. 90 days or max. $100	max. 1 yr or max. $1,000	max. 90 days or max. $100
MISSISSIPPI	max. 6 months or max. $500	max. 6 months or max. $500		max. 10 yrs	max. 6 months or max. $500
MISSOURI	max. 1 yr or max. $500		.	minimum 2 yrs	max. 1 yr or max. $1,000
MONTANA				max. 10 yrs	max. 6 months or max. $500
NEBRASKA	max. 1 yr	max. 6 months or max. $100		max. 20 yrs	max. 90 days or max. $100
NEVADA				max. 6 yrs	max. 1 yr or max. $1,000
NEW HAMPSHIRE	max. 1 yr		max. 1 yr or max. $50	max. 1 yr	max. 1 yr or max. $200
NEW JERSEY	max. 3 yrs and max. $1,000		max. 6 months or max. $500	max. 20 yrs or max. $50,000	max. 3 yrs or max. $1,000
NEW MEXICO		warning the first time; subsequent max. 6 months or max. $100			max. 6 months or max. $100
NEW YORK	max. 3 months or max. $500			*max. 1 yr and/or max. $1,000	
NORTH CAROLINA		max. 6 months or max. $500		max. 10 yrs and/or any fine	
NORTH DAKOTA	max. 3 yrs or max. 1 yr plus $500	max. 1 yr or max. $500	max. 30 dys max. $100	max. 10 yrs	max. 5 yrs and/or max. $1,000
OHIO					max. $250 or max. 30 dys

STATE	ADULTERY	COHABITATION	FORNICATION	SODOMY	PUBLIC LEWDNESS OR INDECENCY
OKLAHOMA	max. 5 yrs or max. $500			max. 10 yrs	max. 5 yrs and/or max. $5,000
OREGON					
PENNSYLVANIA				*max. 2 yrs or max. $5,000	max. 2 yrs or max. $5,000
RHODE ISLAND	max. 1 yr or max. $500		max. $10	max. 20 yrs	max. 1 yr and/or max. $5,000
SOUTH CAROLINA	max. 1 yr and/or max. $500	max. 1 yr and/or max. $500	max. 1 yr and/or max. $500	max. 5 yrs and/or minimum $500	sentence at the court's discretion
SOUTH DAKOTA	max. 5 yrs and/or max. $500			max. 10 yrs	max. 1 yr and/or max. $2,000
TENNESSEE				max. 15 yrs	
TEXAS				max. $200	max. $200
UTAH	max. 1 yr and/or max. $1,000		max. 6 months and/or max. $299	max. 6 months and/or max. $299	max. 6 months and/or max. $300
VERMONT	max. 5 yrs and/or max. $1,000			1-5 yrs	max. 5 yrs or max. $300
VIRGINIA	$20-$100	$50-$500	$20-$100	max. 3 yrs	max. 1 yr and/or max. $1,000
WASHINGTON	max. 2 yrs and/or max. $1,000	max. 1 yr and/or max. $1,000		max. 10 yrs	max. 90 days and/or max. $250
WISCONSIN	max. 3 yrs and/or max. $1,000	max. 1 yr and/or max. $500	max. 6 months and/or max. $200	max. 5 yrs and/or max. $500	max. 1 yr and/or max. $500
WYOMING	max. 3 months and max. $100	max. 3 months and max. $100	max 3 months and max. $100	max. 10 yrs	at court's discretion

*Not outlawed if participants in the act are married. New York is one of the few states that actually defines sodomy as "deviate sexual intercourse," more specifically meaning "contact between the penis and the anus, the mouth and the penis, or the mouth and the vulva."

It should be noted that the definitions of these laws vary substantially from state to state. Some, though on the books for many years, have never been enforced or tested in the courts (e.g. fornication—cohabitation). The term "sodomy" covers such a wide range of sexual acts and circumstances, often utilizing archaic adjectives such as "abominable and detestible," that even in states where no specific sodomy laws exist, sex acts falling into the category are sometimes prosecuted under the umbrella terms of public lewdness or indecency. The element of vagueness in this area of law is so universal that in the end conviction, acquittal, or dismissal depends entirely upon interpretation. Consequently, whatever you choose to do sexually, make certain that you do it in private, or at least, in the presence of witnesses who are parties to the act.

Bibliography

Barbeau, Clayton C. *Art, Obscenity, and Your Children.* St. Meinrad, Ind.: Abbey Press, 1967. 95¢.

Barnett, Walter. *Sexual Freedom and the Constitution: An Inquiry into the Constitutionality of Repressive Sex Laws.* Albuquerque: University of New Mexico Press, 1973. $10.00

Chandos, John, ed. *The Banned Books of England and Other Countires: A study of the conception of literary obscenity.* London: G. Allen & Unwin, Ltd. 1962.

——. *To Deprave and Corrupt.* London: Souvenior Press, 1962.

Craig, Alec. *Above All Liberties.* London: G. Allen & Unwin, Ltd. 1942. Reprint. Plainview, N.Y.: Books For Libraries. 95¢

Csida, June Bundy, and Csida, Joseph. *Rape: How to Avoid It & What to Do About It If You Can't.* Chatsworth, Calif.: Books for Better Living, 1974. $1.50

Dennett, Mary Ware. *Birth Control Laws.* New York: Da Capo Press. $15.00

——. *Who's Obscene?* New York: Vanguard Press, 1930.

De River, J. Paul. *Crime and the Sexual Psychopath.* Springfield, Ill.: C. C. Thomas, 1958. $6.75

Downs, Robert Bingham. *The First Freedom: Liberty and Justice in the World of Books and Reading.* Chicago: American Library Association, 1960. $9.50

Duffy, Clinton T. *Sex and Crime.* Garden City, N.Y.: Doubleday, 1956.

Ellis, Albert. *The Psychology of Sex Offenders.* Springfield, Ill.: C. C. Thomas, 1956.

Ellis, Havelock. *The Reevaluation of Obscenity.* Paris: Hours Press, 1931.

Ernst, Morris L., and Lindley, Alexander. *The Censor Marches On.* New York: Doubleday, Doran & Co., 1940.

Ernst, Morris L., and Schwartz, Alan U. *Censorship: The Search for the Obscene.* New York: Macmillan, 1964. $6.95

Gebhard, Paul H., et al. *Sex Offenders: An Analysis of Types.* New York: Harper & Row, 1965. $15.00

Hart, Herbert Lionel Adolphus. *Law, Liberty, and Morality.* Palo Alto: Stanford University Press, 1963.

Kronhausen, Phyllis, and Kronhausen, Eberhard. *Pornography and the Law.* New York: Ballantine Books, 1964.

Lawrence, D.H. *Pornography and Obscenity.* New York: Knopf, 1930.

——. *Pornography and So On.* London: Faber & Faber, 1936.

Miller, Henry. *Obscenity and the Law of Reflection.* The "Outcast" Chapbooks #11. Yonkers: 1945.

Peckham, Morse. *Art and Pornography: An Experiment in Explanation.* New York: Harper & Row, 1971. Paper $3.95

Rembar, Charles. *The End of Obscenity.* New York: Random House, 1968. $10.95

Ross, Susan. *The Rights of Women: An American Civil Liberties Union Handbook.* Edited by Norman Dorsen and Aryeh Neier. New York: Richard W. Baron, 1973. $1.25

Sagarin, Edward. *The Anatomy of Dirty Words.* Secaucus, N. J.: Lyle Stuart, 1962. $4.95

Schroeder, Theodore A. *A Challenge to Sex Censors.* New York: Free Speech League, 1938.

——. *Witchcraft and Obscenity—Twin Superstitions.* New York: Free Speech League, 1912.

——. *Obscene Literature and Constitutional Law.* Reprint. New York:

Schur, Edwin M. and Bedeau, Hugo. *Victimless Crimes: Two Sides of a Controversy.* New York: Spectrum, $2.45

Sharp, Donald B. *Commentaries on Obscenity.* Metchuen, N. J.: Scarecrow Press, 1970. $7.50

St. John-Stevas, Norman. *Obscenity and the Law.* London: Secker & Warburg, 1956.

Storaska, Frederick. *How to Say No to a Rapist and Survive.* New York: Random House, 1975. $7.95

Supreme Court Obscenity Decisions, The. San Diego: Greenleaf Classics, Inc., 1973. $2.25

United States Government. *The Report of the Commission on Obscenity and Pornography.* Washington: U.S. Government Printing Office; New York: Randon House; New York: Bantam Books.

Sex Discrimination: *A brief guide to written books and other materials dealing with discrimination in all areas because of sex.*

Amundsen, Kirsten. *The Silenced Majority: Women and American Democracy.* Englewood Cliffs N.J.: Prentice-Hall, 1971.

Association of the Bar of the City of New York. "Woman and the Law." *Record 11* (1956): 152-56.

Cassell, Kay Ann. "The Legal Status of Women." *Library Journal* 96 (1971): 2600-03

Eastwood, Mary. "The Double Standard of Justice: Women's Rights under the Constitution." *Valparaiso University Law Review* S(1971): 281-317.

Green, Wayne E. "Sex and Civil Rights." *Wall Street Journal,* May 22, 1967.

McVeety, Jean. "Law and the Single Woman." *Women Lawyers Journal,* January 1967, pp. 10-14.

Ploscowe, Morris. "Sex and the Law." Rev. ed. New York: Ace Books, 1962.

Schulder, Diane. "Women and the Law." *Atlantic,* March 1970, pp. 103-04.

Smith, Solomon D. *Homosexuals and the law—selected writing.* Mimeographed. New Haven: Yale Law School Library, April 1971. 4pp.

——. "Women's Legal Rights in All 50 States." *McCall's,* February 1971, pp. 90-95.

Extracted from The Record of the Association of the Bar of the City of New York: Volume 26, Number 8.

Illustration from a nineteenth century French medical journal accompanying the case history of one Marie-Madeleine Lefort, from childhood to old age

Sex and Medicine

A Glimpse of the Past

*U*ntil recent times, the medical aspects of sex were sadly neglected by physicians. The only angle that was highly developed in ancient times was the psychiatric, so sex got its fair share of attention. However, in Western culture the Judaeo-Christian emphasis on sin and guilt tended to push anything related to sex into the closet and keep it there. Female ailments, going as far back as Hippocrates' time, were generally lumped together under the general heading of hysteria, which grew out of the theory that the uterus became misplaced and wandered through the body, causing all manner of physical and emotional ills. To make matters worse, sexual dysfunctions of all sorts were often as not regarded to be the result of evil spirits, possession, and witchcraft, none of which helped improve health or advance the cause of medicine.

Even in the Far East, prevailing attitudes toward modesty prevented physicians from treating women, and in China examinations were generally done by using anatomical dolls on which the patient indicated where her problem was located, forcing the physician to offer treatment largely by guesswork.

Physical sexual anomalies, of course, received the attention of physicians relatively early in history. Hermaphroditism and pseudo-hermaphroditism attracted special interest, because whenever they occurred the conditions were obvious, thereby easy to study, even during periods of history when medicine was 95 percent art and 5 percent science.

Although relatively obscure to the lay reader, early medical accounts of hermaphroditism do exist and, because of their rarity, are of extreme interest. One of the earlier cases was described in 1686 by a French physician named Dr. Veay of Toulouse. He indicated that outwardly the patient appeared to be a normal, feminine-looking twenty-one-year-old woman with well-formed breasts, a pretty neck, normal-sized hips and thighs. However, "the pudenda is precisely like that of a woman, but the slit is no longer than two fingers breadth, and from the middle of it protrudes a virile member of very considerable thickness, and which, when in a state of erection, comes out about eight inches. This member is well formed, except that it has no prepuce, and is unaccompanied by apparent testicles. The urine and semen issue from it as in men, and what is very extraordinary, the menstrual evacuation is also discharged from the same place. I should have had great difficulty in believing this had I not seen it myself, having examined the party very particularly at a time of menses."

In 1740 two German medical professors, Henry J. Wolfart and Freidrich Christian Cregut, began a bitter controversy over a hermaphrodite that continued for a nine-year period. It began when Professor Wolfart's brother unearthed a scandal involving a fifty-two-year-old hermaphrodite named Sempronia, who was accused of having committed "acts of lewdness" with a girl fifteen years of age. After examining Sempronia, Wolfart found "her" to have a complete set of male and female genitalia. When Cregut examined the subject, he strongly disagreed with Wolfart's findings. Wolfart insisted that Sempronia had a pair of testicles; Cregut, after a more thorough examination, proved that these were not present, and the dispute finally ended.

Another eighteenth century German physician, Martin Schurig, cited the case of a man who married a "female hermaphrodite, by whom he had several children, male and female, and that the individual so considered a woman had frequent connections with the maid servants, and had even gotten them with child."

In *The Parisian Medical Annals of Physiology* in 1789 there appeared an old case history of a bride who could not be deflowered on her wedding night. The article opened with a description of the bridegroom's surprise at the time, "while fondly smoothing his hand over the naked person of his bride, but feeling an object as long as his own member pressing against him. In the utmost of confusion, not to say alarm, he got out of bed, imagining at first that he was bewitched, for in those days the power of sorcery was an article of almost universal and implicit belief."

Thinking at first that his friends had played a rude prank on him and substituted a man for his bride, he leaped out of bed, lit a candle, and made certain that his wife was indeed beside him. The poor young woman was alarmed by her husband's unexpected behavior and begged him to rejoin her beneath the covers. Composing himself he did just that and began once more "to renew his marital duties." Now his astonishment increased "when he found that he could not disengage himself from the arms of his beloved who, in proportion as her passion increased, crushed him still closer and closer to her breast. It was now that he no longer doubted being the victim of witchcraft, for, upon this occasion, by a strange metamorphosis, the man became as it were a woman, while the latter was playing the part of the male gender.

"At length the man, having recovered himself somewhat, began to examine the cause of his embarrassment. He no sooner cast his eyes on his wife's pudenda than a male appendage as long as his own presented itself to him. Questioning his wife upon the subject, she informed him as delicately as she could that she imagined all women to have been formed like herself in those parts. She told him moreover, that during the excessive cold of winter, the clitoris almost entirely disappeared, being at that time neither longer nor thicker than the half of the little finger; but that as the summer heat set in, it became excessively enlarged." The report went on to describe how the husband suggested having the offending part amputated, but his wife would have no part of such an operation and the idea was abandoned.

We are unfortunately left hanging as to the further relations of this couple, but it may be assumed in light of modern-day knowledge that the woman was what is termed a pseudo-hermaphrodite and in possession of an abnormally large clitoris. John Davenport, the nineteenth-century author of *Aphrodisiacs and Anti-Aphrodisiacs*, touched upon this matter, observing that "These are the enormous dimensions which sometimes deceive as to the real character of the sex, and which had occasioned the belief in the existence of real hermaphrodites."

One of the best first-hand descriptions of a true hermaphrodite was written by a nonmedical man, bibliographer Henry Spencer Ashbee, whose attention to detail is worthy of any physician. Describing the person he saw as a fairly attractive woman, he went on to say, "She was about twenty years of age, rather pretty, and quite womanly, with beautiful eyes, a good complexion, and fair hair; her nose was rather masculine and her mouth rather rough and large, with bad teeth; her chest was expansive, and her breasts well developed; the lower part of her legs slightly bowed, and masculine. She possessed, in appearance at least, the organs of both sexes, but neither perfect: a small penis, as in a lad of twelve or fourteen years, and testicles apparently developed; the yard was, however, not perforated. Underneath the testicles was what seemed to be a perfect female vestibule, of which the opening was, however, only large enough to allow her to pass water, but not to receive a man, or even admit the insertion of the end of a quill . . . she had no monthly flow, but felt, nevertheless, a periodic indisposition; she experienced pleasure in the embraces of both sexes, and had even an erection when with a sympathetic female. She could not, of course, satisfy her desires."

In *The Golden Age of Erotica* there is a sensitive summation of the predicament which is most appropriate. "There is something immeasurably tragic about the plight of the hermaphrodite. It is impossible for the so-called normal person to conceive the depths of loneliness, frustration, and misery which imprison these hybrid creatures who are shunned by a society that has no place for them."

No discussion of sex in medicine would be complete without mention of one of history's most charming medical charlatans. He was Dr. James Graham, father of the notorious "celestial bed." He set up practice in London, about the time of the American Revolution, after having traveled extensively both on the continent and in the new world. Consistently attracting patients with such gimmicks as "the electric bath" and the "magnetic throne," his heyday dawned in 1779, when he set up his now legendary Temple of Health. At this point so many wealthy patients flocked to him that his coffers swelled to a point that would make even a contemporary specialist turn green with envy.

His male patients were offered an especially attractive inducement in the person of his assistant, who was billed as Vestina, the Rosy Goddess of Health. Her act consisted of performing sensuous dances in the seminude. During the Temple's first year, she was portrayed by a certain Emma Lyon who eventually slid into the ranks of high society as Lady Hamilton, achieving her permanent niche in history as the mistress of Lord Nelson.

By the year 1781, Graham's establishment was so successful that he moved it to lavish quarters in Pall Mall. It underwent a slight name change, now being known as The Temple of Health and of Hymen. The lighting was definitely theatrical,

Hebe Vestina, the Rosy Goddess of Health seen reclining in Dr. James Graham's Temple of Health and Hymen London, eighteenth century

filtering through colored glass stained to create a variety of moods. Patients were admitted by paying an initial charge of six guineas. This entitled them to an elaborate show, including seductive lighting, appropriate music, lovely dancing girls, and medical lectures by the guru himself.

This was all the impressive come-on. The sting was the good doctor's Celestial Bed. According to all descriptions, it was nine by twelve feet and supported on forty pillars of glittering glass. Surrounding it were intricate rainbow murals and frescoes. Hidden above, in what he called "the super celestial dome," was a reservoir of perfumes which were dispensed automatically. Graham's advertising promised those who reposed in the bed delicious enjoyment amidst a gentle mist of descending voluptuous fragrances. He also claimed to have an amazing "self-playing organ" which supposedly reproduced the music of guitars, flutes, horns, trumpets, oboes, kettle drums, violins, and heaven knows what else. The "super celestial dome" was supported by pillars and bedposts, ornate carvings of swans in shimmering waters, flying birds, waterfalls, flower-strewing nymphs, shepherds and shepherdesses, fountains, and for the devout, a small church. There were no feathers in the mattress, only "sweet new wheat or cut straw with the grain in the ears and mingled with balm, rose leaves, lavender flowers, and oriental spices." The sheets were of satin and silk, with clients being given a choice of colors. The bed's effectiveness, according to Graham, was due essentially to a hidden pile of artificial lodestones which were supposed to produce a mysterious electrical effluvia guaranteed to stiffen matrimonial zeal after it had become limp. One suspects that these alleged lodestones were not unlike ordinary bedsprings for, in the words of the good doctor, upon pressing into them there resulted "that sweet undulating, tittulating [sic], vibratory, soul-dissolving, marrow-melting motion; which is at once so necessary and pleasing."

What Graham guaranteed was that anyone spending a night in the Celestial Bed would beget strong, beautiful, brilliant, nay, double-distilled children. In plain language he billed it as a cure for impotence and sterility. All comers were welcome and a passport in the form of a marriage certificate was not required. The only prerequisite was the price of admission, which ranged from £50 to £500 per night, depending upon the ability of the prospective sleeper to pay.

Contemporary Attitudes

New York Fertility Research Foundation

Today the problems of impotence and sterility are treated either medically or in sex therapy. One of the leading institutions dealing with these problems is the New York Fertility Research Foundation located at 123 East 89th Street, New York, N.Y. 10028. It is a unique, research-oriented nonprofit facility, specializing exclusively in the total investigation of the complexities of infertility. Founded by Dr. Albert Decker in 1962, the foundation combines the expertise of gynecologists, urologists, endocrinologists, geneticists, pathologists, radiologists, sex therapists, and various researchers in a team approach to the problems of childless couples.

Some outstanding members of the foundation and their accomplishments include:

Dr. Albert Decker, recently called the "Sherlock Holmes of Gynecology" by *Quick Magazine*'s German correspondent, Manfred Kreiner, because of Decker's zeal in searching out the causes of infertility in stubborn cases. Dr. Decker invented an instrument and technique in 1942 for examining the inside of a woman's pelvis. Without surgery, it allows him to investigate minute problems that might be upsetting a tiny phase of the reproductive process. Routine examinations can reveal just so much, and when Dr. Decker suspects that there is some obscure pathology, like the hampered efficiency of tiny hairlike projections at the end of the Fallopian tubes called fimbria, he can examine and photograph inside the pelvic area, with minimal discomfort to his patient, with the *Decker culdoscope*.

Information courtesy of New York Fertility Research Foundation.

Dr. Wayne H. Decker, surgeon-in-chief of FRF and son of Dr. Albert Decker, pioneered the technique of freezing and pooling sperm of men with low sperm counts. With his technique, for the first time the man with a low sperm count is offered a 28 percent chance to achieve fatherhood. It is through Dr. Wayne's efforts that the foundation combines all the specialties for comprehensive research and treatment. Dr. Wayne is looking into the possibilities of implantation of the fetus.

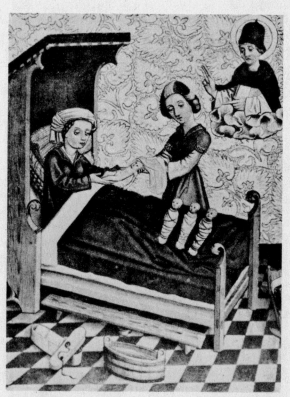

Illustration from a medieval manuscript showing a woman giving birth to quadruplets.

Cover illustration of a contemporary gynecological instrument distributor

some indications that the sex can be determined, and this would require the development of new techniques and the application of already established techniques. His research includes study of fertility of sperm and study of abnormal sperm, *etc.* Dr. Shettles believes he can separate male- and female-producing sperm and can determine when the dice are loaded in terms of some men having a preponderance of male- and female-producing sperm. Dr. Shettles sees this as a population reducer for couples who continue to reproduce beyond their intended family size in the hope of achieving a child of different sex. All research into the causes of infertility will aid in devising better methods of human contraception.

Dr. Masood A. Khatamee, attending gynecologist at FRF, is doing research on the relationship of mycoplasma (newly discovered microorganism found in the genito-urinary tract of women) and infertility. Mycoplasma is thought to cause infertility and spontaneous abortions. Research will indicate whether mycoplasma is a venereal disease and if it is prevalent in women using birth control pills or IUDs.

Dr. Don Sloan and **Stephanie Cook, M.A.**, sexual therapists, assist couples whose problem is a sexual hangup. All couples who come to the foundation are examined and when physical causes of infertility are eliminated and initial investigation reveals the couple has little sex or none at all, they are referred to the sexual therapists for conjoint therapy.

Dr. Ernest Lieber, attending geneticist at FRF, is doing genetic studies of cell cultures (karotypes), which show the arrangement of the chromosomes in the individual cells. Defects show up in magnification. This research is in its beginning stages, but so far 85 percent of the patient couples that have been reviewed thus far, with multiple miscarriages indicating the need for a genetic workup, have been found to have unusual genetic histories—some form of fetal wastage in the first-degree relatives of the husband or wife or both. Dr. Lieber is also doing research in dermatoglyphics—the study of handprints. He is looking at handprints of the couples who have multiple miscarriages to see if they can correlate handprint rearrangements with the genetic history of the couple. Early indications are that genetics research may help prevent abnormal births and may reveal the causes of miscarriages.

Dr. Sidney Shulman, director of immunology at FRF, has said that in up to 30 percent of couples with long-term infertility an immune response to the man's sperm plays a significant role. In researching this problem for treatment of infertility, Dr. Shulman hopes to come up with an effective form of fertility regulation. If he can find out what causes sperm antibodies to appear in infertile persons, then he hopes to isolate the specific antigen on the sperm that stimulates antibody development and prepare a contraceptive "vaccine." Dr. Shulman has also found that in two-thirds of the cases of men who want a vasectomy reversal, immune reactions have developed as a result of the vasectomy. At the moment there is no effective treatment for sperm antibodies in men.

Dr. Landrum B. Shettles, director of research at FRF, is doing work in sperm morphology. Little is known about variations in sperm morphology, but there may be

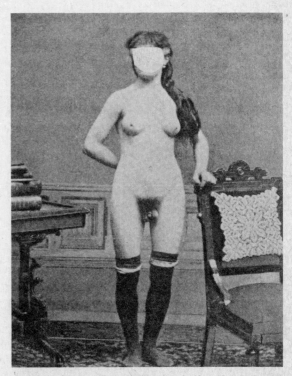

Nineteenth century English photograph of an Hermaphrodite with the face discreetly excised to protect the subject's privacy

V.D. Venereal Disease

Venereal diseases, due to their specific nature, were dealt with at a relatively early stage in the development of medical treatment. Syphilis, in particular, is a matter of controversy among experts, many of whom assert that it did not make its appearance in Europe until 1493, when Columbus returned from the New World. By the seventeenth and eighteenth centuries it was generally referred to as the pox, with the English calling it the French disease, the French calling it the English disease and so on, *ad infinitum*. No great breakthrough in its treatment occurred, however, until Dr. Erlich discovered his "magic bullet"—arsepenimine and bismuth—in the nineteenth century. The greatest advance came during the Second World War, with the advent of sulfa drugs and penicillin, and later with the development of more sophisticated antibiotic specifics. The greatest problem with all venereal disease results from prevailing attitudes of shame and embarrassment, which still are the major hindrance to treatment.

The most spectacular sexual revolution in modern medicine has been in the field of sex-change surgery. The pioneer case was Christine Jorgensen; the most unexpected case was that of Jan Morris. Although there have been a number of books written on the subject of men undergoing sex change operations, little has been written about the opposite side of the coin outside of medical journals. It is relatively easy for surgeons to perform penectomies and to construct artificial vaginas, but the problems involved in surgically transforming a woman into a man are infinitely more difficult. Yet female-to-male surgery has been performed, despite the fact that it is impossible to construct a functional, erectile, artificial penis.

In general, the medical profession has been deficient in dealing with sexuality, and though many significant advances have been made on the laboratory and surgical-research levels, there is still a long road ahead. Too many contemporary physicians have sexual attitudes as troubled and backward as those of laymen. Indeed, Sigmund Freud himself found it so embarrassing to discuss the sexual problems of his patients face-to-face that he developed the technique of placing them on a couch to avoid eye contact. Despite these problems, there is a valuable body of sexual-medical material available at present. One of the best journals in the field is *The Medical Aspects of Human Sexuality*, published by Hospital Publications, Inc., 609 Fifth Avenue, New York, N.Y. 10017. All of the articles that have been published in this valuable periodical are listed in *The Index Medicus*, which may be consulted at any major library or medical school library which permits qualified individuals access to their facilities.

V.D. is an epidemic in the United States. Over two million cases are treated every year, to say nothing of the cases that go undetected. It is a disease that requires professional treatment, and one that can be cured if treated *promptly*. But it will not disappear by itself.

Veneral disease is not *one* disease, but a group of infectious diseases of which syphilis and gonorrhea are the more common. They are spread chiefly through sexual contact. Except for the common cold, gonorrhea has the highest rate of any communicable disease.

Syphilis is produced by a germ called *treponema pallidum* which is transmitted from the body of an infected person to a well person. The germ requires warmth, moisture, and protection from oxygen, which is why the genitals are an ideal place for it to grow. (Occasionally, syphilitic sores are found in the mouth and may be spread by kissing.) Untreated syphilis is a dangerous disease and can result in heart disease, blindness, paralysis, mental illness, and even death.

Gonorrhea is caused by a bacteria known as *gonococci* and can result in sterility, pelvic peritonitis, pharyngitis, and crippling arthritis.

Nonspecific Urethritis (NSU) is like gonorrhea, but takes longer to formulate.

Chancroid produces painful sores on the sex organs and swelling of glands in the groin.

Lymphogranuloma Venereum and **Granuloma Inguinale** both cause ulceration of the genitalia and surrounding areas.

SYMPTOMS

Penicillin and other antibiotics can cure all forms of venereal disease quite easily, if the disease is detected and treated in its early stages.

Just as anybody can get a common cold, anybody can get V.D. The main difference is that V.D. won't go away with an extra large dose of vitamin C. If you think you have V.D., see a doctor. . . . Here are the symptoms that will help you detect early signs.

● **Syphilis** has three main stages. The first sign in both men and women is the appearance of a sore called a chancre (pronounced *shanker*), which appears from ten days to three months after infection. It is usually at the location where the syphilitic germs entered the body. It looks like a pimple, a blister, or a "cold sore," and it is not necessarily painful or irritable. The chancre disappears in from anywhere up to five weeks, but the disease goes on spreading throughout the body. Because the first stage of syphilis causes only very mild physical discomfort it is often ignored. Low fever, sore throat, headache, sore mouth, and inflamed eyes are symptoms of the second stage; also possibly a localized rash as well as patchy bald spots. In later years the disease attacks the vital organs of the body, causing irreparable damage.

● **Gonorrhea.** The first sign among men is usually a discharge from the penis along with a burning or uncomfortable sensation on urination. Women may also notice a discharge, often watery and yellowish in color, although sometimes thick. Often in a woman a discharge is not noticeable, and it is only detected weeks or months later when she feels pain in the lower abdomen.

HOW TO AVOID V.D.

There is no foolproof method, but the use of a prophylactic certainly reduces risk. Washing with soap and water and urinating after sexual relations may be helpful and is recommended.

Abortion

Since the Supreme Court ruling in January of 1973, women have had more freedom to obtain an abortion. The court ruling made most of the existing state laws unconstitutional, forcing state governments to rewrite their laws. However, although special abortion clinics have been springing up all over the country, the controversy rages on. There is still a great difference in opinion on the number of weeks of pregnancy that abortions are safe or moral, this last being the most sensitive issue. For information on where to get an abortion, and the exact legal ruling in your state, contact your local Planned Parenthood Office (see our Contraception Section for Regional Office Listings).

Despite the controversy, however, opinion polls show the majority of women today feel that they should have the right to control their own bodies, and that, if they so decide, they should be able to receive an abortion with all the safe, medical, and sanitary conditions of a clinic, doctor's office, or hospital, without fear of prosecution or the danger of being victimized at the hands of the many back-street abortionists.

Similarly, there should also be laws protecting doctors, as in a recent case in Boston, Massachusetts, where one doctor was charged and convicted of manslaughter for performing an abortion, allegedly murdering the fetus, again raising the issue of whether or not life legally begins at the time of conception, at some later stage of fetal growth, or at the time the child is actually born.

TYPES OF ABORTIONS

Abortions can be categorized into two groups: early abortions which are performed up to the twelfth week of pregnancy, and late abortions, which are performed after the twelfth week of pregnancy.

The best early methods are:

● **Vacuum Aspiration.** This method is performed usually under a local anesthetic (injected into the back of the vagina). A hollow thin tube is then inserted through the cervix into the uterus, and by means of suction, the fetus is vacuumed from the uterine walls. The whole process takes from ten to fifteen minutes, and should cause the woman only minor discomfort, similar perhaps to strong menstrual cramps.

● **Menstrual Extraction.** This is a relatively new method which is performed usually up to eight or ten weeks only. In fact, many women have this process performed without necessarily having received positive pregnancy test results. It is a precaution if they realize they may have had intercourse without proper contraceptive protection and their menstrual period is late. A special tube is also inserted through the cervix into the uterus, and the uterine lining is drawn out. If the woman is pregnant, the fertilized egg will also be removed. It is a very simple and quick method, causing a minimum amount of discomfort, even though anesthetic is not often used. When this method was first developed and began to be practiced widely in London it was nicknamed "the lunch-time abortion," since it was possible for women to receive the extraction during their lunch hour.

● **Dilation and Curettage (D&C)** is another early abortion method. A D&C is used also for other things in addition to terminating pregnancies, such as removing any kind of uterine growth. Doctors differ as to the kind of anesthetic they use, some prefer just a local, while others will administer general anesthetic, putting the patient to sleep. A D&C involves the dilation of the cervix and scraping of the uterine walls with a curette, a spoonlike instrument. The fetus is then removed from the body. This operation also takes only about fifteen minutes, and again the patient may feel severe menstruallike cramps.

● **Saline Injection.** Late abortions are somewhat more complicated and generally require the patient to be hospitalized. The most common method for inducing these late abortions is by saline solution. A salt or concentrated sugar is injected through the abdomen into the uterus. This solution destroys the fetus and induces labor. The patient will experience uterine contractions similar to those experienced in childbirth, which can be painful and can last (as in actual childbirth) anywhere from a few hours to several days.

● **Hysterotomy** is like a miniature Caesarian section operation in which the fetus is removed through an incision made in the uterus through the abdomen. This method is used infrequently, as it involves actual surgery, and the patient may have to be hospitalized for a week or more.

Sterilization

In recent years voluntary sterilization of both men and women has been becoming more popular. It is reported that during 1973 over one million men received vasectomies. A vasectomy is a very minor operation, now often performed in a doctor's office without any hospitalization necessary. It involves the severence of the *vas deferens*—the upper end of the epididymis, the tube in which the sperm passes through and into the seminal fluid. A vasectomy has no physiological effects on a man at all. He continues to create hormones, sperm cells, and seminal fluid as usual; the only difference is that there are no sperm contained in his ejaculation. At present, a vasectomy is irreversible; however, research is going on to find a way that would make it possible for a man to reverse his decision should he later decide to have children.

Tubal ligation is the sealing up of a woman's fallopian tubes. Until recently this was a very complicated operation because fallopian tubes are so deeply implanted in the abdomen. However, Dr. Wheeless of Johns Hopkins Hospital in Baltimore developed a much less complicated operation. A long, thin tube known as a laparoscope (which is equipped with an electronic eyepiece), is inserted into the abdomen through a small incision made just below the navel. The "eye" searches out the fallopian tubes and they are then cut and sealed electronically. This operation is also irreversible, but again research continues.

Miscellany

It is difficult to keep completely abreast of medical research in general, let alone the field of sex. Nevertheless startling new developments are being announced continually.

Several years ago a new drug, L-dopa, was approved by the FDA for treatment of Parkinson's Disease in elderly patients. Inititial results indicated that one of the drug's side effects was to revive a dormant sex drive, and for a while there was quite a furor over its use due to assertions that it might turn out to be a powerful aphrodisiac. The storm finally settled down and the drug is still being successfully used.

A still newer medication, which is quite the opposite side of the coin, has been under study at Johns Hopkins Medical Center. Still in the experimental stages, it is medroxprogesterone acetate, a.k.a. Depo-Provera. A hormone, the compound reduces the body's natural supply of testosterone, and according to early indications, can be a valuable means of treating individuals whose compulsive, hyperactive sex drives lead them to commit sexual offenses. So far all experiments are being conducted under guarded conditions, and Depo-Provera is not available for general use.

One of the most encouraging new surgical techniques was described in an article by Aaron Latham in *New York* Magazine, Feburary 10, 1975, titled *Replaceable You.* The technique in question involved the surgical implantation of collapsible silicone rubber cylinders in the penis which were connected to a similarly implanted reservoir of fluid. The system is operated as a result of connection to a minuscule hand-operated pump. The implantation enables the patient to achieve an erection at will, and was designed by a team of medical researchers at the Baylor College of Medicine for individuals who were unable to achieve erection for purely physiological reasons.

These are merely isolated instances. Still very much the subject of hope on all fronts is the development of an advanced contraceptive "morning after" pill, a male pill, and hopefully an injectible which can have long-lasting effects. We have advanced from the horse and buggy to the spaceship since the turn of the century, and it stands to reason that the future will see parallel progress in the field of medicine.

Hogarth engraving of Mary Toft giving birth to rabbits. London, eighteenth century.

There are many other ways in which mutations can be induced, and prominent among these is increased temperature on the gonads. It has been estimated that if men would wear kilts instead of pants, temperature would be reduced enough to eliminate about half of all genetic defects. On this basis, nuclear power is 8,000 times less dangerous than wearing pants. Tight-fitting trousers warm the gonads somewhat more, so a few days of wearing them does as much damage as a lifetime of exposure to nuclear power.

Dr. Bernard L. Cohen, Director of the Scaife Nuclear Physics Laboratory at the University of Pittsburgh, in an article for Public Utilities Fortnightly, *April 25, 1974*

Bibliography

Airola, Paavo O. *Sex & Nutrition.* New York: University Publishers, 1970. 95¢

Arnstein, Helen. *What Every Woman Needs to Know About Abortion.* New York: Charles Scribner's Sons, 1973.

Boston's Womens Health Collective. *Our Bodies, Ourselves: A Book by and for Women.* New York: Simon & Schuster, 1973.

Breach, M. R. *Sterilization: Methods & Control.* New York: Butterworths, 1968. $2.50

Callahan, Daniel. *Abortion, Law, Choice & Morality.* New York: 1970. $14.95

Elliott, Hazel and Ryz, Kurt. *Venereal Disease, Treatment & Nursing.* Baltimore: Williams & Wilkins, 1972. $8.75

Educational Broadcasting Corporation. *V.D. Blues.* New York: Avon, 1973.

Fleischman, Norman, and Dixon, Peter L. *Vasectomy, Sex, and Parenthood.* Garden City, N.Y.: Doubleday, 1975. $5.95

Gebhard, Paul. *Pregnancy, Birth and Abortion.* New York: Harper & Row, 1958.

Gillette, Paul. *Vasectomy: The Male Sterilization Operation.* New York: Warner Paperback Library, 1972.

Gordon, Sol. *VD Claptrap.* Syracuse, N.Y.: Education University Press, 1972.

Granfield, David. *Abortion Decision.* Garden City, N.Y.: Doubleday, 1971. $1.45

Group for the Advancement of Psychiatry's Committee on Psychiatry and Law. *Right to Abortion: A Psychiatric View.* New York: Charles Scribner's Sons, 1969.

Haggard, Howard W. *Devils, Drugs & Doctors.* New York: Harper & Row, 1945. $6.95

Hall, Robert. *A Doctor's Guide to Having an Abortion.* New York: New American Library, 1971.

Hirschfield, Magnus. *Sexual Pathology: A Study of Disarrangement of the Sexual Instinct.* New York: Emerson, 1939. $5.00

Hoch, Paul H., and Zubin, Joseph, eds. *Psycho-Sexual Development in Health Disease.* New York: Grune & Stratton, 1949.

Jackson, James C. *Sexual Orgasm: Its Healthful Management.* New York: Arno Press, 1974. $15.00

Jacob, François, and Wollman, E., eds. *Sexuality and the Genetics of Bacteria.* New York: Academy Press, 1961. $17.50

Kanaby, Donald, and Kanaby, Helen. *Sex, Fertility and the Catholic.* New York: Alba House, 1964. $2.50

Kando, Thomas. *Sex Change: The Achievement of Gender Identity by Feminized Transsexuals.* Springfield, Ill.: C. C. Thomas, 1973. $7.50

Kasirsky, Gilber. *Vasectomy, Manhood & Sex.* New York: Springer-Verlag, 1972. $5.95

Krafft-Ebing, Richard von. *Psychopathia Sexualis—A Medico Forsenic Study.* Translated by F. J. Rebman. New York: G. P. Putnam's Sons, 1969.

Lader, Lawrence. *Abortion II. Making the Revolution.* Boston: Beacon Press, 1973.

Lader, Lawrence, ed. *Foolproof Birth Control: Male & Female Sterilization.* Boston: Beacon Press, 1973.

Lief, H. I. *Sex Education in Medicine.* New York: Spectrum, 1975.

Mace, David. *Abortion: The Agonizing Decision.* Nashville: Abingdon, 1972.

Mittwoch, Ursula. *Sex Chromosomes.* New York: Academy Press, 1967. $18.50

Money, John, and Green, Richard, eds. *Transsexualism and Sex Re-Assignment.* Baltimore: Johns Hopkins, 1969.

Morton, R. S. *Venereal Disease.* Baltimore: Penguin, $1.25

Neuman, Hans, and Simmons, Sylvia. *The Straight Story on V.D.: A Doctor Answers 201 of the Most Common Questions.* New York: Paperback Library, 1973.

Nicholas, Leslie. *Sexually Transmitted Diseases.* Springfield, Ill.: C. C. Thomas, 1974. $14.50

Noonan, John T., Jr., ed. *The Morality of Abortion: Legal and Historical Perspectives.* Cambridge: Harvard University Press, 1970.

Ohno, S. *Sex Chromosomes and Sex Linked Genes.* New York: Springer-Verlag, 1967. $12.00

Perkins, Robert, L. *Abortion, Pro, Con and Maybe.* Cambridge: Schenkman Publishing, 1974. $7.95 (cloth), $3.95 (paper)

Richard R. *Venereal Disease and Its Avoidance.* New York: Holt Rinehart & Winston, 1974. $2.50

Symbol of fertility. Stained glass window in a German church, fifteenth century

Rosebury, Thedor. *Microbes and Morals. The Strange Story of Venereal Disease.* New York: Viking Press, 1971.

Rosen, Harold., ed. *Abortion in America.* Boston: Beacon Press, 1974. $2.95

Rossman, Isadore. *Sex, Fertility and Birth Control.* New York: Stravon Educational Press, 1967. $6.95

Saltman, Jules, and Zimering, Stanley. *Abortion Today.* Springfield, Ill.: C. C. Thomas, 1973. $7.95 (cloth), $4.95 (paper)

Sarvis, Betty, and Rodman, Hyman, eds. *Abortion Controversy.* New York: Columbia University Press, 1974. $10.00

Scheiman, Eugene. *Sex Can Save Your Heart . . . and Life!* New York: Crown, 1974. $6.95

SIECUS. *Sexuality and Man.* New York: Charles Scribner's Sons, 1970. $6.95

Sloane, Bruce R. *Abortion: Changing Views and Practice.* New York: Grune & Stratton, 1971. $8.50

Steinach, Eugene. *Sex and Forty Years of Biological and Medical Experiments.* 1940. Reprint. Washington: McGrath, 1970. $15.00

Stoller, Robert. *Sex and Gender. On the Development of Masculinity and Femininity.* New York: J. Aronson, 1968. $12.50

Trall, R. T. *Sexual Physiology.* New York: Arno Press, 1974. $16.00

Williams, Walter, W. *Sterility: The Diagnostic Survey of the Infertile Couple.* Baltimore: Williams & Wilkins, 1964. $28.50

Wilson, Robert A. *Sex and Drugs.* Chicago: Playboy Press, 1973. $8.95

Young, William C., ed. *Sex and Internal Secretions.* 2 vols. Baltimore: Williams & Wilkins, 1961. $25.00

Miscellanea Sexualis

THE BATH BOOK

by GREGORY
and BEVERLY FRAZIER

Illustrations by Bruce W. Martin

"*I*f you can't find it anywhere else, it's here." As you peruse this chapter you will discover an olla podrida *of curiosa, verse, games, and serious factual material, from the valuably educational to the wildly outrageous.*

Sex and Advertising

*I*n the definitive article "Sex and Advertising" by Dr. Charles Winick, Professor of Sociology, City College of the City University of New York, which appeared in the April 1971 issue of *Sexual Behavior*, he said, "More than a generation ago Philip Wylie created a sensation when he suggested, in *A Generation of Vipers*, that a central message of much advertising was, 'madam, how good are you in bed?' the latent message of much current advertising, 'dear sir or madam, our product can help you be more sexually with it.' And, 'sexually with it' now has many more meanings than when Wylie's book appeared."

This underlying philosophy applies to virtually every product in the market place from deodorants to automobiles. For example the travel field is with enticing come rife-ons such as "I'm Cindy . . . Fly me," or "Do it the French way," and that airline that "moves its tail for you," to say nothing of the car rental firm that "tries harder." If the sexual theme was taken out of advertising tomorrow, Madison Avenue would be reduced to rubble and the manufacturers and merchants of the world would be suddenly bereft of their most potent selling tool.

Not a great deal has been written on the subject, particularly for the general public. However, here is a list of the most significant recent articles on sex in advertising.

"How Sexy Illustrations Affect Brand Recall" by Major Stadman (Abbott Laboratories Ltd.). *Journal of Advertising Research*. Vol. 9. No. I. Pages 15-19.

"Nudity and Sex in Advertising" by George L. Griffin. *Sexology*. July 1970. Pages 8-11.

"Sex and Advertising" by Charles Winick, Ph.D., *Sexual Behavior*, April 1971. Pages 36-40, 62-64, and 79.

"Sex and the Serpent on Madison Avenue" by Arthur Asa Berger. *Human Behavior*. June 1973. Pages 73-76.

"Sexually Polarized Products and Advertising Strategy" by John R. Stuteville. *Journal of Retailing*. Vol. 47. No. 2. Summer, 1971. Pages 3-13.

In summation it is appropriate to quote the maverick adman Jerry Della Femina, who wrote *From Those Wonderful Folks Who Gave You Pearl Harbor*, an exposé on the advertising industry. Discussing the subject of vaginal sprays, he said: "Let's say that there's this woman who is uptight about herself, really uptight about herself, and consequently she is just not able to enjoy sex. She really feels uncomfortable about herself. And let's say that one day this woman goes out and buys a bottle of Feminique and psychologically she now feels like she is fantastically sparkling clean, bright, or whatever. And let's say that night when her husband comes home or her boyfriend comes in, she jumps on him. And for the first time in her life, she has an orgasm. Now I sold her the Feminique and I created one extra orgasm. I deserve the Nobel Prize."

Sex and Fashion

When *homo sapiens* first donned attire, the primary purpose was to keep warm. In the early development of civilization men and women recognized the seductive value of judiciously covering those parts of the anatomy that in reality they were most anxious to make the focal point of attention. As a consequence, today it is almost universally accepted that appropriate dress is infinitely more attractive to potential sexual partners than total undress.

What could be more illustrative of this than the contemporary world of fashion. One need only turn to the designs of such trend-setters as Rudi Gernreich, Giorgio Di Sant' Angelo, Yves St. Laurent, and Halston, referred to recently by *New York Magazine* as the "High Priest of Sexy." See for yourself, peruse the pages of *Vogue, Harper's Bazaar*, and *Elle*. As the saying goes, one picture is worth a thousand words.

A Rustle of Sheets -the Bed

Merry Eden and Richard Carrington, authors of *The Philosophy of the Bed*, came directly to the point when they said, "about a third of the normal human life is spent in the horizontal position, and from the earliest times man has recognized that this far from inconsiderable period should be passed as pleasurably as possible."

From the straw pallet to the water bed, this essential piece of furniture has been the principal tool for practitioners of the World's Oldest Profession as well as the meeting or mating place for the rest of mankind—the cradle of procreation as well as recreation.

> *Though I be wooden Priapus (as thou see'st),*
> *With wooden sickle and a prickle of wood,*
> *Yet will I seize thee, Girl! and hold thee seized*
> *And this, however gross, withouten fraud*
> *stiffer than lyre-string or than twisted rope*
> *I'll thrust and bury to thy seventh rib.*
>
> *Epigram on Priapus from* Priapeia,
> *London, 1889*

Sex Education

At last we are able to heave a sigh of relief. Some sensible, intelligent, and *accurate* books are being written on the subject of sex education for young children and teenagers, as well as their parents, and guardians' approach on how to instruct children about what is often referred to as "the facts of life."

Mentioned here are several of the more important and explicit books written; for complete listings and advice on books for yourself and your children, contact SIECUS (Sex Information and Education Council of the United States), 122 East 42nd Street, New York City. (Telephone: (212) 661-7010)

SHOW ME

This is a picture book of sex designed for young children and their parents. "It is an explicit, thoughtful, and affectionate picture book designed to satisfy children's curiosity about sex and sexuality—their own as well as that of their elders. In a series of sixty-nine beautiful double-page photographs accompanied by a running commentary assembled from actual reactions of children to the photographs, it explains and illustrates sexual development from infancy through adulthood." It was an original German publication with the explanatory text written by Dr. Helga Fleischhauer-Hardt translated and adapted for the English edition by Hilary Davies. The photography is by Will McBride. *Show Me* drops the euphemistic double-talk of the past in favor of frankness, candor, humor, and love. The authors hope that the book "will serve parents and children as a source of information and facilitate their passage to a more happy sexuality, one marked by love, tenderness, and responsibility." It is published as an oversized book by St. Martin's Press for $12.95.

THE SEX HANDBOOK

This is a guidebook written for teenagers (under eighteen). The book emphasizes practical information, the hard facts about losing your virginity, having sexual intercourse, birth control,

Illustration from the new sex education book for children: Show Me. *Reprinted with permission of St. Martin's Press. English language edition copyright © 1975 by St. Martin's Press, Inc. New York. German language edition © 1974 by Jugenddienst-Verlag Inc.*

Illustration from the new sex education book for children: Show Me.
Reprinted with permission of St. Martin's Press. English language edi-
tion: Copyright © 1975 by St. Martin's Press, Inc., New York.

German Language edition © 1974 by Jugenddienst-Verlag

venereal diseases, homosexuality, abortion, masturbation, orgasm, the law, and every other aspect of a normal, functioning
sex life. The book is written in a very matter-of-fact style; it
does not deal with emotions or love per se, but it *is* very
comprehensive and *accurate*. It should be noted that the language of the book is punctuated with everyday, sexually explicit terms. It is published by Putnam, written by Heidi Handman and Peter Brennan, and is priced at $6.95 and recom-
mended for all level-headed teenagers.

On the subject of adolescent sexuality in America, the *Soren-
son Report* should be consulted. Published by World, *Adolescent Sexuality in Contemporary America* by Robert C. Soren-
son is a total study of the personal values and sexual behavior
of young adults from the ages of thirteen to nineteen. This is
not a sex education book, but a study of the sexual attitudes
of young people.

Other Suggested Sex Education
Reading Materials are: for Children:

Where Do Babies Come From? by Margaret Sheffield and
Sheila Bewley. Published by Alfred A. Knopf, New York.
1972.

For Early Teens:

Girls and Sex by Wardell B. Pomeroy. Published by Delacorte,
New York. 1969.

Boys and Sex by Wardell B. Pomeroy. Published by Delacorte,
New York. 1968.

Sex and Birth Control. by E. J. Lieberman and Ellen Peck.
Published by T. Y. Cromwell, New York. 1973.

For Late Teens, Parents, and Teachers:

The Individual, Sex, and Society by Carlfred B. Broderick and
J. Bernard. Johns Hopkins Press, Baltimore. 1969.

Your Child and Sex by Wardell B. Pomeroy. Delacorte, New
York. 1974.

Sexuality and Man. SIECUS (Sex Education and Information
Council of the U. S.) Scribner's, New York. 1970.

Kiddie Sex

*T*he Guyon Society, 324 South First Street,
Alhambra, California 91802, advocates sexual freedom for
young children. Their slogan is: "Sex by the age of eight or
else it's too late." They favor laws permitting children of
twelve to have sexual relations with anyone they choose,
provided they use contraceptives. For further information,
write the society and send them a #10 size self-addressed
envelope with 20¢ postage.

Hello

Hi,
I'm kind of the "shy type" and this is
really embarrassing for me.
Would it be too forward of me to invite
you over for a kind of "get acquainted"
cocktail?
It would be just swell talking to you about
where you are from, and discussing the
weather and everything, then we could fuck.

A Child's Sexual Bill of Rights

WHEREAS a child's sexuality is just as much a part of cos whole person from birth as the blood that flows in cos veins, making cos sexual rights inherent and inalienable and

WHEREAS the United Nations Organization proclaimed a Universal Declaration of Human Rights in 1948, stating everyone is entitled to all the rights and freedoms encompassed in this Declaration without discrimination of any kind, such as race, color, sex, language, religious opinion, national or social origin, birth, or other status and

WHEREAS a Declaration of the Rights of the Child was proclaimed by UNO in 1959, but no mention was made of the sexual needs and rights of children, and

WHEREAS a child not allowed to express all the instinctive desires nature endowed co with becomes an unhappy, frustrated antisocial being and potential criminal, and

WHEREAS it is time the people of the United States and their lawmakers recognize these facts of life and act accordingly, *Therefore,* the following inalienable rights are specifically set forth, to be implemented by appropriate legislation on a national and state level, and measures taken for the reeducation of the citizenry in every part of the United States, this education to be available free to every citizen, whether school child, or adult:

A Child's Sexual Bill of Rights

1. LEGAL PROTECTION
Every child shall be legally protected in cos sexual rights, regardless of age or status as a legal minor.

2. CHILD'S RIGHT TO COS OWN PERSON
Each child has the right to privacy for cos own personal thoughts, ideas, dreams, and exploration of cos own body without any kind of adult interference, directly or indirectly expressed.

3. SEX INFORMATION
Every child has the right to accurate sex information and to be protected from sex misinformation as soon as co is able to understand this information in simple terms.

4. EMOTIONAL GROWTH
Each child has the right to grow mentally, physically, emotionally, and spiritually as a free, uncrippled happy person in security so co will be tolerant and appreciative of other individuals and their sexuality.

5. SENSUAL PLEASURES
Each child has the right to fully enjoy the sensual pleasures co may feel without shame or guilt.

6. LEARNING THE ART OF LOVE
All children have the right to learn the art of love beginning at any age co is able to understand, just as co is entitled to learn any other art or skill.

7. CHOICE OF A SEX PARTNER
Every child has the right to loving relationships, including sexual, with a parent, sibling, other responsible adult or child, and shall be protected and aided in doing so by being provided with contraceptives and aids to prevent venereal disease.

8. PROTECTION FROM SEX SUPPRESSION
Each child has the right to be protected from any form of sex suppression at home or in society so that in adulthood co will be capable of living cos sex life according to cos natural desires and not according to the dictates of tradition.

A CHILD'S SEXUAL BILL OF RIGHTS was written by Valida Davila, leader and guiding spirit of the San Francisco Sexual Freedom League Childhood Sexuality Circle. In the Bill the new unisexual pronouns are used: co for he/she/him/her, and cos for his/hers.

Sexual Milestones

You've heard of the *Guinness Book of Records*; now we have over 600 sexual superlatives in *The Simons Book of Sexual Records*, originally published in England by W. H. Allen and published in the U.S.A. in 1974 by Pyramid Books, covering everything from the fastest human erection (three seconds) to the youngest incident of voluntary female coitus, aged two.

There is also Pinnacle's *Official Handbook of World Sexual Records,* which is strictly apocryphal.

Soon to be published, Kander's *Erotic File 1975* promises to contain stories, deeds, and accomplishments of unusual sexual or erotic activities, the classifications of which are limited only by the imagination. For information contact Interrelation Research Foundation, P.O. Box 567, Sunset Beach, California 90742.

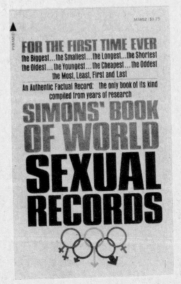

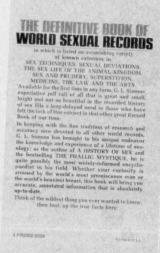

Sex and the Over Fifties

So much of the new sensual awareness and sexuality is directed toward the youth and the under-fifty age bracket. So, often, men and women who have reached the halfway mark lose faith in their own sexuality, their need or desire, and their ability to perform.

According to the studies done on the subject, these fears are totally unfounded and unnecessary. A healthy elderly man or woman can still continue to have a fulfilling sex life even into his or her eighties or older. The only difference is that it may take a little longer, but then, someone sixty doesn't run up the stairs as fast as someone only twenty-five.

For women, menopause has often been misinterpreted as the end of her active sex life, but this is just not true. Some women stride through menopause without even a hesitation, whereas others admittedly suffer definite problems varying from hormone imbalances requiring hormone replacement to treat the hot flashes and nervousness of "change of life" to just being a little extra grumpy in the mornings.

Hormone replacement, incidentally, is something that Masters and Johnson advocate in their book, *Human Sexual Inadequacy*, one of the first works to bring to light startling and revolutionary facts about the sex lives of the over fifties.

One other interesting point that should be made in favor perhaps of our senior years is that because of the lessened ejaculatory demand and better ejaculatory control in most men as they get older, often for the first time in their lives they discover a greater ease in satisfying their partner's need.

Getting older doesn't mean you love someone less. In fact, often the very opposite is true. In Fred Belliveau and Lin Richter's book, *Understanding Human Sexual Inadequacy*, which explains the Masters and Johnson technique, there is an excellent chapter on sex over fifty which ends: "That sexual functioning is normal in older people should be recognized and accepted. They want to maintain their sexual identity while continuing to enjoy the physical and psychological benefits that result. Our culture has conditioned aging men and women not to expect sex or to enjoy sex and it is this attitude that Masters and Johnson hope to change."

A final note. A certain Thomas Paar living in England during the reign of King Charles II was forced to do penance in public for his sexual incontinence at the ripe old age of 110!

Cassette tape recording of Letters to the Happy Hooker, *an abridgment of the bestselling book from Voice Over Books, a unit of R. M. Karen Inc., 200 Park Avenue South, New York, New York 10003*

Sex and the Handicapped

Regrettably, there is not much information available on the subject, but like any other member of our society, handicapped people who can still function sexually should be able to lead fulfilled sex lives. At the National Sex Forum in San Francisco, there have been seminars conducted and films produced specifically dealing with paraplegics and quadiaplegics and the problems they face coping with their sexual identities. For further information we recommend being in contact with the National Sex Forum: 540 Powell Street, San Francisco, California. Additionally, *Penthouse* Magazine, during 1972, ran a series of Letters to the Editor dealing with the handicapped's ways of making love, which is both interesting and informative.

Everything You Wanted to Know About Sex But Can't Find Elsewhere

Subscribe to *Sex News*, a monthly digest of news, views, events, publications, and resources. Published by P.K. Houdek, 7140 Oak, Kansas City, Missouri 64114. One-year subscription $3.00, remittance with order, or $3.50 if invoice and billing are preferred. Back issues are available, twelve for $1.00, payable with order. Please specify desired issues.

"It's like being a bitch in heat. Stand still and you're screwed. Run away and you get bitten in the ass." —
—John V. Lindsay, on being asked what it was like to be Mayor of New York. American Writer's Congress, April 26, 1971.

Provocative Pursuits in Extracurricular Pleasures

"Experts" from the time of Ovid have been pontificating on the hows, whys, and wherefores of making it with spouses (other people's), lovers, and others. Following is a suggested reading list of most recent additions to the field:

The Civilized Couple's Guide to Extramarital Adventure by Dr. Albert Ellis, Peter H. Wyden, 1972, $5.95. Pinnacle Paperback, 1973, $1.25.

The Fine Art of Picking Up Girls by Jim Deane. Pinnacle, 1972, $1.50.

How to Find and Fascinate a Mistress and Survive in Spite of It All by Will Harvey. Pocket Books, 1971, $1.50.

The Girl Watcher's Guide by Don Sauers. Pinnacle, 1972, 95¢.

How to Marry a Married Man by Mary English. Pinnacle, 1971, 95¢.

How to Marry Somebody Else's House Broken Husband by Rosina Francesca. Ashley Books, 1973, $6.95.

The Mating Trade by John Godwin, Doubleday, 1973, $7.95. Pinnacle Paperback, 1974, $1.50.

Men: How to "Make It" 365 Days a Year by Paul Warren. Pinnacle, 1971, $1.25.

Female Impregnates Female

Falling into the "Man Bites Dog" category, this seemingly astounding kind of occurrence has actually taken place from time to time throughout history. One of the earliest cases took place in the late sixteenth century in Salonika, Greece. A physician named Amatus Lusitanus reported that a woman "fresh from carnal connection with her husband" had a lesbian relationship with another woman immediately afterward, resulting in the second woman's pregnancy. A similar case was described by a New York physician in the 1930s, and another was reported in Brazil. In the latter case the patient was furious, having told her doctor, "If it is possible to have a baby by the deed and grace of the Holy Ghost, then I will say nothing. However, never, never have I had contact with a man—nor have I ever thought of such! And never has a doctor uttered such nonsense." Subsequent examination revealed that the patient had an imperforate hymen, and further investigation brought out the fact that the young woman had engaged in homosexual relations with an older woman immediately after the latter had had intercourse with a man. All of which proves that precautions are advisable even in the most unlikely situations.

Latest Word from the Male Chauvinist Pig Department – Judicial Branch

In a recent rape trial in May, 1975, New York Supreme Court Justice Edward J. Greenfield stated that man can use any crafty, manipulative, or deceitful method, from chivalry and gallantry to male chauvinist piggery or any approach short of force, to bed a woman without being guilty of rape but merely be party to a case of seduction.

Included in his ten-page decision, Judge Greenfield states:

"The question in this case is whether the sexual conquest by a predatory male of a resisting female constitutes rape or seduction. It is a fact that since before the dawn of history men with clubs have grabbed women, willingly or unwillingly, by their hair, to have their way with them.

"As we have become more civilized we have come to condemn the more overt, aggressive, and outrageous behavior of some men toward women and labeled it rape. At the same time, we recognize there are some patterns of male aggression which do not deserve the extreme penalty, in which the male objective was achieved through charm, guile, protestations of love, promises, and even deceit—where force was not employed to overcome reluctance and where consent, however reluctant, may be spelled out.

"This we label seduction and society may condone it even as we despair. There is some conduct that comes close to the line between rape and seduction. This is such a case."

When Judge Greenfield penned his decision, perhaps he thought back to what Molière had once said: "*Je prends mon bien ou je le trouve*" or "I take my stuff where I find it."

Off with that girdle . . .
Unpin that spangled breastplate which you wear,
Unlace yourself . . .
Off with that happy busk, which I envie . . .
Licence my roaving hands, and let them go
Before, behind, between, above, below.
O my America! My new found land . . .
How blest I am in this discovering thee . . .
Full nakedness, all joys are due to thee . . .
As liberally, as to a midwife, show
Thyself, cast all, yea, this white lynnen hance,
There is no penance due to innocence.
To teach thee, I am naked first; why then
What needst thou have more covering than a man?

Erotic poem written by John Donne before he took holy orders and wrote his *Devotions*. Written before 1602.

Typical example of the old "eight-pagers." Reprinted courtesy of Lone Wolf, 6311 Yucca Street, Hollywood, California 90028

Sex Comix

Throughout the 1930s and 1940s thousands of clandestinely circulated X-rated comic books, known as "eight-pagers," were eagerly devoured by drooling teenagers throughout the country. Most were parodies of famous comic strip characters. In the sixties and seventies a new variety of underground comics appeared, ranging from pure, unadulterated raunch to biting satire. An interesting series of comic books, essentially educational and feminist in approach, include *Pandora's Box Comix*, formerly *Tits & Clits*, published by Nanny Goat Productions, P.O. Box 845, Laguna Beach, California 92652. 75¢. Age statement required. Nanny Goat also produced *Abortion Eve*: "A discussion about the legality of abortion, what to expect during abortion. Head trips—before and after. And much more." For a complete overview of the entire field, see *A History of Underground Comics* by Mark Estren. Straight Arrow Books, $9.95.

Reproduced by permission of Nanny Goat Productions. Copyright © 1973, Chin Hyvely and Joyce Sutton

Stationery

A unique line of erotic postcards and stationery created by artist Fran Shapolsky is highly decorative. Direct inquiries c/o Downstairs Mail Service, 167 W. 31st Street, New York, New York 10011.

Greeting Cards

Discreetly displayed in the racks of stationery stores operated by the bolder dispensers of prepackaged sentiments and greetings are assorted items that will never find their way into the Mother's Day rush, and only occasionally during other holiday seasons.

Among the most far-out of the genre are produced by a firm headed by Ms. Marcia Blackman, formerly Managing Editor of *Screw*. Her lascivious gems, which include "Pussy Prints" and "Raunchy Riting Pads," are best ordered direct from American Mother Phucker Greeting Card Company, Box 635, Tiburon, California 94920.

Another intriguing line of cards is available from The Pornbroker Collection. Direct inquiries to Photomics, P.O. Box 1267, Radio City Station, New York, New York 10019.

From the Pornbroker collection.

© Jon Stevens 1973.

Reproduced with permission

The Annual Sex Maniac's Diary

The Annual Sex Maniac's Diary was created and written by Ms. Tuppy Owens of London, and elaborately designed by Mr. Robin Ray.

This is an all-inclusive calendar and treasure chest of information, something that no self-respecting sex maniac could possibly do without.

It includes sexy places to stay around the world, a personal chart for your sexual progress, "where to get away with more," "sex games for two or more," such as "sexy forfeits," "panties in your pocket," "body oil slither," "the ravishing rapuse strikes again," "pass the dildoe," and "shuttle suck."

There are recommendations for the best sexual positions for each of the 365 days of the year, witty sayings, and cartoons, not to mention a section at the end to list your favorite "undresses."

For your very own copy or for information as to where it can be purchased in the United States, write: Cand Haven Ltd., 51 South Street, London, W.1. England.

The latest sex manual, from the girl who brought you the Sex Maniac's Diary, *and* The Summer Holiday Sex Manual

The week of December 1st, 1975 from Tuppy Owens' Sex Maniac's Diary. *Copyright © 1974 Tuppy Owens. Reproduced with permission*

The 1975 SEX MANIAC'S DIARY

December Week 1

The whorehouse in Pemberton Lane
Is a place I shan't visit again
They sell fancy vices
At outrageous prices
And my bank account's feeling the strain.

	1 Mon	2 Tue	3 Wed	4 Thur	5 Fri	6 Sat	7 Sun	sex position of the day Tel. nos.
8								
9								
10								
11								
12								
1pm								
2								
3								
4								
5								
6								
7								
8								
9								
10								
11								
12								
1am								
2								
3								
4								
5								
6								
7								

Spirit of Seventy Sex

As America approaches its bicentennial it is appropriate to celebrate the publication of *The Spirit of Seventy Sex* —by Julie and Philip Sinep, who dedicated the book to:

"...the scores of unselfish Americans who bravely tested the sundry dildoes, love creams, vibrators, dongs, dingers, and hundreds of other items..." If you would like to continue on in the true democratic American tradition of sexual exploration, we suggest you write for your very own copy of *The Spirit of Seventy Sex* to Philharmonic Press Limited, 516 Fifth Avenue, New York, N.Y. 10036, sending $8.95 plus $1.50 for postage and a statement that you are twenty-one or older.

How to Become a Mail Order Sex Merchant

Moe Shapiro, who specializes in mailing lists and advertising, promises to make you a bundle if you make enquiry first. Address is 799 Broadway, New York, New York 10003. Phone: (212) 982-8575.

Future Shock

Prelude 2 is the first known vibrator marketed specifically for masturbation. It comes complete with a specifically designed attachment for stimulation of the clitoris, plus other accessories to pleasure other parts of the body, and an informative booklet on how to use Prelude 2 by yourself or with a partner. It is an attractive bright orange color, and is completely silent. It is manufactured by the Sensory Research Corporation in New Jersey and is available for $22.95 plus $1.50 handling charge from Eve's Garden, 115 West 57th Street, New York, New York 10019.

A Knight delights in hardy Deeds of arms;
Perhaps a Lady loves sweet Musick's charms,
Rich men in Store of Wealth delighted be;
Infants love dandling on the Mother's knee
Coy Maids love something, Nothing I'll express,
Keep the first Letters of these lines, and guess.

Acrostic, **John Wilmot,
2nd Earl of Rochester**

"The thing that takes up the least amount of time and causes the most trouble is sex."

—*John Barrymore*

A Unique Boutique for Transvestites

Michael Salem's T.V. Boutique
107 East 59th Street
New York, New York 10017
(212) 371-6877

With its stock of lacy lingerie, frilly feminine apparel, sheer panty hose, and $50 silicone breasts, this unique boutique is on the "must" list for the smart cross-dresser.

Release announcing the first university course ever offered anywhere on pornography, a milestone for the New School for Social Research

THE NATION'S FIRST ILLUSTRATED COLLEGE
PORNOGRAPHY COURSE ARRIVES AT THE NEW SCHOOL OCT. 3

Pornography — or what society labels pornography — can titillate and irritate, please and offend, and the reasons why it triggers these reactions is the subject of this course. The political, economic, moral, legal, artistic, and psychological aspects of pornography are investigated and illustrated in panel discussions and presentations that draw upon experts in the field. The emergence of pornography as a national fad through such films as Deep Throat will be commented upon as well as the Supreme Court's recent anti-pornography ruling. Artists, writers, producers, social critics, actors and actresses, rock musicians, publishers and lawyers as well as activists in the movement against pornography will offer their own views. Surprise guests.

Earl Wilson, Jr., author/composer of **Let My People Come** and defunct Underground Tonight Show hostess, Janet Himselstein. Photo by Lisa Hoffman

Bernhardt J. Hurwood, editor of THE WHOLE SEX CATALOGUE, interviewing Wendy Blodgett, winner of the first Ms. All Bare America pageant, during press conference at Sardi's Restaurant, New York. Photo by Rod Swenson, Jr.

Sic Transit Gloria Department

When former director of publications Michael C. Luckman, at New York's New School for Social Research, offered a course on Pornography in the fall semester of 1973, it included the Kumquats, the world's first erotic puppet show; lectures by such luminaries as Barney Rosset, publisher of Grove Press; Kenneth Norwick of the New York Civil Liberties Union; porno stars Marilyn Chambers and Marc Stevens; playwright Tom Eyen; feminist Claudia Dreifus; Goldstein and Buckley of *Screw*; as well as a performance by topless cellist Charlotte Moorman and a number of prominent female erotic artists. Alas, "it hit the fan." Luckman was fired, the course was canceled, and despite enthusiastic approval of all students and extensive press coverage, prudery and repression emerged triumphant.

Having been thwarted by the New School, the doughty Mike Luckman launched the Underground Tonight Show on Cable T.V., featuring guests from the celebrated Mrs. Miller of Johnny Carson fame to Gerard Damiano, director of *Deep Throat*, not to mention every luminary in the sexual subculture. Once again Luckman's luck failed him; the cable people developed a severe case of "chicken" and canceled the show.

In 1974, entrepreneur Gerry Brandt, who conceived the Electric Circus in the sixties, decided to turn his electricity to eroticism in hopes of topping himself. It was the circus to end all circuses, but the sexy Big Top collapsed in infancy.

Nude Pageants

It was only a matter of time before someone got the idea of spinning off from the chaste and goody-goody Miss America Pageant. To date there have been two, one in the Midwest, and the other on the East Coast. The former, a madcap hyped-up exercise in grist for silly-season journalism, is Dick Drost's annual Miss Nude America bash, held at his Naked City in Roselawn, Indiana. The latter, a more sophisticated affair, took off like a rocket in 1974, with a carefully planned and well-executed approach. It was the first Ms. All Bare America Pageant. Successfully carried out by one of nudism's most articulate spokesmen, Rod Swenson, Jr., emceed by NBC's Don Imus, the Ms. All Bare America Pageants both in 1974 and 1975 were held on the same day as Miss America with resounding press coverage and good-hearted, lavish festivities. It offered the biggest purse in beauty pageants anywhere in the world. The first year's winner, Wendy Blodgett, soared out of obscurity to *Penthouse* cover girl in less than one year. Judging by the success of the first two years, Ms. All Bare America, billed as "America's Honest Beauty Pageant" shows every indication of becoming an established institution.

Sister Marlane and clown at opening of the Erotic Circus. Photo by Lisa Hoffman

Left to right standing: Miss Nude America 1974, Taffy Tamara; Harry Reems; and Randy Lynn; Miss Nude America 1973. Seated, Sheryl and Dick Drost, hosts. Photo by Lionel Perry

An Ultimate Sexual Experience

The cold was intense and the evening darkening. We walked down into the wood and I spread my coat in the snow for her to lie on. Pulled her jodhpurs below her knees and felt the stinging bite of the cold on my buttocks when I let my trousers fall. I pushed into an absolutely incandescent heat. The bush burned white hot but was not consumed. The whole frozen universe was on my back with an irresistible force sinking my cock into that tight bath of incredible fire. It was not so much an illusion as a vision, I believe.

> R.V. Cassill, author of
> best selling *Doctor Cobb's*
> *Game* and forthcoming *Hoyt's*
> *Child*. (Doubleday & Co.)

Games

There are sex games and sex games, and we're not referring to "Doctor" and "House" the way we played them when we were children. Now there are a variety of games related to sexuality and often leading up to the real thing. These are strictly for us post-pubescents, and plenty of them are X-rated. Naturally, for anyone sufficiently inventive to manage without items that come in boxes, the varieties are infinite. It is easy to sexualize any number of kiddie games such as "Truth or Consequences," "Charades," even "Hide-and-go-seek." You don't need any imagination at all to figure out a limitless number of

diversions with a deck of cards, a set of dice, or even a Monopoly set. If you happen to have any literary inclinations, "Dirty-word Scrabble" can provide hours of fun, as can variations on "Perquckey."

On the other hand, provided you know where to find them and how to get them, there are any number of explicit sex games available in the commercial marketplace. There are new twists and wrinkles coming up all the time, and if you keep your eyes open, you can find all sorts of intriguing playthings, sometimes even in your friendly neighborhood bookstore. The following offers a good cross section, and every item listed is readily available through the mail if your local mercantile community happens to be on the uptight side.

A sample of adult entertainment. These games are available from Diplomat Games, Inc. P.O. Box 7333, Van Nuys, California 91406

8. A few long hard ones.

Suggestion: Try starting with 1 down as your key. This crossword features a series of two letter words, one three letter word. Almost all words contain an "o" in them.

ACROSS

DOWN

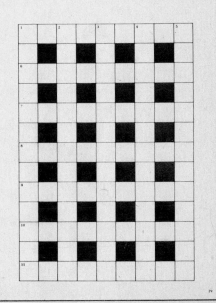

Answer on page 268

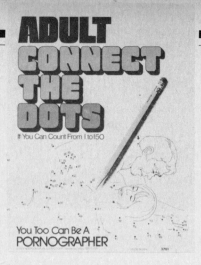

ADULT CONNECT THE DOTS

If You Can Count From 1 to 150

You Too Can Be A
PORNOGRAPHER

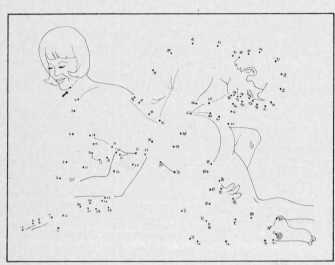

A knowledge of Latin is not necessary to understand the following . . .

*Vulva regit Scotos, vulva
ac tenet ipsa Britannos,*

*Flandros et Batavos nunc
notha vulva regit,*

*Vulva regit populos, quos
regnat Gallia partu.*

*Et fortes Gallos Italia
vulva regit.*

*Hinc furcam furiis, vulvam
conjungate vulvis,*

*Et naturae capox omnia
regina capit.*

Quotes

I think that where a marriage is fruitful and both parties to it are reasonable and decent, the expectation ought to be that it will be lifelong, but not that it will exclude other sex relations. —**Bertrand Russell**, *Marriage and Morals, 1929.*

Man does not live by head alone. —**Al Goldstein.**

Thought from a Feminist Poet, *by Linda Bisgaard*
   Cocktails? Cocktails.
   I'm so tired of male domination.
   For a change, can't we think cunttails instead?

"... as the undressed man becomes a commonplace on the magazine rack, the undressed woman is beginning to put her clothes back on." —**Russell Baker,** *New York Times,* 12/8/74.

There once was a plumber named Lee,
Who was plumbing his girl by the sea.
Said the girl, "Stop your plumbing, I hear someone coming!"
"I know," said the plumber, "It's me."

French
Il y avait plombier Dubois,
Oui Plombait sa femme dans le Bois.
Dit-elle "Arretez!"
J'entende quelqu'un venait."
Dit le plombier, en plomband, "C'est moi."

German
Es Geibt ein Arbeiter von Tinz,
Er schlaft mit ein madel von Linz.
Sei sagt, "Haltsein' plummen,
Ich hore mann kommen."
"Jacht, jacht," sagt der plummer, "Ich binz."

Latin
Prope mare erat tubulator,
Qui virginem ingrediebatur.
Desine ingressus,
Audivi progressus:
Est mihi inquit tubulator.

Graffiti

A good man is hard to find. A hard man is good to find.
(From the wall of the ladies' room at Max's Kansas City, New York)

Speed kills, fuck slow.
(From a men's room wall in a Greenwich Village bar)

The basic difference between a woman in church, and a woman in a bubble bath is that the former has hope in her soul.

Definition: Indecent, sometimes spelled *in decent*—if it's long, hard, and in deep.

Classical Dictionary of the Vulgar Tongue

SIR FRANCIS GROSE, eighteenth century

Abess, or **Lady Abess:** A Bawd, the mistress of a brothel.

Ankle. A girl who is got with child is said to have sprained her ankle.

Apple Dumplin' Shop: A woman's bosom.

Arbor Bitae: A man's penis.

Armour: In his armour, pot valiant; to fight in armour, to make use of Mrs. Phillip's ware. See Cundum (sic).

Backgammon Player: A sodomite.

Basket Making: The good old trade of basket-making; copulation, or making feet for children's stockings.

Bawbels or Bawbles: A man's testicles.

Beard Splitter: A man given to wenching.

Beast with Two Backs: A man and woman in the act of copulation, Shakespeare, in *Othello.*

Benison: The beggar's benison. May your prick and your purse never fail you.

Bite: A cheat, also a woman's privities. Example: The cull wapt the mort's bite; i.e., the fellow enjoyed the wench heartily.

Black Joke: Figuratively, the black joke figures the monosyllable. See Monosyllable.

Blow the Grounsils: To lie with a woman on the floor.

Bob Tail: A lewd woman, or one that plays with her tail; also an impotent man, or an eunuch.

Bottomless Pit: The monosyllable.

To Box the Jesuit and Get Cockroaches: A sea term for masturbation, a crime, it is said, much practiced by the reverend fathers of that society.

Brown Madam, or Miss Brown: The monosyllable.

Buck Fitch: A lecherous old fellow.

Bully Back: A bully to a bawdy house; one who is kept in pay, to oblige the regenters of the house to submit to the impositions of the mother abbess, or bawd; and who also sometimes pretends to be the husband of one of the ladies, and under that pretense extorts money from greenhorns, or ignorant young men, whom he finds with her.

Bun: A common name for a rabbit, also for the monosyllable. To touch bun for luck; a practice observed among sailors before going on a cruise.

Burning Shame: A lighted candle stuck into the parts of a woman, certainly not intended by nature for a candlestick.

Buttered Bun: One lying with a woman that has just lain with another man is said to have a buttered bun.

Buttock Broker: A bawd or matchmaker.

Buttock Ball: The amorous congress.

Capricornfield: Cuckholded, hornified.

Carvel's Ring: The private parts of a woman. Hans Carvel, a jealous old doctor, being in bed with his wife, dreamed the Devil gave him a ring, which, so long as he had it on his finger, would prevent his being made a cuckold. Waking, he found he had got his finger the Lord knows where.

Clicket: Copulation of foxes, used in a canting sense for that of men and women: as, the cull and the mort are at clicks in the dyke; the man and woman are copulating in the ditch.

Cock Bawd: A male-keeper of a bawdy house.

Cock Alley or Cocklane: The private parts of a woman.

Coffee House: To make a coffee house of a woman's ****, to go in and out and spend nothing.

Cool Lady: A female follower of the camp who sells brandy.

Commodity: A woman's commodity, the private parts of a model woman and the public parts of a prostitute.

Covent Garden Nun: A prostitute.

Crackish: Whorish.

Crinkum Crankum: A woman's commodity.

Crinkums: The foul or venereal disease.

CT:** The *xonox* of the Greek, and the *cunnus* of the Latin dictionaries.

Dells: Young buxom wenches, ripe and prone to venery, but who have not lost their virginity, which the upright man claims by virtue of his prerogative; after which they become free for any of the fraternity. Also a common strumpet.

Dildo (From the Italian *diletto*, q.d. a woman's delight, or from our word *dally*, q.d. a thing to play withal): Penis succedanuseum called in Lompardy, Passo Tempo.

To Dock: To lie with a woman. The cull docked the dell all the darkmans: the fellow lay with the wench all night. Docked smack smooth, one who has suffered an amputation of his penis from a venereal complaint.

Domine Do Little: An impotent old fellow.

Doddle Sack: A bagpipe, also the private parts of a woman.

Drury Lane Ague: The venereal disorder.

Duck Fucker: The man who has care of the poultry on board a ship of war.

Dumb Glutton: a woman's privities.

Duchess: A woman enjoyed with her pattens on, or by a man in his boots, is said to be made a duchess.

Face Making: Begetting children.

Flap Dragon: A clap or pox.

Gap Stopper: A whoremaster.

Gobble P....k: A rampant, lustful woman.

Green Gown: To give a girl a green gown, to tumble her on the grass.

To Keep It Up: To prolong a debauch.

Knock: To knock a woman, to have carnal knowledge of her.

Lady Birds: Light or lewd women.

Matrimonial Peace Maker: The sugar stick, or arbor vitae.

Merkin: Counterfeit hair for women's privy parts.

Monosyllable: Woman's commodity.

Mossy Face: The mother of all the saints.

Mutton Monger: A man addicted to wenching.

Nanny House: A brothel.

Nutmegs: Testicles.

Occupy: To occupy a woman, to have carnal knowledge of her.

Pimp Whiskin: A top trader in pimping.

Plug Tail: A man's penis.

Pucker Water: Water impregnated with alum or other ingredients, used by old experienced traders to counterfeit virginity.

Quim: The private parts of a woman; perhaps from the Spanish *quemar*, to barn.

Rantallion: One whose scrotum is so relaxed as to be longer than his penis i.e. whose shot pouch is longer than the barrel of his piece.

To Roger: To bull or lie with a woman, from the name Roger being frequently given to a bull.

Run Goods: A maidenhead, being a commodity never entered.

School of Venus: A bawdy house.

Scotch Warming Pan: Wench.

Shag: To copulate. He is but bad shag, he is no able man for a woman.

Spanish Gout: The pox.

Squirrel: A prostitute: because she, like that animal, covers her back with her tail.

Stallion: A man kept by an old lady for secret services.

State: To lie in state; to be in bed with three harlots.

Strapping: Lying with a woman.

Sugar Stick: The virile member.

Swive: To copulate.

Tackle: A man's tackle, his genitals.

Thorough Good-natured Wench: One who being asked to sit down, will lie down.

Three-Penny Upright: A retailer of love, who, for the sum mentioned, dispenses her favors standing against a wall.

Tuzzy Muzzy: The monosyllable.

Vaulting School: A bawdy house.

Venerable Monosyllable: Pudendum muliebre.

Wap: To copulate.

Westminster Wedding: A match between a whore and a rogue.

Whirlygigs: Testicles.

Whore's Bird: A debauched fellow, the largest of all birds.

Whore-Pipe: The penis.

Windward passage: One who uses or navigates his windward passage, a sodomite.

A Selected Glossary of Common Terms

Abstinence: Watching television.

Anxiety: The impotence of being earnest.

Coition: When Johnson does it to Masters.

Coitus: When Masters does it to Johnson.

Coitus Reservatus: An advance booking in a brothel.

Copulation: Sexual intercourse between a policeman and a detective.

Incest: A family get-together.

In Love: The feeling that still remains even after a man has orgasmed.

Libido: The Italian spelling of liberty.

Love Affair: When you're doing it.

Cheating: When someone else is doing it.

Lust: A feeling we all condemn, but which we would all fight to the death not to lose.

Marriage: The end of a love affair.

Masturbation: Instant sex—not dependent on strangers.

Member: A substitute word used by cowardly writers, referring to the "male."

Orgasm: Summit meeting at the bottom.

Out of Wedlock: The fire escape of marriage.

Passion: An elegant way of spelling lust.

Precoital Fluid: A scotch and soda beforehand.

Premarital Sex: Sex before marrying the man you will most likely never marry.

Premature Ejaculation: A man who has parked his car before he has reached the garage.

Private Parts: The most public part of the body—most written about, most photographed, most poked at by the opposite sex for whom it's supposed to be most private.

Promiscuity: Envy.

Womb: A nice place to go on rainy days.

Yen: A Japanese form of eroticism.

From The Goodlife, Sexually Speaking, *by Sigmund Stephen Miller, published by Prentice Hall, Inc. Copyright © 1972 Sigmund Stephen Miller. Reprinted with permission of the author.*

The Good Hostess. "Take it for yourself — I do just as well with my finger" This illustration is one of 15 beautifully produced prints from a facsimile edition of the folio Die Grenouillère *(1907) by Franz von Bayros (1866-1924). The edition is limited to 250 and is available from the Amorini Gallery, 39 Hertford Street, Mayfair, London W1, England.*

Fuck is perhaps one of the most interesting & exciting words in the English language. Fuck is the one magical word which just by its sound can describe pleasure, pain, hate, and love. Fuck comes from the German word "frikon."

In language, "fuck" falls into many grammatical categories. Fuck can be used as a verb both transitive (He fucked her) and intransitive (She was fucked by him). It can be an active verb (He really gives a fuck) or a passive verb (She really doesn't give a fuck), as an adverb (She is fucking interested in him) and a noun (She is a fine fuck). Fuck can be used as an adjective (She is fucking beautiful). As you can see there is a whole lot of real versatility with "fuck." It pops up everywhere.

Besides its sexual connotation, this lovely word can be used to describe many situations: fraud~I got fucked by that crook ✠ Dismay~Oh, fuck it! ✠ Trouble~I'm fucked now. ✠ Confusion ~What the fuck? ✠ Aggression~fuck you! ✠ Despair~fucked again! ✠ Philosophy~Who gives a fuck? ✠ Incompetence~he's a real fuck-off. ✠ Numerology~Sixty-fuckin'-Nine ✠ Rebellion-fuck it! ✠ Displeasure~What the fuck's going on? ✠ Satisfaction-fuck me again! Also, as: Descriptive anatomy~He's a fuckin' asshole. ✠ To tell time ~It's six-fucking-thirty. ✠ As a prediction~Well, I'll be fucked ✠ A political statement~fuck Washington ✠ Incestuous-Mother fucker. ✠ A put down~fuck off, buster! ✠ All encompassing~fuck 'em all! ✠ Governmental affairs~ fuck the IRS. ✠ A poker hand~A royal fuck ✠ To start a relationship~Let's fuck now ✠ As an acceptance~ fuckin' A! ✠ Enjoyment~fuckin' Wow! ✠ A closing~fuckingly yours.

Use fuck in your daily speech proudly, fuck adds prestige to any conversextion. Put this colorful four letter word to work for you; today, tell someone you know "fuck you"... or "Let's fuck."

Pin-ups, Love Goddesses, and Other Sex Symbols

*T*he definitive work on this vast subject is Mark Gabor's profusely illustrated book, *The Pin-up, a Modest History*, first published in 1972 by Universe Books, New York. He covers the entire range from prehistory to the bizarre, including objects of sexual adoration in the ranks of men, women, and children. Most of us tend to think of this area only in terms of our own experience, but Gabor gives us the works—from medieval woodblocks to posters, theatrical publicity stills, fan and girlie magazines—plus any number of other items less likely to have found their way into the hands of the general public.

Although, in the days before the big Hollywood tub thumpers, the world of show business provided ample sex symbols such as Ziegfeld Girls, Floradora Girls, *et al.,* illustrators contributed their share, notably Charles Dana Gibson, who created the famous Gibson Girl. The big breakthrough, of course, came with the advent of the motion picture starting with Theda Bara, the original "Vamp." There were the Keystone Girls, and such fabled figures as Clara Bow, "The It Girl." The roster becomes never ending—Ann Pennington, Billie Dove, Jean Harlow, Marlene Dietrich, Mae West, Lana Turner, Betty Grable, Rita Hayworth, Marilyn Monroe, Gina Lollobrigida, and Brigitte Bardot, to mention only a few. And how could we possibly ignore the men—Valentino, Gable, Bogart, Navarro, Fairbanks, *père* and *fils.* Erroll Flynn practiced in real life much of what he projected on the screen. Johnny Weismuller caused many a heart to flutter as he swung wailing from the trees. Tyrone Power, Charles Boyer, and Cary Grant, nē Archie Leach, aroused jealousy in the hearts of men around the globe. And Burt Reynolds laid a milestone by being the first big name to pose for a nude magazine centerfold.

There is one fictitious character, however, that should dampen the eyes of any man who served in the armed forces during World War Two—the fabled Miss Lace, created by cartoonist Milton Caniff. This benevolent, sexy, dragon-lady *femme fatale* presided over a feature in *Stars & Stripes* called *Male Call* and literally became den mother to lonesome G.I.'s the world over.

For those who are infected with the Nostalgia Bug it would be wise to note this important address:

YESTERDAY
174-A Ninth Avenue
New York, New York 10011
(212) 691-1615

It is a shop that specializes in old posters, original girlie-magazine cover art, and other tidbits from the past.

"When two people are under the influence of the most violent, most insane, most delusive, and most transient of passions, they are required to swear that they will remain in that excited, abnormal and exhausted condition continuously until death do them part."

—George Bernard Shaw

Sex and Athletics

The sexual overtones in the world of sports have been a dominant factor since ancient times. The athletes of Greece set the tone forever with their emphasis on bodily display and the exaggeration of movement. The gladiators of Rome provided the same thing with the added ingredient of sado-masochism inherent in the bloody fights to the death that aroused spectators to the ultimate heights of sexual release—even St. Augustine in his *Confessions* alludes to the fact.

Today, although the elements of sex and death are not played up, the morbid appetite of the crowd is as present as it was when the walls of the Coliseum rang with the roars of ferocious beasts and bloodthirsty Romans. Circus audiences watching scantily clad acrobats performing on the high wire without nets sit eagerly on the edges of their seats, waiting for the opportunity to witness the horrible spectacle of sudden death. Hockey fans reach orgasmic peaks of excitement when skulls are cracked and blood flows. Similarly devotees of boxing are frequently seen, tense, wet-lipped, and sexually aroused by the sight of glistening naked flesh, blood, and pain. Television transformed wrestling from a legitimate sport to an absurd parody, and among the most fanatical fans were grandmothers.

When Americans still had a veneer of innocence, sports and athletes were held up as examples of clean living, honor, and gentlemanly valor. There are still some who cling to the tattered dream.

Today, Jocks constitute the largest single body of male sex symbols to be found anywhere. Their debaucheries contribute as much to their charisma now as their spotless image did not so many years ago. This is not to be construed as an attack on athletes. They are human, and so are their fans. It is merely that the time has come for us to be honest and admit that we are sexual creatures and that our sexuality pervades all aspects of life, even those once erroneously and hypocritically deemed as chaste.

There once was a girl from Milpetas,

Who was very adept at coitus.

She went out on a date,

With a jock from Cal State,

And ended with athlete's foetus.

Memorandum

To: All Personnel
From: The Administration
Subject: Early Retirement

As a result of automation (as well as a declining workload) the Administration must of necessity take steps to reduce our workforce. A reduction-in-force plan has been developed which appears to be the most equitable under the circumstances. Under the plan older employees will be placed on early retirement, thus permitting the retention of employees who represent the future of the agency.

A program to phase out older personnel by the end of the current year through early retirement will be placed into effect immediately. The program will be known as *Retire Aged Personnel Early* (RAPE).

Employees who are raped will be given the opportunity to seek other jobs within the company, provided that while they are being raped, they request a review of their employment status before actual retirement takes place. This phase of the operation is called *Survey of Capabilities of Retired Early Workers* (SCREW).

All employees who have been raped and screwed may also apply for a final review; this will be called *Study by Higher Authority Following Termination* (SHAFT).

Program policy dictates that employees may be raped once and screwed twice, but may get the shaft as many times as the agency deems appropriate.

Think A Piece

How many chain letters have you gotten over the years, promising that if you don't break the chain you will receive anything from riches to an avalanche of trading stamps? We don't guarantee that you'll get anything if you send this one out—but who knows what interesting pen pals you might unearth. To save yourself some typing you might just place this face down on a photocopying machine and make the necessary number of copies.

* *

"Now has come the time of day, when work is done, it's time to play. Gazing at my martini glass [Non drinkers may substitute the words, "joint of grass" Ed.] I wish I had a piece of ass."

This prayer has been sent to you for good sex luck. The original copy came from Denmark. It has been sent around the world sixty-nine times. The luck has been sent to you. You are to receive a good piece of ass within four days after receiving this copy.

This is no joke. You will receive a good piece of ass. Please do not send money. Do not keep this letter. It must leave within 96 hours after you receive it.

A U.S. Army officer scored with a famous movie star. A prostitute received the biggest tip of her life—but lost it because she broke the chain. While in the Philippines, General MacArthur's testicles fell off six days after receiving this copy. He failed to circulate this prayer. However, before his death, he received an artificial pair.

Please send twenty copies and see what happens to you on the fourth day. Delete the first name, add your name to the bottom, buy a bottle of penicillin tablets, and get ready for the biggest screwing of your life.

Illustration by Wallace Smith to Ben Hecht's Fantazius Mallare

Mister Midwife of Texas

For a quarter of a century now, people have called Norman Casserley by the name of Mister Midwife. In September 1974 he filed an application in a Houston court to officially register this change of name. He said this action would help draw attention to the merits of lay nonmedical midwifery.

Mister Midwife, a U.S. certified, registered, licensed midwife, has delivered over 3,500 bundles of joy. He practices only Natural Homebirth, a term he trademarked in 1949 and has now filed federally in Washington. His mothers disdain the use of drugs and surgery, which often cause more complications than they allegedly cure, says the world's only male midwife. And he's right, because he has never had a death, complication, hemorrhage, flesh tear, ambulance case or hospital referral, malpractice suit, or citizen complaint!

He delights in proving that many cases scheduled as high-risk complications can be delivered normally by drawing on the body's normal physiology rather than routine interference of drugs and surgery.

Many of his clients are physician referrals, since physicians rarely visit the home nowadays. Most of his cases are either first births, pregnancies previously scheduled for Caesarian, or subteenage mothers.

In an era of ever-increasing technological complexity, there is still a place for simpler things which have proven their success over the centuries.

International Association for the Advancement of Lay Nonmedical Midwives
2890 Kerrwood Drive, Columbus, Ohio 43229
William Franklin Decker, *Chairman*

Who's Who in Sex

An all-inclusive "Who's Who in Sex" would of necessity develop into something approaching the size of *Webster's Biographical Dictionary.* The Whole Sex Catalogue "Who's Who in Sex" is an arbitrarily selected list that spans the centuries, including, along with the obvious and the celebrated, a number of lesser-known personalities whom the editors believe deserve a niche in the annals of sexuality—regardless of whether they achieved fame or notoriety in the eyes of historical arbiters past or present.

Eve (In the beginning . . .): Little need be said about this celebrated lady, other than the fact that she is regarded by fundamentalists as the mother of all mankind. However, the chief reason for her inclusion here is that she is considered to be the first woman ever to lead man astray.

Sappho (circa 600 B.C.): The immortal Greek lyric poet of Lesbos, she was also an eloquent philosopher, and her discourses made her a favorite not only of the women in her time but throughout the ages. Though she certainly did not invent lesbian love, she propagated it and declared it superior to any other form. The feminist of today would say, "Sappho was a right-on woman."

Cleopatra (69-30 B.C.): The celebrated Queen of Egypt and notorious lover of Julius Caesar and Marc Antony was certainly one of the first women in history to use her sexuality for political gain.

Tiberius Nero Caesar (42 B.C.-37 A.D.): Roman Emperor from 14 A.D. Best described by Suetonius: "In his retirement in Capri he furnished himself with whores and catamites and lewd discoverers of unnatural and bestial postures and motions: these he called Spinctria, the Incendiaries of his lust. He entertained himself in seeing them in three several rows abusing each other; thereby to excite his decayed appetite. He provided several chambers also hung about with filthy pictures and infamous statues, and furnished with the abominable books of 'Elephantis.' He invented likewise in the woods, walks, and grottoes proper for the benefits of debauchery, where young people of both sexes prostituted themselves in the masquerade of Nymphs and Satyrs. . . . He . . . debauched young children yet in innocence and ignorance (calling them his Little Fry), teaching them to play between his thighs while he swam, to lick and tongue, and sometimes suck him like infants not yet weaned; and indeed the impotency of his age and bestiality of his nature might excite in him those inclinations to such unmanly and abominable follies."

Valeria Messalina (died 48 A.D.): Roman Empress, third wife of Emperor Claudius. Notorious for her profligacy and vices, she abandoned herself to such frenetic prostitution that she was condemned to death. During her lifetime she had executed countless persons who refused to submit to her desires.

Queen of Sheba (circa 950 B.C.): Legendary Queen of Ethopia who refused to share King Solomon's bed on the grounds that if she gave up her virginity she would lose her throne and power.

Mary Magdalene (first century A.D.): The reformed prostitute who, as a result of her meeting with Jesus Christ, became a holy woman and was privileged to be the first to witness the Resurrection.

Ovid (43 B.C.-17 A.D.): Roman poet, the first writer of major stature to grow up under the empire. Although his greatest work, *Metamorphoses,* is a reflection of the disillusionment of his era, his *Ars Amatoria,* or *The Art of Love*, qualifies as the first sex manual in history (2 B.C.). Not only does it give information on how to flirt, attract lovers, and become a successful adulterer, it also gives precise and explicit details about virtually every conceivable position in the art of sexual lovemaking.

Salome (before 62 A.D.): Daughter of Herodias and granddaughter of Herod. Probably the arche type of all exotic dancers to follow her. Her great claim to fame (or infamy) is that she received the head of John the Baptist as a reward for her act.

Sabina Poppaea (died 65 or 66 A.D.): The mistress of Nero, she has been regarded by historians as a suitable partner for a madman of such depravity. She died as a result of a violent kick from her lord and master.

Petronius Arbiter (Gaius or Titus Petropius) (died 65 A.D.): Roman voluptuary poet and the reputed author of *The Satyricon,* the first Western European novel. He distinguished himself in military and political affairs but his chief talent lay in the "pursuit of pleasure." He carried on with such refined elegance that he was given the official title of the Emperor Nero's "arbiter of elegance" (*arbiter elegantiae*). He was ordered to commit suicide after being suspected of conspiracy against the Emperor and spent his last hours performing various "social pleasures and amusements" as well as compiling a catalogue of Nero's debaucheries. *Satyricon (Satyricon liber. Book of Satyrlike Adventures)* is a "picaresque" romance, relating the wanderings and escapades of a disreputable trio of adventurers.

Empress Theodora (approximately 508-547 A.D.): Said to be the daughter of a bear-feeder at the amphitheater in Constantinople, she began life as a courtesan and actress. Eventually she married the Emperor Justinian and became one of the most powerful women in the world of her day, exercising great influence over her husband. A tyrannical and capricious matchmaker, she forced men and women to take husbands and wives at the slightest whim, and as a precursor of modern feminists, she appointed herself protectress of adulterous wives despite cries of outrage from cuckolded husbands. Whatever her shortcomings, her beauty and intellectual powers sustained her until the end of her life.

Giovanni Boccaccio (1313-1375): Italian writer and humanist, one of the greatest figures of European literature. Born in Paris, he spent his early childhood and teens in Florence, then went to Naples where the King, Robert Anjou, delighted himself by being surrounded by men of letters.

Boccaccio's most celebrated work. *The Decameron,* deals largely with the sexual peccadilloes of a group of people who secluded themselves during the great plague of 1348.

Giovanni Francesco Poggio Bracciolini (1380-1459): Italian humanist, known chiefly for his literary detective work, and amazing ability to survive the deadly politics of his time. He is distinguished as having written a book, *Liber Facetiarum*, not only the first authentic best seller in Western literature (having coicided with the invention of movable type), but also the first collection of bawdy stories which became the blueprint for future authors of the genre such as Marguerite of Navarre, and Rabelais.

Thomas Parr (1483-1500): The archetypal "dirty old man," who was forced to do public penance for his uncontrolled sexual behavior at the age of 110.

John Scoggin (1480-1500): Court Jester to Edward IV of England, notorious for his ribaldry and pranks of sexual and scatological nature.

Marguerite of Navarre (1492-1549): The sister of Francis I of France and Queen of Navarre. A political activist, mysticist, and brilliant writer of poetry and prose, much of which is considered to this day as among the ranking works of lusty eroticism. It is said by some historians that her personal life was filled with episodes of debauchery.

Pietro Aretino (1492-1556): Italian author, often referred to as the "journalist of the century," the father of public relations and the greatest blackmailer of all times. His scurrilous attacks on the powerful, rich, and influential figures of his times incurred sufficient enmity to force his eventual retreat to a palatial villa in Venice, where he was safe from the numerous assassination attempts of his enemies. For his successful ventures in blackmail against royalty he was called by Ariosto "the scourge of Princes." His sensual nature and lusty life-style were reflected in the explicit sexuality of his prose. One of the great ironies in history is that he intimidated the great Michelangelo to use his likeness in a mural in the Sistine chapel, in which he appeared as Saint Bartholomew.

Aphra Behn (1640-1689): English novelist, dramatist, and spy. The first female professional writer whose often coarse novels raised eyebrows in her own time and for centuries to come. She grew up in the Dutch West Indies; Charles II of England put her fluent Dutch to work by making her a secret agent in Holland.

Charles II, (Stuart) King of England (1630-1685): Best known as the "Merry Monarch." Forced into exile during the rule of Cromwell, he ascended the throne in 1660, heralding the Restoration. The puritan era of repression in England exploded into a period of merry debauchery and sexual freedom the likes of which it had never seen before. His life was testimony to his belief that "God will never damn a man for allowing himself a little pleasure." His mistresses, the most famous of which was Nell Gwynn, bore him fourteen acknowledged offspring, all of whom he ennobled.

John Wilmot, 2nd Earl of Rochester (1647-1680): The most outstanding rake of his time, and favored courtier of King Charles II. In the words of his biographer, Charles Norman, "He blazed out his youth and health in lavish voluptuousness." As the most controversial member of Charles Stuart's court, Rochester was called in his time, "the greatest of sinners, whose tongue would tempt the angels to a second fall . . . the prince of all the devils in town . . . who delights in nothing but rapes and riots . . . the delight and wonder of men, and the dove and dotage of women . . ." and "the man in all England who has the least honour but the greatest wit." A brilliant practical joker and master of disguises, he fooled friends and strangers with equal success as he seduced women and perpetrated outrageous pranks on men. His wild irreverence and explicitly licentious language notwithstanding, he has been recognized as one of the greatest poets produced by England. He never composed his so-called obscenities to arouse, but to satirize and lampoon. As a contemporary, Robert Woleseley, wrote of Rochester, "Never was his pen drawn, but on the side of good sense, and usually employed, like the arm of ancient heroes, to stop the progress of arbitrary oppression." His addiction to drink and his sexual appetites were his downfall. Plagued periodically by bouts with the pox, he once remained drunk for a full five years, finally succumbing to the ravages of old age at thirty-three.

Nell Gwynn (1650-1687): The most popular English actress of her time, and favorite mistress of Charles II. A true child of the London streets, she was illiterate to her death, but due to her position in the heart of the King, a living antithesis of England's earlier puritanical society. It is presumed that she remained faithful to Charles II during their intimacy and subsequently to his memory after his death. On his deathbed the King begged of his brother, "Let not poor Nellie starve," and James II faithfully carried out the late Monarch's last wish, paying Nell sizable sums each month, thus settling all her debts. In 1687 she suffered a stroke and died several months later. At her funeral Thomas Tenninson (later the Archbishop of Canterbury) eulogized her, saying, "Joy shall be in heaven over one sinner that repenteth, more than over ninety and nine just persons who had no repentence."

Emund Curll (1675-1747): English publisher and bookseller who was continually in trouble with the authorities for his alleged "filthy libels" and "obscene publications," immortalized in history as "the abominable Curll." He was convicted of obscenity in 1728 for publishing a book entitled *Venus in the Cloister* or the *Nun in Her Smock;* an attack on the church, it supposedly exposed hidden sexual orgies in the confessional. No man to take his slings and arrows without a fight, he published circulars proclaiming that he was the subject of persecution for vindicating the memory of the late Queen Anne. Thus on the day he spent in the pillory he was cheered rather than reviled and emerged a hero to his readers.

Sir Francis Dashwood (Lord of Despencer) (1708-1781): Founder of Medmenham Abbey, better known as The Hellfire Club. Notorious for his predilection for practical jokes of the crudest nature, irreverence, blasphemy, drink, and womanizing, Dashwood founded his notorious club on the ancestral estate and turned it into a private preserve of lush opulence that was the scene of the most infamous orgies of his time. It was written of him that "he far exceeded in licentiousness anything exhibited since the days of Charles II." The decor was straight out of a novel by de Sade. The servants were sworn to secrecy, and the club members, or "Monks of Medmenham Abbey," numbered among their ranks members of the most influential families in Britain—Lord Sandwich, politician John Wilkes, Thomas Potter, son of the Archbishop of Canterbury. And among the illustrious foreign guests was none other than the American Ambassador, Benjamin Franklin. A contemporary writer said of Medmenham, "There was not a vice for the practising of which he [Dashwood] did not make provision. The cellars were stored

with the choicest wines, the larders with the delicacies of every climate. The cells although otherwise fairly plain, were fitted up for all purposes of lasciviousness, for which the proper objects were also provided."

John Cleland (1709-1789): English scholar, diplomat, and linguist, Cleland entered the pages of history when he wrote the notorious *Fanny Hill* while serving time in debtor's prison. The fifty guineas for which he sold this erotic masterpiece temporarily bailed him out of his financial difficulty, but the uproar created by publication of the book was his eventual salvation. As a result of the public outrage at *Fanny Hill*, the authorities forced Cleland to sign an agreement promising never to write such a scandalous work again, for which he was granted a pension of one hundred pounds a year for life.

Jeanne Antoinette Poisson Pompadour (Marquise de Pompadour) (1721-1764): Fourth and most famous of the acknowledged mistresses of Louis XV of France. At a masked ball at Versailles she attracted the attentions of Louis XV. Her reputation as a *Femme fatale* preceded her, and her talents for entertaining in music and drama some of the leading writers of the day, including Voltaire and Fontenelle, made her salon famous. Louis XV made her a Marquise, and in September of 1745 she was formally presented to the Queen at Versailles, thus being recognized as the King's *maîtresse en titre*. A little known fact concerning Pompadour's career is that after studying under the tutelage of France's finest artists she became a skilled etcher and engraver. A number of her works were highly erotic. One collection of her etchings, consisting of 65 plates, was published the year she died, 1764. Its title in literal translation was *My Leisures, dedicated to My Friends, a small collection to excite the fervor of the faithful, to the Matins of Cythera. By an Amateur of the Office.*

Giovanni Jacopo Casanova (1725-1798): Venetian adventurer, philanderer, lover, and sensualist. His peripatetic wanderings took him from one end of Europe to another. He consorted with royalty and rogues, made and lost fortunes, forever leaving in his wake scandal and broken hearts. In addition to their great entertainment value, his memoirs are considered to be of great historical significance. The fact that his name has come into the language as a noun meaning "great lover" attests to his permanent niche in the annals of sexual history.

Catherine the Great (1729-1796): Empress of Russia from 1762 to 1796. Her private life was the object of curiosity and interest throughout Russia and her scandalous affairs with agents, ministers, and friends at her court later became the talk of Europe. Catherine succeeded to the throne after the Grand Duke (her husband) had reigned for a short time. She and one of her lovers, Grigrior Grigorievich Orlov and his brother, Aleksei, persuaded the guards to undertake a coup d'état, and secretely escorted her to St. Petersburg where she was acclaimed as Empress. Her only son, Peter, is presumed the son of the Grand Duke solely because of their incredible physical likeness. It is said that Catherine had almost insatiable sexual appetites and that she would mount or be mounted by virtually anything from a horse to a cossack regiment.

Restif de la Bretonne (1734-1806): French novelist and contemporary of the Marquis de Sade, nicknamed "The Rousseau of the Gutter" and the "Voltaire of Chambermaids." A number of his works were distinctly pornographic, notably *"The Anti-Justine"* or *"The Memoirs of a Good Natured Libertine,"* written as a protest to the cruelties depicted in the works of Sade. His mammouth work, *Monsieur Nicholas,* is regarded to this day as providing the definitive picture of life in the streets of Paris during his time.

Compte Donatien Alphonse François de Sade (better known as the Marquis de Sade) (1740-1814): French nobleman, soldier, author, and philosopher. A direct descendant of Laura de Sade, immortalized in the poetry of Petrarch, Sade was an extremely handsome young man, betrothed at an early age by his impecunious family to the daughter of a wealthy middle class mercantile family anxious for a liaison with the nobility. By making the unfortunate error of falling in love with the wrong sister, he incurred the everlasting emnity of his mother-in-law, a forceful, determined, and powerful woman. It was due largely to her efforts that he spent much of his life in prison, where he channeled all of his bitterness, hatred, and frustration into his literary works. Once in his life did he actually become personally involved in a situation which today would be called sado-maschostic—the notorious Rose Keller affair. Although he did, during his brief periods of freedom, participate in orgies and produce sexually oriented plays which he had written, his chief efforts were devoted to the novels which earned him everlasting notoriety. While imprisoned in the Bastille during the French Revolution, he incited mobs to violence by hanging inflammatory banners and slogans out the windows. Eventually gaining his freedom during the height of the Revolution, he was regarded as an acceptable aristocrat as "Citizen Sade," and given an official position. His bitterness, however, was too firmly ingrained, and after the ascent of Napoleon to the throne of the first empire, he again made enemies in high places and was committed to a fashionable Paris insane asylum, where he spent the rest of his life writing and producing plays with inmates as performers. Despite his infidelities, his wife remained fiercely loyal to the end. What few people know about de Sade is that despite his reputation, he was one of the most prominent literary figures to advocate the abolition of capital punishment, saying that to execute a murderer accomplished nothing more than to make society a murderer as well.

Thomas Bowdler (1754-1825): A simple-minded English physician who in the year 1818 had the effrontery to publish a ten-volume edition of William Shakespeare's works "in which nothing is added to the original text; but those words and expressions are omitted which cannot with propriety be read aloud in a family." After having profited somewhat by this outrage upon immortal literature, he performed a similar castration on Gibbon's *Decline and Fall of the Roman Empire*. As a result of his rapacity against the printed word Bowdler's name entered the language as a synonym for censorship or expurgation as in *to bowdlerize.*

Lady Emma Hamilton (1761-1815): Born Emma Lyon, Lady Hamilton's incomparable beauty preceded her reputation and led to many famous affairs with the infamous and influential of her times, including the period when she attained notoriety as "Vestina, the Rosy Goddess of Health" while in the employ of the charlatan, Dr. James Graham. A series of underground drawings for which she posed in the nude, known as "Lady Hamilton's Postures," were for a time the rage of London collectors of erotica. The affair that shocked London and Europe the most was her long-standing relationship with Lord Nelson. Her life of art, beauty, and charm, after Nelson's death at Trafalgar, despite his "bequest of her to the nation," plunged her tragically into debt and debilitation. But despite her unhappy end, she lives on in history as a glittering symbol of glamour and sensuality.

Madame Restell (18 -1878): Before, during, and after the Civil War, Madame Restell was the most notorious and successful abortionist in New York. Having amassed a fortune by the 1870s, she purchased a palatial mansion on Fifth Avenue and continued to pursue her career until driven to suicide by the fanatical Anthony Comstock in 1878.

Sir Alexander James Edmund Cockburn (1802-1880): Eminent British judge who eventually became Lord Chief Justice and who was responsible in 1857 for an act enabling the police to seize and destroy "obscene" publications, works "Written with the single purpose of corrupting the morals of youth, and other nature calculated to shock the feeling of decency in any well-regulated mind." He was the man who first used the phrase "to deprave and corrupt" in connection with allegedly obscene literature.

Wilhelmine Schröder Devrient (1804-1860): Best known to the music world for her electrifying portrayal of "Pamina" in Mozart's *Magic Flute*. She is alleged to have written a private memoir discovered posthumously by a nephew who later had it published. According to this manuscript she lost her virginity in Frankfurt immediately after her Viennese debut. After this her autobiographical reminiscence seemed to come straight out of Krafft-Ebing. Her exploits involved lovers of both sexes and all sexual persuasions. It describes orgies, and debaucheries from bestiality to necrophilia. If this memoir is indeed authentic, it is miraculous that she survived to the age of fifty-six.

Joseph Smith (1805-1844): Founder of the Mormon Church, despotically ruling his small group of followers, he was eventually arrested and imprisoned in Carthage, Illinois, by non-Mormon enemies who objected to his doctrine of polygamy. Seized and taken from jail by a lynch mob on June 27, 1844, he was shot to death, leaving behind a multitude of widows. Although the church eventually repudiated polygamy, Brigham Young, who led the Mormons to Utah, had 26 wives. Though indicted for polygamy in 1871, he was never convicted.

John Humphrey Noyes (1811-1886): Graduate of Dartmouth College, his mother was the aunt of United States President Rutherford B. Hayes and an orthodox religious reformer. He formed a commune in 1836, expounding the gospel of perfectionism which included pure communism (in 1848 he published a tract entitled *Bible Communism*). Among his beliefs were group marriage, regarded as scandalous free love by his contemporaries. Forced to flee his original community in Putney, Vermont, in 1848, he founded the Oneida Community in New York State where, thanks to the industriousness and single-minded purpose of the commune members, a flourishing business was established in the manufacture of mouse traps and fine silver, which to this day is marketed as Oneida Community silverware. Noyes eventually was forced to flee to Canada to avoid prosecution for adultery. He died in Niagara Falls, Ontario.

Lola Montez (1818-1861): Celebrated British dancer and adventuress of great beauty and magnetic personality. As mistress of Louis the First of Bavaria, she was granted the titles of Baroness of Rosenthal and Countess of Lansfeld. After attaining too much power over the Bavarian government she was eventually ousted by the Jesuits and other Austrian political opponents. From that time on, she resumed her stage career and eventually wrote a book *The Art of Beauty*, afterwards devoting her life to helping "fallen women."

Edward Sellon (1818-1866): Commencing his career as an officer in the British East India Company, Sellon is referred to by G. Rattray Taylor in *Sex in History* as "the greatest pornographer since the days of Rome," asserting that he was the author of "the most lascivious book ever written," called *The Romance of Lust*, erroneously attributed by Pisanus Fraxi to one William S. Potter, a well-to-do collector of erotica and world traveler. Sellon's autobiography, *The Ups and Downs of Life*, was a romance of lust in itself. Preferring Indian women to all others, he wrote, "It is impossible to describe the enjoyment I experienced in the arms of these syrens [sic]. I have had English, French, German, and Polish women of all grades of society since, but never, never did they bear a comparison with those salacious, succulent houris of the Far East." After returning to England and entering into an unsuccessful marriage, he plunged into a final round of debauchery, eventually committing suicide in a Piccadilly hotel in April, 1866.

Sir Richard Francis Burton (1821-1890): Celebrated British explorer, orientalist, anthropoligist, and linguist. His voluminous writing included translations of the great erotic classics, both of the East and the West, *e.g.*, *The Thousand and One Nights, Kama Sutra, The Perfumed Garden, Il Pentamerone*, and others. Burton was the first "infidel" to make a successful pilgrimage to the Holy City of Mecca disguised as an Arab. His wife, a devoted Roman Catholic, though loyal to the end regarded the greater body of his work as "extremely indecent" and after his death burned many of his manuscripts and had published a severely expurgated edition of *The Thousand and One Nights*, thereby making this monumental work available for women and children of the Victorian era, who might otherwise never have seen it. It is doubtful if the world of letters and science will ever again see a man of Burton's intellect and energy.

Paolo Mantegazza (1831-1910): Pioneer Italian physician and sexologist who was one of the first recognized authorities to experiment with cocaine. After chewing coca leaves, he once said, "I prefer a life of ten years with coca to a life of centuries without coca." While a professor of general pathology at the University of Pavia, still in his twenties, he became a pioneer of testicular transplantation (1860) during a series of successful experiments with frogs. In the field of sexual research his works are referred to frequently by Krafft-Ebing, Hermann Heinrich Ploss, Ivan Bloch, Magnus Hirschfeld, and Havelock Ellis. As one biographer put it, "When Mantegazza wrote about love, he could not be calm. For everywhere he saw sex, the source of the profoundest of human emotions, bringing tragedy instead of happiness to mankind." An early crusader for the intelligent approach to sexuality he once said, "Know that I have the courage to work in the open, and that I have never been among those who . . . place fig leaves on Greek statues." His principal works were *The Physiology of Love, The Hygiene of Love*, and the comprehensive anthropological study, *The Sexual Relations of Mankind*.

Henry Spencer Ashbee (1834-1900): A successful London merchant, scholar, and bibliophile, Ashbee was best known for compiling his three-volume bibliography of the erotic and the pornographic *Index Libronum Prohibitorum*, 1877; *Centuria Librorum Absconditorum*, 1879; *Catena Librorum Tacendorum*, 1885. All three books reflected not only his own extensive collection of erotic literature and art but those of many prominent contemporaries. Ashbee also possessed the finest and most extensive collection of the first editions of the works of Miguel Cervantes. In his will he donated the Cervantes collection to the British Museum with the stipulation that in order to receive it they must also accept his private collection of erotica, thereby preserving it for future generations.

The Chevalier Leopols von Sacher-Masoch (1836-1905): Son of a police commissioner in Lemburg, Austria, Masoch was descended from Spanish nobility on his father's side and from Polish gentry on his mother's. His early childhood profoundly influenced his sexual proclivities, which were eventually labeled with his name as *masochism* by Krafft-Ebing. In all of his relationships with women, he was the classic "slave," demanding total humiliation as a prelude to sexual satisfaction. This became the underlying theme in all of his novels, notably *"Venus in Furs,"*

perhaps the best known of his works. During the height of his career as a novelist, he was hailed by critics as the most promising practitioner of German prose since Goethe, all of which involved the theme of a dominant female interwoven with fanciful tales of brutality and torture based upon Slavic folklore. Toward the end of his life, as his health began deteriorating, he retired to a modest estate near a sinister-appearing ruined tower, said by the natives to be haunted by restless spirits of witches who had been tortured to death in medieval times. The house was filled with chains, nail-studded whips, fetters, authentic old-time torture instruments, and paintings depicting the whip-bearing, fur-clad Amazons of his erotic fancy. Despite a certain amount of suspicion toward him by his neighbors, he was, in the words of Havelock Ellis, "a kind of Tolstoy to them." Encouraging cultural life and education, he even arranged a new water system. He was influential in preventing the hostility between Jews and Christians from erupting into violence. However, as he declined he developed a dangerous lust for shedding the blood of creatures he loved. Declared by a psychiatrist to be a dangerous homicidal psychotic, he was confined for the rest of his life in secret to a mental hospital in Mannheim on March 9, 1895, at which time, because of his international literary reputation, his death was announced, although he actually lived in confinement until 1905.

Victoria Claflin Woodhull (1838-1927): United States feminist reformer and first woman presidential candidate. Born in Ohio and raised with a background of "spiritualism," she traveled with her family from town to town demonstrating spiritualism. At fifteen, she married Canning Woodhull but continued her career, traveling with the Claflin Family medicine and fortune telling show, and later became a clairvoyant with her sister, Tennessee. In 1864 she divorced Woodhull and married James Blood, with whose help she started the *Woodhull & Claflin's Weekly* in 1870 with her sister. It was a weekly newspaper that strongly advocated equal rights for women and a single standard of morality for both sexes. Her open advocacy of free love made her very suspect to the women's suffrage movement of her time, but her speech in front of the House Judiciary Committee in 1871 won her favor, and the National Radical Reformers made her their candidate for president.

Krafft-Ebing, Baron Richard Von (1840-1902): German neuropsychiatrist, best known for his work in sexual psychopathology. Educated in Germany and Switzerland he was appointed Professor of Psychiatry at Strasbourg, and subsequently held similar positions at Graz and Vienna. His work focused mainly on the genetic functions in insanity, and in sexual deviations. He established a relationship between syphilis and general paralysis. He performed experiments using hypnosis, and studied epilepsy, paralysis agitaris, and hemicrania. His best-known work is *Psychopathia Sexualis* (1886).

Anthony Comstock (1844-1914): Quite conceivably the most outrageous bigot ever to appear on the American scene. A relentless crusader against what he regarded as vice, his untiring efforts eventually resulted in the passing of the so-called Comstock Law in New York State, which rendered virtually anything to do with sex in art or literature illegal. Not only did he devote himself to assaulting the fundamental rights granted under the first amendment, he managed to acquire police powers during his tenure. Typical of Comstock's fanatical behavior was his infamous raid on The Art Students' League. We may all sleep more comfortably in our beds knowing that he is firmly implanted six feet beneath the ground, but we must be perpetually on our guard to thwart the efforts of his spiritual descendants who still creep about the woodwork in their tennis shoes, ready to pounce upon and hack to pieces our freedom of speech and expression.

Oscar Wilde (1854-1900): The infamous Irish poet and dramatist who delighted London's society with his witty conversation and elaborate manners. He was an advocate of the "art for art's sake" movement in London, a contemporary aesthetic group of people whose affectations included long hair, eccentric dress (hence Wilde's green carnation), walking sticks, and effeminate manners.

In 1884 he married Constance Lloyd and she bore him two children, both boys. In 1891 he published his first and only novel, *A Picture of Dorian Gray*, which was highly criticized for its "alleged morality." Later that year he met and became friends with Lord Alfred Douglas, the third son of the 9th Marquess of Queensberry. It was a friendship that eventually led his life to disaster because of his arrest on homosexual offenses under the Criminal Law Amendment act of 1885. At his first trial the jury disagreed, but at the second he was found guilty and was sentenced to two years hard labor on May 25, 1895. During his imprisonment he wrote many letters of recrimination to Douglas, which were later published in 1905 as *De Profundis*. After his release from prison he spent the rest of his life living with a small circle of friends in France and Italy, sometimes under the assumed name of Sebastian Melmouth. Among his most known works are, *The Importance of Being Earnest, Ideal Husband, A Woman of No Importance, Lady Windemere's Fan, Happy Prince and Other Stories, Lord Arthur.*

Sigmund Freud (1856-1939): Austrian neurologist, and founder of psychoanalysis. Forced to leave Vienna after the invasion of the Third Reich, he moved to London and Paris, where he worked on the treatment of hysteria by hypnosis (which served as a structural basis for his psychoanalysis). Later he replaced hypnosis by free association of ideas. He believed that the complexities of repressed and forgotten impressions underlie all emotional disturbances and that the mere revelation and acceptance of these impressions often effects a cure. He also expounded a theory that dreams are the unconscious representation of repressed desires, particularly sexual desires.

Henry Havelock Ellis (1859-1939): British physician, essayist, and editor. Best known for his studies in human sexual behavior. At fifteen, Ellis had a mystical experience when he claimed to have seen the "universe as beauty" and through his writings he went on to preach these feelings and try to eliminate any thoughts of "ugliness" in the world. In his own inability to express feelings of "love," he became preoccupied with the problem of "the ugliness and beauty of sex," which he felt could be solved only in a scientific spirit. He later became a doctor, but never really practiced medicine. His most famous works are: *Man & Woman* (1894), *Studies in the Psychology of Sex* (7 volumes), *The Nationalization of Health* (1892), *The Task of Social Hygiene* (1912), and *The Erotic Rights of Women* (1918). He emerged throughout his career and writing as one of the most influential men involved in "the rights and emancipation of women and of sex education."

Magnus Hirschfield (1868-1935): The famous sexologist and one of the foremost pioneers in the sexual revolution of the tabooed science, of which he said, "Let us admit once and for all that *sex* is the basic principle around which the rest of human life with all its institutions is pivoted." Prior to the overthrow of Germany by the Nazis, he worked at the Institute of Sexology in Berlin, but then later had to flee for his life after the Third Reich destroyed the Institute and all of Hirschfield's

papers and work. Arriving in America as a refugee he spent the rest of his life studying, writing, and traveling the globe, lecturing on the sex lores of the world's cultures. Two of his most known and read works are *The Sexual History of the World War* and *Sex in Human Relationships*.

Grigori Efimovich Rasputin (1871-1916): Often referred to as the Mad Monk, this son of poor peasants from Tobolsk, Siberia, had little formal education. After leaving home in 1904 and devoting his full energies to religion he soon gained a reputation among the peasants as a holy man. Moving to St. Petersburg in 1907, his charismatic personality quickly gained him entrance to the inner circles of the royal family. Rapidly achieving a position of ascendency over the Czar Nicolas and his Czarina, he now began interfering with secular as well as church politics, while at the same time living a life of lustful debauchery. His crudity and ignorance outraged a group of influential Russian noblemen who assassinated him on December 31, 1916, with great difficulty for his constitution was so strong that he ingested enough strychnine to kill several horses while at the same time absorbing more than enough bullets to kill ten men.

Ivan Bloch (1872-1922): German scientist and sexologist. Little need be said of Ivan Bloch that his comprehensive writings don't already express. A forerunner in sexual liberation, his books, *Sexual Life in England* and *The Sexual Life of our Time: A complete encyclopedia of the sexual-sciences in their relationship to modern civilization*, were extremely important contributions to the sexual sciences of the early 1900s.

Bertrand Arthur William Russell (1872-1970): English mathematician philosopher, famous for his eloquent championship of "individual liberty," which made his position in the intellectual life of his time comparable with that of Voltaire in the eighteenth century and J. S. Mill in the nineteenth century. He was awarded the Nobel prize in literature in 1950 for his extensive writings in many areas such as *Marriage and Morals* (1929), *Education and the New Social Order* (1932), *In Praise of Idleness* (1935), and *The Analysis of Mind* (1921).

Margaret Sanger (1883-1966): A trained nurse by profession, she was the American pioneer of the birth-control movement, and founder and first president of the (American Birth Control League) Planned Parenthood Federation. In 1915 she was indicted for sending "pleas for birth control" through the mail, which did not deter her efforts. In 1921 she organized the first American Birth Control Conference. She wrote many books, articles, and pamphlets all relating to contraception and population control.

D. H. Lawrence (David Herbert) (1885-1930): English novelist, poet, essayist, and playwright. In 1914 Lawrence married Freida von Richthofen, cousin of Baron Manfred von Richthofen, the Germany military aviator. The following year his book, *The Rainbow*, was condemned as obscene. His most notorious novel, *Lady Chatterley's Lover*, published in 1928, became a historical landmark in the censoring of literature. His most read works, many of which have been made into successful motion pictures, are *Sons & Lovers, The Lost Girl, Women in Love, The Plumed Serpent, The Virgin and the Gypsy*. In 1930, just before his death, he wrote a study dealing with censorship called *Pornography and Obscenity*.

Henry Valentine Miller (1891-   ): Miller has been called "the heir of D. H. Lawrence" in his struggle to write and publish freely. His most read works, *Tropic of Cancer, Tropic of Capricorn, Black String, Cosmological Eye, Colossus of Maroussi*, have earned him a place in the literary archives of philosophy, despite consistent attempts from the authorities to ban them on grounds of "obscentiy."

Alfred Charles Kinsey (1894-1956): Famed scientist and sexologist whose name became an American household word. Born in Hoboken, New Jersey, on June 23, 1894. In 1938 he coordinated the first marriage course while he was a professor at Indiana University and later went on to continue his ground-breaking work in the area of sex research, finally founding the Institute for Sex Research at the university, now known as the Kinsey Institute. His two landmark volumes, *Sexual Behavior in the Human Male* (1948) and *Sexual Behavior in the Human Female* (1953), revolutionized people's thinking and understanding of their own sexual behavior.

Polly Adler (1900-1962): Polly Adler was probably America's most famous "Madam" in the 1920s and '30s. Her establishments were the rendezvous for many famous celebrities, from movie stars, writers, and politicians to some of the more prominent gangsters of her era. In her autobiography, *A House Is Not a Home*, she said of herself, "as Miss Pearl Adler, the reformed procuress and honest citizen, I was a social outcast, as Madam Polly, the proprietress of New York's most opulent bordello, society came to me."

Hugh Marston Hefner (1926-   ): Born on April 9 in Chicago, Illinois, Hefner founded *Playboy* in 1953 after resigning a minor editorial job at *Esquire*. It was an immediate success and rapidly transcended the "girlie" magazine image by publishing serious fiction, features, and interviews by and about top men in the world of art, letters, sports, and politics. He immortalized the "bunny" as a sex symbol, and in the process created an international empire of publishing, merchandising, hotels, clubs, films, and television production.

Ralph Ginzburg (1929-   ): Born in Brooklyn, New York, he became the "famed publisher" of the quarterly erotic magazine *Eros*, whose suppression by the authorities led to a ten-year literary *cause celèbre* climaxed by his imprisonment on March 9, 1972, for a four-year sentence. He was released eight months later, and is serving the rest of his sentence paroled and on probation. He is now the publisher of a consumers' guide magazine, *Moneysworth*, as well as the author of *100 Years of Lynching*, and *An Unhurried View of Erotica*.

Robert Guccione (1930-   ): Brooklyn-born photographer and artist who followed in the footsteps of Hugh Hefner and launched *Penthouse* magazine in London in 1965. After initial difficulties the publication became an "overnight success" and exploded on the American newsstands, appropriately enough, in 1969. He revolutionized publishing by legitimizing the display of pubic hair in photographs. Today a multimillionaire, his other publications, *Viva* and *Penthouse Forum*, can be obtained in almost every major city in the world.

Al Goldstein (1939-   ): This bearded, rotund, self-styled sex maniac might never have achieved his position in the "fifth estate of flesh" had he not flunked the police academy physical. His debut in publishing was with the now defunct *New York Free Press*. While working there as managing editor, he met Jim Buckley and to quote Claudia Dreifus,

"*Screw* emerged out of the wet dreams" of these two gentlemen. Coming from a straight middle-class Jewish suburban background, Goldstein once actually worked as a photographer for the *New York Daily Mirror* before his fall into debauchery. Commenting on that phase of his life, he once said, "I've just been such a whore all my life that I absolutely refuse to compromise with *Screw*. I am a true believer about that paper." After achieving national infamy for his pungent style and scurrilous attacks on all who dared cross swords with him, he went so far as to practice what he preaches by playing a role in the porno farce, *It Happened in Hollywood*. Today Goldstein modestly admits to being the kingpin of a fourteen-million-dollar empire of flesh.

Dr. William Masters and Virginia Johnson: A husband and wife team, they are renowned sex therapists and founders of the Biological Reproductive Foundation in Missouri. They have made extensive physiological tests on men and women to determine the varieties and levels of sexual satisfaction achieved through orgasm. Their theories and the techniques they have developed to help people who are facing sexual problems or dysfunctions have revolutionized the field of sex therapy.

Drs. Phyllis and Eberhard Kronhausen: Husband and wife team of psychologists, sexologists, authors, and film-makers, who founded their own brand of "family milieu therapy," a technique for treating severe emotional disturbances (i.e. schizophrenics, psychotics) and who consider themselves more like "gurus" than "shrinks" — "Psychotherapy is probably eighty percent art and intuition and only twenty percent science anyway," they say. The owners of probably the largest collection of erotic art in the world, both contemporary and classical, in 1972 after two years of litigation against the United States government, they founded the first International Museum of Erotic Art in San Francisco, which houses this collection. They have written several important books, the most noted of which are *Pornography and the Law, The Sexually Responsive Woman, Erotic Fantasies—A Study of the Sexual Imagination,* and two volumes of their art collection, *Erotic Art I* and *Erotic Art II*. They have produced and directed several erotic films, including *Freedom to Love* and *The Hottest Show in Town*.

Many of the people listed here are not necessarily part of the so-called "sex establishment," but are listed because of the fact that they have made valuable contributions to enlightening society and advancing the ongoing need for a greater understanding of human sexuality.

Robert Ardrey: Screenwriter, author, best known for *African Genesis*, whose territorial imperative threw great light on the integral element of sex both in animals and humans as related to territory and possessions.

Johann Jarob Bachofen: Author of *Myth, Religion, and Mother Right*. The *Locus Classicus* of "matriarchy" theories and of much feminist ideology.

Fred Belliveau: Vice President of the Medical Division of the publishing house Little, Brown & Company, Belliveau and colleague Lin Richter were the original editors of Masters and Johnson's work, and authors of the book *Understanding Human Sexual Inadequacy*, which translated into lay terminology the experiments and writings of Masters & Johnson.

Eric Berne: Psychiatrist and author of the best seller *Games People Play* and *Sex in Human Loving*, and founder of the school of transactional analysis.

Harry Benjamin: Gerontologist and sexologist, one of the leading experts in the treatment of the transsexual, he has demonstrated as many as nine specific ways of gender determination: anatomic, chromosomal, endocrinal, genetic, germinal, gonadal, legal, psychological, and social.

Walter Benton: Author of the sensitive, erotic *This Is My Beloved*, which when published in 1943 inflamed the passions of more maidens than anyone since Lord Byron.

Ed Brecher: Award-winning science writer whose landmark book, *The Sex Researchers*, was the first serious in-depth study of sex therapy, therapists, and their techniques.

Helen Gurley Brown: Married, author of *Sex and the Single Girl*, editor of *Cosmopolitan*, and closet reader of *Playgirl, Viva*, etc.

Jim Buckley: Co-founder of *Screw* and producer of *It Happened in Hollywood* among other accomplishments in the sexual subterranean.

Mary Calderone: Dr. Calderone is the head of SIECUS and one of the country's outspoken advocates of sex education.

Frank S. Caprio: One-time staff psychiatrist at Walter Reed Hospital in Washington, D.C., Caprio has devoted his career to the problems of sex and marriage. Author of nearly thirty books on the subject and numerous magazine articles, he is a staunch advocate of sex education for adults.

Charles Carrington: Paris-based publisher and dealer in erotica and pornography with a heavy emphasis on flagellant literature, who dominated the English language pornography market from 1895 to 1917.

Eduardo Cemano: New York-based artist and film-maker, who has won awards for his straight television commercials. In the erotic film field he has been acclaimed for the artistic quality of his productions, especially those involving exotic choreography, some of which have been seen on television. His *Madame Zenobia* was the first sexually explicit film to win an award at the prestigious Cannes Film Festival.

Marilyn Chambers: From the chaste boxes of Ivory Snow, this clean-cut all-American sexpot catapulted her way to fame from *Behind the Green Door* to the *Resurrection of Eve* and beyond.

Robert Chartham: Prolific British writer and sexologist whose gems of wisdom include such revealing information as "if a man and woman stimulate each other to orgasm without penis-vagina contact, it is called 'heavy petting.'"

Eustace Chesser: British psychologist and gynecologist whose controversial *Love Without Fear* published in 1940 resulted in the prosecution of Dr. Chesser and his publisher for publishing "an obscene libel." At the end of the trial the jury returned a not guilty verdict for both defendants, and the book, written in straightforward language designed for the layman, went on to achieve immense international success.

Alex Comfort: Today a senior fellow at the Center for the Study of Democratic Institutions in Santa Barbara and author of *Joy of Sex* and *More Joy*.

Harvey Corman: Handsome, pioneering inventor of the "menstrual extraction" contraceptive and abortion method, continuously in trouble with the authorities for carrying out his work without the protective armor of having the necessary initials after his name. He spends a great deal of his time in India and other Asian continents, where he teaches his methods.

Alistair Crowley: Outrageous Satanist and author whose bizarre sexual activities scandalized Europe, especially the British upper class from which he sprang.

Gerard Damiano: Producer/director of *Deep Throat* and *The Devil in Miss Jones*, two of the most significant milestones in X-rated cinema.

Simone De Beauvoir: Brilliant French writer, essayist, philosopher, and author of *The Second Sex*, a milestone book reevaluating the role of woman in society in the highest of intellectual terms. Her book, *Must We Burn Sade*, offered great enlightenment on the life, work, and literary validity of the Marquis de Sade.

Betty Dodson: One of the leading American erotic artists, forerunner of the new sexual freedom, and the guru of female masturbation.

François Duyckaerts: Author of *The Sexual Bond (Le Formation Du Lien Sexual)*; professor of Dynamic and Developmental Psychology at the University of Liege, Belgium; believes that "the establishment of a true and lasting sexual union would . . . represent a victory over the forces of hate and perversion."

Dr. Albert Ellis: Executive director of the Institute for Rational Living, and director of services for the Institute for Advanced Study in Rational Psychotherapy. Author and/or editor of over thirty books, two of the most important being *Sex without Guilt* and the *Encyclopedia of Sexual Behavior*.

Don Fass: Former disc jockey and newsman, the youngest reporter to have covered the early space shoots at Cape Canaveral, founder and president of the National Bisexual Liberation Organization.

Julius Fast: Author of *Body Language*, the best-selling book that scored high points in breaking down the barriers of sexual communications, and *Incompatibility of Man and Women, and How to Overcome It*, whose children think he's a groovy dad because he wrote a book about the Beatles and wears a beard.

Roberta Findlay: The only woman in porno films who writes, produces, directs, photographs, and edits feature hard-core films, her most recent being *The Wetter, The Better*, a parody on the motion picture, *Shampoo*.

Stanley Fleischman: Lawyer and author, considered to be one of the nation's leading first amendment crusaders, and defender of constitutional rights.

Betty Freidan: One of the principal founders of N.O.W. (National Organization of Women), whose book *The Feminine Mystique* advocated the need for married women to find their place in society outside of the kitchen.

Erich Fromm: Author of *The Art of Loving: An enquiry into the nature of love* and *Sigmund Freud's Mission: An analysis of his personality and influence*.

John H. Gagnon: Colleague of Dr. Kinsey *et al.* and author with William Simon of *Sexual Conduct: A Human Social of Human Sexuality* and editor of *Sexual Deviance* (with William Simon).

Ken Gaul: Writer, former advertising man, and one-time managing editor of *Screw*. This iconoclastic entrepreneur created the First New York Erotic Film Festival in 1971 with an eye toward making the event the annual "Cannes" of erotica.

Paul H. Gebhard: Colleague of Dr. Kinsey *et al.* and author of *Sex Offenders*.

Joan Garrity: Author of the best-selling *Sensuous Woman* and popularizer of whipped cream as an adjunct to lovemaking.

Maurice Girodias: Son of Jack Kahane, the notorious London "booklegger"; Girodias' famous green Traveller's Companion Series of explicit sexual novels, many written by impecunious authors of stature, rapidly became the bane of customs' officials throughout the English-speaking world. These masterpieces of class pornography were smuggled into the United States by many a nervous student during the '50s until Girodias was forced to leave Paris at the insistence of Madame DeGaulle who was an avid crusader against "smut." Establishing himself in New York, he continued his publishing career, once stating publicly, "It is my business to deprave and corrupt." Actually, Girodias has carved himself a permanent niche in the field of letters by having been the first publisher with sufficient courage to publish the works of men such as Henry Miller, Nabokov, Donleavy, and Burroughs, as well as other anonymous erotica by authors with such exotic pseudonyms as Akbar del Piombo and Marcus von Heller.

Germaine Greer: One of the pioneer feminists to explore a woman's sexual role in her book, *The Female Eunuch*.

Alan F. Guttmacher: Specialist in gynecology and obstetrics, has held professorships at Johns Hopkins, Mount Sinai Medical School, and Albert Einstein Medical School. President of Planned Parenthood Federation (1962) and leader in the field of family planning and birth control. His books include, *Babies by Choice or Chance, The Complete Book of Birth Control, Birth Control and Love*, and *Understanding Sex*.

René Guyon: French jurist whose radical ideas on sexuality and children inspired a California-based group to adopt his name and call themselves the Guyon Society, their principal philosophy being to encourage sexual activity for children at an early age.

Beverly Harrell: Brooklyn-born Nevada madam, once banished from Los Angeles by the head of the vice squad, who gained national attention by being the first of her profession to seek political office as a candidate for the Nevada State Legislature in 1974.

Frank Harris (deceased): Irish-born, prominent editor and writer and member of the London literary elite, Harris' five-volume autobiography, *My Life and Loves*, is considered one of the most revealing

sexual biographies of his age. Not published in full until approximately thirty years after his death, the book stands apart for its literary excellence. Harris was an early friend of feminists, in that he believed rights for women were equally important sexually, economically, and politically. Harris was also the definitive biographer of Oscar Wilde.

Hartman and Fithian (William and Marilyn): A team of sex therapists often referred to as the West Coast Masters and Johnson, and authors of the book, *Treatment of Sexual Dysfunctions: A Bio-psychosocial Approach.*

Lisa Hoffman: European born photo-journalist who has become a female Boswell to the New York sexual subculture.

Xaviera Hollander: Better known as The Happy Hooker. The only hooker in history who has turned her profession into a personal cottage industry.

Morton Hunt: Philadelphia born author and journalist, Hunt deserves his place in sexual archives, essentially for his scholarly and comprehensive book, *The Natural History of Love,* of which he says, "this is neither a Perfumed Garden, nor a historian's Kinsey report, but primarily a history of the emotional relationships between the sexes."

Jill Johnston: Author of *Lesbian Nation* and other books, columnist for *The Village Voice,* and militant lesbian feminist.

Erica Jong: Author, poet, and lecturer, and innovator of the "zipless fuck" in her best-selling book, *Fear of Flying.*

James Joyce: Brilliant Irish poet and novelist, the fiery writer of *Ulysses,* which sent shock waves around the literary world, resulting in one of the landmark obscenity trials of the century, from which he eventually emerged triumphant.

Carl Gustave Jung: Psychiatrist and early colleague of Freud who violently disagreed with the Freudian theory that the libido was a manifestation of the sex instinct, holding instead that it was a will to live and that neurosis was better understood by analyzing patients' immediate problems than by delving into their childhood.

Ed Lange: One of the founders of the Elysium Institute and a leading figure in the Sensual Awareness movement.

Gershon Legman: G. Legman, as he calls himself, is without a doubt the greatest living authority in the field of erotic folklore literature and bibliography. One of the few literary snows whose attitude is totally justified, Legman is the author of numerous scholarly books, one of the most important being *The Horn Book—Studies in Erotic Folklore and Bibliography,* and *The Rationale of the Dirty Joke.*

Claude Levi-Strauss: Distinguished French anthropologist, he has held professorships in the United States and Europe and is associated with major anthropological and scientific institutes around the world. A member of the Legion of Honor, he is author of many significant works contributing to the understanding of sex and and its relationship to culture, and he has never been seen wearing Levi's in Paris or New York.

John and Mimi Lobell: Architects, swingers, and leading advocates of group sex; authors of *John and Mimi* and *The Complete Handbook for a Sexually Free Marriage.*

Linda Lovelace: If anyone has the right to go down in history, Linda Lovelace does.

Alexander Lowen: A disciple of Wilhelm Reich and founder of the school of bioenergetic analysis and author of *Love and Orgasm* which elaborates on Reich's theory on the orgasm.

Michael C. Luckman: Luckman, fired in September, 1974, for teaching the nation's first illustrated college course in pornography at the New School of Social Research, launched the first American Sex Festival "Eros 75" in June, 1975, where he introduced the "Tonguey" to the world as the equivalent of the Emmy, Oscar, and Tony.

Ted McIlvenna: An ordained Protestant Minister, Rev. McIlvenna is one of the founders of the National Sex Forum, which is sponsored by the Genesis Ecumenical Church of San Francisco, and a director of the International Museum of Erotic Art housing the Kronhausen collection.

Bronislaw Malinowski: Distinguished anthropologist, author of many books in which sex and repression in savage society and the sexual life of savages in northwestern Melanesia shed great light on the subject.

Herbert Marcuse: German-born, neo-Marxist philosopher and professor at the University of California at San Diego. Marcuse regards bodily repression, particularly sexual repressions, as among the most significant attributes of the exploitative social order. He argues that the ruling classes, recognizing a revolutionary potential in sexuality, have throughout history forced puritanical sexual ethics on the masses, thereby channeling their energies into substitute methods of gratification, *i.e.* sports, and other popular entertainments. Among his works are *Reason and Revolution, Eros and Civilization,* and *Counter-Revolution and Revolt.* He is regarded by many as the spiritual godfather of the Hippie generation.

Del Martin & Phyllis Lyon: Authors of the definitive book on lesbians, *Lesbian Woman.*

Rollo May: Psychiatrist, lecturer, and author of *Love and Will.*

Margaret Mead: One of the most prominent American anthropologists in the world, assistant curator of ethnology at the American Museum of Natural History, and author of many books, including *Sex and Temperament in Three Primitive Societies,* which was an immense contribution toward establishing the validity of accepting the vast differences that exist from culture to culture.

Merle Miller: Screen and television writer, and author of *Only You, Dick Daring* and the best-selling book of conversation with President Harry Truman, *Plain Speaking.* Miller's courageous public statement on his own homosexuality proved that by challenging society with dignity one does not have to lose stature.

Kate Millett: Author of *Sexual Politics* and *Flying*—leading feminist, lecturer, and organizer.

Mitchell Brothers: Two of the leading cine-moguls of porn, the Mitchell Brothers, headquartered in San Francisco, are responsible for the meteoric rise of Marilyn Chambers and known chiefly for their lavish and ambitious productions.

John Money: Professor of medical psychology at Johns Hopkins Uni-

versity, associate professor of pediatrics, and president of the Society of Scientific Study of Sex. His principal books in the field are *Sex Errors of the Body: Dilemmas, Education, Counseling* and *Sex Research: New Developments.*

Ashley Montagu: Noted anthropologist and lecturer, whose book *The Natural Superiority of Women* speaks for itself.

Desmond Morris: Noted British zoologist, whose book *The Naked Ape* makes it plain that we are all lovable beasts at heart.

George & Nena O'Neill: The husband and wife, anthropologist and sociologist, team, whose book *Open Marriage* was the first book to explore a sexually honest and open relationship within the confines of marriage.

Phil Osterman: Rags to riches entrepreneur who fought his way up in show business, finally making the big breakthrough as producer and director of *Let My People Come.*

Vance Packard: Author and journalist, whose name became a household word with the publication of his books *The Hidden Persuaders* and *The Status Seekers.* He earned his niche in sex with the publication of *The Sexual Wilderness* in 1958.

Ellen Peck: Author of *The Baby Trap* and founder of the Non-Parent Organization, whose main advocacy is marriage without children.

Anton Perich: Yugoslavian-born, electronic Boswell of the New York sexual subculture, whose videotaped excursions into voyeurism have revolutionized cable television by their heavy sexual content.

Wardell Pomeroy: Psychologist and protegé of Dr. Alfred Kinsey, author of the definitive biography of Kinsey.

Rolf S. Reade: Anagram of Alfred Rose, bibliographer of erotica of the British Museum Private Case and the Enfer de la Biblioteque Nationale, Paris, and other collections, published in 1936 as *Registrum Librorum Eroticorum.*

Harry Reems: In reviewing Harry's short screen life in his autobiography, *Here Comes Harry Reems*, Harry himself admits to have "erupted one gallon, two quarts, one pint, and fifteen ounces of jism for the cameras." Need anything more be said about this nice Jewish boy from Westchester County? He also freely admits that "he'd rather spend time on his farm in Pennsylvania and collecting antiques."

Wilhelm Reich: Radical psychoanalyst belonging to the second generation of Freudian critics. His greatest discovery was the function of the orgasm and it became a focal point around which he eventually "interpreted the entire cosmos." He shook up Freudians by substituting the word genital for sexual as Freud used it, and his use of Marxist terminology influenced Marcuse. Reich asserted that not every sexual climax was a true orgasm, the latter being strictly the total release of a dammed-up libido. It would be unfair to Reich and his followers to cause confusion by dealing inadequately with his further work, especially his controversial Orgone therapy, which is best understood by reading his works. He was such a radical that among his enemies were the Communists, the Fascists, the A.M.A., and the U.S. Government, which finally sent him to prison in 1956. Among his most significant works are *The Discovery of the Orgone, The Function of the Orgasm: Sex,*

Economic Problems of Biological Energy, The Mass Psychology of Fascism, and *The Sexual Revolution Toward Sex Governing Character Structure.*

Charles Rembar: Lawyer, author, and civil libertarian; among his most famous cases were his successful defenses of *Lady Chatterley's Lover* and *Fanny Hill*, an account of which can be read in his book, *The End of Obscenity.*

Alex De Renzy: Outstanding producer of porno films, whose work has been regarded by critics as a considerable cut above the average "quick and dirty." In the words of William Rostler, author of *Contemporary Erotic Cinema*, he is "one of the few pros whose technical standards match those of the major Hollywood productions."

Dr. David Reuben: The man who gave us everything we wanted to know about sex, but were afraid to ask.

Robert Rimmer: Author of the book, *The Harrad Experiment*, a novel that triggered a controversial storm on the campuses throughout the United States, the theme of which encouraged sexual freedom in the dormitory.

Andrew Rock: Male disciple of Betty Dodson and serious advocate of male masturbation, Rock conducts bodysex workshops for men, patterned after those of his mentor.

Barney Rossett: Proud possessor of two children and a German shepherd, he is the founder and president of Grove Press, and of the late, lamented *Evergreen Review.* One of the most courageous publishers in America, Rossett has rushed in where others feared to tread. A perfect example was his successful fight against the United States Government in the now classic *Lady Chatterley's* case. Always placing emphasis on literary significance over profit motive, Rossett has frequently placed himself and his company in financial jeopardy, yet he has always practiced his pioneering publishing philosophy. Branching out into the precarious area of film distribution, he followed a parallel course beginning with the importation of *I Am Curious (Yellow)*, and today his film division distributes one of the most extensive aggregates of quality sexually oriented motion pictures.

Samuel Roth: American publisher and, in the words of Charles Rembar, a man of "considerable culture," Roth was a pioneer in the publication of erotic fiction much of which was of little literary value but which also included the works of Joyce and Schnitzler. He was prosecuted and convicted on obscenity charges in New York State under the Comstock Act and to quote from Rembar, "The Roth case was hailed as a victory for those bent on suppression."

William Rotsler: Nationally known figure photographer, author of over 200 hundred magazine articles on erotic film, writer, director of twenty-six erotic feature films and film critic. His book *Contemporary Erotic Cinema* is one of the most comprehensive works on the subject.

Tina Russell: Star of countless porno features and loops, Tina certainly ranks among the top ten in her field. She is also the author of an autobiography, *Porno Star.*

Barbara Seaman: One of the most rational and free-thinking members of the feminist movement and author of *The Doctor's Case Against the*

Pill and *Free and Female*, in which she punched holes in many male pronouncements about the female orgasm.

William Shutz: A fellow of Esalen and author of the best-selling book *Joy*. He probably was one of the prime movers who put Esalen on the map in so far as the general public is concerned.

Charles W. Socarides: Psychiatrist, author, who remained at odds with the rest of his colleagues after the American Psychiatric Association declared homosexuality neither a sickness nor a mental disorder, by continuing to maintain the position that homosexuality is "a deviant form of sex, and harmful to all society."

Georgina Spelvin: Georgina graduated from the circus and the Broadway musical to the silver screen of porn by a curiously circuitous route. Hired as the production cook for Damiano's *Devil in Miss Jones*, she inherited the lead when the star went down with a sore throat, and from there it has been all uphill.

Margo St. James: She may be the happiest hooker of them all, founder of *Coyote*, a political activist "hooker's union" that is single-mindedly fighting for the decriminalization of prostitution.

Martha Stein: Author of *Lovers, Friends, Slaves . . . the nine male sexual types*, a psycho-sexual study of the transactions between call girls and their clients, based on actual observation of over four thousand cases, director of Psycho-Sexual Research Center, Inc., and associate of sex-information and education organizations.

Gloria Steinem: Leading sex symbol of the feminist movement . . . like it or not. And editor of *Ms* Magazine, writer and lecturer . . . (And she's come a long way.)

Marc Stevens: Marc Stevens, cocky veteran porno star, modestly claims in his autobiography *10½!*, "My cock is the biggest and the best in the New York blue movie industry." If you want to find out for yourself, feel free to write, Marc Stevens Fan Club, 210 E. 35th Street, New York, New York 10016—however, Marc says he is booked up solidly for the next six months.

Marie Stopes: English author, paleobotanist, and pioneering advocate of birth control, she co-founded the Mother's Clinic for Constructive Birth Control in 1921. Principal books: *Married Love, Contraception: Its Theory, History, and Practice, Sex and the Young*, and *Sex and Religion*.

Emerson and Caroline Symonds: Founders and coordinators of the Sensory Awareness Centers in California and pioneers in the training of sex-surrogates.

Gay Talese: Outstanding journalist and best-selling author of *The Kingdom and the Power* and *Honor Thy Father*, Talese found his way into the annals of the sex world while researching his eagerly awaited forthcoming book on *Sex in America*.

Stith Thompson: The most important folklorist since Sir James Frazer. Thompson's monumental six-volume motif-index of *Folk Literature* is the definitive source for all social scientists of the sexual themes universal in all cultures of the human race.

Lionel Tiger: British anthropologist and author of *Men in Groups* and *Imperial Animal* (in collaboration with Robin Fox), both publications exploring sex roles in human behavior.

Abigail Van Buren and Ann Landers: Twin sisters each with her own syndicated column of advice laden with lighthearted and witty pronouncements, a heavy proportion of which deal with the sexual dilemmas of their devout readers.

Theodore H. Van De Velde: Pioneer medical author on sex and marriage; principal works *Fertility and Sterility in Marriage, Ideal Marriage: Its Physiology and Technique*, and *Sexual Tensions in Marriage*.

Marco Vassi: Author of a number of well-received erotic novels for Maurice Girodias, as well as a picaresque nonfiction account of his prodigious sexual exploits, *The Stored Apocalypse* (Trident), and currently editor of the Penthouse Book Club.

Andy Warhol: Avant-garde artist and member of the super-hype, this externally bland Svengali to would-bes and never-will-bes has aroused bitter controversies and passions of love and hate, even to being the target of a near assassination. Given to banal utterances, he believes that "everyone should be famous for at least fifteen minutes."

Earl Wilson, Jr.: Former singer, and now successful songwriter/lyricist who has established a solid reputation on his own merits the hard way, *i.e.* without capitalizing on the name of a celebrated father. His tuneful, witty, and explicit lyrics in the hit show *Let My People Come* run the gamut from tender to outrageous.

To all those living or dead who feel they have deserved a place in the sexual Who's Who, but were omitted— our apologies.

General Bibliography

$\mathcal{A}$s you have seen throughout THE WHOLE SEX CATALOGUE, we have provided individual bibliographies and suggested reading lists subject by subject. Some books mentioned in the text may have been excluded, having been adequately covered within the context of individual chapters. Every effort has been made to avoid duplications or omissions. Here we have not broken the bibliography down into categories. Instead, we have focused our attention on the entire spectrum of the subject, with particular emphasis on the most current titles. You will note that wherever possible we have indicated prices and information as to whether a book is out of print or rare, and for the most part we have restricted ourselves to books published in English.

Adburgham, Alison. *A Punch History of Manners and Modes 1841-1940.* London: 1961.

Alexander, Shana. *Women's Legal Rights.* Los Angeles: Wollstonecraft Inc., 1974. $9.95 (cloth), $5.95 (paper).

Anchell, Melvin. *Sex and Sanity.* New York: Macmillan, 1971. $6.95

Anderson, A. J. *Library Problems in Intellectual Freedom and Censorship.* New York: R. R. Bowker Co., 1974. $10.95

Andreas, Carol. *Sex and Caste in America.* Englewood Cliffs, N.J.: Prentice-Hall, 1971. $5.95

Aphrodite, J. [pseud.]. *To Turn You On.* Secaucus, N.J.: Lyle Stuart, 1974. $8.00

Athearn, Louise Montague. *What Every Formerly Married Woman Should Know.* New York: David McKay, 1974. $6.95

Atkins, John. *Sex in Literature: The Erotic Impulse from the Classics to the Present Day.* New York: Grove Press, 1972. $2.95

Atkins, Thomas R., ed. *Sexuality in the Movies.* Bloomington: Indiana University Press, 1975.

Saint Augustine. *Confessions.* Reprint. Baltimore: Penguin Books, 1961.

Barbach, Lonnie Garfield. *For Yourself: The Fulfillment of Female Sexuality. A Guide to Orgasmic Response.* Garden City, N.Y.: Doubleday, 1975. $7.95

Barnett, Walter. *Sexual Freedom and the Constitution.* Albuquerque: University of New Mexico Press, 1973. $10.00

Barriere, Albert, and Leland, Charles G. *A Dictionary of Slang, Jargon and Cant.* 2 vols. Edinburgh: 1889-90.

Barton, Stuart. *The Human Swop Shop.* Lyle Publications, 1972.

Basler, Roy P. *Sex, Symbolism & Psychology in Literature.* New York: Octagon Books, 1967. $10.50

Beach, Frank A., ed. *Sex and Behavior.* Huntington, N.Y.: Krieger, 1974. $18.50

Beamer, Roger L. *The Sexually Liberated Marriage.* Chatsworth, Calif.: Alpha Library Press, 1974. $3.95

Berger, Evelyn Miller. *Triangle: The Betrayed Wife.* Chicago: Nelson-Hall, 1974. $7.95

Bergler, Edmund. *Laughter and the Sense of Humor.* New York: Grune and Stratton, 1956. $11.75

Bernard, Jessie. *Sex Games: Communication Between the Sexes.* New York: Atheneum, 1972. $3.95

Berne, Eric. *Sex in Human Loving.* New York: Simon & Schuster, 1970. $6.95

Bestic, Alan. *Sex and the Singular English.* New York: Taplinger, 1972. $5.95

Birchall, Ellen F., and Gerson, Noel B. *Sex and the Adult Woman.* New York: Simon & Schuster, 1965. $1.25

Bosch, Vernon. *Sexual Dimensions: The Fact and Fiction of Genital Size.* New York: Penthouse Book Club, 1974. $9.95

Braden, Beatrice. *Sex Was More Fun When....* Los Angeles: Price/Stern/Sloan, 1973. $2.50

Brady, Frank. *Hefner.* New York: Macmillan, 1974. $7.95

Brend, W. A. *Sacrifice to Attis: A Study of Sex and Civilization.* London: Heinemann, 1936.

Brenton, Myron. *Sex Talk.* New York: Fawcett, Crest, 1973. $1.25.

Briffault, R. *Sin and Sex.* London: Allen & Unwin, 1931 (Macaulay, 1931).

Brooks, Charles V. W. *Sensory Awareness.* New York: Viking, Esalen Books, 1974. $8.95

Brooks, Robert. *Sex: Black & White.* New York: Dell, 1971. $1.25

Browne, W. F. *The Importance of Women in Anglo-Saxon Times.* S.P.C.K., 1919

Bruce, Lenny. *How to Talk Dirty and Influence People.* Reprint. Chicago: Playboy Press, 1974. $1.50

Bullough, Vern L. *The Subordinate Sex.* Baltimore: Penguin Books, 1974. $2.95

Bry, Adelaide. *Sexually Aggressive Woman.* New York: David McKay, 1975.

Burton, Sir Richard. *The Erotic Traveller.* Edited by E. Leigh. New York: G. P. Putnam's Sons, 1967. $4.95

Calderone, Mary. *Sexuality and Human Values.* New York: Association Press, 1974. $7.95

Campanelli, Louise. *Sex and All You Can Eat.* Secaucus, N.J.: Lyle Stuart, 1975. $7.95

Casler, Lawrence. *Is Marriage Necessary?* New York: Behavioral Publications, Human Sciences Press, 1975. $8.95

Chambers, Marilyn. *Marilyn Chambers: My Own Story.* New York: Warner Paperback Library, 1975. $1.95

Chanter, A. G. *Sex Education in the Primary School.* New York: St. Martin's Press, 1966. $5.95

Chapman, A. H. *Sexual Maneuvers and Stratagems.* New York: G. P. Putnam's Sons, 1969. $5.95

Chou, Eric. *The Dragon and the Phoenix.* London: Michael Joseph, 1971.

Cole, William. *Sex and Love in the Bible.* Deer Park, New York: Brown Book Company, $6.50

Colton, Helen. *Sex After the Sexual Revolution.* New York: Association Press, 1973. $7.95

Connell, Noreen. *Rape: First Sourcebook for Women.* New York: New American Library, Plume Books, 1975. $3.95

Cooper, Boyd. *Sex Without Tears.* New York: Bantam Books, 1974. $1.50

Corey, Robert E. *The Book of Love and Sex.* Los Angeles: Sherbourne Press, 1974. $9.95

Craig, Alex. "The Bibliography of Nudism." *Sun and Health* 14 (1954).

Crouch, Joseph. *Puritanism and Art: An Inquiry into a Popular Fallacy.* London: 1910.

Csicsery, George. *Sex Industry.* New York: New American Library, Signet, 1973. $1.25

Cunnington, C. Willett. *Why Women Wear Clothes.* London: 1941.

Cunnington, C. Willett, and Cunnington, Phillis. *The History of the Underclothes.* London: 1951.

Dallas, D. M. *Sex Education in School and Society.* Atlantic Highlands, N.J.: Fernhill House Ltd., 1972. $2.25

Dalrymple, Willard. *Sex is for Real: Human Sexuality and Sexual Responsibility.* New York: McGraw-Hill, 1969. $5.95

Daniell, Rosemary. *A Sexual Tour of the Deep South.* New York: Holt, Rinehart and Winston, 1975. $6.95 (cloth), $3.95 (paper).

Darwin, Charles H. *The Origin of Man and Sexual Natural Selection.* Stuttgart: 1919.

Davenport, John. *Curiositates Erotica Physiologiae; or Tabooed Subjects Freely Treated.* London: 1875.

Davidson, Michael. *Sex Surrogates.* New York: New American Library, 1973. $1.25

De Archenholtz, W. *A Picture of England.* London: 1797.

Decter, Midge. *The New Chastity and Other Criticisms of Women's Liberation.* New York: Coward, McCann and Geoghegan, 1972. $5.95

De la Cruz, Felix F., and LaVeck, Gerald D. *Human Sexuality and the Mentally Retarded.* Baltimore: Penguin Books, Pelican Books, 1974. $1.50

De Ropp, Robert S. *Sex Energy.* New York: Dell, Delta Books, 1971. $2.45

Discreet Gentleman's Guide to the Pleasures of Europe, The. Simplified Travel Books. New York: Bantam Books, 1975. $1.95

Drzazge, John. *Sex Crimes.* Springfield, Ill.: C.C. Thomas, 1960. $7.05

Durgnat, Raymond. *Eros in the Cinema.* Atlantic Highlands, N.J.: Fernhill House Ltd., 1966. $5.50

Eller, Vernard. *Sex Manual for Puritans.* Nashville: Abingdon Press, 1971. $3.00

Ellison, Alfred. *Oral Sex and the Law.* New York: Penthouse Book Club, 1974. $30.00

Elsom, John. *Erotic Theatre.* New York: Taplinger, 1974. $10.00

Etzioni, Amitai, *Genetic Fix.* New York: Macmillan, 1973. $7.95

Farren, David. *Sex and Magic.* New York: Simon & Schuster, 1975. $6.95

Felstein, Ivor. *Sex in Later Life.* Baltimore: Penguin Books, 1974. $1.45

Ferenczi, Sandor, and Rank, Otto. *Sex in Psycho-Analysis.* Translated by Ernest Jones. Reprint. New York: Dover Publications, 1937. $3.50

Filene, Peter Gabriel. *Him/Her/Self. Sex Roles in Modern America.* New York: Harcourt Brace Jovanovich, 1975. $10.00

Fleming, Alice L. *Conception, Abortion, Pregnancy.* Nashville: Thomas Nelson, 1974. $5.95

Flitch, J. E. Crawford. *Modern Dancing and Dancers.* London: 1912.

Francoeur, Robert T. *Eve's New Rib: Twenty Faces of Sex, Marriage and Family.* New York: Dell, Delta Books, 1973. $2.65

——. *Utopian Motherhood: New Trends in Human Reproduction.* Cranbury, N.J.: A. S. Barnes & Co., 1973. $2.95

Francoeur, Robert T. and Francoeur, Anna K. *The Future of Sexual Relations.* Englewood Cliffs, N.J.: Prentice-Hall, Spectrum Books, 1974. $7.95 (cloth, $2.45 (paper).

——. *Hot and Cool Sex.* New York: Harcourt Brace Jovanovich, 1975. $7.95

Freeman, Sally; Johnson, Paul; Logan, Tom; and Sheridan, Sharon. *The Bulbous, Juicy, Sprouted, Alternative, Yeasty, Bio-Dynamic, Perennial, Carnivorous, Succulent, Pithy, Heliotropic, Insectivorous, Photosynthetic, Mulchable, Deep-Rooted, Bloomin', Low Down, Dirty, Plant Book.* New York: G.P. Putnam's Sons, 1975. $5.00

Fried, Edrita. *On Love and Sexuality.* New York: Grove Press, 1975. $1.95

Freud, Sigmund. *Sexual Enlightenment of Children.* Reprint. New York: Collier, 1963. $1.50

Gerber, Albert B. *Sex, Pornography & Justice.* Secaucus, N.J.: Lyle Stuart, 1965. $10.00

Gerhart, Sally, and Johnson, William R. *Loving Men/Loving Women: Gay Liberation and the Church.* San Francisco: Glide Publications, $6.95

Gersoni-Stavn, Diane. *Sexism & Youth.* New York: R.R. Bowker Co., 1974. $4.95

Ghiselin, Michael T. *The Economy of Nature and the Evolution of Sex.* Berkeley: University of California Press, 1975. $12.95

Gilder, George F. *Sexual Suicide.* New York: Quadrangle, 1973. $7.95

Goode, William J., and Price, Steven D. *The Second-Time Single Man's Survival Handbook.* New York: Praeger, 1975. $6.95

Goodland, R. *A Bibliography of Sex Rites and Customs.* London: Routledge, 1931.

Gordon, Sol. *The Sexual Adolescent.* Belmont, Calif.: Duxbury Press, 1974. $6.95 (cloth), $3.50 (paper).

Gorer, Geoffrey. *Hot Strip Tease and Other Notes on American Culture.* London: 1937.

——. *The Life and Ideas of the Marquis De Sade.* Owen, 1953.

Graves, Robert. *Lars Porsena or the Future of Swearing and Improper Language.* London: Kegan Paul, 1927.

Greene, Graham. *Lord Rochester's Monkey.* New York: Viking, 1975. $15.95

Gregersen, E. A. *Sex, Culture, & Society.* New York: Gordon Press, 1974. $12.50

Grotjahn, Martin. *Beyond Laughter.* New York: McGraw-Hill, 1957.

Gunther, Max. *Virility 8.* Chicago: Playboy Press, 1975. $7.95

Guyon, René. *The Ethics of Sexual Acts.* New York: 1934.

Haeberle, Erwin J. *Sex Atlas: A New Illustrated Guide.* New York: Seabury Press, 1974. $12.50

Hageman, Alice. *Sexist Religion and Women in the Church: No More Silence.* New York, Pocket Books, 1973. $1.50

Haggarty, John. *Sex in Prison.* New York: Ace Books, 1975. $1.50

Halacy, D. S. *Genetic Revolution: Shaping Life for Tomorrow.* New York: Harper & Row, 1974. $6.95

Halcomb, Ruth. *Sex and the Single Ms.* Chatsworth, Calif.: Books for Better Living, 1974. $1.25

Hall, Carrie A. *From Hoopskirts to Nudity.* Caldwell I., 1938.

Hall, Robert E. *Sex: An Advanced Primer.* New York: Doubleday, 1974. $4.95

Hamilton, Michael, ed. *The New Genetics and the Future of Man.* Grand Rapids: Wm. B. Eerdmans, 1972. $6.95

Harrell, Beverly, and Bishop, George. *An Orderly House.* New York: Dell, 1975. $1.50

Harrison, Barbara Grizzuti. *Unlearning the Lie: Sexism in School.* New York: William Morrow, 1974. $2.95

Harris, Mervyn. *The Dilly Boys: The Game of Male Prostitution in Piccadilly.* New Perspectives, 1974. $6.95.

Hayds, H. R. *The Dangerous Sex: The Myth of Feminine Evil.* London: 1966.

Hayn, H. *Bibliotheca Germanorum Erotica et Curiosa.* Munich: 1912-29.

Hellman, Hal. *Biology in the World of the Future.* New York: M. Evans, 1971. $5.95

Hemming, James, and Maxwell, Zena. *Sex and Love.* New York: Praeger, 1974. $5.95

Hernton, Calvin C. *Sex and Racism in America.* New York: Grove Press, 1966. $1.95

Hettlinger, Richard. *Sex Isn't That Simple: The New Sexuality on Campus.* New York: Seabury Press, 1974. $6.95

Himes, Norman E. *Medical History of Contraception.* Medical Aspects of Human Fertility. London: 1936.

Hirsch, Arthur H. *Sexual Misbehavior of the Upper Cultured.* Westport, Conn.: Greenwood Press, 1973. $17.50

Hodgson, Leonard. *Sex and Christian Freedom: An Enquiry.* Naperville, III.: Alec R. Allenson Inc., 1967. $1.95

Hollander, Xaviera. *The Happy Hooker on the Best Part of a Man.* New York: New American Library, 1975. $1.50

Holmes, Ronald M. *Sexual Behavior: Extramarital, Non-marital, Co-marital.* Berkeley: McCutchan, 1971. $3.95

Holt, Peggy. *The Lover's Astrology Cookbook.* Los Angeles: Price/Stern/Sloan, 1974. $2.00

Hopson, Barrie, and Hopson, Charlotte. *Intimate Feedback.* New York: Simon & Schuster, 1975. $7.95

Hooper, Columbus B. *Sex in Prison: The Mississippi Experiment with Conjugal Visiting.* Baton Rouge: Louisiana State University Press, 1969. $5.95

Hoque, Richard. *Sex, Satin, & Jesus.* Nashville: Broadman. $4.95

Horner, Tom. *Sex in the Bible.* Rutland, Vt.: C. E. Tuttle, 1974. $7.50

Houdek, P. K. *A Sourcebook for Adult Sex Education.* Kansas City, Mo.: Planned Parenthood. $1.00

Hunold, Gunther. *Sexual Pleasures from A to Z.* New York: Pent-r-Books, 1974. $12.95 (cloth), $7.95 (paper)

Hunt, Morton. *Sexual Behavior in the '70s.* Chicago: Playboy Press, 1975. $10.00

Jeanniere, Abel. *The Anthropology of Sex.* New York: Harper & Row, 1967.

Jefferson, John Cordy. *Lady Hamilton and Lord Nelson.* 2 vols. London: 1888.

Jonas, David and Jonas, Doris. *Sex and Status.* New York: Stein and Day, 1975. $8.95

Jones, E. *On the Nightmare.* London: Hogarth, 1931. As *Nightmare, Witches and Devils*, New York: W. W. Norton, 1931.

Julty, Sam. *Male Sexual Performance.* New York: Grosset & Dunlap, 1975. $8.95

Kane, Paula, and Chandler, Christopher. *Sex Objects in the Sky.* Chicago: Follett, 1975. $5.95

Kanowitz, Leo. *Sex Roles in Law and Society: Cases and Materials.* Albuquerque: University of New Mexico Press, 1974. $8.50

Karlen, Arno. *Sexuality and Homosexuality: A New View.* New York: W. W. Norton, 1971. $15.00

Kay, Harvey. *Male Survival.* New York: Grosset & Dunlap, 1975. $7.95

Kelly, G. L. *Sexual Feeling in Married Men and Women.* New York: Permabooks, 1961.

Kelman, Stanley. *Sexuality, Self and Survival.* New York: Random House, 1972. $5.95

Kent, Saul. *Future Sex.* New York: Warner Paperback Library, 1975. $1.50

Keown, Ian M. *Lovers' Guide to America.* New York: Macmillan, 1974. $7.95 (cloth), $3.95 (paper).

King, Francis. *Sexuality, Magic and Perversion.* Secaucus, N.J.: Lyle Stuart, 1974. $3.95

Kinkade, Kathleen. *A Walden Two Experiment: The First Five Years of Twin Oaks Community.* New York: William Morrow, 1972. $7.95

Knight, R. Payne. *An Account of the Remains of the Worship of Priapus etc.*, London: 1786.

Koestenbaum, Peter, *Existential Sexuality.* Englewood Cliffs, N.J.: Prentice-Hall, Spectrum Books, 1974. $6.95 (cloth), $2.95 (paper)

Kreps, Juanita. *Sex in the Market Place.* Baltimore: Johns Hopkins Press, 1971. $6.00

Landis, Carney. *Sex in Development.* Washington: McGrath, 1970. $16.50

Langdon-Davies, John. *The Future of Nakedness.* London: 1929.

Lanval, M. *Les Mutilations sexuelles dans les religions anciennes et modernes.* Brussels: Le Laurier, 1936.

Laurence, Theodor. *Satan, Sorcery and Sex.* Englewood Cliffs, N.J.: Prentice-Hall, Parker Publishing, 1974. $6.95

Laver, James. *Taste and Fashion from the French Revolution to the Present Day.* London: 1929.

Lea, H. C. *A History of Sacerdotal Celibacy in the Christian Church.* Williams & Norgate, 1907.

Lee, John Alan. *Colours of Love. An Explanation of the Ways of Loving.* Don Mills, Ont.: General Publishing Co., 1975, $9.95

Lehrman, Nat, ed. *The Playboy Book of Sex: A Contemporary Guide to Making Love.* Chicago: Playboy Press, forthcoming.

Lester, William. *Morality Anyone?* New Rochelle, N.Y.: Arlington House, 1975. $7.95

Levy, Howard S., and Chang, Ching-Seng. *Sex Histories: China's First Modern Treatise on Sex Education.* New York: Paragon Reprint Corp., 1967. $5.00

Lewis, Barbara. *Sexual Power of Marijuana.* New York: Wyden, 1970. $5.95

Lewis, C. S. *The Allegory of Love.* New York: Clarendon Press, 1936.

Lippard, Vernon W., ed. *Family Planning, Demography and Human Sexuality in Medical Education.* New York: Sea Cliff Press, 1975. $9.00 (cloth), $4.50 (paper).

Lloyd, C. B., ed. *Sex Discrimination and the Division of Labor.* New York: Columbia University Press, 1975.

Longworth, T. C. *The Devil a Monk Would Be: A Survey of Sex and Celibacy in Religion.* Joseph, 1936.

Lorraine, John A. *Sex and the Population Crisis. An Endocrinologist's View.* St. Louis: C. V. Mosby, 1970. $7.75

Losoney, Mary Jane, and Losoney, Lawrence. *Sex and the Adolescent.* Notre Dame, Ind.: Ave Maria Press.

Lucka, Emil. *Eros: The Development of the Sex Relation Through the Ages.* New York: G. P. Putnam's, 1975. Reprint. New York: AMS, 1974. $20.00

——. *The Evolution of Love.* London: Alien & Unwin, 1923.

Lynch, W. Ware. *Rape: One Victim's Story.* Chicago: Follett, 1975. $6.95

Mann, William Edward. *Orgone, Reich and Eros: William Reich's Theory of Life Energy.* New York: Simon & Schuster, 1974. $3.95

Marcus, Steven. *The Other Victorians: A Study of Sexuality and Pornography in Mid-Nineteenth-Century England.* New York: Basic Books, 1975. $10.95

Marcuse, Herbert. *Eros and Civilization.* Boston: Beacon Press, 1955. $8.95

Martin, Cy. *Whiskey and Wild Women.* New York: Hart Publishing, 1975. $15.00

Masters, R. E. L. *Patterns of Incest*. New York: 1963.

Masters, R. E. L., and Lea, Edward. *Sex Crimes in History*. New York: Matrix House, 1970. $9.50

Mathis, James L. *Clear Thinking About Sexual Deviations: A New Look at an Old Problem*. Chicago: Nelson-Hall, 1974. $6.95

McCarthy, Barry W.; Johnson, Fred W.; and Ryan, Mary A. *Sexual Awareness: A Practical Approach*. San Francisco: Scrimshaw Press, 1975. $8.95

McCary, James Leslie. *Freedom and Growth in Marriage*. New York: Hamilton Publishing, 1974. $12.95

Mellen, Joan. *Women and Their Sexuality in the New Film*. New York: Dell, Laurel, 1975. $1.25

Miles, Herbert J. *Sexual Understanding Before Marriage*. Grand Rapids: Zondervan, 1972. $1.25

Milton, J. L. *On Spermatorrhea*. Renshaw, 1881.

Moll, Albert. *Sexual Life of the Child*. Norwood: Norwood Editions, 1912. $10.00

Money, John, and Tucker, Patricia. *Sexual Signatures*. Boston: Little, Brosn, 1975. $6.95

Montagu, Ashley, ed. *The Practice of Love*. Englewood Cliffs, N.J.: Prentice-Hall, Spectrum Books, 1974. $7.95 (cloth), $2.95 (paper).

Morris, Jan. *Conundrum*. New York: New American Library, Signet, 1975. $1.50

Muncy, Raymond L. *Sex & Marriage in Utopian Communities: Nineteenth Century America*. Bloomington: Indiana University Press, 1973. $10.00

Murphy, Charles, and Day, Linda. *Sex: A Book for Teenagers*. New York: Seabury Press, 1970. $1.75

Murstein, Bernard I. *Love, Sex and Marriage Through the Ages*. New York: Springer, 1974. $16.95

National Lampoon. The Job of Sex. New York: Warner Paperback Library, 1974. $1.25

Nicolli, Allardyce. *Masks, Mimes and Miracles: Studies in the Popular Theater*. London: 1931.

Nohl, J. *The Black Death: A Chronicle of the Plague*. London: Allen & Unwin.

Norwick, Kenneth P. *Lobbying for Freedom: A Citizen's Guide to Fighting Censorship at the State Level*. New York: St. Martin's Press, 1975. $8.95 (cloth), $3.95 (paper)

Oakley, Anne. *Sex, Gender and Society*. New York: Harper & Row, 1973. $2.95

Oliven, J. F. *Sexual Hygiene and Pathology*. Philadelphia: J. B. Lippincott, 1965. $14.00

Ollendorf, Robert. *The Juvenile Homosexual Experience*. New York: Julian Press, 1967. $7.00

Omega, Kane. *Cosmic Sex*. Secaucus, N.J.: Lyle Stuart, 1974. $5.95

O'Reilly, Edward. *Sexercises: Isometric & Isotonic*. New York: Crown, 1967. $4.95

Paine, Lauran. *Sex in Witchcraft*. New York: Taplinger, 1972. $6.50

Pallavicino, Ferrante. *Whore's Rhetorick*. New York: Obolensky, 1961.

Papin, Edwin R. *Sex, Symbolism & the Bible*. New York: Vantage. $3.95

Parkes, A. S. *Sex, Science & Society*. Chester Springs, Pa.: Dufour Editions, 1968. $10.50

Partridge, Eric. *A Dictionary of Slang and Unconventional English*. 5th ed. New York: Macmillan, 1970. $18.50

Paul, Leslie. *Eros Rediscovered*. New York: Association Press, 1970. $5.95

Phallic Worship. A Description of the Mysteries of the Sex Worship of the Ancients. 1886.

Phallism: A Description of the Worship of Lingam-Yoni in Various Parts of the World. London: 1889.

Phelan, Nancy, and Volin, Michael. *Sex and Yoga*. New York: Harper & Row, 1968. $4.95

Phipps, William E. *Sexuality of Jesus*. New York: Harper & Row, 1973. $5.95

Pierson, Elaine C. *Sex is Never an Emergency: A Candid Guide for Young Adults*. Philadelphia: J. B. Lippincott, 1973. $3.95

Ploss, H. H.; Bartels, M.; and Bartels, P. *Woman*. Edited by J. Dingwall. London: Heinemann, Medical Books, 1936.

Plummer, Kenneth. *Sexual Stigma*. London: Routledge & Kegan Paul, 1975

Poland, Jefferson, ed. *Sex Marchers*. Los Angeles: Panu Publishing Co., 1968. $5.95

Pomeroy, Sarah B. *Goddesses, Whores, Wives, and Slaves*. New York: Schocken Books, 1975. $8.95

Pope, Michael. *Sex and the Undecided Librarian: A Study of Librarians' Opinions on Sexually Oriented Literature*. Metuchen, N. J.: Scarecrow Press, 1974. $6.00

Porteous, Helen. *Sex & Identity*. New York: Bobbs-Merrill, 1972. $7.95

Purdy, Al. *Sex and Death*. Toronto: McClelland & Stewart Ltd., 1973. $2.95

Rainer, Jerome, and Rainer, Julia. *Sexual Adventure in Marriage*. New York: Pocket Books, 1973. $1.50

Raskin, Lyn. *Diary of a Transsexual*. New York: Olympia Press, 1971.

Reade, Brian, ed. *Sexual Heretics*. New York: Coward, McCann, 1971. $12.50

Reich, Wilhelm. *The Sexual Revolution*. New York: Noonday Press, 1945.

Reiche, Reimut. *Sexuality and Class Struggle*. New York: Praeger, 1971. $6.95

Reinhardt, J. N. *Sex Perversions and Sex Crimes*. Springfield, Ill.: C. C. Thomas, 1957. $5.95

Richardson, Betty. *Sexism in Higher Education*. New York: Continuum Books, 1975. $7.95

Robie, W. F. *The Art of Love*. Ithaca: Rational Life Press, 1925.

———. *Rational Sex Ethics*. Ithaca: Rational Life Press, 1927.

Rogers, Rex, ed. *Sex Education: Rationale and Reaction*. New York: Cambridge University Press, 1974. $15.50.

Rose, Al. *Storyville, New Orleans*. University: University of Alabama Press, 1975. $17.50

Rosenberg, Charles *et al*., eds. *Sex, Marriage and Society*. 35 vols. New York: Arno Press, 1974. $535.00

Rowse, A. L. *Sex and Society in Shakespeare's England*. New York: Charles Scribner's Sons, 1975. $9.95

Rubin, Isadore. *Sexual Life After Sixty*. New York: Basic Books, 1965.

Ruitenbeck, Hendrik. *The New Sexuality*. New York: Franklin Watts, 1975. $4.95

Rushdoony, Rousas J. *The Politics of Pornography*. New Rochelle, N.Y.: Arlington House, $6.95

Ryan, M. *Prostitution in London with a Comparative View of that in Paris, New York, etc.* Bailliere, 1839.

Sachs, Curt. *World History of the Dance*. Translated by Bessie Schonberg. London: 1938.

Sagarin, Edward, and Sellin, Thorsten. *Sex and the Contemporary American Scene*. Philadelphia: American Academy of Political & Social Science, 1968. $3.00

Saltzman, Janet. *Chafetz: Masculine/Feminine or Human?* New York: Peacock, 1974.

Sarvis, Betty, and Rodman, Hyman. *The Abortion Controversy*. 2nd ed. New York: Columbia University Press, 1975. $3.95

Savage, Brian. *Sex and Violence*. New York: Dell, 1973. $10.75

Saxe, Louis P., and Gerson, Noel B. *Sex and the Mature Man*. New York: Simon & Schuster, 1964. $5.95

Scanzoni, John. *Sexual Bargaining: Power Politics in the American Family*. Englewood Cliffs, N.J.: Prentice-Hall, Spectrum, 1972. $2.45

Scanzoni, Letha. *Sex and the Single Eye*. Washington: Canon Press, 1975.

Scheimann, Eugene, *Sex Can Save Your Heart . . . and Life*. New York: Crown, 1975. $6.95

Scheingold, Lee Dreisinger, and Wagner, Nathaniel. *Sound Sex and the Aging Heart*. New York: Behavioral Publications, Human Sciences Press, 1975. $7.95

Schmidt, J. E. *Cyclopedic Lexicon of Sex.* New York: Penthouse Book Club. $10.00

Schoenfeld, Eugene. *Dr. Hip's Natural Food and Unnatural Acts.* New York: Dell, Delacorte Press, 1975. $7.95

Schofield, Michael. *Sexual Behavior In Young Adults.* Boston: Little, Brown, 1973. $11.50

Scholes, Percy A. *The Puritans and Music in England and New England.* London: 1934.

Scott, Harold. *The Early Doors: Origins of the Music Hall.* London: 1946.

Secondi, John J. *For People Who Make Love.* New York: Bantam Books, 1975. $1.50

See, Carolyn. *Blue Money.* New York: David McKay, 1974. $6.95

Selzer, Joae Graham. *When Children Ask About Sex.* Boston: Beacon Press, 1975. $6.95

Seruya, Flora; Losher, Susan; and Ellis, Albert. *Sex and Sex Education: A Bibliography.* New York: R. R. Bowker Co., 1974. $15.50

Seward, Georgene, and Williamson, Robert G., eds. *Sex Roles in a Changing Society.* New York: Random House, 1970. $10.95

Sex and the Spinal Cord Injured: Some Questions and Answers. Washington: Veteran's Administration, 1974. 60¢

Sex Role Stereotyping in the Schools. West Haven: National Education Association, 1973. $2.50

Sexual Heretics. Edited by Brian Reade. New York: Coward, McCann, 1971. $12.50

Sexuality in the Movies. Edited by Thomas R. Atkins. Bloomington: Indiana University Press, 1975.

Sexual Problems: Diagnosis and Treatment in Medical Practice. Edited by Charles W. Wahl. New York: Free Press, 1967. $8.95

Sherman, Allan. *The Rape of the Ape.* Chicago: Playboy Press, 1973. $9.95

Simons, G. L. *Sex and Superstition.* New York: Barnes & Noble, 1973. $8.95

Singer, Laura J., and Buskin, Judith. *Sex Education on Film: A Guide to Visual Aids & Programs.* New York: Teachers College Press, 1971. $3.95

Slattery, William J. *The Erotic Imagination: Sexual Fantasies of the Male Adult.* Chicago: Henry Regnery, $7.95

Smith, William H. [Long, H.W.]. *Sane Sex Life and Sane Sex Living.* New York: Eugenic Publishing Co., 1922.

Snyder, Robert. *This is Henry—Henry Miller from Brooklyn.* Los Angeles: Nash Publishing, 1974. $5.95

Spacks, Patricia Meyer. *The Female Imagination.* New York: Alfred A. Knopf, 1975. $10.00

Spurrier, William A. *Natural Law and the Ethics of Love.* Philadelphia: Westminster Press, 1975. $5.95

Stein, Ralph. *The Pin-Up.* Chicago: Playboy Press, 1974. $17.95

Stein, Robert. *Incest and Human Love: The Betrayal of the Soul in Psychotherapy.* Baltimore: Penguin Books, $2.95

Steinman, Anne, and Fox, David. *The Male Dilemma: How to Survive The Sexual Revolution.* New York: J. Aronson, 1975. $12.50

Stiller, Richard. *The Love Bugs: A Natural History of the VDs.* Nashville: Thomas Nelson, 1975. $5.95 (cloth), $2.95 (paper)

Stone, H. M. and Stone, A. S. *A Marriage Manual.* Rev. ed. New York: Simon & Schuster, 1953.

Stonehouse, Bernard, *et al. The Way Your Body Works.* New York: Crown, 1975. $9.95

Terman, Lewis M., and Miles, Catherine C. *Sex and Personality: Studies in Masculinity and Femininity.* New York: Atheneum, Russell & Russell, 1968. $15.00

Thomas. P. *Karma Kalpa.* Bombay: D. B. Taraporevala Sons & Co., 1960.

Thomson, W. A., ed. *Sex and Its Problems.* New York: Longman, 1968. $3.00

Valentini, Norberto, and Di Meglio, Clara. *Sex and the Confessional.* Translated by Melton S. Davis. New York: Stein & Day, 1975. $6.95

Van Cleef, Monique. *House of Pain.* Secaucus, N.J.: Lyle Stuart, 1974. $7.95

Van Gulik, Robert H. *Sexual Life in Ancient China.* New York: Humanities Press, 1961. $21.50

Vogliotti, Gabriel R. *The Girls of Nevada.* Secaucus, N.J.: Lyle Stuart, 1975. $7.95

Wahl, Charles W., ed. *Sexual Problems: Diagnosis and Treatment in Medical Practice.* New York: Free Press, 1967. $8.95

Wall, Otto A. *Sex and Sex Worship.* Washington: McGrath, 1920. $47.00

Walsh, Molly. *Sex and the People We Really Are.* Paramus, N.J.: Paulist/Newman Press, 1967. $1.25

Walters, Ronald G. *Primers for Prudery: Sexual Advice to Victorian America.* Englewood Cliffs, N.J.: Prentice-Hall, 1974. $6.95

Ward, Edward. *The London-Spy Compleat.* 2d ed. London: 1704.

Watts, Alan. *Erotic Spirituality: The Vision of Konarek.* New York: G. P. Putnam's Sons, 1974. $9.95

Wayne, Alice, and Harper, John. *Games Singles Play.* New York: Popular Library, 1975. $1.25

Weber, Nancy. *The Life Swap.* New York: Dial Press, 1974. $6.95

Wells, John Warren. *Total Sexuality.* New York: Warner Paperback Library, 1974. $1.50

Wershub, Leonard P. *Sexual Impotence in the Male.* Springfield, Ill.: C. C. Thomas, 1959. $5.95

Whelan, Elizabeth. *Sex and Sensibility.* New York: McGraw-Hill, 1974. $6.95

Whittaker, Peter. *The American Way of Sex.* New York: Berkley, 1975. $1.50

Wikler, Revy, and Grey, Peg S. *Sex and the Senior Citizen.* New York: Frederick Fell, 1968. $5.95

Wile, I. S., ed. *Sex Life of the Unmarried Adult.* New York: Vanguard, 1934.

Williams, George C. *Sex & Evolution.* Princeton: Princeton University Press, 1974. $4.95

Wilson, Paul. *Sexual Dilemma: Abortion, Homosexuality, Prostitution and Criminal Threshold.* Lawrence, Me.: University of Queensland Press, 1971. $9.25

Wilson, Robert A. *The Book of the Breast.* Chicago: Playboy Press, 1974. $8.95

Wolfe, Linda. *Playing Around: Women and Extramarital Sex.* New York: William Morrow, 1975. $7.95

Wood, H. Curtis, Jr. *Sex Without Babies.* Ardmore, Pa.: Whitemore, 1967. $5.00

Wright, Helen. *Sex and Society.* Seattle: University of Washington Press, 1969. $4.95

Wright, Helena. *More About the Sex Factors in Marriage.* London: Ernest Benn, 1969.

Wright, Thomas. *Anglo-Saxon and Old English Vocabularies.* 2 vols. Edited and collected by Richard Paul Wulcker. London: 1884.

Wroth, Warwick. *The London Pleasure Gardens of the 18th Century.* London: 1896.

Zablocki, Benjamin. *The Joyful Community.* Baltimore: Penguin Books, 1971. $2.15

End Note

*H*opefully, by the time you have reached this page your sexual horizons will have been expanded to infinity. We have offered you keys to doorways of the past, a wide-angle view of the present, and a springboard to the future. In short, we have tried to provide you with an overview of the erogenous zones of the globe. But when all is said and done, it all boils down to the old dictum: *the most erogenous zone of them all is the human mind.*

Acknowledgments

*I*t goes without saying that a job as monumental as *The Whole Sex Catalogue* could never have been accomplished without the help and encouragement of others—many others. I would like to thank all of those who made the seemingly impossible become a reality. Andrew Ettinger, Editor-in-Chief of Pinnacle Books, who conceived the idea originally and had enough confidence in me to assign the project. My editor, Ann Kearns, whose meticulous editing, unbelievable energy, and constant drive managed to survive while bearing the brunt of all the external pressures and enduring my personal idiosyncrasies to the point of frequently being driven up the walls. Shirley Craig, my assistant through thick and thin, who tackled all the drudgery without complaint, contributed many valuable ideas throughout, and perpetually brought order out of chaos. I must give special thanks to Fred Jordan of Grove Press, whose behind the scenes help is impossible to sum up in one or two lines. I must also express special thanks to Drs. Phyllis and Eberhard Kronhausen, who in addition to writing the Introduction to this book, made available their entire personal art collection, and gave continuous advice and moral support from beginning to end. As for the others who gave so much of their time and selves, space prohibits my going into detail, but I give them all my deepest thanks. Pauline Abrams, Marjorie Bair, Ruth Beasley of the Institute for Sex Research, Indiana University, Hugh Beeson, Fred Belliveau, Dian Dincin Buchman, Marcia Blackman, Jane Bloom, Carol Botwin, Jerry Bukzin, William Corson, Tony Crawley, Barbara Ekstrom, Janice Epp, Will Faller, Don Fass, Bernice Fisher, Stanley Fleischman, Mark Gabor, Ken Gaul, Mr. & Mrs. Lawrence Gichner, Dana Greene, Donald J. Haley and the Pussycat Theatres, Dr. William Hartman and Marilyn Fithian, Jane Heil, Jean-Noel Herlin, Ted Hurwood, Judith Jobin, Doug Johns, Chuck Jones, Kay Kim of the New York Public Library, Shell and Barry Kugler, Ellis Levine, Jeri Logan, George Mair, Allan H. Mankoff, Joseph Mask of the New York Public Library, Patrick M. McGrady, Jr., Phoebe McKay, Merrill Miller, Robert Massey, Neal Olson, Tuppy Owens, David Paris, Captain Jack Parker of the Los Angeles Police Department, John Raymond, Harry Reems, Bryan Wilson-Rich, The Sandstoners, Ed and June Seeman, Jerry Schneiderman, Dr. Don Sloan, Edie Solow, Irwin Spector, Rod Swenson Jr., Emerson Symonds, Gay Talese, Michele Urry, Gene Webster, Lynn Yates, and Sandy Zane. I must also offer my warmest gratitude to the entire staff of Pinnacle Books, who treated an outsider like a member of the family during the entire course of this project—and all of whom contributed immeasurably beyond the call of duty. And last but definitely not least, a very special thanks to Frank Curcio whose superb design finally pulled the book together.

Bernhardt J. Hurwood
July 1975
New York